## 4TH EDITION

# UNDERSTANDING AND MANAGING DIVERSITY

## Readings, Cases, and Exercises

**Carol P. Harvey**

*Assumption College*

**M. June Allard**

*Assumption College*
*Worcester State College Professor Emerita*

PEARSON
Prentice Hall

Upper Saddle River, New Jersey 07458

**Library of Congress Cataloging-in-Publication Data**

Harvey, Carol P.
  Understanding and managing diversity : readings, cases and exercises
/ Carol P. Harvey, M. June Allard. — 4th ed.
      p. cm.
  Includes index.
  ISBN-13: 978-0-13-206910-6
  ISBN-10: 0-13-206910-5
  1. Minorities—Employment—United States. 2. Multiculturalism—United States. 3. Personnel
management—United States.  I. Allard, M. June. II. Title.

HF5549.5.M5H37 2008
658.3008—dc22                                                                                        2007052506

**AVP / EIC:** David Parker
**Product Development Manager:** Ashley Santora
**Project Manager, Editorial:** Kristen Varina
**Marketing Manager:** Nikki Jones
**Marketing Assistant:** Ian Gold
**Senior Managing Editor:** Judy Leale
**Associate Managing Editor:** Suzanne DeWorken
**Project Manager, Production:** Karalyn Holland
**Senior Operations Specialist:** Arnold Vila
**Operations Specialist:** Carol O'Rourke
**Cover Design:** Studio Indigo
**Cover Illustration/Photo:** Getty Images, Inc.
**Manager, Rights and Permissions:** Charles Morris
**Composition:** Aptara
**Full-Service Project Management:** Nitin Agarwal/Aptara
**Printer/Binder:** R.R. Donnelly-Harrisonburg

Credits and acknowledgments borrowed from other sources and reproduced, with permission, in this text-
book appear on appropriate page within text.

Pearson Education Ltd., London
Pearson Education Singapore, Pte. Ltd
Pearson Education, Canada, Inc.
Pearson Education–Japan
Pearson Education Australia PTY, Limited

Pearson Education North Asia, Ltd., Hong Kong
Pearson Educación de Mexico, S.A. de C.V.
Pearson Education Malaysia, Pte. Ltd
Pearson Education Upper Saddle River, New Jersey

10 9 8 7 6 5 4 3 2 1
ISBN-13: 978-0-13-206910-6
ISBN-10: 0-13-206910-5

**This book is dedicated to our contributors, without whose knowledge and hard work this text would not be possible.**

# CONTENTS

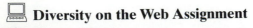

**Diversity on the Web Assignment**

**Points of Law**

**Diversity on the Web Assignment**
**Points of Law**

⌨ **Diversity on the Web Assignment**

🏛 **Points of Law**

🖥 **Diversity on the Web Assignment**

🏛 **Points of Law**

**Diversity on the Web Assignment**

**Points of Law**

# PREFACE

## Understanding and Managing Diversity: Change and Inclusion

Since the third edition of *Understanding and Managing Diversity: Readings, Cases, and Exercises* was published in 2005, workplace diversity has become a more complex issue, characterized by a need for meaningful organizational *change* and management practices that promote the *inclusion* of diverse workers. Consequently, the fourth edition is based on understanding the forces for and against these changes, and the application of the theories and practices that lead to inclusive management.

Although many organizations now have a more diverse workforce—at least at some levels—this does not mean that managers know how to work productively with people whose values, life styles, motivators, and communication styles may be quite different from their own. There are simply more people of color, women, working parents, immigrants, openly gay, people with disabilities, and older workers employed in twenty-first-century organizations. Global business negotiations are now widespread and technological innovations have made intercultural communication a major issue.

To be successful in terms of managing diversity, organizations need to move beyond the segmented reactive approach, where diversity initiatives are largely a human resource issue and avoiding lawsuits is the prime objective. While organizations need the variety of perspectives and creativity that differences can bring, managers need the skills to understand the needs of their workers and deal with the conflicts that may arise when people are free to express dissenting views. When this is done well, workers feel more committed to accomplishing the mission and objectives of their organizations. If diversity is to be an asset to an organization, it must be seen as a human capital issue that changes how people are led and the way that businesses manage employees, deal with customers, and negotiate with suppliers.

At the same time, there is a movement to document the business case for diversity—i.e., to prove that diversity is a competitive advantage and not just the right thing to do. Making the business case is a complex, controversial, and long-term issue, and still a work in progress. In the meantime, successful organizations, are implementing changes to the way work is structured, improving interpersonal communication, and learning that just having the numbers is not enough.

Our objectives for the fourth edition are as follows:

- To provide interesting, accurate, and timely readings, cases, and exercises that will help clarify the complexity of managing and working in a changing and increasingly diverse workplace

- To help students to realize how multiple social identities may affect productivity, communication, motivation, retention, and inclusion in organizations

- To illustrate the innovative practices and strategies that can be used to make diversity an organizational asset

## NEW PEDAGOGICAL AND CONTENT FEATURES

In terms of pedagogy, the fourth edition incorporates innovations to meet the need for assessment, integrate the use of technology in the classroom, and provide material that is not available from any other sources. For example, the fourth edition includes

- An extensive *pre- and post-course assessment package* that enables instructors to measure students' learning and progress in terms of course goals

- *Integration of technology* into teaching and learning about diversity through an interactive Web-based diversity exercise (DIVERSITY!), and a new feature, *Diversity on the Web* assignments

- Extensive material on the use of popular *films* that can be used to illustrate diversity concepts throughout the course

- *Six new cases,* such as Pitney Bowes and the Air Force Academy

- Reprinted material from *The Harvard Business Review*, the *Managing Diversity* newsletter, *DiversityInc*, The Brookings Institute, and Ivey Publishing

- The integration of "Points of Law"—short explanations of diversity-related law inserted into relevant readings and cases

- Writing assignments designed to encourage critical thinking

- New topics such as immigration, utilization of human capital, flexible work arrangements, weight and appearance, family and work-life issues, supplier diversity, and intercultural negotiation

## REVISIONS AND DIVERSITY CLASSICS

Much of the content from the third edition has been revised and/or updated, including articles on ethics, African Americans, Hispanics, Asians, women, social classes, and older workers. In addition to this new material, you will find the classic seminal articles for which our books are known and updates of other favorite course materials. We think that it would be difficult to teach a meaningful diversity course without Minor's *Nacerima*, Peggy McIntosh's *White Privilege and Male Privilege*, Sowell's *World View of Cultural Diversity*, and Deborah Tannen's *The Power of Talk*. To these we have added a recent piece by R. Roosevelt Thomas, Jr.: *Redefining Diversity*.

Other articles have been revised to reflect current diversity issues and practices, such as *How Canada Promotes Workplace Diversity; Generational Diversity; Organizational Innovations for Older Workers; Progress and Backlash: Making Sense of Lesbian, Gay, Bisexual and Transgender Issues in the Workplace; Media Messages;* and *Evaluating Diversity and Inclusion in the Real World: Conducting a Diversity Audit, etc.*

## SUPPLEMENTS PACKAGE

As instructors we appreciate your need for supportive teaching materials. The fourth edition is accompanied by a complete supplemental package and an online Web site for instructors (www.prenhall.com/Harvey) complete with Power Point slides and a test bank. The Instructor's Manual includes a topic outline detailed teaching notes for each article, case, and exercise; instructions for conducting course assessments; answers to the discussion questions; and supplemental teaching materials, such as four extra cases reprinted from the third edition that can be used as additional class or written assignments: *Tailhook; Briarwood; Believability: A Case of Diversity in Law Enforcement;* and *Dilemmas at Valley Tech.*

## ACKNOWLEDGMENTS

The most important people to thank are our contributors. Because we believe that diversity is a multidisciplinary subject, we think that it is important to have articles written from the perspectives of psychologists, historians, and sociologists, etc., as well as by management faculty, diversity practitioners/consultants, and managers who work with diversity issues on a daily basis. Their depth of knowledge on specific topics enriches the text in ways that no individual author could do. Special thanks go to Peter Kerr of the Pitney Bowes Corporation, who was so helpful in opening the channels of communication at his organization.

In additition, several people from Assumption College contributed technical research and clerical expertise to this final product. Specifically, we would like to thank Lynn Cooke from the Information Technology Center, and Carole Myles, Larry Spongberg, Calle Curran, and Dawn Thistle from the college library, as well as Maria Alicata, the secretary in the Business Studies department.

We appreciate the assistance from the staff at Prentice Hall, particularly David Parker, editor-in-chief; Ashley Santora, product development manager; Kristen Varina, assistant editor; and Judy Leale, senior managing editor.

Carol P. Harvey, EdD
Assumption College
Department of Business Studies
500 Salisbury Street
Worcester, MA 01609
charvey@assumption.edu

M. June Allard, PhD
24 Curtis Street
Auburn, MA 01501
jallard0322@yahoo.com

# ABOUT THE AUTHORS

**Carol P. Harvey, EdD**, is a professor and former chair of the Business Studies Department at Assumption College. Her doctorate is from the University of Massachusetts in Teaching and Learning in Higher Education with a specialization in Organizational Behavior. She has an MBA and Certificate of Advanced Studies from Northeastern University and a MA in Psychology.

Formerly employed as a manager at the Xerox Corporation, her research interests include implementing diversity initiatives in organizations and improving critical thinking skills in higher education. Her teaching currently includes both undergraduate- and graduate-level courses in Managing Diversity, International Communication, Organizational Behavior, Training and Development, and Small Business Management.

She is the corecipient of the 2004 Roethlisberger Memorial Award from the Organizational Behavior Teaching Society for the best article, from the *Journal of Management Education,* "Critical Thinking in the Management Classroom: Bloom's Taxonomy as a Learning Tool" and the 2002 recipient of the Volunteer of the Year Award from the Center for Women in Enterprise.

**M. June Allard** is *professor emerita* from Worcester State College, where she served as chair of the Psychology and the Social and Behavioral Science departments. She holds a PhD from Michigan State University in Social Psychology with a specialization in cross-cultural research. She is the recipient of nine national fellowships and numerous Distinguished Service and Outstanding Teaching awards and is listed in a number of national and international directories of scientists and women leaders.

Dr. Allard has conducted program reviews and evaluations for over 30 years and is a recognized expert in this field. She currently maintains a consulting practice designing and conducting research and program evaluations. Formerly employed as a senior scientist in the research and development industry in Washington, D.C., she has directed a wide range of projects on government contracts in industry as well as in university research institutes. She is a site visitor for the New England Association of Schools and Colleges for collegiate accreditation and for the Accreditation Visiting Committee for the American Psychological Association (APA) as well as a member of the APA Undergraduate Consulting Service.

A lifelong world traveler, she brings expertise on evaluation to the international education arena, where she lectures on research and program evaluation internationally in countries such as Morocco, Costa Rica, Poland, Mexico, Turkey, Trinidad,

Nicaragua, Bolivia, Brazil, Guatemala, South Korea, and Sicily and has conducted research and evaluation projects for the U.S. Peace Corps, UNESCO, and the U.S. Agency for International Development. She is an examiner for the International Baccalaureate Organization (IBO) and a specialist with the APA Panel of Experts, Commission on Ethnic Minority Recruitment, Retention and Training. Dr. Allard has published extensively and has authored encyclopedia articles on the educational systems of various countries.

We encourage instructors who use this text to contact us with suggestions and comments on how to improve future editions. We welcome copies of your syllabi, so that we can better understand how our text is used in your classrooms.

# Introduction to the Text

**W**elcome to the fourth edition of *Understanding and Managing Diversity: Readings, Cases, and Exercises*. Because of the demographic, economic, technical, and global changes that are occurring in today's workplace, and the debate over the business case for diversity, we are using the themes of change and inclusion for this edition. Diversity has moved beyond the Affirmative Action/Equal Employment Opportunity model, where the numerical representation of single dimensions such as race, gender, age, etc. (i.e., numbers of diverse people) in organizations and avoiding lawsuits were the primary goals.

Today, diversity management is a far more complex issue than it was when the last edition of this text was published. First, twenty-first-century workers, customers, co-workers, and suppliers are often the products of multiple social identity group influences that have a range of salience, and many of these social identities are not even visible. For example, a young worker, white, male, and born in America, may not appear to be the product of a diverse socialization process. However, assume that this employee spent his childhood moving from country to country because his father worked for a global corporation. In addition, this employee was educated at foreign schools where English was a second language and his being Jewish often made him feel different from his friends. Having experienced a lack of inclusion may influence the development and importance of some of his social identities. In turn, his experiences can create a broad range of values, lifestyles, motivators, and communication styles that make it more complex to manage this employee.

Managing as one would like to be managed (called the Golden Rule—treat people as you would like to be treated) and/or treating all employees alike is no longer an effective leadership style. The segments of today's workforce that are increasing are women, non-Christians, nonwhites, immigrants, older, and openly gay employees. The complexity of multiple social identities—combining ethnicity, religion, gender, etc.—makes effective management and inclusion in the twenty-first century an ongoing challenge.

Second, there is a movement to document that diversity provides a measurable competitive advantage in terms of creativity, quality decision making, product development, and so on—i.e., making what is often called "the business case for diversity." The dilemma here is that most organizations are in the process of grappling with these workplace changes, but not yet at the inclusion stage where all people, despite their differences, feel that they are a vital part of the organization. Consequently, it is difficult to measure the impact of diversity on the bottom line.

This is why it is so difficult to prove that diversity matters in terms of measuring the business case, i.e., the specific value that diversity brings to an organization. It is difficult to measure that which is in flux, constantly changing. With most organizations in the process of change but not at the inclusion stage, managers need three types of diversity skills that correspond to the three main sections of this text.

## SECTION I

Provides an *Understanding* of the basics that underlie diversity learning: the influences that are driving workplace changes; the various approaches to understanding the impact of differences; the need to consider several definitions of diversity; and the differences between stereotypes, prejudice, discrimination, and privilege, with an emphasis on understanding the influence of one's own perceptions.

## SECTION II

Focuses on *Information* about the context of the identity group socialization processes and experiences that may influence people from diverse and multiple social identity groups with an emphasis on the fact that these may vary significantly from individual to individual within these groups.

## SECTION III

Provides students with an opportunity to *Apply* what they have learned about diversity to the change process through the development, evaluation, and implementation of inclusion strategies and programs that are appropriate for particular organizational cultures.

Throughout the text, there are Diversity on the Web exercises, Writing Assignments, and Points of Law explanations that illustrate the concepts from the readings. The text is enriched by the "Resources for Teaching about Diversity" in this last section, which is entirely new with this edition. This section features assessment tools to measure learning and provides details for utilizing film to illustrate diversity concepts in the classroom.

## SECTION IV

Features assessment tools to measure learning and provides details for utilizing film to illustrate diversity concepts in the classroom.

# SECTION I

# A Framework for Understanding Individual Perspectives of Diversity

## Introduction

**Goals of Section I**

- To understand why it is so important to be knowledgeable about diversity and inclusion in the workplace

- To be aware of the historical and legal contexts for workplace diversity

- To understand the differences between stereotypes, prejudice, discrimination, and privilege

- To clarify how the articles and exercises in Section I fit together in terms of learning about workplace diversity

## WORKPLACE DIVERSITY AND CHANGE IN THE TWENTY-FIRST CENTURY

While there is no universal agreement about what workplace diversity means, for the purposes of this text we define diversity as *the ways in which people differ that may affect their organizational experience in terms of performance, motivation, communication, and inclusion.* This definition reflects the need to recognize the impact of multiple dimensions of diversity. For example, a white male worker may appear to lack diversity, but his health problems, religion, sexual orientation, and/or age may be diversity issues for him. Often, in the workplace, people have salient differences that may be important to their organizational experiences. In today's highly competitive global workplace, organizations must do all that they can to adapt their management policies and practices to the changing needs of the twenty-first-century worker.

> Diversity is about business and the bottom line and about leveraging the skills and talents of all employees to enable the organization to compete. Diversity is not about reaching quotas and hiring unqualified minorities for the sake of "having diversity" (SHRM, 2007).

■ 1 ■

**W**orkplace diversity can be a misunderstood and controversial subject. The United States was founded on the principle that "all are created equal," but women and African Americans were excluded from this equality for many years. As articles in this text will substantiate, the workforce is becoming increasingly older, nonwhite, non–native born, non-Christian, and female. Some of the factors driving these changes include: growth in nonwhite populations, immigration, more working parents, employees staying in the workplace past traditional retirement age, global business initiatives, the presence of multiple generations in organizations, more openness about one's sexual orientation, etc.

## THE HISTORICAL AND LEGAL CONTEXT FOR WORKPLACE DIVERSITY

Although most people associate the origins of American workplace diversity with the passage of Title VII of the Civil Rights Act (1964), the United States has always been a nation of immigrants, with a mixture of ethnicities, races, and religions that have not always lived and worked together amicably. From the oppression of slavery, the internment of the Japanese-Americans and Italian-Americans during WWII, the segregated public schools in the South, the anti-Semitism of the 1950s, the 1969 Stonewall incident, the killing of Matthew Shephard, the Los Angeles race riots, etc., to the firing of radio host, Don Imus, differences have often led to conflicts.

Throughout the text you will find many "Points of Law," i.e., features that detail specific legislation pertaining to particular readings and cases. The first one, which illustrates the major U.S. Equal Employment laws, follows. Canadian employment law is explained in Hunt's "How Canada Promoted Workplace Diversity" article.

However, in the twenty-first century, these differences "are being defined less by political action than by daily experience, in the schools, in sports arenas, in pop culture, and at worship, and especially in the workplace"(NY Times, 2007).

Hewlett-Packard's Diversity Value Chain and statement exemplifies the ideal but not the reality for diversity progress in most organizations.

> At HP we have recognized that creating a diverse, inclusive work environment is a journey of continuous renewal. Each step in the process has an important significance to remember as we move forward into the twenty-first century. Together the steps create a diversity value chain upon which we are building our winning global workforce and workplace (Hewlett-Packard, 2007).

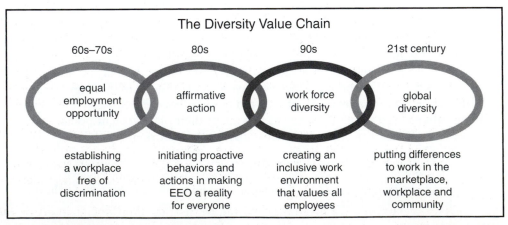

The Diversity Value Chain

| 60s–70s | 80s | 90s | 21st century |
|---|---|---|---|
| equal employment opportunity | affirmative action | work force diversity | global diversity |
| establishing a workplace free of discrimination | initiating proactive behaviors and actions in making EEO a reality for everyone | creating an inclusive work environment that values all employees | putting differences to work in the marketplace, workplace and community |

Reprinted with permission of Hewlett-Packard

## Points of Law

### Major U.S. Federal Equal Employment Opportunity Legislation

| | |
|---|---|
| **Equal Pay Act (1963)** | States that males and females must be paid same salary for jobs that require equal skill, effort, & responsibility |
| **Civil Rights Act (Title VII - 1964)** | Prohibits discrimination in employment in terms of hiring, promoting, firing, etc., on the basis of race, sex, national origin, religion, and color |
| **Executive Order 11246 (amended by 11375) (1965)** | Requires organizations that accept federal funds and those with $50,000 in federal contracts in a year to have a written Affirmative Action plan |
| **Age Discrimination in Employment Act (1974)** | Protects workers over forty from discrimination in terms of hiring, firing, salary, benefits, and other employment decisions |
| **Americans with Disabilities Act (1994)** | Prohibits discrimination against people with physical or mental disabilities who are termed as "qualified disabled" in terms of hiring, firing, advancement, training, pay, participation in social activities, etc., and requires that an employer make reasonable accommodations for the disability |
| **Civil Rights Act (1991)** | Gives additional legal protection in terms of increased compensatory and punitive damages, jury trials for those claiming intentional discrimination, and extends the time limits on age discrimination claims |

*Adapted from http://www.dol.gov/esa/regs/compliance/*

To move an organization into the third and fourth stages of this value chain, where the different perspectives that diverse employees bring to decision making can become a competitive advantage, managers need to create an inclusive working environment. Being "inclusive" means that diverse employees feel that they are vital contributors to the organizational mission, not marginalized or tolerated. Movement into this stage is crucial, because until it happens, organizations cannot tap into the richness of a diverse workforce. Because so many organizations have not achieved this inclusive stage, it explains why it is so difficult to establish the business case for diversity, i.e., to "prove" or "measure" that diversity can be a competitive advantage that enhances the organization's bottom line.

While the equal employment laws and affirmative action initiatives of the 1960s were the catalysts for organizational change, legislation is simply not enough. "Any company that systematically discriminates against a subset of the population, pays a price in employee quality for hiring inferior candidates from the majority in preference to more talented minority candidates" (DeLong, 2006).

Diverse workers are no longer willing to give up their social identities to assimilate into the workplace. Today, they value their individuality. So the "melting pot" metaphor accepted as fact in the past is recognized for the myth that it represents.

## PREJUDICE, STEREOTYPES, DISCRIMINATION, AND PRIVILEGE

Prejudice, stereotypes, discrimination, and privilege, are forces that work against diversity inclusion. Bringing diverse workers into an organization is not a seamless transition. Since these terms are often used interchangeably with negative connotations, knowing the fundamental differences between them is vital to understanding the dynamics of workplace diversity. *Prejudice* is preconceived, evaluative *attitudes* about someone based on his or her group memberships. To illustrate these differences, we will follow the situation at Terrin Industries.

---

**┌─ Diversity at Terrin Industries — Part One ──────────**

Keith starts to read e-mail about the experience and qualifications of his new manager, Sage Wilson. As he reads on, Keith realizes that this new person is not a male as he expected. He will have a female manager for the first time in his career. Because he thinks that men are logical and women are emotional (a preconception), even though he has never met Sage, he may find himself thinking negatively about her, in that she will make business decisions based more on emotions than logic.

---

Our prejudices can come from many sources, including our socialization as children, the media, our peers, etc. While prejudices can be positive, neutral, or negative, it is the negative ones that most often lead to the stereotypes that can be problematic in the workplace. If a person is a member of a group that we identify with and in which membership is important to us, this is called an in-group membership, and there is a tendency to see other members of this group in a positive way. For example, a student athlete may find herself thinking positively about all student athletes because of their need to balance both academic and athletic responsibilities. However, a nonathlete, being an out-group member, may think negatively that all athletes are stupid and are not taking their education seriously.

Although the term *stereotype* originally referred to an eighteenth century printing process used to make reproductions of prints (Ashmore & Del Boca, 1981), today it means an overgeneralized belief that categorizes all members of a social identity group as "typical" of that group. Like prejudices, stereotypes are learned and not innate and can be positive, neutral, as well as negative. However, negative stereotypes are "more likely in groups with unbalanced representation of subgroups, i.e., when there is a minority" (Chen & DiTomaso, 1996). The psychologist, Gordon Allport wrote that, "The human mind must think with the aid of categories, . . .(which are) the basis for normal prejudgment. We cannot possibly avoid this process. Orderly living depends on it" (p. 20, 1954).

Research studies confirm that knowledge of negative stereotypes actually can change the beliefs that group members have about themselves, by decreasing self-confidence and causing them to internalize the popular stereotype.

> Stereotypes seem to most effect the best and the brightest. Only if you are Black and care about academics, or female and care about math, will you care if society thinks that you are bad at those things (Begley, 2003).

Gregory Sawin (1991) uses complexity-identity theory to clarify the influence of stereotypes on our thinking by making the analogy of stereotypes as "mental maps." He writes that the accuracy of our perceptions and judgments depend on the quality and quantity of the direct experiences we have had with people who represent a category, i.e., a social identity group. The more we have experienced what he calls "the territory," the more able we are to know that the people within that category are not all alike and in fact exhibit a wide range of behaviors. This should improve the accuracy of our "map," or categorization of that person. Section II of the text will present a wealth of information about social identity group memberships that will help you to understand people unlike yourself.

---

### Terrin Industries—Part Two

When Sage arrives, Keith also sees that she is an African American woman. He grew up in a diverse neighborhood, went to racially integrated schools and has had African American teachers, friends, and college roommates, so Keith has a wide range of past experiences to draw upon when he thinks of Sage in terms of her race. Whatever her management style, Keith's wealth of experience in terms of race, should give him a more accurate "mental map" of African Americans, which will help him *not* to stereotype Sage's actions as being typical or as having anything to do with her race.

---

While stereotypes are mental processes, they can lead to ***discrimination***, which is a *behavior* that occurs when members of a social identity group are treated unfairly or unequally, because of their group memberships. Negative stereotypes can be particularly problematic in the workplace because they may influence important decisions (i.e., become the basis for discriminatory actions) in hiring, promotions, performance appraisals, etc. If we acknowledge our prejudices, it can help us to avoid conscious or unconscious discriminatory actions. If we deny our prejudices, we are more apt to discriminate against people from a social identity group about which we have negative stereotypes and to treat too well those belonging to groups we think positively about or identify with (i.e., the halo effect).

Pincus (2000) delineates three levels of discrimination:

- ***Individual discrimination***—when a person discriminates against another because of the latter's social group membership, such as a specific ethnicity, religion, etc.
- ***Structural***—when organizations, such as corporations, *unintentionally* discriminate against members of social identity groups by their policies and practices.

- *Institutional*—when discrimination is *intentional* and embedded in an institution's ways of thinking because of the predominance of the dominant group's power, such as at the military academies.

These distinctions are important to understand because many people feel that they personally don't "discriminate" against specific groups, but they fail to realize that they need to work to eliminate these two other forms of discrimination that can cause serious problems in the workplace. Part III of the Terrin Industries case provides an example of such a policy.

---

**Terrin Industries—Part Three**

It has been two years since Sage came to the Midwest regional office. Her performance has been outstanding, and she is facing a career planning session with her boss, Aaron Lucey, the vice president of sales. He has spoken about Sage's performance at the senior staff meetings, where the consensus was that she should be groomed for the position of vice president of marketing. However, the company has a policy that all vice presidents should have work experience in each of the company's three divisions. This would require that Sage work a two-year assignment at the manufacturing facility located in Malaysia.

When Aaron presents this idea to Sage, she tells him that she will have to turn this opportunity down, because she can't move that far away. She is a divorced mother of two children and shares her children's custody with her ex-husband, but she does not feel comfortable revealing that her custody agreement states that the children must live no more than 500 miles from her ex-husband. Sage argues that because she has already had management level manufacturing and international management experience at another company, this policy should be waived. Aaron makes it clear that this requirement has been in place for twenty years and that all of the other vice presidents have worked in Malaysia. After thinking about this meeting, Sage realizes that because of this policy, in order to rise to the next level, she will have to get a position at a different company. The next morning she calls a corporate recruiter and starts her job search.

---

The previous example illustrates how structural (unintentional) discrimination can be detrimental to a business decision and cost an organization a good diverse employee.

*Privilege* is an unearned, socially constructed advantage that gives group members who have it economic, political, and/or social power that is not necessarily dependent on majority status. In American society, being male, white, able-bodied, middle-class, Christian, and straight are the more powerful and therefore privileged groups. Those who experience privilege are usually unaware that they have this unearned status and think that everyone else experiences the world as they do, i.e., as an individual.

However, those who lack privilege are well aware of their less powerful position and are often defined in terms of their group memberships. Have you ever heard anyone say, "I just interviewed *a qualified white applicant*"? Probably not. But have you ever heard someone say, "I just interviewed a qualified Black, Hispanic, or Asian applicant"?

What a society holds to be the more valuable assets and privileges are socially constructed, i.e., dependent upon time and place. In South Africa during apartheid, whites experienced racial privilege because they had more power even though they were in the numerical minority. In the Middle Ages, heavy women were considered to be more attractive than thin women; in Asian and Native American cultures, older people are revered for their wisdom. Today, being thin and having a youthful appearance give one more power in the workplace.

---

### Terrin Industries — Part 4

The corporate managers at Terrin Industries are shocked when Sage submits her resignation. Because she feels uncomfortable about raising the issue of her family situation, she simply writes that she has "received a better opportunity" at the vice presidential level at another local corporation. At the board meeting, the discussion centers around how much the organization had invested in her and how women often make emotional decisions. The theme of the discussion is that minorities and women don't understand how business works, don't appreciate the opportunities that they have today, and lack organizational loyalty.

---

At Terrin Industries, little effort was made to understand that today's workforce has changed. Sage's reluctance to talk to management about her family obligations as a reason for leaving, may indicate that she does not feel valued enough, i.e., "included," to risk revealing that this is a major issue for her. Being able to uproot one's family to a foreign country to further a career is a privilege that many of today's workers don't have. As a result, the organization lost a valuable diverse employee. More importantly, because diversity wasn't understood and/or managed well here, this may reinforce negative stereotypes in the future about promoting minorities and women to high-level positions.

Section I of this text continues with readings and exercises that are designed to provide a foundation for your study of workplace diversity. Aurelio and Laib (#1), Allard (#3), Bowman (#4), Minor (#5), and Harvey (#6) will help you to broaden your self-awareness in terms of understanding stereotypes, prejudice, and privilege. Thomas (#2) provides an inclusive framework for a new vision of workplace diversity. McIntosh (#8) explains in more detail the notion of "privilege" and Parker (#7) provides guidelines for dealing with the conflicts that may occur when heterogeneity is introduced into work groups and these differences are not well managed. These readings and exercises will prepare you for the study of the social identity groups (Section II) and the application of organizational diversity and inclusion to the changing organizations of the twenty-first century (Section III).

## BIBLIOGRAPHY

Allport, G. (1954). *The nature of prejudice.* Reading, MA: Addison-Wesley.

Ashmore, R.D., and DelBoca, F.K. (1981). Conceptual approaches to stereotypes and stereotyping. In D.L. Hamilton (Ed.), *Cognitive processes in stereotyping and inter-group behavior* (pp. 1-35). Hillsdale, NJ: Erlbaum.

Begley, S. (2003). The stereotype trap. In S. Plous (Ed.), *Understanding prejudice and discrimination,* (p. 109). McGrawHill: Boston.

Chen, C., and DiTomaso, N. (1996). Performance appraisal and demographic diversity: Issues regarding appraisals, appraisers and appraising. In *Managing diversity: Human resource strategies for transforming the workplace*, E. Kossek & S. Lobel (Eds.), Blackwell Business: Cambridge, MA.

DeLong, T. (2006). A framework for pursuing diversity in the workplace. Harvard Business School reprint, #9-407-029. Harvard Business School Publishing: Cambridge, MA.

Hewlett-Packard. *The diversity value chain*. Retrieved August 27, 2007 from http://www.hp.com/cgi-bin/pf-new.cgi?IN=referer

Pincus, F.L. (2000). Discrimination comes in many forms: individual, institutional and structural. Chapter 4, *Readings for diversity and social justice: An anthology on racism, sexism, anti-semitism, heterosexism, classism, and abelism*. Maurianne Adams et al. (eds.) New York: Routledge.

Sawin, G. (1991, Summer). How stereotypes influence opinions about individuals. *ETC: A Review of General Semantics, 48*(2), 210-212. Retrieved August 20, 2007, from Academic Search Premier database.

SHRM. (2007). *Recruiting for workplace diversity: a business strategy*. Society for Human Resource Management: Alexandria, VA.

The New York Times, *How race is lived in America*. Retrieved August 26, 2007, from www.nytimes.com/library/national/race.

---

**Diversity on the Web**

Go to http://www.understandingprejudice.org/iat/ and take the Implicit Association Tests for race and gender. Over 1,000,000 people have taken these tests. What did these tests teach you about yourself in terms of your conscious and unconscious beliefs?

# DIVERSITY!

Jeanne Aurelio
*Bridgewater State College*


Christopher Laib
*University of Massachusetts, Dartmouth*

Most Americans in the workplace experience people who are very different from themselves on a daily basis. Those differences certainly include temperament and personality, but also areas of diversity, such as cultural, gender, ethnic, religious, sexual orientation, ability, age, and size differences that are the subject of this book. Much is known about the kinds of differences people possess; far too much knowledge for any individual person to know everything about diversity. What is needed is openness to differences and the understanding that everyone's behavior is partially influenced by their diversity profiles. In the interest of being able to work with others (and they with us), we must continually strive both to educate ourselves on what is known about how and why people are different and to keep an open mind.

## PURPOSE

The purpose of the game **DIVERSITY!** is to teach some facts about many areas of diversity, plus provide information about the laws that govern the United States regarding these differences. The game tests current knowledge of many of the aforementioned areas. Because the game is played in teams, it will also enable students to get to know one another. In addition, **DIVERSITY!** is intended to provide a window into the enormous quantity of knowledge available on differences among people.

The authors hope that the **DIVERSITY!** game will interest you in learning about diversity so that you will have an increased acceptance and understanding of people, especially in the workplace. The game has the serious intent of showing you both familiar and unfamiliar areas of knowledge. This game may give you ideas about where to focus your study during this course.

**How To Play**

1. Choose a team of 4–5 people or more, as directed by your instructor. Be sure to sit close together so that you can confer quietly. One team will randomly be chosen to select the first question category and level. All teams will debate their answers internally, and one team member will raise a hand or use his or her assigned team noisemaker when the team is ready to answer.

2. The moderator (instructor), or helper, will call on the first team to respond. If their answer is correct, they will receive the number of points indicated, and choose the next question category and level. If their answer is incorrect, the moderator will call upon the second quickest team to respond, and so on.

3. In the event that no team answers the question correctly, the instructor will give the correct response. The team that chose last still has control of the board and should choose the next question. Scores will be recorded by the moderator, and the winner announced at the end of one or two rounds of 25 questions each, depending upon the time available. As the class goes through the various questions, make note of those you would like to discuss at the conclusion of the game.

## PRACTICE QUESTIONS AT VARIOUS LEVELS (ANSWERS APPEAR IN BOX BELOW.)

1. *Level 2:* In 1983, this astronaut became the first American woman in space.
2. *Level 3:* The number of languages known to be spoken in the world is _____.
3. *Level 4:* In this religion, men may have multiple wives while women must remain monogamous.

## DISCUSSION QUESTIONS

1. Are there any **DIVERSITY!** questions you would like to discuss further?

2. What is one thing you learned as a result of this game that you did not know prior to playing it?

3. In which categories did you notice that you and/or class members were particularly knowledgeable? In which categories did you and/or class members lack knowledge?

4. What is your reaction to this experience?

5. How do you think this experience ties in with the purpose of this course?

*Answer to Practice Questions*

1. Sally Ride   2. 6,800   3. Islam

# Redefining Diversity

## R. Roosevelt Thomas, Jr.

Every decade or so, people who concern themselves with the vigor of U.S. business organizations fasten onto a particular word or phrase that surfaces from a general, wide-ranging issue. For a time, the buzzword is extra hot.

Before long, the word begins to take on a symbolic meaning: It serves as a simple verbal code for the complex problem from which it originated, but no one is really sure any longer what it actually means.

We have seen this happen recently with the word diversity. For the general public it has become verbal shorthand for a workforce that is multiracial, multicultural, and multiethnic—which means it comes preloaded with people's own individual perceptions and biases. For HR managers, it has become a kind of semantic umbrella that encompasses an assortment of HR programs. Senior management and managers of other functions tend to use the word more generally, but they too are essentially referring to workforce demographics.

I think it's time to look at diversity in a new light. In this broader version, diversity applies not only to a company's people concerns, but to many other critical areas as well.

## WHAT DOES DIVERSITY MEAN?

Diversity refers to any mixture of items characterized by differences and similarities. Reproduced with permission from *Managing Diversity*, December 2002, vol. 2, number 3.

Simple enough, on the surface. But like many simple notions, its implications are significant. If we are to put it into operation, we must fully understand what it means.

**Diversity is not synonymous with differences, but encompasses differences and similarities.** Because we are so accustomed to thinking of diversity in terms of workforce demographics, and equating it with the minority constituencies in that workforce, we tend to think diversity means the qualities that are different. Therefore, even when people expand the concept of diversity to include the whole range of strategic issues, they still tend to focus on the differences. But the definition that is put forth here includes not only differences but also similarities.

This is a crucial distinction. It means that when making managerial decisions, you no longer have the option of dealing only with the differences or similarities present in the situation; instead, you must deal with both simultaneously. One way

Reproduced with permission from *Managing Diversity*, December 2002, vol. 2, number 3.

of conceptualizing this is to think in terms of a macro-micro continuum. A micro perspective looks at the individual component and a macro perspective looks at the mixture. To get at the true nature of diversity (comprising differences and similarities) requires an ability to assume both perspectives simultaneously; the micro facilitates identification of differences, and the macro enhances the ability to see similarities.

**Diversity refers to the collective (all-inclusive) mixture of differences and similarities along a given dimension.** When you are dealing with diversity, you are focusing on the collective picture, not just pieces of it. To highlight this notion of mixture, visualize a jar of red jelly beans; now imagine adding some green and purple jelly beans. Many would believe that the green and purple jelly beans represent diversity. I suggest that the diversity instead is represented by the resultant mixture of red, green, and purple jelly beans.

It is easy to see these jelly beans as a metaphor for employees. Of course, it works equally well as a metaphor for any other aspect of the organization that you might be concerned with: It could as easily represent a mixture of product lines, functions, marketing strategies, or operating philosophies.

**The component elements in diversity mixtures can vary, and so a discussion of diversity must specify the dimensions in question.** The components of a diversity mixture can be people, concepts, concrete items, or abstractions. If you are reflecting on the many ways your employees can vary (by race, gender, age, education, sexual orientation, geographic origin or employment, tenure), that's a mixture whose components are people, individuals categorized along multiple dimensions.

But consider your colleague who is struggling to create an environment where various functions (marketing, research, manufacturing, and finance) can do their best work. In that mixture, the components are abstractions known as organizational units or functions. One may argue that functions are composed of individuals, which is true, but the general manager of multiple functions does not experience this as a mixture of people but rather as a mixture of organizational units.

So it is no longer sufficient to say "I'm working on diversity issues," you must also specify which dimension you are dealing with. Otherwise you are very likely to fall into a fruitless discussion of apples and oranges.

## DIVERSITY MANAGEMENT

**The Diversity Management Process** is versatile enough to deal with any of these problems. It is also powerful enough to deal with more than one at the same time. Once you have mastered the use of this tool, you can quickly apply it to other situations:

Step 1:  **Get clear on the problem.** What changes are occurring in the environment your company does business in and how important are they? What do you need to do to succeed in your organizational mission, and what is interfering with your achieving success?

This is not as easy as it sounds. Being able to see clearly, without prejudgments or personal bias, what is happening while you are in the midst of it is an important skill. Future thinking—being able to understand what you see and project its implications—is one hallmark of leaders.

Step 2:  **Analyze the diversity mixture.** The next step is to analyze the set of circumstances you are dealing with. Your goal is to be able to define the situation in terms of a diversity mixture. What are the elements of the mixture at hand? This may be—probably is—a new concept for you.

For example, if your concern is a mixture of product lines, they may be similar (or different) in the mechanisms used to manufacture them, in distribution channels, in profitability ratios, in customer bases, in development costs, and so on.

**Step 3:** **Check for diversity tension.** Ask yourself two questions: Am I seeing tension here as a result of this diversity mixture? And if so, do I need to do anything about it? Diversity tension refers to the conflict, stress, and strain associated with the interactions of the elements of the mixture. Tension of some sort often accompanies a diversity mixture—but not always. When it is present diversity tension is usually easy to spot.

The real question is, does it require attention? Not all tension is bad. "Good" tension produces new ideas, new products, new processes. Good tension acts like fine-grit sandpaper, polishing rough ideas into a gleaming finished product. Tension is a problem only when it interferes with your ability to achieve objectives.

Counterproductive tension is usually obvious. Dysfunctions abound: Interpersonal relationships disintegrate into constant squabbling; petty rivalries between departments end up paralyzing work; functions and work groups that are nominally collaborating are in fact sabotaging each other. Even when goodwill is intact, the complex nature of the situation can create tensions that cripple productivity.

**Step 4:** **Review action options.** Your task at this point is to dispassionately review what is being done to address your primary problems and decide how well that approach is working. If it is not working well, it's time to try something else.

To help managers find that "something else," I developed a structure called the Diversity Paradigm, which is the heart of the diversity management process (see below). Once managers have figured out the essence of the problem, they can review the eight action options and choose one (or more) that seems to offer the best hope of solving it.

### The Diversity Paradigm's Action Options

| Option | Description |
| --- | --- |
| Include/Exclude | Include by expanding the number and variability of mixture components. Or exclude by minimizing the number and variability of mixture components. |
| Deny | Minimize mixture diversity by explaining it away. |
| Assimilate | Minimize mixture diversity by insisting the "minority" components conform to the norms of the dominant factor. |
| Suppress | Minimize mixture diversity by removing it from your consciousness—by assigning it to the subconscious. |
| Isolate | Address diversity by including and setting "different" mixture components off to the side. |

*Continued*

| | |
|---|---|
| **Tolerate** | Address diversity by fostering a room-for-all attitude, albeit with limited superficial interactions among the mixture components. |
| **Build relationships** | Address diversity by fostering quality relationships—characterized by acceptance and understanding—among the components. |
| **Foster mutual adaptation** | Address diversity by fostering mutual adaptation in which all components change somewhat for the sake of achieving common objectives. |

## DISCUSSION QUESTIONS

1. R. Roosevelt Thomas, Jr., has been a well-respected diversity author and consultant for more than twenty years. After reading this article, what surprises you about his "redefinition of diversity"?

2. After reviewing Thomas' eight (8) action options in the Diversity Paradigm model, which of these could be characterized as good management practices even when diversity is not an issue?

3. Because Thomas writes that diversity management has to go beyond legal compliance, do you think that he would or would not support the repeal of Civil Rights legislation? Why?

---

**Diversity on the Web**

Go to the Web address that follows and read Thomas' 2006 article "Diversity Management: An Essential Craft for Leaders."
According to this article, how do the views of managers in other countries differ from a more traditional American approach to diversity management?
Which approach do you think he considers to be best for twenty-first-century organizations? Why?

*http://www.leadertoleader.org/knowledgecenter/journal.aspx?ArticleID=94*

---

# I AM . . .

## M. June Allard

*Assumption College*
*Worcester State College Professor Emerita*

---

**Instructions**

1. Think about how you would describe yourself to someone you have never met. On each line below, write a single-word description.

*I am a(an)*

_____        _____

_____        _____

_____        _____

_____        _____

_____        _____

_____        _____

_____        _____

_____        _____

_____        _____

2. Place a star by the three most important descriptors.

# Increasing Multicultural Understanding: Uncovering Stereotypes

John R. Bowman

*University of North Carolina at Pembroke*

**Instructions Prior to Class**

1. Turn to the Uncovering Stereotypes Worksheet: (Worksheet A).
2. Follow your instructor's directions for completing the blank category boxes that reflect different special populations.
3. Working individually:
   - Complete the **First Thought/Judgment** column by writing your first thought about or judgment of each category. Refer to the example given on Worksheet A.
   - Rate each thought/judgment as positive ($+$), negative ($-$), or neutral (0), and enter these ratings in the **Rating** column.
   - Complete the **Sources** column by indicating the source of your judgment for each category.

**Instructions for Working as a Group in Class:**

- Turn to the Uncovering Stereotypes Group Summary Sheet: (Worksheet B).
- Five categories (Family, Media, Experience, Work Experience, Friends) have already been listed on the summary sheet. Add additional categories (derived from your group discussions) to the sheet.
- Take a quick count of the number of positive, negative, and neutral thoughts/judgments made by your group for each of the Source Categories and enter totals on the last line.
- As a class, discuss which sources lead to positive, which to negative, and which to neutral judgments.
- Discuss the implications of having negative or positive stereotypes/judgments from different perspectives; for example, among workers, between managers and workers, and at the corporate level.

## Worksheet A: Uncovering Stereotypes

| Category | First Thought/Judgment | Rating* | Sources |
|---|---|---|---|
| Working Mother | Neglects children, busy, tired | −, 0, 0 | Own experience, movies |
| Southerner | | | |
| AIDS Carrier | | | |
| Smoker | | | |
| Hispanic | | | |
| Muslim Female | | | |
| Gay African American President of the U.S. | | | |

*(+) = positive
 (−) = negative
 (0)  = neutral

**Worksheet B: Uncovering Stereotypes Group Summary Sheet**

| Source Categories | Positive (+) Thoughts/Judgments | Negative (−) Thoughts/Judgments | Neutral (0) Thoughts/Judgments |
|---|---|---|---|
| Family | | | |
| Media | | | |
| Experience | | | |
| Work Experience | | | |
| Friends | | | |
| Other | | | |
| | | | |
| | | | |
| Total | | | |

**— Diversity on the Web —**

1. Take and score the multicultural quiz found on the Web site listed at the bottom of this box.

2. Think about your score on this quiz and your responses to Bowman's "Uncovering Stereotypes" exercise.
   a) What are your primary sources of information about social identity groups that you do not belong to?
   b) How accurate is your knowledge about these groups?
   c) How could a lack of correct information contribute to the formation of stereotypes?

*http://www.edchange.org/multicultural/quizzes.html*

# Body Ritual Among The Nacirema

## Horace Miner

The anthropologist has become so familiar with the diversity of ways in which different peoples behave in similar situations that he is not apt to be surprised by even the most exotic customs. In fact, if all of the logically possible combinations of behavior have not been found somewhere in the world, he is apt to suspect that they must be present in some yet undescribed tribe. This point has, in fact, been expressed with respect to clan organization by Murdock (1949:71). In this light, the magical beliefs and practices of the Nacirema present such unusual aspects that it seems desirable to describe them as an example of the extremes to which human behavior can go.

Professor Linton first brought the ritual of the Nacirema to the attention of anthropologists twenty years ago (1936:326), but the culture of this people is still very poorly understood. They are a North American group living in the territory between the Canadian Cree, the Yaqui and Tarahumare of Mexico, and the Carib and Arawak of the Antilles. Little is known of their origin, although tradition states that they came from the east. According to Nacirema mythology, their nation was originated by a culture hero, Notgnihsaw, who is otherwise known for two great feats of strength—the throwing of a piece of wampum across the river Pa-To-Mac and the chopping down of a cherry tree in which the Spirit of Truth resided.

Nacirema culture is characterized by a highly developed market economy which has evolved in a rich natural habitat. While much of the people's time is devoted to economic pursuits, a large part of the fruits of these labors and a considerable portion of the day are spent in ritual activity. The focus of this activity is the human body, the appearance and health of which loom as a dominant concern in the ethos of the people. While such concern is certainly not unusual, its ceremonial aspects and associated philosophy are unique.

The fundamental belief underlying the whole system appears to be that the human body is ugly and that its natural tendency is to debility and disease. Incarcerated in such a body, man's only hope is to avert these characteristics through the use of the powerful influences of ritual and ceremony. Every household has one or more shrines devoted to this purpose. The more powerful individuals in the society have several shrines in their houses and, in fact, the opulence of a house is often referred to in terms

*Reproduced by permission of the American Anthropological Association from the *American Anthropologist,* vol. 58, June 1956. Not for further sale or reproduction.

of the number of such ritual centers it possesses. Most houses are of wattle and daub construction, but the shrine rooms of the wealthy are walled with stone. Poorer families imitate the rich by applying pottery plaques to their shrine walls.

While each family has at least one shrine, the rituals associated with it are not family ceremonies but are private and secret. The rites are normally only discussed with children, and then only during the period when they are being initiated into these mysteries. I was able, however, to establish sufficient rapport with the natives to examine these shrines and to have the rituals described to me.

The focal point of the shrine is a box or chest, which is built into the wall. In this chest are kept the many charms and magical potions without which no native believes he could live.

These preparations are secured from a variety of specialized practitioners. The most powerful of these are the medicine men, whose assistance must be rewarded with substantial gifts. However, the medicine men do not provide the curative potions for their clients, but decide what the ingredients should be and then write them down in an ancient and secret language. This writing is understood only by the medicine men and by the herbalists who, for another gift, provide the required charm.

The charm is not disposed of after it has served its purpose, but is placed in the charm-box of the household shrine. As these magical materials are specific for certain ills, and the real or imagined maladies of the people are many, the charm-box is usually full to overflowing. The magical packets are so numerous that the people forget what their purposes were and fear to use them again. While the natives are very vague on this point, we can only assume that the idea in retaining all the old magical materials is that their presence in the charm-box, before which the body rituals are conducted, will in some way protect the worshipper.

Beneath the charm-box is a small font. Each day every member of the family, in succession, enters the shrine room, bows his head before the charm-box, mingles different sorts of holy waters in the font, and proceeds with a brief ritual of ablution. The holy waters are secured from the Water Temple of the community, where the priests conduct elaborate ceremonies to make the liquid ritually pure.

In the hierarchy of magical practitioners, and below the medicine men in prestige, are specialists whose designation is best translated "holy-mouth-men." The Nacirema have an almost pathological horror of and fascination with the mouth, the condition of which is believed to have a supernatural influence on all social relationships. Were it not for the rituals of the mouth, they believe that their teeth would fall out, their gums bleed, their jaws shrink, their friends desert them, and their lovers reject them. They also believe that a strong relationship exists between oral and moral characteristics. For example, there is a ritual ablution of the mouth for children which is supposed to improve their moral fiber.

The daily body ritual performed by everyone includes a mouth-rite. Despite the fact that these people are so punctilious about care of the mouth, this rite involves a practice which strikes the uninitiated stranger as revolting. It was reported to me that the ritual consists of inserting a magic bundle of hog hairs into the mouth, along with certain magical powder, and then moving the bundle in a highly formalized series of gestures.

In addition to the private mouth-rite, the people seek out the holy-mouth-man once or twice a year. These practitioners have an impressive set of paraphernalia, consisting of a variety of augers, awls, probes, and prods. The use of these objects in the exorcism of the evils of the mouth involves almost unbelievable ritual torture of the client.

The holy-mouth-man opens the client's mouth and, using the above mentioned tools, enlarges any holes, which may have been created in the teeth. Magical materials are put into these holes. If there are no naturally occurring holes in the teeth, large sections of one or more teeth are gouged out so that the supernatural substance can be applied. In the client's view, the purpose of the ministrations is to arrest decay and to draw friends. The extremely sacred and traditional character of the rite is evident in the fact that the natives return to the holy-mouth-man, despite the fact that their teeth continue to decay.

It is to be hoped that, when a thorough study of the Nacirema is made, there will be careful inquiry into the personality structure of these people. One has but to watch the gleam in the eye of a holy-mouth-man, as he jabs an awl into an exposed nerve, to suspect that a certain amount of sadism is involved. If this can be established, a very interesting pattern emerges, for most of the population shows definite masochistic tendencies. It was to these that Professor Linton referred in discussing a distinctive part of the daily body ritual which was performed only by men. This part of the rite involves scraping and lacerating the surface of the face with a sharp instrument. Special women's rites are performed only four times during each lunar month, but what they lack in frequency is made up for in barbarity. As part of this ceremony, women bake their heads in small ovens for about an hour. The theoretically interesting point is that what seems to be a preponderantly masochistic people have developed sadistic specialists.

The medicine men have an imposing temple, or latipso, in every community of any size. The more elaborate ceremonies required to treat very sick patients can only be performed at this temple. These ceremonies involve not only the thaumaturge but a permanent group of vestal maidens who move sedately about the temple chambers in distinctive costume and headdress.

The latipso ceremonies are so harsh that it is phenomenal that a fair proportion of the really sick natives who enter the temple ever recover. Small children whose indoctrination is still incomplete have been known to resist attempts to take them to the temple because "that is where you go to die." Despite this fact, sick adults are not only willing but eager to undergo the protracted ritual purification, if they can afford to do so. No matter how ill the supplicant or how grave the emergency, the guardians of many temples will not admit a client if he cannot give a rich gift to the custodian. Even after one has gained admission and survived the ceremonies, the guardians will not permit the neophyte to leave until he makes still another gift.

The supplicant entering the temple is first stripped of all his or her clothes. In everyday life the Nacirema avoids exposure of his body and its natural functions. Bathing and excretory acts are performed only in the secrecy of the household shrine, where they are ritualized as part of the body-rites. Psychological shock results from the fact that body secrecy is suddenly lost upon entry into the latipso. This sort of ceremonial treatment is necessitated by the fact that the excreta are used by a diviner to ascertain the course and nature of the client's sickness. Female clients, on the other hand, find their naked bodies are subjected to the scrutiny, manipulation, and prodding of the medicine men.

Few supplicants in the temple are well enough to do anything but lie on their hard beds. The daily ceremonies, like the rites of the holy-mouth-men, involve discomfort and torture. With ritual precision, the vestals awaken their miserable charges each dawn and roll them about on their beds of pain while performing ablutions, in the formal movements of which the maidens are highly trained. At other times they insert magic wands in the supplicant's mouth or force him to eat substances which are supposed to be healing. From time to time the medicine men come to their clients and jab magically treated needles into their flesh. The fact that these ceremonies may not cure, and may even kill the neophyte, in no way decreases the people's faith in the medicine men.

There remains one other kind of practitioner, known as a "listener." This witch-doctor has the power to exorcise the devils that lodge in the heads of people who have been bewitched. The Nacirema believe that parents bewitched their own children. Mothers are particularly suspected of putting a curse on children while teaching them the secret body rituals. The counter-magic of the witch-doctor is unusual in its lack of ritual. The patient simply tells the "listener" all his troubles and fears, beginning with the earliest difficulties he can remember. The memory displayed by the Nacirema in these exorcism sessions is truly remarkable. It is not uncommon for the patient to bemoan the rejection he felt upon being weaned as a babe, and a few individuals even see their troubles going back to the traumatic effects of their own birth.

In conclusion, mention must be made of certain practices which have their base in native esthetics but which depend upon the pervasive aversion to the natural body and its functions. There are ritual fasts to make fat people thin and ceremonial feasts to make thin people fat. Still other rites are used to make women's breasts larger if they are small, and smaller if they are large. General dissatisfaction with breast shape is symbolized in the fact that the ideal form is virtually outside the range of human variation. A few women afflicted with almost inhuman hypermammary development are so idolized that they make a handsome living by simply going from village to village and permitting the natives to stare at them for a fee.

Reference has already been made to the fact that excretory functions are ritualized, routinized, and relegated to secrecy. Natural reproduction functions are similarly distorted. Intercourse is taboo as a topic and scheduled as an act. Efforts are made to avoid pregnancy by the use of magical materials or by limiting intercourse to certain phases of the moon. Conception is actually very infrequent. When pregnant, women dress so as to hide their condition. Parturition takes place in secret, without friends or relatives to assist, and the majority of women do not nurse their infants.

Our review of the ritual life of the Nacirema has certainly shown them to be a magic-ridden people. It is hard to understand how they have managed to exist so long under the burdens which they have imposed upon themselves. But even such exotic customs as these take on real meaning when they are viewed with the insight provided by Malinowski when he wrote (1948:70).

Looking from far and above, from our high places of safety in developed civilization, it is easy to see all the crudity and irrelevance of magic. But without its power and guidance, early man could not have advanced to the higher stages of civilization.

## DISCUSSION QUESTIONS

1. What general message do you think the author was trying to convey in his description of this culture?

2. Why are some behaviors described as "magic"?

3. Why are some behaviors described as "rituals"? Do you think this is a fair label?

4. Does the humorous approach to this culture bother you? Do you feel that the description is belittling or sarcastic in tone?

5. Imagine that you are a member of the author's culture described in this article. What stereotypes could you have about this culture and its people if this reading is your only source of information?

---

**Diversity on the Web**

# NACIREMA EXTENDED

You are a member of a team of anthropologists studying a large and rather diverse group of people. These people have a primitive information and communication system called "Internet" that will provide you with a first glimpse of their culture. To begin examining this culture, the team decides to scan "Internet" for information on their rituals.

1. Read the *Body Ritual Among the Nacirema* article in this text by Miner.
2. Using the Web sites listed at the bottom of this box as a starting point, investigate ("scan") Internet for descriptions of one ritual. Be complete in your investigation, searching for symbolism and note how the ritual relates to a holiday or event. What does the ritual celebrate? Are there special roles in the event? Who participates?
3. Using a style similar to Miner's, record your perceptions of one of the events from the list that follows. A sample description ("Observation of the Cultural Event Called Halloween") appears on the next page.
4. Based *solely* on the information in your report, what kinds of stereotypes of American culture could result from these observations?

### College Graduation Ceremonies

- http://brownielocks.com/graduation_ceremony.html
- http://www.wrightwood.com/college.htm
- http://timesofindia.indiatimes.com/Delhi_times/An_underwater_degree_ceremony/articleshow/22050.cms

### National Political Conventions

- http://people.howstuffworks.com/political-convention.htm
- http://wikipedia.org/wiki/united_states_presidential_nominating_convention
- http://en.wikiedia.org/wiki/political_convention

| | |
|---|---|
| **Saint Patrick's Day Parade** | http://saintpatricksdayparade.com |
| **Mardi Gras Parade** | http://www.holidays.net/mardigras/parades.htm |
| **Thanksgiving Parade** | http://www.nyctourist.com/macys_menu.htm |
| **Easter Parade** | http://www.ny.com/holiday/easter |
| **Rose Parade** | http://www.tournamentofroses.com/aboutus/officialPhotos.asp |

Adapted from Nacirema Extended by M. J. Allard from C. P. Harvey & M. J. Allard: *Understanding and Managing Diversity,* 3rd ed. Prentice Hall, 2005.

## BIBLIOGRAPHY

Linton, Ralph. (1936). *The study of man*. New York: D. Appleton-Century Co.

Malinowski, B. (1948). *Magic science and religion*. Glencoe, IL: The Free Press.

Murdock, G. P. (1948). *Social structure*. New York: The MacMillan Company.

## SAMPLE DESCRIPTION

### Observation of Cultural Event Called Halloween

Halloween is a very strange custom. It doesn't appear to be a holiday; it is more like an event—an event characterized by at least two rituals and many symbols. There seem to be no special roles for males, females, or elders. The chief rituals appear to be the 1) Ritual of the Pumpkins and 2) Ritual of the Begging.

**Ritual of the Pumpkins.**

The pumpkin vegetable, which apparently is eaten at other times of the year, is not eaten at this event. Instead, the people paint strange faces on pumpkins or carve faces on empty pumpkin shells. Lighted candles are placed inside the carved pumpkins. Decorated pumpkins appear in windows facing outdoors or on display outside of homes.

**Ritual of the Begging.**

This is a special ritual for children. On Halloween night, children dress up in costumes that frequently represent mythical characters—ghosts, witches, monsters, ghouls, cartoon characters. They wear masks to hide their identities. After dark the children go begging from house to house, calling out "Trick or treat." People then open their doors and give candy to the children. Sometimes the children play pranks on the people.

**Symbols.**

Among the prominent symbols of Halloween are ghosts, skeletons, spiders, witches, black cats, grave yards and monsters, all of which seem to be very frightening, gory, ugly, or sinister in character. Not only are these symbols displayed in the costumes the children wear, but many houses are adorned on the outside with displays of them, particularly witches and ghosts.

Sometimes people visit "haunted houses" (eerie houses where frightening creatures lurk in dark corners to scare people). Sometimes, too, people attend social events called Halloween parties where they play strange games such as dunking their heads in buckets of water while trying to catch an apple in their teeth.

These events are sometimes for adults and sometimes for children.

# Exploring Diversity in Your Organization

## Carol P. Harvey
### *Assumption College*

Agood beginning to a course in diversity is to analyze how diversity or lack of diversity could affect an organization with which you are quite familiar. Your instructor can assign either Option A, which is relevant to exploring diversity on a college campus, or Option B, which is appropriate for an organization where you are or have been recently employed.

## INSTRUCTIONS

### *Option A — Exploring Diversity on Your College Campus*

1. **Organizational Leadership.** Using the catalog, Web page, or other resources, research your college to determine who has the power to make important decisions in the organization. How diverse is this college in terms of its board of trustees and senior staff such as vice presidents, provosts, deans, and above?

2. **Faculty.** Using the catalog, Web page, or other resources, research your college's faculty to determine how diverse they are. Contrast the effects of having a more homogeneous faculty and a more heterogeneous faculty in terms of: (a) your learning experiences, (b) your advising/mentoring experiences, or (c) any other aspects of your college life, such as athletics, extracurricular activities, and so on.

3. **Student Body.** Compare the student body with the organizational leadership and faculty. In most cases, the students are younger and less educated, but are there other obvious differences such as race, gender, or ethnicity? How does the student body compare with the community in which the college is located? (Check www.census.gov.) If there are major differences, how can these be an advantage or a disadvantage to your college experience? Explain your answer.

4a. If your college is diverse in terms of leadership, faculty, and/or students, how does diversity contribute to your learning experience and/or personal development?

**or**

4b. If your college isn't diverse, how does the lack of diversity affect your learning experience and/or personal development?

### *Option B—Exploring Diversity in Your Work Organization*

1. **Organizational Leadership.** Using the organizational chart, Web page, or other resources, research your company to determine who has the power to make important decisions in the organization. How diverse is this organization in terms of its board of directors and senior managers such as vice presidents, area managers, and above? *(Note: The criteria for defining diversity may be related to the location and the mission of your company. For example, if you are working in a racially diverse city, such as Detroit, you may find more African Americans. If you are working in fashion retail, you may find more women in leadership positions. Although many aspects of diversity aren't visible, the purpose here is more to determine if there are obvious groups that are not represented in the leadership of the company.)*

2. **Lower-level and/or hourly workers.** How does the diversity of the board and management of your organization compare with the composition of the various levels of your organization? What types of issues does this raise? Provide specific examples.

3. **Customers.** If your organization works with consumers and clients, how do your target markets compare with the management and staff of your organization in terms of diversity?

4. In the future, how could diversity or lack of diversity affect your career and/or the ability of the organization to meet customer/client needs?

# The Emotional Connection of Distinguishing Differences and Conflict

Carole G. Parker

In recent years, diversity in organizations has been an exciting, stimulating, frustrating, and intriguing topic. Some organizations continue to struggle for diversity, whereas others have a fully integrated diverse workforce. The challenge to increase and manage diversity continues to be critical to organizational goals, particularly as more organizations, large and small, transact business internationally. Some organizations work to appreciate diversity and value differences, whereas others continue to discount differences and diversity. Smart managers today realize the importance of balance in work groups. Attempts to incorporate differences in age, gender, race, culture, sexual preference, and styles of being in their organizations to capitalize on the incredible potential diversity offers are occurring. Managing differences requires energy, commitment, tolerance, and finally, appreciation among all parties involved. Differences among people are not inherently good or bad; there is no one "right" way to deal with differences. Learning to manage and ultimately appreciate differences requires learning, emotional growth, and stretching the boundaries of all participants. Although differences can be challenging, they also lead to very important benefits, both to individuals, groups and organizations.

## HOW DIFFERENCES ARE OFTEN MANAGED

What action and factors must be uppermost in selecting the most appropriate approach to addressing differences? Often avoidance or repression is used to manage differences. The avoidance of differences often takes the form of associating with individuals of similar backgrounds, experiences, beliefs, and values. This strategy enables an environment of mutual support and predictability. Those who are adverse to risk or challenges are apt to select this strategy. Another avoidance strategy is to separate individuals who create sparks between each other. Although this strategy may reduce tension, it minimizes the opportunity for individuals and the organization to learn and grow.

The repression of differences occurs when an individual or organization refuses to allow disagreements to emerge. Top management often influences the culture by stressing conformity, which naturally affects diversity. Statements by managers such as: "We must work on this project in a professional and collegial manner," or "By working together cooperatively, we will succeed during these difficult times," create the boundaries for behavior limited to cooperation, collaboration, and loyalty and limit the opportunity for challenging assumptions, testing new ideas, and strategies for success. Repression is quite costly. Resistances develop that have both organizational and individual consequences. Blocking strong feelings and repressing differences may result in desensitization and loss of productivity. When individual differences come together, managers exert control to reduce conflict.

Both appropriate times and dangers are associated with the use of avoidance and repression in managing differences. Teams or work groups faced with tight deadlines may want to limit the number and type of ideas generated. Avoidance may be an appropriate interim strategy for dealing with differences by enabling an individual to learn more about a person or situation before advancing a stance. The challenge to management is to decide when it is most appropriate to use these approaches. The skill level of the manager, rather than an overt choice, may also influence the decision. Avoidance can lead to groupthink, which occurs when everyone in a group agrees with everyone else, even though there are different opinions, values, beliefs, and perceptions among group members. Groupthink is the result of not challenging ideas, opinions, values, or beliefs. Individuals may not believe it is safe (concerns about advancing or retaining one's job) to challenge, particularly if management does not model this behavior.

Still another danger in avoiding differences is overcompatibility. When overcompatibility exists in an organization, it may be due to a strong need for support, reassurance, or security, or a need to eliminate perceived threats. In an organization, this can severely hamper the development of new ideas, productivity, growth, and development. Avoidance and repression of differences are not viable solutions. When differences are present, they must be expressed and worked through. If not, unnecessary conflict will result.

## POSITIVE ASPECTS OF DIFFERENCES

- Differences are opportunities. The old adage "Two heads are better than one" has merit. When combining multiple perspectives, one gains a richer set of experiences, and the variability of these often leads to a more creative approach than could be achieved independently.
- Differences are tests to the strength of a position. One needs to be sure all the perspectives, opinions, and perceptions enhance the final product.

A healthy interaction among differences (gender, age, race, culture, etc.) could address the preceding concerns. Two factors influence the treatment of differences: first, the needs, wants, and goals of the individual; and second, the value placed on the relationship. People are often motivated by the desire to meet their needs and satisfy their wants and desires. The stronger the motivation, the greater the likelihood of addressing differences. Furthermore, when the persons involved are important to each other, or valued, the tendency to manage the differences increases to preserve the relationship. The reverse is likely when there is no value in the relationship. Once these factors are assessed, it becomes necessary to recognize behavior and attitudes that *will* be helpful in managing the differences.

Differences are not problems to be solved; they are dilemmas to be managed. Successful managers of difference reduce their judgments and accept the difference as legitimate. Clear boundaries between self and others, a willingness and interest in being influenced, and an awareness of choice with the ability to make choices are also helpful. Using strong language such as *ought to, cannot, necessary, impossible, requirement,* or *mandate* will diminish success.

Differences are experienced from contact with others who are dissimilar. A range of life experiences and success in interpersonal relationships support the ability to deal with differences. Individuals who have traveled nationally and internationally, or who have had unusual experiences beyond the normal scope of their daily activities tend to develop an appreciation for differences, even though at the time of initial contact there may have been challenges, fear, and longing for what is familiar. Managing differences is not an individual process; it is interactive among individuals. When only one individual is attempting to deal with the difference, the result is coping behavior. Dealing with differences evokes emotion. A range of emotions for human interaction that leads to awareness of differences is necessary. These emotions can lead to conflict, but conflict is *not* a prerequisite to managing differences.

Differences evoke emotions at different levels, ranging from small or minor to large and major. An inverted triangle graphically shows the escalating intensity in each level of emotion as differences are encountered (see Figure 1).

This model is based on the assumption that difficulties will likely result from contact with differences. The first level involves an awareness of the difference. Here the parties are exploring and learning about each other—what is similar, what is not, and what is discomforting; the second level may result. One becomes uncomfortable

**FIGURE 1   The Escalation of Differences into Conflict**

Conflict/War
Hostility
Anger
Open Disagreement
Frustration
Heightened Tension
Irritation
Annoyance
Discomfort
Awareness of Differences

ESCALATING INTENSITY

with boundaries being pushed while values or beliefs are challenged. When the differences appear to be greater than the similarities, annoyance occurs. The parties are not able to appreciate how their differences may be beneficial to each other. Irritation, on the next level, may result from continued exploration, possibly through a dialectic process. Tension is heightening as more contact occurs; there is possibly an overlay of fear. The boundaries of self are threatened (What will happen to me if I continue with this encounter?), and frustration leading to open disagreement develops.

Anger, often a protective strategy, shifts the emotions to the next level, and hostility erupts while the dispute solidifies. Each party has a firm stance reflecting his or her position. The final level is conflict or war, where each party works hard to repress, neutralize, or destroy the other. In Figure 1, we suggest that an individual, group, organization, or society may, depending on the situation, traverse through each of these emotional levels when encountering differences. The process is not necessarily a linear one. Emotions run deep on various issues and could erupt immediately from awareness to hostility or anger or any other step on the triangle. In fact, awareness can lead to avoidance, tolerance, or appreciation.

Recent history lends itself to application of the triangle. In February 1993, terrorists, who have different values and beliefs than most Americans, bombed the New York City World Trade Center. The explosion caused six deaths, 1,042 injuries, and nearly $600 million in property damage. Americans were shocked, and then-President Clinton declared that every effort should be taken to bring those responsible to justice. Swift actions led to the prosecution and conviction of four of seven co-conspirators. Yet the American public, although outraged and frightened by the experience, only demonstrated minimal awareness that there were dramatic differences between the U.S. foreign policy and those on the receiving end of the policy. Not until seven years later, with the attacks on the World Trade Center again, along with the Pentagon in Washington, D.C., did awareness shift to outrage, anger, hostility, and, ultimately, conflict/war.

During the aftermath of the events of September 11, 2001, when thousands of people from many countries met their peril in the attack on the World Trade Center, the United States unified against all who would harm her. In many instances, those who disagreed with the policy to go to war with those responsible for this terrorist act were afraid to speak out. It was considered anti-American to express different opinions about how to handle terrorist activity focused on the United States. Such behavior is an example of groupthink, mentioned earlier in this chapter. The government is particularly susceptible to groupthink where patriotism must be at the highest, yet evidence of dissent tends to make its way to the media, newsprint, or television. Still, individuals may be reluctant to speak candidly against the actions of government policy.

Conflict, at the top of the triangle, may result or emerge from differences. There are many definitions of conflict. Listed here are typical examples of definitions:

1. Conflict exists when two or more parties want the same thing or their wants are incompatible in some way.
2. Conflict must involve emotionality; it is a disturbing emotion within ourselves and may involve feelings of anger and frustration.
3. The higher the stakes, the greater the conflict; one must *care* to have conflict.
4. Conflict can be internal: within oneself, a group, or between groups. Conflict involves competition of wants and viewpoints.
5. Conflict can be enjoyable.

It is important to distinguish conflict from difference. Difference and conflict are both important and necessary ingredients in human interaction and, if valued, can lead to opportunity, creativity, and appreciation. Difference is a component of diversity, which is a constant in our environment. Managers and the workforce are grappling with this constant and learning that appreciating or valuing differences opens the door to new and creative ways of addressing organizational challenges. For example, when a group of salaried and union personnel from the automotive industry were invited to identify adjectives they associate with conflict, most of the language was highly charged, emotional, and violent. The list generated for differences was dramatically broader, more varied, and less emotionally charged, and contained language of hope (see Table 1).

The autoworkers pointed out that differences can lead to conflict and cited examples, including the inability to motivate employees to complete their assigned jobs, poor communication, pressures concerning time, inequity in work assignments, differences of opinions, and methods for getting work done. They further pointed out how important it is for people to listen to each other and pay attention to differences, incorporating the differences into the process of solving a problem or completing a task, not just engaging in conflict because of a difference.

It was believed that when a diverse team worked together, there was greater creativity and innovation, a sense of connectedness, more risk taking, less boredom, higher productivity, and greater cooperation. On the other hand, the mismanagement of differences or engaging in conflictual behavior in the organization would most likely lead to higher stress, individual withdrawal, limited learning, less risk taking, overcompatibility, interpersonal tension, and decreased communication.

## THE EMOTIONAL CONNECTION

Emotional intelligence is one key to developing the ability to manage and appreciate differences. Emotional intelligence involves at least five elements: awareness of self, the ability to recognize personal emotions when they are occurring; managing self, which involves awareness of and engaging in emotions that are appropriate to a situation; self-motivation, putting emotional energy into action for a useful purpose and controlling

| Table 1.1 | Distinguishing Difference and Conflict |
| --- | --- |

| Conflict | Difference |
| --- | --- |
| Anger | Opinions |
| War | Ideas |
| Tension | Options |
| Frustration | Methods |
| Kill | Skills |
| Hostility | Race |
| Shouting | Gender |
| | Jobs |
| | Age |
| | Interpretation |
| | Values |
| | Environment |

emotions when necessary; awareness of emotions in others, which involves empathy and demonstrating caring when appropriate; and finally, managing interpersonal relationships, which involves dealing with both self and others in social, professional, and personal interactions (Goleman, 1995). Emotional intelligence, then, is the ability to be aware of, name, and manage individual experience of emotions. The triangle in Figure 1 illustrates the escalating intensity of emotions when differences are mismanaged or misunderstood and develop into conflict. Managers must recognize that it is the diversity in styles of interaction and the particular way a person or group makes meaning of his or her experience that creates the experience of difference. Difference enables choice and opportunity as much as it may create tension and insecurity; this also enables the organization to achieve its objectives. Differences provide opportunities to develop our emotional intelligence. According to Cherniss and Goleman (2001), managers and workers who develop their emotional intelligence may be able to improve their effectiveness at work and potential for advancement. In addition, personal relationships will improve and strengthen when an individual develops emotional intelligence.

The family is an excellent and readily accessible unit for exploring and experimenting with emotional intelligence. Our home life is often a place where we must manage differences with significant consequences for either harmony or unrest. One answer to understanding the emotional impact of encountering differences at home or in the work environment may come with knowledge of three major transitions occurring in contemporary society. Fritz Capra (1982) suggests that a paradigm shift in the thoughts, perceptions, and values that form a particular view of reality is essential if the world is to survive. This is a pattern or paradigm shift involving moving from certainty to uncertainty, closed to open systems, truth to no truth, and a realization of multiple realities coexisting in a complex society. Recognition and mastery of this paradigm shift may prove to be a motivation for developing the emotional skills necessary for valuing diversity and managing differences.

Historically, it has not been acceptable for professionals to exhibit emotions in the workplace; with the introduction of emotional intelligence, there is more acceptance of the whole person and the resulting complexity. When managing diversity or differences, one has at least four options for guiding behavior: avoidance, conflict, tolerance, and appreciation. Avoidance provides an opportunity to learn more about the difference before declaring a stance. In this sense, avoidance as a strategy for managing differences may facilitate new learning and greater opportunity for future interaction of a productive nature. On the other hand, avoidance may be a survival strategy between different status levels within the organization. Clearly, a manager may tell a subordinate to "sit down and just be quiet." Under these circumstances, the worker could jeopardize his or her position with the organization if the worker chooses noncompliance.

Tolerance as a strategy may be influenced by status within the organization. Managers generally have the power and authority to get their viewpoints adopted. Nonmanagers often must compromise or tolerate the views of their managers, even when they feel the freedom to express an opposing viewpoint. Oftentimes, adopting tolerance is necessary, because it allows for the expression of differences; however, when there is an imbalance of power, the options for influence are limited. The upside of tolerance is an individual's opportunity to express a point of view that is active involvement, rather than passive participation, in an event. Conflict as a strategy may also serve some purpose. Conflict involves direct and active resistance to another, and may involve judgments of good, bad, right, or wrong. Often conflict occurs more openly among managers, who have higher status and more latitude than subordinates to resist a point of view or the directives of each other and top management. Finally, appreciation of differences or diversity demonstrates a high degree of personal development and growth at the individual level. The process of appreciation involves a collaborative interaction among various parties with differences. When differences are appreciated, there are usually organizational norms that support the freedom of expression without fear of reprisal. With the ability to discuss differences openly, using a dialectical process, parties are often able to employ multiple strategies, resulting ultimately in appreciation. Appreciation results from applying the skills of emotional intelligence mentioned earlier.

## CONCLUSION

Developing healthy ways to acknowledge and respond to diversity (differences) and the emotions evoked increases our ability to not only manage ourselves, but also to manage others in workplace and personal settings. Employing a combination of strategies, such as conflict, avoidance, tolerance, and appreciation, may demonstrate the capacity of an individual to manage differences and value diversity.

## DISCUSSION QUESTIONS

1. How can one distinguish difference from conflict?

2. What are some of the dangers of avoiding and repressing differences?

3. Think of an experience that you had in an organization or social setting involving avoidance or repression of differences. What was the outcome? How did you feel about the outcome?

4. What are some positive aspects of difference?

5. What roles do emotions play in our ability to manage differences?

6. How can you develop the skills needed to increase your emotional intelligence?

## BIBLIOGRAPHY

Cherniss, C., & Goleman, D. (2001). *The emotionally intelligent workplace*. San Francisco: Jossey-Bass.

Capra, F. (1982). *The turning point*. New York: Bantam.

Goleman, D. (1995). *Emotional intelligence*. New York: Bantam.

---

### Diversity on the Web

Research the history of a major class-action lawsuit, such as Bell South, Texaco, Denny's, Georgia Power, Wal-Mart, etc. Develop a time line of the events that led to these lawsuits.

Do the events listed on the time line indicate escalating conflict as illustrated by Parker's triangle?

What actions or interventions could have been taken to prevent these conflicts from escalating into costly lawsuits?

# White Privilege and Male Privilege: A Personal Account of Coming to See Correspondences through Work in Women's Studies

Peggy McIntosh

*Wellesley College*

**T**hrough work to bring materials and perspectives from Women's Studies into the rest of the curriculum, I have often noticed men's unwillingness to grant that they are over privileged in the curriculum, even though they may grant that women are disadvantaged. Denials which amount to taboos surround the subject of advantages which men gain from women's disadvantages. These denials protect male privilege from being fully recognized, acknowledged, lessened, or ended.

Thinking through unacknowledged male privilege as a phenomenon with a life of its own, I realized that since hierarchies in our society are interlocking, there was most likely a phenomenon of white privilege which was similarly denied and protected, but alive and real in its effects. As a white person, I realized I had been taught about racism as something which puts others at a disadvantage, but had been taught not to see one of its corollary aspects, white privilege, which puts me at an advantage.

I think whites are carefully taught not to recognize white privilege, as males are taught not to recognize male privilege. So I have begun in an untutored way to ask what it is like to have white privilege. This paper is a partial record of my personal observations, and not a scholarly analysis. It is based on my daily experiences within my particular circumstances.

I have come to see white privilege as an invisible package of unearned assets which I can count on cashing in each day, but about which I was "meant" to remain oblivious. White privilege is like an invisible weightless knapsack of special

*©1988 Peggy McIntosh. May not be reprinted without permission of the author. mmcintosh@wellesley.edu

provisions, assurances, tools, maps, guides, codebooks, passports, visas, clothes, compass, emergency gear, and blank checks.

Since I have had trouble facing white privilege, and describing its results in my life, I saw parallels here with men's reluctance to acknowledge male privilege. Only rarely will a man go beyond acknowledging that women are disadvantaged to acknowledging that men have unearned advantage, or that unearned privilege has not been good for men's development as human beings, or for society's development, or that privilege systems might ever be challenged and *changed*.

I will review here several types or layers of denial which I see at work protecting, and preventing awareness about, entrenched male privilege. Then I will draw parallels, from my own experience, with the denials which veil the facts of white privilege. Finally, I will list 46 ordinary and daily ways in which I experience having white privilege, within my life situation and its particular social and political frameworks.

Writing this paper has been difficult, despite warm receptions for the talks on which it is based.[1] For describing white privilege makes one newly accountable. As we in Women's Studies work to reveal male privilege and ask men to give up some of their power, so one who writes about having white privilege must ask, "Having described it, what will I do to lessen or end it?"

The denial of men's over-privileged state takes many forms in discussions of curriculum-change work. Some claim that men must be central in the curriculum because they have done most of what is important or distinctive in life or in civilization. Some recognize sexism in the curriculum but deny that it makes male students seem unduly important in life. Others agree that certain *individual* thinkers are blindly male-oriented but deny that there is any systemic tendency in disciplinary frameworks or epistemology to over-empower men as a group. Those men who do grant that male privilege takes institutionalized and embedded forms are still likely to deny that male hegemony has opened doors for them personally. Virtually all men deny that male over-reward alone can explain men's centrality in all the inner sanctums of our most powerful institutions. Moreover, those few who will acknowledge that male privilege systems have over-empowered them usually end up doubting that we could dismantle these privilege systems. They may say they will work to improve women's status, in the society or in the university, but they can't or won't support the idea of lessening men's. In curricular terms, this is the point at which they say that they regret they cannot use any of the interesting new scholarship on women because the syllabus is full. When the talk turns to giving men less cultural room, even the most fair-minded of the men I know well tend to reflect, or fall back on, conservative assumptions about the inevitability of present gender relations and distributions of power, calling on precedent or sociobiology and psychobiology to demonstrate that male domination is natural and follows inevitably from evolutionary pressures. Others resort to arguments from "experience" or religion or social responsibility or wishing and dreaming.

After I realized, through faculty development work in Women's Studies, the extent to which men work from a base of unacknowledged privilege, I understood that much of their oppressiveness was unconscious. Then I remembered the frequent charges from women of color that white women whom they encounter are oppressive. I began to understand why we are justly seen as oppressive, even when we don't see ourselves that way. At the very least, obliviousness of one's privileged state can make a person or group irritating to be with. I began to count the ways in which I enjoy unearned skin privilege and have been conditioned into oblivion about its existence, unable to see that it put me "ahead" in any way, or put my people ahead, over-rewarding us and yet also paradoxically damaging us, or that it could or should be changed.

My schooling gave me no training in seeing myself as an oppressor, as an unfairly advantaged person, or as a participant in a damaged culture. I was taught to see myself as an individual whose moral state depended on her individual moral will. At school, we were not taught about slavery in any depth; we were not taught to see slaveholders as damaged people. Slaves were seen as the only group at risk of being dehumanized. My schooling followed the pattern which Elizabeth Minnich has pointed out: Whites are taught to think of their lives as morally neutral, normative, and average, and also ideal, so that when we work to benefit others, this is seen as work which will allow "them" to be more like "us." I think many of us know how obnoxious this attitude can be in men.

After frustration with men who would not recognize male privilege, I decided to try to work on myself at least by identifying some of the daily effects of white privilege in my life. It is crude work, at this stage, but I will give here a list of special circumstances and conditions I experience which I did not earn but which I have been made to feel are mine by birth, by citizenship, and by virtue of being a conscientious law-abiding "normal" person of good will. I have chosen those conditions which I think in my case *attach somewhat more to skin-color privilege* than to class, religion, ethnic status, or geographical location, though of course all these other factors are intricately intertwined. As far as I can see, my Afro-American co-workers, friends, and acquaintances with whom I come into daily or frequent contact in this particular time, place, and line of work cannot count on most of these conditions.

1. I can if I wish arrange to be in the company of people of my race most of the time.
2. I can avoid spending time with people whom I was trained to mistrust and who have learned to mistrust my kind or me.
3. If I should need to move, I can be pretty sure of renting or purchasing housing in an area which I can afford and in which I would want to live.
4. I can be pretty sure that my neighbors in such a location will be neutral or pleasant to me.
5. I can go shopping alone most of the time, pretty well assured that I will not be followed or harassed.
6. I can turn on the television or open to the front page of the paper and see people of my race widely represented.
7. When I am told about our national heritage or about "civilization," I am shown that people of my color made it what it is.
8. I can be sure that my children will be given curricular materials that testify to the existence of their race.
9. If I want to, I can be pretty sure of finding a publisher for this piece on white privilege.
10. I can be pretty sure of having my voice heard in a group in which I am the only member of my race.
11. I can be casual about whether or not to listen to another woman's voice in a group in which she is the only member of her race.
12. I can go into a music shop and count on finding the music of my race represented, into a supermarket and find the staple foods which fit with my cultural traditions, into a hairdresser's shop and find someone who can cut my hair.

13. Whether I use checks, credit cards, or cash, I can count on my skin color not to work against the appearance of financial reliability.
14. I can arrange to protect my children most of the time from people who might not like them.
15. I do not have to educate my children to be aware of systemic racism for their own daily physical protection.
16. I can be pretty sure that my children's teachers and employers will tolerate them if they fit school and workplace norms; my chief worries about them do not concern others' attitudes toward their race.
17. I can talk with my mouth full and not have people put this down to my color.
18. I can swear, or dress in second-hand clothes, or not answer letters, without having people attribute these choices to the bad morals, the poverty, or the illiteracy of my race.
19. I can speak in public to a powerful male group without putting my race on trial.
20. I can do well in a challenging situation without being called a credit to my race.
21. I am never asked to speak for all the people of my racial group.
22. I can remain oblivious of the language and customs of persons of color who constitute the world's majority without feeling in my culture any penalty for such oblivion.
23. I can criticize our government and talk about how much I fear its policies and behavior without being seen as a cultural outsider.
24. I can be pretty sure that if I ask to talk to "the person in charge," I will be facing a person of my race.
25. If a traffic cop pulls me over or if the IRS audits my tax return, I can be sure I haven't been singled out because of my race.
26. I can easily buy posters, postcards, picture books, greeting cards, dolls, toys, and children's magazines featuring people of my race.
27. I can go home from most meetings of organizations I belong to feeling somewhat tied in, rather than isolated, out-of-place, outnumbered, unheard, held at a distance, or feared.
28. I can be pretty sure that an argument with a colleague of another race is more likely to jeopardize her chances for advancement than to jeopardize mine.
29. I can be pretty sure that if I argue for the promotion of a person of another race, or a program centering on race, this is not likely to cost me heavily within my present setting, even if my colleagues disagree with me.
30. If I declare there is a racial issue at hand, or there isn't a racial issue at hand, my race will lend me more credibility for either position than a person of color will have.
31. I can choose to ignore developments in minority writing and minority activist programs, or disparage them, or learn from them, but in any case, I can find ways to be more or less protected from negative consequences of any of these choices.
32. My culture gives me little fear about ignoring the perspectives and powers of people of other races.
33. I am not made acutely aware that my shape, bearing, or body odor will be taken as a reflection of my race.
34. I can worry about racism without being seen as self-interested or self-seeking.
35. I can take a job with an affirmative action employer without having my coworkers on the job suspect that I got it because of my race.

36. If my day, week, or year is going badly, I need not ask of each negative episode or situation whether it has racial overtones.
37. I can be pretty sure of finding people who would be willing to talk with me and advise me about my next steps, professionally.
38. I can think over many options, social, political, imaginative, or professional, without asking whether a person of my race would be accepted or allowed to do what I want to do.
39. I can be late to a meeting without having the lateness reflect on my race.
40. I can choose public accommodation without fearing that people of my race cannot get in or will be mistreated in the places I have chosen.
41. I can be sure that if I need legal or medical help, my race will not work against me.
42. I can arrange my activities so that I will never have to experience feelings of rejection owing to my race.
43. If I have low credibility as a leader I can be sure that my race is not the problem.
44. I can easily find academic courses and institutions which give attention only to people of my race.
45. I can expect figurative language and imagery in all of the arts to testify to experiences of my race.
46. I can choose blemish cover or bandages in "flesh" color and have them more or less match my skin.

I repeatedly forgot each of the realizations on this list until I wrote it down. For me, white privilege has turned out to be an elusive and fugitive subject. The pressure to avoid it is great, for in facing it I must give up the myth of meritocracy. If these things are true, this is not such a free country; one's life is not what one makes it; many doors open for certain people through no virtues of their own. These perceptions mean also that my moral condition is not what I had been led to believe. The appearance of being a good citizen rather than a troublemaker comes in large part from having all sorts of doors open automatically because of my color.

A further paralysis of nerve comes from literary silence protecting privilege. My clearest memories of finding such analysis are in Lillian Smith's unparalleled *Killers of the Dream* and Margaret Andersen's review of Karen and Mamie Fields' *Lemon Swamp*. Smith, for example, wrote about walking toward black children on the street and knowing they would step into the gutter; Andersen contrasted the pleasure which she, as a white child, took on summer driving trips to the south with Karen Fields' memories of driving in a closed car stocked with all necessities lest, in stopping, her black family should suffer "insult, or worse." Adreinne Rich also recognizes and writes about daily experiences of privilege, but in my observation, white women's writing in this area is far more often on systemic racism than on our daily lives as light-skinned women.[2]

In unpacking this invisible knapsack of white privilege, I have listed conditions of daily experience which I once took for granted, as neutral, normal, and universally available to everybody, just as I once thought of a male-focused curriculum as the neutral or accurate account which can speak for all. Nor did I think any of these perquisites as bad for the holder. I now think that we need a more finely differentiated taxonomy of privilege, for some of these varieties are only what one would want for everyone in a just society, and others give license to be ignorant, oblivious, arrogant, and destructive.

Before proposing some more finely-tuned categorization, I will make some observations about the general effects of these conditions on my life and expectations.

In this potpourri of examples, some privileges make me feel at home in the world. Others allow me to escape penalties or dangers which others suffer. Through some, I escape fear, anxiety, or a sense of not being welcome or not being real. Some keep me from having to hide, to be in disguise, to feel sick or crazy, to negotiate each transaction from the position of being an outsider or, within my group, a person who is suspected of having too close links with a dominant culture. Most keep me from having to be angry.

I see a pattern running through the matrix of white privilege, a pattern of assumptions which were passed on to me as a white person. There was one main piece of cultural turf; it was my own turf, and I was among those who could control the turf. I could measure up to the cultural standards and take advantage of the many options I saw around me to make what the culture would call a success of my life. *My skin color was an asset for any move I was educated to want to make.* I could think of myself as "belonging" in major ways, and of making social systems work for me. I could freely disparage, fear, neglect, or be oblivious to anything outside of the dominant cultural forms. Being of the main culture, I could also criticize it fairly freely. My life was reflected back to me frequently enough so that I felt, with regard to my race, if not to my sex, like one of the real people.

Whether through the curriculum or in the newspaper, the television, the economic system, or the general look of people in the streets, we received daily signals and indications that my people counted, and that others *either didn't exist or must be trying not very successfully, to be like people of my race.* We were given cultural permission not to hear voices of people of other races, or a tepid cultural tolerance for hearing or acting on such voices. I was also raised not to suffer seriously from anything which darker-skinned people might say about my group, "protected," though perhaps I should more accurately say *prohibited,* through the habits of my economic class and social group, from living in racially mixed groups or being reflective about interactions between people of differing races.

In proportion as my racial group was being made confident, comfortable, and oblivious, other groups were likely being made inconfident, uncomfortable, and alienated. Whiteness protected me from many kinds of hostility, distress, and violence, which I was being subtly trained to visit in turn upon people of color.

For this reason, the word *privilege* now seems to me misleading. Its connotations are too positive to fit the conditions and behaviors which "privilege systems" produce. We usually think of privilege as being a favored state, whether earned, or conferred by birth or luck. School graduates are reminded they are privileged and urged to use their (enviable) assets well. The word *privilege* carries the connotation of being something everyone must want. Yet some of the conditions I have described here work to systemically over-empower certain groups. Such privilege simply *confers dominance,* gives permission to control, because of one's race or sex. The kind of privilege which gives license to some people to be, at best, thoughtless and, and at worst, murderous should not continue to be referred to as a desirable attribute. Such "privilege" may be widely desired without being in any way beneficial to the whole society.

Moreover, though "privilege" may confer power, it does not confer moral strength. Those who do not depend on conferred dominance have traits and qualities which may never develop in those who do. Just as Women's Studies courses indicate that women survive their political circumstances to lead lives which hold the human race together, so "underprivileged" people of color who are the world's majority have survived their oppression and lived survivor's lives from which the white global minority can and must learn. In some groups, those dominated have actually become strong through *not* having all of these unearned advantages, and this gives them a great deal to teach the others. Members of the so-called privileged groups can seem foolish, ridiculous, infantile, or dangerous by contrast.

I want, then, to distinguish between earned strength and unearned power conferred systemically. Power from unearned privilege can look like strength when it is in fact permission to escape or to dominate. But not all of the privileges on my list are inevitably damaging. Some, like the expectation that neighbors will be decent to you, or that your race will not count against you in court, should be the norm in a just society and should be considered as the entitlement of everyone. Others, like the privilege not to listen to less powerful people, distort the humanity of the holders as well as the ignored groups. Still others, like finding one's staple foods everywhere, may be a function of being a member of a numerical majority in the population. Others have to do with not having to labor under pervasive negative stereotyping and mythology.

We might at least start by distinguishing between positive advantages which we can work to spread, to the point where they are not advantages at all but simply part of the normal civic and social fabric, and negative types of advantage which unless rejected will always reinforce our present hierarchies. For example, the positive "privilege" of belonging, the feeling that one belongs within the human circle, as Native Americans say, fosters development and should not be seen as privilege for a few. It is, let us say, an entitlement which none of us should have to earn; ideally it is an *unearned entitlement.* At present, since only a few have it, it is an *unearned advantage* for them. The negative "privilege" which gave me cultural permission not to take darker-skinned others seriously can be seen as arbitrarily conferred dominance and should not be desirable for anyone. This paper results from a process of coming to see that some of the power which I originally saw as attendant on being a human being in the United States consisted in *unearned advantage* and *conferred dominance,* as well as other kinds of special circumstance not universally taken for granted.

In writing this paper I have also realized that white identity and status (as well as class identity and status) give me considerable power to choose whether to broach this subject and its trouble. I can pretty well decide whether to disappear and avoid and not listen and escape the dislike I may engender in other people through this essay, or interrupt, take over, dominate, preach, direct, criticize, or control to some extent what goes on in reaction to it. Being white, I am given considerable power to escape many kinds of danger or penalty as well as to choose which risks I want to take.

There is an analogy here, once again, with Women's Studies. Our male colleagues do not have a great deal to lose in supporting Women's Studies, but they do decide whether to commit themselves to more equitable distributions of power. They will probably feel few penalties whatever choice they make; they do not seem, in any obvious short-term sense, the ones at risk, though they and we are all at risk because of the behaviors which have been rewarded in them.

Through Women's Studies work I have met very few men who are truly distressed about systemic, unearned male advantage and conferred dominance. And so one question for me and others like me is whether we will be like them, or whether we will get truly distressed, even outraged, about unearned race advantage and conferred dominance and if so, what we will do to lessen them. In any case, we need to do more work in identifying how they actually affect our daily lives. We need more down-to-earth writing by people about these taboo subjects. We need more understanding of the ways in which white "privilege" damages white people, for these are not the same ways in which it damages the victimized. Skewed white psyches are an inseparable part of the picture, though I do not want to confuse the kinds of damage done to the holders of special assets and to those who suffer the deficits. Many, perhaps most, of our white students in the United States think that racism doesn't affect them because they are not people of color; they do not see "whiteness" as a racial identity. Many men likewise think that Women's Studies does not bear on their own existences because they are not female; they do not see themselves as having gendered identities. Insisting on the universal *effects* of "privilege" systems, then, becomes one of our chief tasks, and being more explicit about the *particular* effects in particular contexts is another. Men need to join us in this work.

In addition, since race and sex are not the only advantaging systems at work, we need to similarly examine the daily experience of having age advantage, or ethnic advantage, or physical ability, or advantage related to nationality, religion, or sexual orientation. Professor Marnie Evans suggested to me that in many ways the list I made also applies directly to heterosexual privilege. This is a still more taboo subject than race privilege: the daily ways in which heterosexual privilege makes married persons comfortable or powerful, providing supports, assets, approvals, and rewards to those who live or expect to live in heterosexual pairs. Unpacking that content is still more difficult, owing to the deeper imbeddedness of heterosexual advantage and dominance, and stricter taboos surrounding these.

But to start such an analysis I would put this observation from my own experience: The fact that I live under the same roof with a man triggers all kinds of societal assumptions about my worth, politics, life, and values, and triggers a host of unearned advantages and powers. After recasting many elements from the original list I would add further observations like these:

1. My children do not have to answer questions about why I live with my partner (my husband).
2. I have no difficulty finding neighborhoods where people approve of our household.
3. My children are given texts and classes which implicitly support our kind of family unit, and do not turn them against my choice of domestic partnership.
4. I can travel alone or with my husband without expecting embarrassment or hostility in those who deal with us.
5. Most people I meet will see my marital arrangements as an asset to my life or as a favorable comment on my likability, my competence, or my mental health.
6. I can talk about the social events of a weekend without fearing most listener's reactions.
7. I will feel welcomed and "normal" in the usual walks of public life, institutional, and social.
8. In many contexts, I am seen as "all right" in daily work on women because I do not live chiefly with women.

Difficulties and dangers surrounding the task of finding parallels are many. Since racism, sexism, and heterosexism are not the same, the advantaging associated with them should not be seen as the same. In addition, it is hard to disentangle aspects of unearned advantage which rests more on social class, economic class, race, religion, sex, and ethnic identity than on other factors. Still, all of the oppressions are interlocking, as the Combahee River Collective statement of 1977 continues to remind us eloquently.[3]

One factor seems clear about all of the interlocking oppressions. They take both active forms which we can see and embedded forms which as a member of the dominant group one is taught not to see. In my class and place, I did not see myself as racist because I was taught to recognize racism only in individual acts of meanness by members of my group, never in invisible systems conferring unsought racial dominance on my group from birth. Likewise, we are taught to think that sexism or heterosexism is carried on only through individual acts of discrimination, meanness, or cruelty toward women, gays, and lesbians, rather than in invisible systems conferring unsought dominance on certain groups. Disapproving of the systems won't be enough to change them. I was taught to think that racism could end if white individuals changed their attitudes; many men think sexism can be ended by individual changes in daily behavior toward women. But a man's sex provides advantage for him whether or not he approves of the way in which dominance has been conferred on his group. A "white" skin in the United States opens many doors for whites whether or not we approve of the way dominance had been conferred on us. Individual acts can palliate, but cannot end, these problems. To redesign social systems we need first to acknowledge their colossal unseen dimensions. The silences and denials surrounding privilege are the key political tools here. They keep thinking about equality or equity incomplete, protecting unearned advantage and conferred dominance by making these taboo subjects. Most talk by whites about equal opportunity seems to me now to be about equal opportunity to try to get in to a position of dominance while denying that *systems* of dominance exist.

It seems to me that obliviousness about white advantage, like obliviousness about male advantage, is kept strongly inculturated in the United States so as to maintain the myth of meritocracy, the myth that democratic choice is equally available to all. Keeping most people unaware that freedom of confident action is there for just a small number of people props up those in power, and serves to keep power in the hands of the same groups that have most of it already. Though systemic change takes many decades, there are pressing questions for me and I imagine for some others like me if we raise our daily consciousness on the perquisites of being light-skinned. What will we do with such knowledge? As we know from watching men, it is an open question whether we will choose to use unearned advantage to weaken hidden systems of advantage, and whether we will use any of our arbitrarily-awarded power to try to reconstruct power systems on a broader base.

## DISCUSSION QUESTIONS

1. What does the author mean by the concept of "white privilege"?

2. Reread the author's list of 46 examples of white privilege. Select the five examples that seem the most significant in helping you to understand that white people are privileged. Explain your selections.

3. In addition to white privilege, the author also cites examples of heterosexual privilege. In a similar manner, develop a list of privileges that the able-bodied enjoy that the physically challenged do not experience.

4. Most of us have experienced privilege in some form. Describe an example from your experience.

5. How does this article help you to understand the oppression that members of other groups may experience?

---

**Diversity on the Web**

Peggy McIntosh writes about the notion of racial, gender, and straight privilege and makes it clear that most people are unaware of their privileges. Watch "The Miniature Earth" video at: www.miniature-earth.com

What does this short video teach you about your educational and social class privileges?

What are the global and future implications of the data presented in the video?

---

## Endnotes

1. This paper was presented at the Virginia Women's Studies Association conference in Richmond in April 1986 and the American Educational Research Association conference in Boston in October 1986 and discussed with two groups of participants in the Dodge Seminars for Secondary School Teachers in New York and Boston in the spring of 1987.

2. Andersen, Margaret, "Race and the Social Science Curriculum: A Teaching and Learning Discussion." *Radical Teacher,* November 1984, pp. 17–20; Smith, Lillian. 1949. *Killers of the Dream.* New York: W.W. Norton.

3. "A Black Feminist Statement." The Combahee River Collective. In Hull, Scott, and Smith (eds.). *All the Women Are White, All the Blacks Are Men. But Some of Us Are Brave: Black Women's Studies.* The Feminist Press, 1982, pp. 13-22.

# A Framework for Understanding Social Identity Perspectives of Diversity

## Introduction

### Goals of Section II

■ To understand why some people are treated differently in the workplace because of their group memberships

■ To provide a theoretical framework for understanding the socialization process

■ To clarify that there is a range of saliency and variation among the members of any social identity group

■ To understand the complexity of multiple group identities

■ To understand why changes in the workforce have led to issues of inclusion for some employees and managers

In Section II, we bridge the introductory material on prejudice discrimination, stereotypes, conflict, and privilege by providing information that should help you to understand the relationship between social identity group memberships and people's experiences in the workplace. Like it or not, the reality is that our memberships in certain gender, age, religion, race, etc., groups give each of us an identity that affects how others interact with us and how we experience the world. Coworkers, customers, managers, etc., may value different things, have different needs, hold different values, communicate in different ways, etc. Although there has been a shift from more blatant forms of discrimination to more subtle forms, discrimination still exists, as many of the articles in this section will illustrate.

To complicate managing diversity in the twenty-first century, within the social identity categories there is also a wide range of differences among group members.

Section II provides students with information about these groups to give you a better understanding of the experiences of these memberships.

## MACRO/MACRO LEVEL DIFFERENCES

In terms of economic, social, and political power, all societies have what are considered to be dominant (or agent) and nondominant (or target) groups. The distinction between the two groups is socially constructed (i.e., dependent on time and place), and not necessarily related to numerical minority status. Dworkin and Dworkin define nondominants as being identifiable because of some characteristic(s), having less power than the dominants, experiencing more discrimination, and being aware of their nondominant status in society. In contrast, dominants can blend into society better, hold more of the power in society's institutions, are less apt to experience being the targets of discrimination, and are often unaware of their dominant status (i.e., privileges) in society (1999).

> Harassment, discrimination, exploitation, marginalization and other forms of differential and unequal treatment are institutionalized and systemic. These acts often do not require the conscious thought or effort of individual members of the agent group but are rather part of business as usual that becomes embedded in social structures over time
>
> (Hardiman & Bailey, p. 17).

When a nondominant group member excels at something (Barak Obama), he is often seen as an exception. When one performs poorly (Carley Fiona of Hewett Packard), the failure can reflect on all group members (e.g., generalizing that women are not capable of leading large corporations).

## SOCIALIZATION AND SALIENCY

Through our developmental experiences with the social institutions of society such as families, education, religion, cultures, workplaces, etc., we learn what are considered acceptable and unacceptable behaviors. Additionally, we may experience this socialization process differently because of our subgroup memberships. In most societies there are different expectations, roles, norms, etc., for many of the groups to which we belong, such as being young or being old, being female or being male, etc. We learn these ways of thinking, evaluating, and acting in subtle ways through our life experiences.

An individual's **social identity** is his/her "self-concept that derives from his or her membership in a particular social group and the value and emotional significance attached to that group membership" (Tatum, 1997). For example, if you identify strongly with your Jewish heritage and religion, it will be salient (i.e., important) to whom you are, how you behave, and how you experience the world. On the other hand, if you were born into the Jewish religion but your family did not practice the religion, follow the customs and traditions, etc., and this really doesn't matter much to you, your social identity as Jewish may be less important to you as an individual than it is to other Jews. However, in spite of the fact that individuals experience a wide range of influence in terms of the saliency of their social identities, people who know that you are "Jewish" may generalize their expectations, prejudices, and stereotypes, (positive, negative, or neutral), based on social identity group memberships.

An additional factor to consider is that most workers have memberships in multiple social identities. A white male coworker is a member of two dominant groups in terms of race and gender. However, he may also belong to nondominant groups because of his age (50), physical ability (lack of mobility), and sexual orientation (gay)—all social identities that still experience considerable systemic discrimination and inclusion issues in the workplace.

Just as there is no consensus about definitions of diversity, there is little agreement on the social identity classifications. A popular typography is Marilyn Loden's division of social identities in terms of primary and secondary dimensions (see chart that follows). **Primary dimensions** are considered to be more fixed, visible, and relevant to an individual's identity. **Secondary dimensions** are considered to be more fluid, and less central to one's social identity. However useful this model is, it may not account for individual saliency. For example, to a working mother, her status as a parent (secondary) may be more relevant to her performance, decisions, career motivation, etc., than her gender (primary).

---

### Dimensions of Diversity

| Primary Dimensions | Secondary Dimensions |
| --- | --- |
| Age | Geographic Location |
| Gender | Military & Work Experience |
| Mental/Physical Abilities | Family Status |
| Race | Income, Religion |
| Ethnic Heritage | First Language, Education |
| Sexual Orientation | Organizational Role & Level |
| | Communication & Work Styles |

Adapted from Loden, M. (1996) *Implementing Diversity*.

---

In this text, we have tried to be as inclusive as possible in terms of the readings, cases, and exercises that will help you to understand why diverse coworkers, customers, and managers may experience the workplace differently than you do. In addition to race, gender, ethnicity, sexual orientation, social class, age differences, physical/mental abilities, and religion, we have added coverage of the new workplace diversity challenges: immigrant status, weight/appearance, family/work life, etc. This section closes with material designed to help you to understand the complexity of integrating these multiple dimensions of diversity into organizational life both today and in the future.

## BIBLIOGRAPHY

Dworkin, A.G. & Dworkin, R.J. (1999). *The minority report*, 3rd ed., Orlando, Florida: Harcourt Brace.

Hardiman, R. Jackson, B.W. (1997). Conceptual foundations for social justice courses. From *Teaching for Diversity and Social Justice*, Maurianne Adams, et al., eds., New York: Routledge, pp. 16–29.

Loden, M. (1996). *Implementing diversity*. Chicago: Business One Irwin, p. 16.

Tatum, B. D. (1997). *Why are all the black kids sitting together in the cafeteria*? New York: Basic Books, p. 63.

# Are African Americans Still Experiencing Racism?

Joyce McNickles

*Anna Maria College*

Carlo M. Baldino

*Sutton, Massachusetts*

**M**any white Americans may have been surprised when a recent Gallup survey asked African Americans if they felt they were treated fairly in the United States. Only 38% of the African Americans surveyed felt as though they were, while 76% of the whites surveyed felt African Americans were treated fairly (Gallup, 2004). These statistics are indicative of the perception gap that exists between whites and African Americans when it comes to matters of race and racism.

The good news is that the same Gallup survey revealed that 46% of African Americans and 59% of whites acknowledged that relations between the two groups had generally improved. Seventy percent of whites and 80% of African Americans surveyed supported interracial marriages and 57% of whites and 78% of African Americans reported that they prefer living in racially mixed neighborhoods. These numbers show a significant decrease in prejudicial attitudes within both groups, compared with previous Gallup polls on civil rights and race relations.

## A MATTER OF TERMINOLOGY—PREJUDICE AND RACISM

Whites may wonder that if their personal prejudice has decreased, why do so many Africans Americans still believe that they are treated unfairly? Tim Wise, a well-known white antiracism writer, activist, and national lecturer, recently suggested that if one is trying to understand why conversations about race and racism are so difficult between African Americans and whites, it is because they often are not talking about the same thing. According to Wise (2006), most whites see racism in terms of negative individual and interpersonal behavior such as "the uttering of a prejudicial remark or bigoted slur." For African Americans, it is much more. It is the policies and practices in various social institutions that create inequities for them. Dealing with an individual's personal prejudice can be frustrating for anyone, but confronting racial disparities in the judicial system, the education system, the health care system, and the workplace have the potential to create far more significant consequences than the personal prejudice of one individual.

Allport (1954) defined prejudice as a feeling, favorable or unfavorable, toward a person which was not based on actual experience (p. 7). Prejudice based on race is referred to as **racial prejudice** (Andersen & Taylor, 2006, p. 243). Prejudice and racism are not the same thing. An important distinction must be made between *racial prejudice* and *racism*. Racial prejudice resides within the individual; racism resides within society's structures and institutions. It is true that individuals make up society's institutions and in order for racism to exist in any institution there has to be some individual racial prejudice. However, racism extends far beyond any individual and his or her personal prejudice. It results from one racial group having the social power to act on a racial prejudice and have a detrimental impact on the lives of another racial group (Tatum, 1997). One example of this is the illegal practice of seeing what happens when real estate agents steer African American homebuyers away from homes in white neighborhoods based on a desire to keep the makeup of that neighborhood mostly white (Galster & Godfrey, 2005).

Racism can also be seen as a system of advantage based on race (Wellman, 1977). Beverly Tatum (1997) finds this definition of racism useful because

> It allows us to see that racism, like other forms of oppression, is not only a personal ideology of racial prejudice, but also a system involving cultural messages and institutional policies and practices as well as the belief of individuals. In the context of the United States, this system clearly operates to the advantage of Whites and to the disadvantage of people of color (p. 7).

**Institutional racism** is another term that is often used to describe the system of advantage operating within various societal institutions, such as the criminal justice system, the education system, the health care system, and the workplace (Andersen & Taylor, 2006, p. 245; Wijeyesinghe, Griffin, & Love, 1997). Institutions may have policies, practices, and procedures that confer advantages to whites and disadvantages to African Americans and other people of color. For example, much of the standard curriculum in U.S. public schools is centered on the contributions and culture of white Americans rather than that of African Americans. This gives white students a psychological advantage, because they have many opportunities to see themselves and their racial group reflected in history, literature, the arts, and the sciences (Nieto, 2004).

Conversely, this disadvantages African Americans because, aside from Black History Month programs, often they do not see themselves reflected in the curriculum. It is important to note that these policies, practices, and procedures may be unintentional or intentional, overt or covert.

Diller (2004) describes racism as "the manipulation of social institutions to give preferences and advantages to whites and at the same time restrict the choices, rights, mobility and access of people of color" (p. 30). Feminist scholar Peggy McIntosh (1990) referred to the advantages whites receive as "white privilege" and believes that these privileges are invisible to most whites. African Americans and other people of color cannot count on these privileges.

Institutionalized racism promotes disparities and inequities between whites and African Americans. It also promotes disparities between whites and other people of color. Although this essay highlights the racial experiences of African Americans, this is not to suggest that other people of color such as Latinos, Asians, and Native Americans do not experience racism in the Unites States.

## RACIAL DISPARITIES AND INEQUITIES IN THE WORKPLACE

In recent years, African Americans have certainly made gains in the workplace, but they are still underrepresented at the higher levels of management in just about every professional field. African Americans, along with other racial minorities, make up about 1% of the most powerful positions in corporate America (Carr-Ruffino, 2006, p. 4). Research studies suggest that white men in organizations are more likely to be promoted over African Americans with the same education (Dewitt, 1995; Zwerling & Silver, 1992). Despite affirmative action initiatives and federal employment laws against racial discrimination, many African Americans still confront subtle and sometimes overt institutional racism in the workplace. The Gallup (2004) survey reported that only 12% of African Americans felt they had equal job opportunities as whites, while 61% of whites surveyed felt they did.

Catalyst (2004), a leading research organization working to advance women in business, conducted a survey of over 900 African American women working in FORTUNE 1000 companies and found that African American women at various professional levels faced institutional barriers related to their race. Many women described these institutional barriers as a "concrete ceiling" (p. 3), highlighting how much more impenetrable they are than the barrier of the glass ceiling which many white women face. More than half of the women surveyed held graduate degrees yet reported facing racial stereotyping, scrutiny of their work, and repeated questioning of their authority and credibility. They also reported a lack of support from their organizations and exclusion from informal networks. Even though many women reported that their companies had diversity recruitment initiatives, many believed the initiatives did little to address institutional racism.

A Princeton University workplace study examined discrimination in hiring young minority males and male ex-offenders in entry-level, low-wage jobs. The researchers sent African American, Latino, and white male testers (applicants) to over 1,500 private employers in New York City during a nine-month period. The applicants were given fake résumés indicating equal educational and work experience. In several situations, the résumés also indicated an 18-month prison term. The study showed that the white males with a criminal record had a slightly better chance of getting a job than an African American male with no criminal record. Young white male high school graduates were twice as likely to receive a positive response (a callback or interview) from the employers as equally qualified African American males (Pager & Western, 2005).

Research suggests that African American names may also make people the target of institutional racism. Researchers from the University of Chicago and

Massachusetts Institute of Technology (Bertrand & Mullainathan, 2004) sent 5,000 fictitious résumés in response to 1,300 help wanted ads in the Boston and Chicago newspapers. They randomly assigned "white-sounding" first names to half the résumés.

Names such as Emily, Jill, Kristen, Allison, and Laurie were given to the female applicants; males were given names such as Brett, Todd, Neil, Greg, Brendan, Jay, and Brad. The other half of the résumés were assigned "African American–sounding" names such as Ebony, Lakisha, Tamika, Keisha, Latoya, and Kenya to female applicants and Jamal, Hakim, Leroy, Tyrone, Darnell, and Jermaine to male applicants. Aside from the difference in names, the résumés reflected the same experience, education, and skills for both groups. The study found that applicants with the "white-sounding names" received 50% more callbacks for interviews than applicants with "African American–sounding names." The disparities were consistent across occupation, industry, and company size. The researchers concluded that African Americans may be screened out of the hiring process in favor of white applicants before they even have a chance to be interviewed.

## RACIAL DISPARITIES AND INEQUITIES IN HEALTH CARE

Several studies found that African Americans and other racial minorities tended to receive lower quality health care than whites, even when they had the same insurance and income as whites (Jha, 2005; Smedley, Stith, & Nelson, 2003; Sonel et al., 2005). In a major study conducted by the Institute of Medicine, researchers found in interviews with doctors that even though most doctors are well-intentioned, subconscious racial bias against African Americans influenced their medical decisions (Smedley et al., 2003; Stolberg, 2002). Research also suggests that doctors tend to view African American patients as less intelligent than whites and less likely to follow medical advice and engage in follow-up care (van Ryn & Burke, 2000). The Institute of Medicine study reviewed one hundred previous research studies and concluded that racial minorities are less likely to be given appropriate medication for heart disease and to undergo bypass surgery, less likely to receive kidney dialysis and transplants than whites, but three times more likely to have lower limb amputations as a result of diabetes than whites. In terms of mental health, African Americans are more likely to be diagnosed as psychotic, but less likely to be given antipsychotic medication. They are more likely to be hospitalized involuntarily and placed in restraints, compared with whites (Smedley et al., 2003). When African American women use illicit drugs during pregnancy, they are ten times more likely to be reported to child welfare agencies for prenatal use than are white women (Neuspiel, 1996).

## RACIAL DISPARITIES AND INEQUITIES IN THE JUSTICE SYSTEM

Perhaps in no other institution are there more blatant examples of institutional racism than in law enforcement and the criminal justice system. Racial profiling is a major concern for African Americans. **Racial profiling** is the use of race alone as a criterion by police officers as a reason for stopping and detaining someone who appears suspicious of criminal activity. It has become so common that African

Americans call it the crime of "DWB," short for "**Driving While Black.**" Many police departments attempt to justify racial profiling by using statistics that point to a higher proportion of crimes committed by African Americans than whites. Every year at least 90% of African Americans who are stopped by police are not arrested, which means that there's only a 10% probability that a black driver in a car has actually committed a crime (Andersen & Taylor, 2006).

Statistics show that 8 out of 10 automobile searches conducted by state troopers over a 10-year period on the New Jersey Turnpike were on cars driven by African American and Latinos. The vast majority of these searches found no evidence of crimes or illegal materials (Kocieniewski & Hanley, 2000).

Andersen and Taylor's (2006) review of the research on African Americans and the criminal justice system revealed several examples of institutional racism. African Americans are often the victims of **police brutality,** or the use of excessive force by police officers. Most cases of police brutality are perpetrated against people of color and there are usually no penalties or consequences for the officers guilty of this practice. Disparities continue after African Americans are arrested. They are faced with higher bails and are not as likely as whites to be given the opportunity to plea bargain. After going to trial, they are found guilty more often than whites, are likely to get longer sentences, and are less likely than whites to get probation—even when they come from the same economic background and have similar arrest records (Andersen & Taylor, 2006, p. 174).

Race is also a factor in capital punishment. Blacks are disproportionately placed on death row. In 2003, blacks constituted just 12% of the total U.S. population, yet made up 42% of the nearly 3,500 prisoners on death row nationally (U.S. Bureau of Justice Statistics, 2004). Research shows that when whites and African Americans commit the same crime against a white victim, the African American offender is more likely to receive the death penalty. African Americans who kill whites get the death penalty at a 300% higher rate than if they kill another African American (Paternoster & Brame, 2003).

African American youths face similar disparities in the criminal justice system. A 2000 California study showed minority youths are more than twice as likely as their white counterparts to be transferred out of California's juvenile justice system and tried as adults. Once in the adult system, the study found that African American juvenile offenders are 18.4 times more likely to be jailed than whites for equivalent crimes (Males & Macallair, 2000). Similar racial disparities were found throughout the United States (Butterfield, 1995).

The Sentencing Project study, based on Justice Department statistics, reported that even though African Americans constituted just 13% of all monthly drug users, they represented 35% of arrests for drug possession, 55% of the convictions, and 74% of the prison sentences. Data from the U.S. Sentencing Commission found that crack cocaine sentences are the single most significant factor contributing to racial disparity in federal sentencing (The Sentencing Project, 2006a).

Len Bias, the college basketball star drafted first by the Boston Celtics, died of a drug overdose in 1986. His death was a key stimulus for the federal crack cocaine mandatory sentencing laws. In 1988 Congress adopted the Anti–Drug Abuse Act, which included new mandatory sentences for low-level crack offenses. Defendants convicted with just five grams of crack cocaine were subject to a five-year mandatory minimum sentence. The same penalty was triggered for powder cocaine only when an offense involved at least 500 grams (Gest, 1995). Twenty years later, we see the racial disparities created by these laws. According to the Sentencing Project, more than 80 percent of the defendants prosecuted for a crack offense are African-American, despite the fact that more than two-thirds of crack users are white or Latino (The Sentencing Project, 2006b). Perhaps the ultimate irony in the Len Bias case is that he did not in fact die of a crack overdose, but rather from snorting powder cocaine (Gest, 1995).

## THE FUTURE

African Americans and white Americans have made steps toward understanding and accepting each other's differences. They work side by side in many American workplaces and live in racially mixed neighborhoods with each other. However, much work needs to be done to improve the experiences of African Americans as they enter American institutions. This can begin with whites acknowledging that institutional racism still exists and that it puts African Americans as a racial group at a disadvantage. Until this acknowledgement happens, it will be very difficult for the two racial groups to have any meaningful dialogue to improve race relations.

## DISCUSSION QUESTIONS

1. According to the authors, what explains the perception gap that exists between whites and African Americans when it comes to matters of race and racism?

2. What is the difference between racial prejudice and racism?

3. In what societal institutions can institutional racism be found?

4. How do Arab Muslims suffer biases and prejudices similar to African Americans in a post 9/11 America?

5. How does the factual evidence presented in this article lend support to affirmative action programs and policies?

6. What must white people acknowledge in order for race relations to improve?

## BIBLIOGRAPHY

Allport, G. W. (1954). *The nature of prejudice.* Cambridge, MA: Addison-Wesley.

Andersen, M. L., & Taylor, H. F. (2006). *Sociology: The essentials* (4th ed.). Belmont, CA: Thomson/Wadsworth.

Bertrand, M., & Mullainathan, S. (2004). Are Emily and Greg more employable than Lakisha and Jamal? A field experiment on labor market discrimination. *American Economic Review, 94*(4), 991–1013.

Butterfield, F. (1995, October 5). More blacks in their 20's have trouble with the law. *The New York Times*, p. A8.

Carr-Ruffino, N. (2006). *Managing diversity: People skills for a multicultural workplace* (7th ed.). Boston, MA: Pearson.

Catalyst. (2004). Advancing African American women in the workplace: What managers need to know. New York: Catalyst. Retrieved October 30, 2006, from http://www.catalyst.org/.

Dewitt, K. (1995, April, 20). Blacks prone to job discrimination in organizations. *The New York Times,* p. A19.

Diller, J. V. (2004). *Cultural diversity: A primer for the human services.* Belmont, CA: Wadsworth.

Gallup Organization. (2004). *Civil rights and race relations.* Princeton, NJ: The Gallup Organization. Retrieved October 30, 2006, from http://assets.aarp.org/rgcenter/general/civil_rights.pdf.

Galster, G., & Godfrey, E. (2005). By words and deeds: Racial steering by real estate agents in the U.S. in 2000. *American Planning Association. Journal of the American Planning Association, 71*(3), 251–268.

Gest, T. (1995, November 6). New war over crack. *U.S. News & World Report, 119,* 81.

Jha, A. K. (2005). Racial trends in the use of major procedures among the elderly. *The New England Journal of Medicine, 353*(7), 683.

Kocieniewski, D., & Hanley, R. (2000, November 28). Racial profiling was the routine, New Jersey finds. *The New York Times,* p. A1.

Males, M., & Macallair, D. (2000). *The color of justice: An analysis of juvenile adult court transfers in California.* Washington, DC: Justice Policy Institute. Retrieved October 30, 2006, from http://www.buildingblocksfor-youth.org/colorofjustice/coj.html.

Mauer, M., & Huling, T. (1995). *Young black Americans and the criminal justice system.* Washington, DC: The Sentencing Project. Retrieved September 23, 2006, from http://www.sentencingproject.org/pdfs/rd_youngblack_5yrslater.pdf.

McIntosh, P. (1990). White privilege: Unpacking the invisible knapsack. *Independent School, 49*(2), 31.

Neuspiel, D. R. (1996). Racism and perinatal addiction. *Ethnicity & Disease, 6*(1–2), 47.

Nieto, S. (2004). *Affirming diversity: The sociopolitical context of multicultural education* (4th ed.). Boston, MA: Allyn and Bacon.

Pager, D., & Western, B. (2005). *Discrimination in low wage labor markets: Evidence from New York City.* Paper presented at the Population Association of American Annual Meeting. Retrieved September 17, 2006, from http://paa2005.princeton.edu/download.aspx?submissionId=50874.

Paternoster R., Brame, R., Bacon, S., Ditchfield, A., et al. (2003). *An empirical analysis of Maryland's death sentencing system with respect to the influence of race and legal jurisdiction.* University of Maryland, Department of Criminology. Retrieved January 1, 2007, from http://www.newsdesk.umd.edu/pdf/finalrep.pdf.

Sentencing Project. (2006a). *Race and class penalties in crack cocaine sentencing.* Washington, DC: The Sentencing Project. Retrieved October 30, 2006, from http://www.sentencingproject.org/pdfs/5077.pdf.

Sentencing Project. (2006b). *Crack cocaine sentencing policy: Unjustified and unreasonable.* Washington, DC: The Sentencing Project. Retrieved October 30, 2006, from http://www.sentencingproject.org/pdfs/1003.pdf.

Smedley, B. D., Stith, A. Y., & Nelson, A. R. (2003). *Unequal treatment: Confronting racial and ethnic disparities in health care.* Washington, DC: National Academy Press.

Sonel, A. F., Good, C. B., Mulgund, J., Roe, M. T., Gibler, W. B., Smith, S. C., et al. (2005). Racial variations in treatment and outcomes of black and white patients with high-risk non-ST-elevation acute coronary syndromes: Insights from CRUSADE (can rapid risk stratification of unstable angina patients suppress adverse outcomes with early implementation of the ACC/AHA guidelines?). *Circulation, 111*(10), 1225–1232.

Stolberg, S. G. (2002, March 21). Race gap seen in health care of equally insured patients. *New York Times,* p. A1.

Tatum, B. D. (1997). *Why are all the black kids sitting together in the cafeteria? and other conversations about race.* New York: Basic Books.

---

**Diversity on the Web**

1. Go to the Internet address below and identify three examples of institutional racism. You may also click on the links within "in this section" for additional examples.

   Using the definitions from the chapter, explain why your choices qualify as examples of institutional racism.

   *http://www.aclu.org/racialjustice/index.html*

2. Proponents of affirmative action argue that it is still needed because racism and discrimination continue. Go to the Internet address below and view the myths and facts about affirmative action.

   Do you think the facts presented here would be enough to change the minds of affirmative action opponents? Why or why not?

   *http://www.aapf.org/focus/*

3. African Americans are not the only racial minority experiencing racism in the United States. Go to the Internet address below and take the test on Native Americans.

   What was your score? Why do think you did or did not do well on this test? Which of the answers on the test surprised you the most? Why?

   *http://www.understandingprejudice.org/nativeiq/*

4. Go to the Internet address below and identify three issues of concern to members of the Latino community. How are these issues different from or similar to the ones confronting African Americans?

   *http://www.nclr.org/content/topics/detail/498/*

---

 **Points of Law**

The most important diversity-related legislation is Title VII of the Civil Rights Act of 1964. This law prohibits discrimination in organizations with 15 or more employees in terms of the hiring, promotion, and treatment of employees (later amended to include customers and suppliers) on the basis of race, color, religion, sex, or national origin. Title VII legislation is administered by the Equal Employment Opportunity Commission (EEOC).

*http://www.eeoc.gov/policy/vii.html*

# Inventing Hispanics

## A Diverse Minority Resists Being Labeled

Amitai Etzioni

Thirty years ago immigrants from Latin America who settled in the United States were perceived in terms of their home nation—as, for example, Cuban Americans or Mexican Americans, just as European newcomers were seen as Italian Americans or Polish Americans. Today the immigrant flow from Central and South America has grown substantially, and the newcomers are known as Hispanics.

Some observers have expressed concern that efforts to make Hispanics a single minority group—for purposes ranging from elections to education to the allocation of public funds—are further dividing American society along racial lines. But attempts, both incidental and ideological, to forge these American immigrants into a strongly defined minority are encountering an unanticipated problem. Hispanics by and large do not see themselves as a distinct minority group; they see themselves as Americans.

## HISPANICS AND AFRICAN AMERICANS

Hispanics are particularly important for understanding the future of diversity in American society. Already they have overtaken African Americans to become the nation's largest minority, and immigration patterns ensure that the number of Hispanics will continue to grow more rapidly than that of African Americans.

U.S. race relations have long been understood in terms of black and white. Until recently, many books on the subject did not even mention other races, or did so only as a brief afterthought. Now recognition is growing that Hispanics are replacing blacks as the primary minority. But whereas blacks have long been raising their political consciousness, Hispanics have only just begun to find their political legs.

Recent increases in minority populations and a decline in the white majority in the United States have driven several African-American leaders, including Jesse Jackson and former New York City Mayor David Dinkins, along with a few Hispanics, such as Fernando Ferrer, a candidate for the 2002 mayoral election in New York City, and some on the white left (writing in *The American Prospect)* to champion a coalition of minorities to unseat the "white establishment" and become the power-holders and shapers of America's future. The coalition's leaders are systematically encouraging Hispanics (and Asian Americans) to see themselves as victims of discrimination and racism—and thus to share the grievances of many African Americans. Whether they will succeed depends much on how Hispanic Americans see themselves and are viewed by others.

## HISPANICS AND THE CENSUS

For several decades now, the Census Bureau has been working to make Hispanics into a distinct group and—most recently—into a race. In 1970, a 5 percent sample of households was asked to indicate whether their origin was Mexican, Puerto Rican, Cuban, Central or South American, or other Spanish. But it was only in 1980, that "Hispanics" became a distinct statistical and social category in the census, as all households were asked whether they were of "Spanish/Hispanic origin or descent." Had no changes been made in 1980, we might well have continued to think of Hispanics as we do about other white Americans, as several ethnic groups, largely from Mexico and Cuba.

The next step was to take Hispanics, who were until recently multiple ethnic groups that were considered racially white, and make them into a unique, separate group whose members, according to the census, "can be members of any race." This unusual status has had several notable results. One is the flurry of headlines following the release of new census data in March 2001 announcing that "California Whites Are a Minority"—even though 59.5 percent of Californians, including many Hispanics, chose white as their race. The only way for whites to be proclaimed a minority in California is for no Hispanics to be counted as white—even those 40 percent, or more than four million people, who specifically marked white as their race on the census form. Another curious result is the awkward phrase "non-Hispanic whites," by which the media now refer to the majority of Americans.

Because of their evolving status in the census, Hispanics are now sometimes treated not as a separate ethnic group, but as a distinct race. (Race marks sharper lines of division than ethnicity.) Often, for example, when national newspapers and magazines, such as the *Washington Post* and *U.S. News and World Report,* graphically depict racial breakdowns on various subjects, they list Hispanics as a fourth group, next to white, black, and Asian. Much less often, but with increasing frequency, Hispanics are referred to as "brown" Americans, as in a *Newsweek* article that noted a "Brown Belt" across America. The result is to make the country seem more divided than it is.

Should one mind the way the census keeps its statistics? Granted, social scientists are especially sensitive to the social construction of categories. But one need not have an advanced degree to realize that the ways we divide people up—or combine them—have social consequences. One may care little how the census manipulates its data, but those data are what we use to paint a picture of the social composition of America. Moreover, the census categories have many other uses—for college admissions forms, health care, voting, and job profiles, government budget allocations, and research. And the media use the census for guidance. In short, the census greatly influences the way we see each other and ourselves, individually and as a community.

This is not to suggest that the Census Bureau has conspired to split up the nation. The recategorizations and redefinitions reflect, in part, changes in actual numbers (large increases in the nation's Hispanic population might arguably justify a separate category); in part, efforts to streamline statistics (collapsing half-a-dozen ethnic groups into one); and, in part, external pressures to which all government agencies are subjected. To be sure, the Census Bureau is a highly professional agency whose statistics are set by scientific considerations. But there is as yet no such thing as a government agency that has a budget set by Congress, that needs public cooperation for carrying out its mission, and that is fully apolitical. Likewise, the Office of Management and Budget, which sets the racial categories, is among the less political branches of the White House, yet still quite politically attuned.

## HISPANICS IN THEIR OWN EYES

How do Hispanics see themselves? First of all, the vast majority prefer to be classified as a variety of ethnic groups rather than as one. The National Latino Political Survey, for example, found that three out of four respondents chose to be labeled by country of origin, rather than by "pan-ethnic" terms such as "Hispanic" or "Latino." Hispanics are keenly aware of big differences among Hispanic groups, especially between Mexican Americans (the largest group) and Cuban Americans, the latter being regarded as more likely to be conservative, to vote Republican, to become American citizens, and so on.

America has, by and large, dropped the notion that it will tell you what your race is, either by deeply offensive blood tests or by examining your features and asking your neighbors (the way the census got its figures about race until 1950). We now allow people to indicate which race they consider themselves to be by marking a box on a census form. Many Hispanics resist being turned into a separate race or being moved out of the white category. In 1990, the census allowed people to buy out of racial divisions by checking "other" when asked about their racial affiliation. Nearly 10 million people — almost all of them Hispanics — did so.

When the Census Bureau introduced its "other" category, some African-American leaders objected because, as they correctly pointed out, the resulting diminution in minority figures both curtails numerous public allotments that take race into account and affects redistricting. So the 2000 census dropped "other" and instead allowed people to claim several races (but not to refuse to be racially boxed in). The long list of racial boxes to be checked ended with "some other race," with a space to indicate what that race was. Many of the 18 million people who chose this category, however, made no notation, leaving their race as they wanted it — undefined.

Of those who chose only "some other race," almost all (97 percent) were Hispanic. Among Hispanics, 42.2 percent chose "some other race," 47.9 percent chose white (alone) as their race, 6.3 percent chose two or more races, and 2 percent chose black (alone). In short, the overwhelming majority of Hispanics either chose white or refused racial categorization, clearly resisting the notion of being turned into a separate race.

## A MAJORITY OF MINORITIES

As I have shown in considerable detail in my recent book, *The Monochrome Society,* the overwhelming majority of Americans of all backgrounds have the same dreams and aspirations as the white majority. Hispanic and Asian immigrants and their children (as well as most African Americans) support many of the same public policies (from reformed health insurance to better education, from less costly housing to better and more secure jobs). In fact, minorities often differ more among themselves than they do with the white majority. Differences among, say, Japanese Americans and Vietnamese Americans are considerable, as they are among those from Puerto Rico and Central America. (Because of the rapid rise of the African-American middle class, this group, too, is far from monolithic.)

Intermarriage has long been considered the ultimate test of relationships among various groups in American society. Working together and studying together are considered low indicators of intergroup integration; residing next to one another, a higher one; intermarriage—the highest. By that measure, too, more and more Hispanic (and Asian) Americans are marrying outside their ethnic group. And each generation is more inclined to marry outside than the previous ones.

In the mid-1990s, about 20 percent of first-generation Asian women were intermarried, compared with slightly less than 30 percent of the second generation and slightly more than 40 percent of the third generation. Hispanic intermarriage shows a similar trend. More and more Americans, like Tiger Woods, have relatives all over the colorful ethnic-racial map, further binding America into one encompassing community, rather than dividing it along racial and ethnic lines.

In short, there is neither an ideological nor a social basis for a coalition along racial lines that would combine Hispanics, Asians, and African Americans against the white majority to fashion a radically different American society and creed.

## DIVERSITY WITHIN UNITY

Immigrants to America have never been supra-homogenized. Assimilation has never required removing all traces of cultural difference between newcomers and their new homeland. The essence of the American design—diversity within unity—leaves considerable room for differences regarding to whom one prays and to which country one has an allegiance—as long as it does not conflict with an overarching loyalty to America. Differences in cultural items from music to cuisines are celebrated for making the nation, as a community of communities, richer.

Highly legitimate differences among the groups are contained by the shared commitments all are expected to honor: the Constitution and its Bill of Rights, the democratic way of government, peaceful resolution of conflict, and tolerance for differences. These shared bonds may change as new Americans join the U.S. community, but will do so in a largely gradual, continuous, and civil process, rather than through rebellion and confrontation. I write "largely" because no country, the United States included, is completely free of troublesome transitions and we have had our share.

No one can be sure what the future holds. A prolonged downward turn in the economy (a centerpiece of most radical scenarios) would give efforts to enlist new immigrants into a majority-of-minorities coalition a better chance of succeeding. But unlike some early Americans who arrived here as slaves, most new immigrants come voluntarily. Many discover that hard work and education do allow them to move up the American economic and social ladders. That makes a radicalization of Hispanics (and Asian Americans) very unlikely. As far as one can project the recent past into the near future, Hispanics will continue to build and rebuild the American society as a community of communities, rather than dividing it along racial lines.

## DISCUSSION QUESTIONS

1. What values that tend to be strong in Hispanic cultures, contribute to popular stereotypes about Hispanic workers? How could these values contribute to a perception that Hispanics lack the initiative and drive so valued in today's workplace?

2. What are the common stereotypes about Hispanics? How could these stereotypes affect career mobility for Hispanics?

3. What role has the popular media (television, newspapers, movies, music, etc.) played in the perpetuation of these stereotypes?

# To Be Asian in America

## Angela Johnson Meadows

C. N. Le barely remembers fleeing Vietnam for the United States when he was 5. Sketchy images of riding a cargo ship to Guam, having his documents processed, and boarding a plane that would take him to Arkansas are all that remain of the life-altering experience.

But the reason for leaving his war-ravaged homeland is crystal clear. After military pressure from communist North Vietnam caused the South Vietnamese government to collapse in 1975, Le's family was in jeopardy.

"The U.S. government knew that those who worked for the U.S. military were going to be persecuted pretty harshly if they stayed back in Vietnam," says Le, whose parents both were U.S. military workers. "So [the U.S. government] made arrangements for their Vietnamese employees and their families to be evacuated."

Le and his family spent their initial days in the United States at Fort Chaffee, an Arkansas military base that served as a processing center for Vietnamese refugees.

"We had a little playground there that kids would play on, so in a lot of ways my experience was more of a typical kid's experience . . . than a refugee experience," recalls Le, a visiting assistant professor at the University of Massachusetts, Amherst.

"Adults who had more of a recognition of what was going on would probably tell you, like my parents have said, it was a pretty traumatic experience for them, having to leave their country, leave everything behind and try to start life in a whole new country," Le says.

Le's status as a refugee is different from that of Chinese, Asian Indians, Japanese, and some other Asians who have come to America, yet regardless of country of origin or mode or time of arrival, the majority of these immigrants share a common goal—a better life. For some, that means educational or professional opportunities they were denied in their homelands; for others, it's escaping political turmoil; and for others still, it's sacrificing the comforts of middle-class life to provide better chances for their children. It is the quintessential U.S. immigrant story.

There are nearly 12 million people of Asian heritage living in the United States. Asian Americans (a term used by *DiversityInc* to describe both immigrant and American-born Asians) represent East Asian nations such as China, Japan, and Korea;

Reprinted with permission from *DiversityInc,* April 2005, pp. 29–47.

South Asian countries including India, Pakistan, and Nepal; and Southeast Asian nations such as Thailand, Vietnam, and Malaysia.

Still only 4.6 percent of the U.S. population, the Asian-American segment, is experiencing astronomical growth. Between 2000 and 2050, the population is expected to surge 213 percent, according to the U.S. Census Bureau. The projected general-population growth during the same time? A paltry 49 percent.

But this growth isn't a 21st–century phenomenon. Historians have traced their presence in the land that evolved into the United States of America as far back as 1763, when Filipinos traveling aboard Spanish galleons jumped ship in New Orleans to escape imprisonment and fled into the Louisiana bayou to establish the first recorded Filipino settlement in America. Some argue their history in the United States dates back to the 1400s.

The Chinese were the first group of Asians to arrive in great numbers, appearing in the mid-1800s. The lure? The potential economic prosperity of the 1848 California Gold Rush and job opportunities associated with agriculture and the building of the intercontinental railroad.

Asian Americans were recruited as laborers—mostly men who were enticed by the opportunity to earn money to support their families or indentured servants who were sent to work off the debts of other Asians back home.

"These people were often deceived," says Gary Okihiro, director of the Center for the Study of Ethnicity and Race and a professor of international and public affairs at Columbia University. "Although these [work and payment] conditions were spelled out to them, they were oftentimes unfulfilled."

Many planned to return to their homelands when their contracted work period ended, but were prevented by U.S. immigration laws.

"They locked those that were here in the U.S.," says Okihiro. "Their remittances were crucial for the sustenance of their families back in Asia, so they were oftentimes trapped into remaining in the U.S."

Subsequent Asians came in waves, with the largest population arriving after the 1965 passage of the Immigration and Nationality Act. Immigrants and their offspring from China, the Philippines, India, Vietnam, Korea, and Japan now account for the largest Asian populations in the country.

## A BRAVE NEW WORLD

W.E.B. DuBois once described the African-American experience as one of a double-consciousness, rooted in the need to navigate between one's own culture and that of the mainstream. It is an experience that rings true for Asian immigrants and their descendants as well.

"When they arrive, they begin to realize that they're different," says John Kuo Wei Tchen, the founding director of the A/P/A Studies Program and Institute at New York University. "Identities get challenged and they have to deal with what it means to be American or resident alien."

Some Asian Americans relied on assimilation as a means of blending in with American society and as an attempt to escape anti-Asian sentiments that heightened during World War II. "This question about how much they wanted to or did assimilate is a question of how much they were permitted to assimilate," says Okihiro.

Today, ties to home remain strong for new Asian immigrants; however, many families experience acculturation—the process of assimilating new ideas into an existing cognitive structure—with U.S.-born generations.

"Parents would like to think their children are going to be very embracive and very welcoming of the parents' own culture," says Franklin Ng, a professor in the anthropology department at California State University–Fresno. "Parents may have these kinds of supportive mechanisms, encouraging them to go to a temple, or ethnic church, so their children will become familiar with their ethnic culture . . . [but] the youth are having their own trajectory."

Growing up in a Southern California suburb, Le struggled with his Vietnamese name. By the time he reached high school, racial and ethnic tensions had set in and Le decided to go by the name Sean. "At that age, you just want to fit in and be like everyone else," he says.

But a college course on race and ethnicity changed his thinking. "That's when I became more socially conscious . . . and really began to see that my identity . . . was a source of strength . . . rather than a source of embarrassment. I wanted to go back to my Vietnamese name. The name Sean didn't really fit my identity," says Le, who is also the founder of Asian-Nation.org, an online resource for Asian-American historical, demographic, political, and cultural issues.

Today, Le uses his first and middle initials, a way to keep his Vietnamese name—Cuong Nguyen—without having to face the pronunciation problems of non-Asians.

This balancing act isn't limited to language issues. Many struggle with the expectations of both their family and mainstream society.

"We were raised in the family to be in a very consistent way with the traditional Chinese culture." says Lora Fong, a third-generation Chinese American. "We spoke Chinese in the home and ate Chinese food in the home. The home life was one thing, but going out into the regular world, you have to fit in; there is a certain amount of biculturalism."

When Fong's father died in 1984, her Chinese and American worlds collided. She was working at IBM at the time, a company that often assisted employees in making funeral arrangements for loved ones.

"I was a team leader, I was frequently running projects and giving assignments and keeping people on task," says Fong, now an attorney at Greenbaum, Rowe, Smith & Davis in Woodbridge, N.J. Fortunately, Fong had a Chinese-American supervisor who understood that her professional persona was in stark contrast to her status within her traditional Chinese family.

"He knew that I could not take on a role of being in charge [in my family]." Fong recalls. "He just said, 'She's the daughter. She's the youngest. She's not running things. The company does not have a role there, so just back off.' And that was really antithetical to the way the company took on a role in an employee's personal life. That was such a dichotomy."

## STRIVING FOR SUCCESS

Despite viewing America as the proverbial land of opportunity, the path to a better life has not been without roadblocks, particularly for those who arrived prior to 1965. Chinese in the United States were denied citizenship in the late 1800s, while immigration of all Asians, except for Filipinos (whose residence in a U.S. territory gave them the status of nationals), was halted in 1924 through the National Origins Act. It wasn't until the Immigration and Nationality Act of 1965 that Asian Americans were accepted into the country in larger numbers. The gates to the United States were opened, particularly to those with expertise in the medical, science, and technology fields, explaining in part the proliferation of Asian Americans in those disciplines today.

In the face of language barriers, cultural adjustments and government and societal oppression, Asian Americans as a whole appear to have done quite well in America. A look at demographic data shows that Asian Americans as a group surpass all other racial and ethnic groups in the country in median household income and education levels. And while many marketers are turned off by the small size and myriad languages of the population, the buying power of Asian Americans is projected to jump 347 percent between 1990 and 2009, compared with a modest 159-percent increase for the overall population.

For aspirational Asian Americans, social mobility is a priority and education often is viewed as the method of achievement. This focus contributes to the group's economic success.

"Researchers suggest that one legacy of Confucianism in many Asian countries (notably China, Korea, Japan, and Vietnam) is the notion that human beings are perfectible if they work to improve themselves," write Yu Xie and Kimberly A. Goyette, authors of *Demographic Portrait of Asian Americans.* "Given this cultural heritage, some Asian Americans may be more likely than whites to believe that hard work in school will he rewarded."

"In China, you have a kind of high-stakes testing," adds Tchen, referring to the country's civil-service system. "The emperor constantly recruits the best to come to the capital or to work . . . It's not so odd for higher education to be seen as the modern variation of that practice."

Mia Tuan's mother and father encouraged higher learning. "Even though my parents knew nothing about the U.S. educational system . . . it was always assumed that I would go to college," says Tuan, an associate professor of sociology at the University of Oregon.

Tuan's mother wanted her daughter to be the next Connie Chung. "Connie opened that door and parents encouraged us to go through that same door," says Tuan.

"I chose to not be the next Connie Chung, but a whole cohort of Asian-American women did hear that call and answered that call . . . When I told them I was going into sociology, they didn't know what the hell that was, but it was a Ph.D., so that counted for something."

But educational attainment isn't a priority for all Asians in America. "If you come from a rural society where schooling and education was not such a benefit to your ability to raise crops . . . your emphasis on education would be different," says Tchen. "That would be true for Hmong or Southeast Asians . . . They don't necessarily relate to higher education as a way to better themselves."

This is played out in the educational statistics of Asian Americans. For example, in 2000, 76 percent of Asian Indians and 67 percent of Chinese Americans between the ages of 25 and 34 had a college degree or higher, compared with 43 percent of Filipino Americans and 27 percent of Vietnamese Americans.

## FIGURE 2–1

### How They Score Class of 2003 SATs

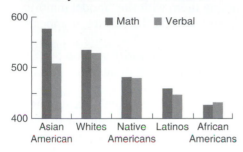

■ Math  ■ Verbal

600
500
400

Asian American | Whites | Native Americans | Latinos | African Americans

### U.S. Asian Population

12.5 Other
7.8 Japanese
10.5
10.9 Vietnamese
16.2 Asian Indian
18.3 Filipino
23.8% Chinese

### Educational Attainment
People 25 years and older, 2004

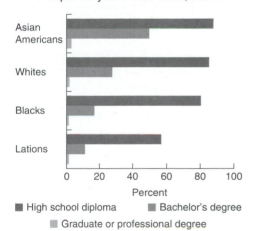

Asian Americans

Whites

Blacks

Lations

0   20   40   60   80   100
Percent

■ High school diploma   ■ Bachelor's degree
■ Graduate or professional degree

### Median Family Incomes
In U.S. Population 25+

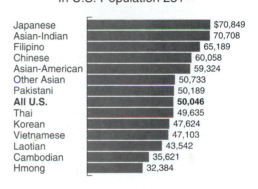

| Japanese | $70,849 |
| Asian-Indian | 70,708 |
| Filipino | 65,189 |
| Chinese | 60,058 |
| Asian-American | 59,324 |
| Other Asian | 50,733 |
| Pakistani | 50,189 |
| **All U.S.** | **50,046** |
| Thai | 49,635 |
| Korean | 47,624 |
| Vietnamese | 47,103 |
| Laotian | 43,542 |
| Cambodian | 35,621 |
| Hmong | 32,384 |

### Asian-American Buying Power
Projected rate of increase 1990-2009

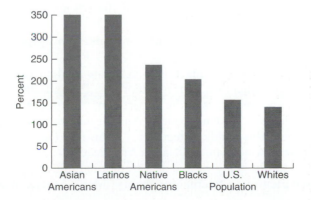

350
300
250
200
150
100
50
0

Percent

Asian Americans | Latinos | Native Americans | Blacks | U.S. Population | Whites

## THE MODEL MINORITY AND OTHER MYTHS

While the myths of universal affluence and intelligence among Asian Americans are just that, it hasn't stopped society from pinning them with the "model minority" label. They are seen as smart, wealthy and successful, and on the surface, it appears to be a positive perception.

"My parents' generation? They liked the model minority stereotype," says Tuan. "In their mind, it has served us well . . . They saw it as the price you pay for being an outsider and it was a price they were willing to pay."

But a look behind the stereotype and its implications reveals a troubling story. "A lot of these [income] statistics can be misleading," says Le. "Family median income is mainly inflated because Asian-American families tend to have more workers . . . They're more likely to live in urban areas where salaries are higher, but the cost of living is also higher."

Per capita income for Asian Americans in the 2000 census measured $20,719, compared with $21,587 for the overall population.

A look at Fortune 500 companies illustrates that an intense focus on education really doesn't guarantee professional success. Despite high education levels, Asian Americans represent less than 1 percent of senior-management ranks or corporate boards.

"Everybody cites the success of Asian Americans, yet if you compared the level of education and position with that of white people, they come below white people," says Okihiro. "Their investment in education does not pay off. There's a glass ceiling for them."

Tuan's father was a diplomat with the Taiwanese government; however, after the U.S. office closed, he found it wasn't easy to translate his skills. He ended up opening a pizza shop.

"They lost a lot of status," says Tuan of her parents, whose migration to the United States erased the prestige of their advanced degrees. "That put pressure on the next generation to make it worthwhile."

The belief that Asian Americans can succeed on their own dilutes the notion that some could benefit from programs ranging from Medicaid to affirmative action. Thirteen percent of all Asian Americans live in poverty. Twenty-three percent of Asians outside of the six largest groups are impoverished, rivaling the 24 percent of blacks of this economic status.

"With this spotlight on the talented tenth, there is neglect of those who may be in the lower tiers," says Ng.

Tuan recalls a meeting with faculty members and graduate students in her department.

"At one point [during the meeting] a graduate student said, 'We take issue with the fact that the department isn't hiring minorities,' " says Tuan, who was one of three recently hired Asian Americans in the department. "I was stunned when the student said that, and I said, 'So, do we not count?' And his answer was basically [that] we didn't, that Asians were this middle category . . . In his mind a minority hire would have been Latino, African American, and Native American."

In addition to not being viewed as a traditional minority, Asian Americans also have an imposed identity as "eternal foreigners." Many American-born Asians have at least one story of being asked about their origins. A reply such as Fresno or Washington, D.C., is often met with the incredulous response of: "No, where are you *really* from?"

Even high-profile American-born Asians can't escape the stereotype. When Tara Lipinski defeated Michelle Kwan in the 1998 Winter Olympics figure-skating competition, MSNBC ran a headline that read: "American beats out Kwan." Kwan, who was born in Torrance, Calif., is just as American as Lipinski.

This misconception has some basis in truth, says Le. Approximately two-thirds of Asian Americans are immigrants. "But the social implications are that when someone is judged to be a foreigner, it is easier for that person to be treated as if they're not a real American . . . It becomes easier to deny them the same rights and privileges that are given to real Americans."

Asian Americans also face the perception that they are all the same. When Ng first settled in Fresno, Calif., he was taunted by a group of teenagers who ordered him to "Remember Pearl Harbor Day," an allusion to Japan's attack on the United States. As a child growing up in a Chicago suburb during the Korean War era, Tchen received the label of "gook," a disparaging term for Southeast Asians. Both Ng and Tchen are Chinese.

But perhaps the most notable misidentification occurred in 1982, when 27-year-old Vincent Chin visited a suburban Detroit strip club to celebrate his impending nuptials. While there, Chin encountered a couple of disgruntled autoworkers, one of whom had recently been laid off. The autoworkers hurled insults at Chin and blamed him for the demise of Detroit's auto industry. After Chin left the club, the two men met up with Chin in front of a fast-food restaurant and beat him with a baseball bat. Chin, who was Chinese—not Japanese, as his attackers had assumed—slipped into a coma and died five days later.

## THE ASIAN-AMERICAN IDENTITY IN AMERICA

Asian Americans represent nearly 25 countries and speak at least as many languages; however, it is the challenges stemming from stereotypes, misconceptions, discrimination, and exclusion that help this disparate group to unite under the umbrella term of "Asian American."

"The experience of being treated as foreigners, exotics, outsiders, hordes, dangerous, those kinds of images that are recycled in American media . . . perpetuate some kind of basis for people of different backgrounds to come together," says Tchen.

"A pan-Asian orientation is useful as sort of an instrument for coalition building for political advancement," adds Ng. "Asian Americans are ignored in the corridors of power, and collectively they can have more impact and can address issues that are more common."

Although Fong identifies first as a Chinese American, she's also concerned about broader Asian-American issues.

"We are all sharing a unique experience in terms of people's pre-conceived notion of who we are and what we should or shouldn't be doing in this society," says Fong, who is a past president of the Asian Pacific American Lawyers Association of New Jersey.

In addition to fighting shared struggles, Asian Americans have been able to collectively celebrate the accomplishments of Asian Americans of various backgrounds.

Norman Mineta, U.S. Secretary of Transportation, and Elaine Chao, U.S. Secretary of Labor, are two of the highest-ranking Asian Americans in the Bush administration. Andrea Jung, chairman of the board and CEO of Avon Products, and Indira Nooyi, president and chief financial officer at PepsiCo, are just a few people who have broken what career consultant Jane Hyun describes as the "bamboo ceiling" of corporate America. And the presence of Asian Americans in sports and entertainment continues to flourish.

"When I was growing up . . . there was not exactly a wide range," says Tuan. "But if you were to ask—and I do ask these questions of the students—to name five prominent Asian-American public figures, they can come up with them now . . . I can only see that as being a good thing, because it shifts this notion of what's possible or who or what an Asian American is or what they're capable of. That's very powerful to me."

## DISCUSSION QUESTIONS

1. In what ways have Asian Americans experienced "target" status?

2. Why are Asian Americans sometimes not thought of as a minority group?

3. As a group, Asian Americans have the highest SAT scores and the highest college graduation rates. Then, how do you account for the fact that Asian Americans have found more success in small businesses than they have in FORTUNE 500 companies?

4. How does the educational success of Asian Americans contribute to popular prejudices about these groups?

# A World View of Cultural Diversity

## Thomas Sowell

**D**iversity has become one of the most often used words of our time—and a word almost never defined. Diversity is invoked in discussions of everything from employment policy to curriculum reform and from entertainment to politics. Nor is the word merely a description of the long-known fact that the American population is made up of people from many countries, many races, and many cultural backgrounds. All this was well known long before the word *diversity* became an insistent part of our vocabulary, an invocation, an imperative, or a bludgeon in ideological conflicts.

The very motto of the country, *E. Pluribus Unum,* recognizes the diversity of the American people. For generations, this diversity has been celebrated, whether in comedies like *Abie's Irish Rose* (the famous play featuring a Jewish boy and an Irish girl) or in patriotic speeches on the Fourth of July. Yet one senses something very different in today's crusades for "diversity"; certainly not a patriotic celebration of America and often a sweeping criticism of the United States, or even a condemnation of Western civilization as a whole.

At the very least, we need to separate the issue of the general importance of cultural diversity—not only in the United States but in the world at large—from the more specific, more parochial, and more ideological agendas that have become associated with this word in recent years. I would like to talk about the worldwide importance of cultural diversity over centuries of human history before returning to the narrower issues of our time.

The entire history of the human race, the rise of man from the caves, has been marked by transfers of cultural advances from one group to another and from one civilization to another. Paper and printing, for example, are today vital parts of Western civilization, but they originated in China centuries before they made their way to Europe. So did the magnetic compass, which made possible the great ages of exploration that put the Western hemisphere in touch with the rest of mankind. Mathematical concepts likewise migrated from one culture to another: Trigonometry from ancient Egypt, and the whole numbering system now used throughout the world

Reprinted by permission of Springer and Transaction Publications from *Society*, Volume 29, No. 1, 1991, pp. 37–44, "A World View of Cultural Diversity," by Thomas Sowell. With kind permission from Springer Science and Business Media.

originated among the Hindus of India, though Europeans called this system *Arabic numerals* because it was the Arabs who were the intermediaries through which these numbers reached medieval Europe. Indeed, much of the philosophy of ancient Greece first reached Western Europe in Arabic translations, which were then retranslated into Latin or into the vernacular languages of the West Europeans.

Much that became part of the culture of Western civilization originated outside that civilization, often in the Middle East or Asia. The game of chess came from India, gunpowder from China, and various mathematical concepts from the Islamic world, for example. The conquest of Spain by Moslems in the eighth century A.D. made Spain a center for the diffusion into Western Europe of the more advanced knowledge of the Mediterranean world and of the Orient in astronomy, medicine, optics, and geometry.

The later rise of Western Europe to world preeminence in science and technology built upon these foundations, and then the science and technology of European civilization began to spread around the world, not only to European offshoot societies such as the United States or Australia, but also to non-European cultures, of which Japan is perhaps the most striking example.

The historic sharing of cultural advances, until they became the common inheritance of the human race, implied much more than cultural diversity. It implied that some cultural features were not only different from others but better than others. The very fact that people—all people, whether Europeans, Africans, Asians, or others—have repeatedly chosen to abandon some feature of their own culture in order to replace it with something from another culture implies that the replacement served their purposes more effectively. Arabic numerals are not simply different from Roman numerals, they are better than Roman numerals. This is shown by their replacing Roman numerals in many countries whose own cultures derived from Rome, as well as in other countries whose respective numbering systems were likewise superseded by so-called Arabic numerals.

It is virtually inconceivable today that the distances in astronomy or the complexities of higher mathematics should be expressed in Roman numerals. Merely to express the year of the declaration of American independence as MDCCLXXVI requires more than twice as many Roman numerals as Arabic numerals. Moreover, Roman numerals offer more opportunities for errors, as the same digit may be either added or substracted, depending on its place in sequence. Roman numerals are good for numbering kings or Super Bowls, but they cannot match the efficiency of Arabic numerals in most mathematical operations—and that is, after all, why we have numbers at all. Cultural features do not exist merely as badges of identity to which we have some emotional attachment. They exist to meet the necessities and to forward the purposes of human life. When they are surpassed by features of other cultures, they tend to fall by the wayside or to survive only as marginal curiosities like Roman numerals today.

Not only concepts, information, products, and technologies transfer from one culture to another. The natural produce of the earth does the same. Malaysia is the world's leading grower of rubber trees—but those trees are indigenous to Brazil. Most of rice grown in Africa today originated in Asia, and its tobacco originated in the Western hemisphere. Even a great wheat-exporting nation like Argentina once imported wheat, which was not an indigenous crop to that country. Cultural diversity, viewed internationally and historically, is not a static picture of differentness but a dynamic picture of competition in which what serves human purposes more effectively survives while what does not tends to decline or disappear.

Manuscript scrolls once preserved the precious records, knowledge, and thought of European or Middle Eastern cultures. But once paper and printing from China became known in these cultures, books were clearly far faster and cheaper to produce and drove scrolls virtually into extinction. Books were not simply different from scrolls; they were better than scrolls. The point that some cultural features are better than others must be insisted on today because so many among the intelligentsia either evade or deny this plain reality. The intelligentsia often use words like *perceptions* and *values* as they argue in effect that it is all a matter of how you choose to look at it.

They may have a point in such things as music, art, and literature from different cultures, but there are many human purposes common to peoples of all cultures. They want to live rather than die, for example. When Europeans first ventured into the arid interior of Australia, they often died of thirst or hunger in a land where the Australian aborigines had no trouble finding food or water, within that particular setting, at least, the aboriginal culture enabled people to do what both the aborigines and Europeans wanted to do—survive. A given culture may not be superior for all things in all settings, much less remain superior over time, but particular cultural features may nevertheless be clearly better for some purposes—not just different.

Why is there any such argument in the first place? Perhaps it is because we are still living in the long, grim shadow of the Nazi Holocaust and are, therefore, understandably reluctant to label anything or anyone "superior" or "inferior." But we do not need to. We need only recognize that particular products, skills, technologies, agricultural crops, or intellectual concepts accomplish particular purposes better than their alternatives. It is not necessary to rank one whole culture over another in all things, much less to claim that they remain in that same ranking throughout history. They do not.

Clearly, cultural leadership in various fields has changed hands many times. China was far in advance of any country in Europe in a large number of fields for at least a thousand years and, as late as the sixteenth century, had the highest standard of living in the world. Equally clearly, China today is one of the poorer nations of the world and is having great difficulty trying to catch up to the technological level of Japan and the West, with no real hope of regaining its former world preeminence in the foreseeable future.

Similar rises and falls of nations and empires have been common over long stretches of human history—for example, the rise and fall of the Roman Empire, the "golden age" of medieval Spain and its decline to the level of one of the poorest nations in Europe today, the centuries-long triumphs of the Ottoman Empire intellectually as well as on the battlefields of Europe and the Middle East, and then its long decline to become known as "the sick man of Europe." Yet, while cultural leadership has changed hands many times, that leadership had been real at given times, and much of what was achieved in the process has contributed enormously to our well-being and opportunities today. Cultural competition is not a zero-sum game. It is what advances the human race.

If nations and civilizations differ in their effectiveness in different fields of endeavor, so do social groups. Here is especially strong resistance to accepting the reality of different levels and kinds of skills, interests, habits, and orientations among different groups of people. One academic writer, for example, said that nineteenth-century Jewish immigrants to the United States were fortunate to arrive just as the garment industry in New York began to develop. I could not help thinking that Hank Aaron was similarly fortunate that he often came to bat just as a home run was due to be hit. It might be possible to believe that these Jewish immigrants just happened to be in the right place at the right time if you restricted yourself to their history in the United States. But, again taking a world view, we find Jews prominent, often predominant, and usually prospering, in the apparel industry in medieval Spain, in the Ottoman Empire, in the Russian Empire, in Argentina, in Australia, and in Brazil. How surprised should we be to find them predominant in the same industry in America?

Other groups have excelled in other special occupations and industries. Indeed, virtually every group excels at something. Germans, for example, have been prominent as pioneers in the piano industry. American piano brands like Steinway and Knabe, not to mention the Wurlitzer organ, are signs of the long prominence of Germans in this industry, where they produced the first pianos in Colonial America. Germans also pioneered in piano-building in Czarist Russia, Australia, France, and England. Chinese immigrants have, at one period of history or another, run more than half the grocery stores in Kingston, Jamaica, and Panama City and conducted more than half of all retail trade in Malaysia, the Philippines, Vietnam, and Cambodia. Other groups have dominated the retail trade in other parts of the world—the Gujaratis from India in East Africa and in Fiji or the Lebanese in parts of West Africa, for example.

Nothing has been more common than for particular groups—often a minority—to dominate particular occupations or industries. Seldom do they have any ability to keep out others and certainly not to keep out the majority population. They are simply better at the particular skills required in that occupation or industry. Sometimes we can see why. When Italians have made wine in Italy for centuries, it is hardly surprising that they should become prominent among winemakers in Argentina and in California's Napa Valley. Similarly, when Germans in Germany have been for centuries renowned for their beermaking, how surprised should we be that in Argentina they became as prominent among brewers as Italians among winemakers? How surprised should we be that beermaking, in the United States arose where there were concentrations of German immigrants in Milwaukee and St. Louis, for example? Or that the leading beer producers to this day have German names like Anheuser-Busch or Coors, among many other German names?

Just as cultural leadership in a particular field is not permanent for nations or civilizations, neither is it permanent for given racial, ethnic, or religious groups. By the time the Jews were expelled from Spain in 1492, Europe had overtaken the Islamic world in medical science, so that Jewish physicians who sought refuge in the Ottoman Empire found themselves in great demand in that Moslem country. By the early sixteenth century, the sultan of the Ottoman Empire had on his palace medical staff 42 Jewish physicians and 21 Moslem physicians.

With the passage of time, however, the source of the Jews' advantage—their knowledge of Western medicine—eroded as successive generations of Ottoman Jews lost contact with the West and its further progress. Christian minorities within the Ottoman Empire began to replace the Jews, not only in medicine but also in international trade and even in the theater, once dominated by Jews. The difference was that these Christian minorities—notably Greeks and Armenians—maintained their ties in

Christian Europe and often sent their sons there to be educated. It was not race or ethnicity as such that was crucial but maintaining contacts with the ongoing progress of Western civilization. By contrast, the Ottoman Jews became a declining people in a declining empire. Many, if not most, were Sephardic Jews from Spain, once the elite of the world Jewry. But by the time the state of Israel was formed in the twentieth century, those Sephardic Jews who had settled for centuries in the Islamic world now lagged painfully behind the Ashkenazic Jews of the Western world—notably in income and education. To get some idea what a historic reversal that has been in the relative positions of Sephardic Jews and Ashkenazic Jews, one need only note that Sephardic Jews in colonial America sometimes disinherited their own children for marrying Ashkenazic Jews.

Why do some groups, subgroups, nations, or whole civilizations excel in some particular fields rather than others? All too often, the answer to this question must be: Nobody really knows. It is an unanswered question largely because it is an unasked question. There is an uphill struggle merely to get acceptance of the fact that large differences exist among peoples, not just in specific skills in the narrow sense (computer science, basketball, or brewing beer) but more fundamentally in different interests, orientations, and values that determine which particular skills they seek to develop and with what degree of success. Merely to suggest that these internal cultural factors play a significant role in various economic, educational, or social outcomes is to invite charges of "blaming the victim." It is much more widely acceptable to blame surrounding social conditions or institutional policies.

But if we look at cultural diversity internationally and historically, there is a more basic question than whether blame is the real issue. Surely, no human being should be blamed for the way his culture evolved for centuries before he was born. Blame has nothing to do with it. Another explanation that has had varying amounts of acceptance at different times and places is the biological or genetic theory of differences among peoples. I have argued against this theory in many places but will not take the time to go into these lengthy arguments here. A world view of cultural differences over the centuries undermines the genetic theory as well. Europeans and Chinese, for example, are clearly genetically different. Equally clearly, China was a more advanced civilization than Europe in many ways, scientific, technological, and organizational, for at least a thousand years. Yet over the past few centuries, Europe has moved ahead of China in many of these same ways. If those cultural differences were due to genes, how could these two races have changed positions so radically from one epoch in history to another?

All explanations of differences between groups can be broken down into heredity and environment. Yet a world view of the history of cultural diversity seems, on the surface at least, to deny both. One reason for this is that we have thought of environment too narrowly, as the immediate surrounding circumstances or differing institutional policies toward different groups. Environment in that narrow sense may explain some group differences, but the histories of many groups completely contradict that particular version of environment as an explanation. Let us take just two examples out of many that are available.

Jewish immigrants from Eastern Europe and Italian immigrants from southern Italy began arriving in the United States in large numbers at about the same time in the late nineteenth century, and their large-scale immigration also ended at the same time, when restrictive immigration laws were passed in the 1920s. The two groups arrived here in virtually the same economic condition—namely, destitute. They often lived in the same neighborhoods and their children attended the same schools, sitting side by side in the same classrooms. Their environments, in the narrow sense in which the term is commonly used, were virtually identical. Yet their social histories in the United States have been very different.

Over the generations, both groups rose, but they rose at different rates, through different means, and in a very different mixture of occupations and industries. Even wealthy Jews and wealthy Italians tended to become rich in different sectors of the economy. The California wine industry, for example, is full of Italian names like Mondavi, Gallo, and Rossi, but the only prominent Jewish winemaker, Manishewitz, makes an entirely different kind of wine, and no one would compare Jewish winemakers with Italian winemakers in the United States. When we look at Jews and Italians in the very different environmental setting of Argentina, we see the same general pattern of differences between them. The same is true if we look at the differences between Jews and Italians in Australia, or Canada, or Western Europe.

Jews are not Italians and Italians are not Jews. Anyone familiar with their very different histories over many centuries should not be surprised. Their fate in America was not determined solely by their surrounding social conditions in America or by how they were treated by American society. They were different before they got on the boats to cross the ocean, and those differences crossed the ocean with them.

We can take it a step further. Even Ashkenazic Jews, those originating in Eastern Europe, have had significantly different economic and social histories from those originating in Germanic Central Europe, including Austria as well as Germany itself. These differences have persisted among their descendents not only in New York and Chicago but as far away as Melbourne and Sydney. In Australia, Jews from Eastern Europe have tended to cluster in and around Melbourne, while Germanic Jews have settled in and around Sydney. They even have a saying among themselves that Melbourne is a cold city with warm Jews while Sydney is a warm city with cold Jews.

A second and very different example of persistent cultural differences involves immigrants from Japan. As everyone knows, many Japanese-Americans were interned during the Second World War. What is less well known is that there is and has been an even larger Japanese population in Brazil than in the United States. These Japanese, incidentally, own approximately three-quarters as much land in Brazil as there is in Japan. (The Japanese almost certainly own more agricultural land in Brazil than in Japan.) In any event, very few Japanese in Brazil were interned during the Second World War. Moreover, the Japanese in Brazil were never subjected to the discrimination suffered by Japanese-Americans in the decades before the Second World War.

Yet, during the war, Japanese-Americans overwhelmingly remained loyal to the United States and Japanese-American soldiers won more than their share of medals in combat. But in Brazil, the Japanese were overwhelmingly and even fanatically loyal to Japan. You cannot explain the difference by anything in the environment of the United States or the environment of Brazil. But if you know something about the history of those Japanese who settled in these two countries, you know that they were culturally different in Japan before they ever got on the boats to take them across the Pacific Ocean and they were still different decades later. These two groups of immigrants left Japan during very different periods in the cultural evolution of Japan itself. A modern

Japanese scholar has said: "If you want to see Japan of the Meiji era, go to the United States. If you want to see Japan of the Taisho era, go to Brazil." The Meiji era was a more cosmopolitan, pro-American era; the Taisho era was one of fanatical Japanese nationalism.

If the narrow concept of environment fails to explain many profound differences between groups and subgroups, it likewise fails to explain many very large differences in the economic and social performances of nations and civilizations. An eighteenth-century writer in Chile described that country's many natural advantages in climate, soil, and natural resources and then asked in complete bewilderment why it was such a poverty-stricken country. The same question could be asked of many countries today.

Conversely, we could ask why Japan and Switzerland are so prosperous when they are both almost totally lacking in natural resources. Both are rich in what economists call "human capital"—the skills of their people. No doubt there is a long and complicated history behind the different skill levels of different peoples and nations. The point here is that the immediate environment—whether social or geographic—is only part of the story.

Geography may well have a significant role in the history of peoples, but perhaps not simply by presenting them with more or less natural resources. Geography shapes or limits peoples' opportunities for cultural interaction and the mutual development that comes out of this. Small, isolated islands in the sea have seldom been sources of new scientific advances of technological breakthroughs, regardless of where such islands were located and regardless of the race of people on these islands. There are islands on land as well. Where soil, fertile enough to support human life, exists only in isolated patches, widely separated, there tend to be isolate cultures (often with different languages or dialects) in a culturally fragmented region. Isolated highlands often produce insular cultures, lagging in many ways behind the cultures of the lowlanders of the same race—whether we are talking about medieval Scotland, colonial Ceylon, or the contemporary montagnards of Vietnam.

With geographical environments as with social environments, we are talking about long-run effects not simply the effects, of immediate surroundings. When Scottish highlanders, for example, immigrated to North Carolina in colonial times, they had a very different history from that of Scottish lowlanders who settled in North Carolina. For one thing, the lowlanders spoke English while the highlanders spoke Gaelic on into the nineteenth century. Obviously, speaking only Gaelic in an English-speaking country affects a group's whole economic and social progress.

Geographical conditions vary as radically in terms of how well they facilitate or impede large-scale cultural interactions as they do in their distribution of natural resources. We are not even close to being able to explain how all these geographical influences have operated throughout history. This too is an unanswered question largely because it is an unasked question, and it is an unasked question because many are seeking answers in terms of immediate social environment or are vehemently insistent that they have already found the answer in those terms.

How radically do geographic environments differ, not just in terms of tropical versus arctic climates, but also in the very configuration of the land and how this helps or hinders large-scale interactions among peoples? Consider one statistic: Africa is more than twice the size of Europe, and yet Africa has a shorter coastline than Europe. This seems almost impossible. But the reason is that Europe's coastline is far more convoluted, with many harbors and inlets being formed all around the continent. Much of the coastline of Africa is smooth, which is to say, lacking in the harbors that make large-scale maritime trade possible by sheltering the ships at anchor from the rough waters of the open sea.

Waterways of all sorts have played a major role in the evolution of cultures and nations around the world. Harbors on the sea are not the only waterways. Rivers are also very important. Virtually every major city on earth is located either on a river or a harbor. Whether it is such great harbors as those in Sydney, Singapore, or San Francisco; or London on the Thames, Paris on the Seine, or numerous other European cities on the Danube—waterways have been the lifeblood of urban centers for centuries. Only very recently has man-made, self-powered transportation, like automobiles and airplanes, made it possible to produce an exception to the rule like Los Angeles. (There is a Los Angeles River, but you do not have to be Moses to walk across it in the summertime.) New York has both a long and deep river and a huge sheltered harbor.

None of these geographical features in themselves create a great city or develop an urban culture. Human beings do that. But geography sets the limits within which people can operate and in some places it sets those limits much wider than in others. Returning to our comparison of the continents of Europe and Africa, we find that they differ as radically in rivers as they do in harbors. There are entire nations in Africa without a single navigable river—Libya and South Africa, for example.

"Navigable" is the crucial word. Some African rivers are navigable only during the rainy season. Some are navigable only between numerous cataracts and waterfalls. Even the Zaire River, which is longer than any river in North America and carries a larger volume of water, has too many waterfalls too close to the ocean for it to become a major artery of international commerce. Such commerce is facilitated in Europe not only by numerous navigable rivers but also by the fact that no spot on the continent, outside of Russia, is more than 500 miles from the sea. Many places in Africa are more than 500 miles from the sea, including the entire nation of Uganda.

Against this background, how surprised should we be to find that Europe is the most urbanized of all inhabited continents and Africa the least urbanized? Urbanization is not the be-all and end-all of life, but certainly an urban culture is bound to differ substantially from non-urban cultures, and the skills peculiar to an urban culture are far more likely to be found among groups from an urban civilization. Conversely, an interesting history could be written about the failures of urbanized groups in agricultural settlements.

Looking within Africa, the influence of geography seems equally clear. The most famous ancient civilization on the continent arose within a few miles on either side of Africa's longest navigable river, the Nile, and even today the two largest cities on the continent, Cairo and Alexandria, are on that river. The great West African kingdoms in the region served by the Niger River and the long-flourishing East African economy based around the great natural harbor on the island of Zanzibar are further evidences of the role of geography. Again, geography is not all-determining—the economy of Zanzibar has been ruined by government policy in recent decades—but nevertheless, geography is an important long-run influence on the shaping of cultures as well as in narrow economic terms.

What are the implications of a world view of cultural diversity on the narrower issues being debated under that label in the United States today? Although "diversity" is used in so many different ways in so many different contexts that it seems to mean all things to all people, there are a few themes that appear again and again. One of these broad themes is that diversity implies organized efforts at the preservation of cultural differences, perhaps governmental efforts, perhaps government subsidies to various programs run by the advocates of diversity.

This approach raises questions as to what the purpose of culture is. If what is important about cultures is that they are emotionally symbolic, and if differentness is cherished for the sake of differentness, then this particular version of cultural diversity might make some sense. But cultures exist even in isolated societies where there are no other cultures around—where there is no one else and nothing else from which to be different. Cultures exist to serve the vital, practical requirements of human life—to structure a society so as to perpetuate the species, to pass on the hard-earned knowledge and experience of generations past and centuries past to the young and inexperienced in order to spare the next generation the costly and dangerous process of learning everything all over again from scratch through trial and error—including fatal errors. Cultures exist so that people can know how to get food and put a roof over their head, how to cure the sick, how to cope with the death of loved ones, and how to get along with the living. Cultures are not bumper stickers. They are living, changing ways of doing all the things that have to be done in life.

Every culture discards over time the things that no longer do the job or which do not do the job as well as things borrowed from other cultures. Each individual does this, consciously or not, on a day-to-day basis. Languages take words from other languages, so that Spanish as spoken in Spain includes words taken from Arabic, and Spanish as spoken in Argentina has Italian words taken from the large Italian immigrant population there. People eat Kentucky Fried Chicken in Singapore and stay in Hilton Hotels in Cairo. This is not what some of the advocates of diversity have in mind. They seem to want to preserve cultures in their purity, almost like butterflies preserved in amber. Decisions about change, if any, seem to be regarded as collective decisions, political decisions. But this is not how cultures have arrived where they are. Individuals have decided for themselves how much of the old they wished to retain, how much of the new they found useful in their own lives.

In this way, cultures have enriched each other in all the great civilizations of the world. In this way, great port cities and other crossroads of cultures have become centers of progress all across the planet. No culture has grown great in isolation—but a number of cultures have made historic and even astonishing advances when their isolation was ended, usually by events beyond their control.

Japan was a classic example in the nineteenth century, but a similar story could be told of Scotland in an earlier era, when a country where once even the nobility were illiterate became, within a short time as history is measured, a country that produced world pioneers in field after field: David Hume in philosophy, Adam Smith in economics, Joseph Black in chemistry, Robert Adam in architecture, and James Watt, whose steam engine revolutionized modern industry and transport. In the process, the Scots lost their language but gained world preeminence in many fields. Then a whole society moved to higher standards of living than anyone ever dreamed of in their poverty-stricken past.

There were higher standards in other ways as well. As late as the eighteenth century, it was considered noteworthy that pedestrians in Edinburgh no longer had to be on the alert for sewage being thrown out the windows of people's homes or apartments. The more considerate Scots yelled a warning, but they threw out the sewage anyway. Perhaps it was worth losing a little of the indigenous culture to be rid of that problem. Those who use the term "cultural diversity" to promote a multiplicity of segregated ethnic enclaves are doing an enormous harm to the people in those enclaves. However they live socially, the people in those enclaves are going to have to compete economically for a livelihood. Even if they were not disadvantaged before, they will be very disadvantaged if their competitors from the general population are free to tap the knowledge, skills, and analytical techniques Western civilization has drawn from all the other civilizations of the world, while those in the enclaves are restricted to what exists in the subculture immediately around them.

We need also to recognize that many great thinkers of the past—whether in medicine or philosophy, science or economics—labored not simply to advance whatever particular group they happened to have come from but to advance the human race. Their legacies, whether cures for deadly diseases or dramatic increases in crop yields to fight the scourge of hunger, belong to all people—and all people need to claim that legacy, not seal themselves off in a dead-end of tribalism or in an emotional orgy of cultural vanity.

## DISCUSSION QUESTIONS

1. Most people have grown up with the United States leading the world in many areas, such as technology, standard of living, medicine, and education. Is it important that the U.S. always lead in these areas? How can diversity in the workforce help any country advance? Has the U.S. made good use of its social capital in the past? Why or why not? In end of question #2 add "of the U.S." to end of question #2.

2. The United States regularly exchanges scientists, business leaders, and technology with countries all over the world. Would the author think this is a good idea, or will this just help other countries get ahead?

3. In America, the management of workers by "assimilation into the workforce" is being replaced by the "integration of diversity." How would the author explain this shift in approach?

4. The author states that "What serves human purposes more effectively survives, while what does not, tends to decline or disappear." What aspects of American culture in general do you think may decline? What aspects of American business culture may decline?

5. List things that we have now or the ways things are done now that differ markedly from your parents' or grandparents' generation.

6. It has been said that English is the international language of business; Italian is the international language of music; French is the international language of diplomacy. What explanation would the author give for this? Might this change?

# Cultural Transmission Today:

## Sowell Revisited

M. June Allard

*Assumption College*
*Worcester State College Professor Emerita*

Cultures enrich each other through communication—communication through travel,
trade, and migration, and communication through print and electronic media.

In *A World View of Cultural Diversity* (in this text), Sowell paints a global picture of how the "entire history of the human race, the rise of man from the caves, has been marked by transfers of cultural advances from one group to another and from one civilization to another. Tracing the historic transfer of "concepts, information, products, and technologies" from one culture to another, the role geographic and social environmental factors play in shaping cultures and in transmission among cultures is described. These factors however, are only part of the story, for in Sowell's words, they fail to explain "many very large differences in the economic and social performances of nations and civilizations." It is from the sharing of cultural features, leading people to adopt superior features of other cultures and relinquishing less useful features of their own, that advances come.

In today's world, new avenues of cultural transmission continue to evolve that even more transcend the boundaries of geography. Cultural sharing and transfer now occur extensively through print and electronic media as well as through modern avenues of travel, international trade, and migration. Cultural transfer through print and electronic media is examined in the *Media Messages* article and its exercises found in this text, while the discussion here examines the transfer occurring through travel and migration.

## Travel and Tourism

Travel is a traditional medium of cultural contact. Even today such in-person contacts are important, especially so in high context cultures, such as those in Asia and South America, where it is the social situation that provides the "cues" to the meaning of the words and silences in communication. From the U.S., travel to nearly all parts of the world constantly increases in the form of tourism, cultural and scientific exchanges, study abroad, business trips, and other short-term, more transitory contacts. Business and personal travel tend to be avenues of cultural contact more or less restricted to the more "privileged, industrialized first-world subjects" (Nakamura, 2000), but this is not so with longer term contact.

**Migration and immigration** provide longer term, more sustained cross-national contact. Unlike travel and tourism, migration occurs for people of all economic levels. The poor and those with restricted opportunities move in search of greener pastures, and rich and poor alike leave home countries in times of turmoil. But for whatever reasons they leave one culture for another, immigrants bring with them their home cultures—customs, religions, languages, and ways of looking at the world—and so begins cultural transfer.

Government, industry, and academic leaders generally *seek* transfer of knowledge and products not only by promoting scientific, educational, and cultural exchanges, but also by crafting immigration laws to facilitate visitation and immigration of the talented and educated from other countries. Certainly the competition among the victorious WWII allies for securing the German rocket scientists even before the end of the war bears witness to this. The scientists (at least their skills) were so valued that they were sought out long before the war was over and their politics (they *were* the enemy) were ignored; they were eagerly sought as "prizes of war." In many countries today, however, politics does not always encourage such exchange—sometimes even acting to interfere. Fearing to admit terrorists or striving to preserve native culture, governments sometimes stem the flow of scientists and students. Past activities or suspected political connections can result in visas that never seem to arrive.

In the U.S., the native educated and businesses alike lobby strongly that the scientific and technical expertise and innovativeness these talented people bring are very badly needed (Anderson, 2007; Viscarolasaga, 2007) contending further that foreign students we have already educated should be allowed to stay permanently. "Indeed, foreign science, engineering, and medical students who stay in the U.S. after completing their education…are a major source of skilled immigrants" (Friedman & Tomaso, 1996). A report from the Kauffman Foundation makes the case even stronger when they report that "most immigrants who founded technology and engineering companies in the United States received degrees from U.S. universities" (MHT, 2007).

Although the "import" of technology and expertise through skilled immigrants may generally be encouraged, the "import" of their cultural baggage, language especially, is frequently not welcomed. "Anti-immigrant sentiment has greeted every wave of immigrants" (DeGroat, 2006). Anti-immigration rallies and headlines such as "English Language Lost Under the Stampede of Immigration" are not uncommon. (Worcester Telegram and Gazette, August, 2006). Hate groups are activated and local communities enact ordinances to deter immigrants from settling. Hardly welcoming notes.

## THE IMMIGRANTS

Before the attacks of 9/11, U.S. immigration gates were open wide. In the decade of the 1990s, almost 10 million foreigners came to the U.S. (Borjas, 1996) and "in the last 30 years, the United States…absorbed the biggest wave of immigrants since the turn of the [last] century…By 2004, approximately 34.2 million Americans were foreign born—about 12 percent of the population" (Gilgoff, 2006).

The past decade witnessed a U.S. labor force filled with foreign-born workers representing "diversity in every sense of the word—from skin color, nationality and ethnicity to culture, religion, language, age, orientation and ability" (Ortiz, 2006). In terms of skill and education, immigrants range from a top layer composed of the educated elite to a bottom layer of those with little or no education. They differ too, in economic status. Contrary to popular belief, not all immigrants are poor. Many are wealthy—note for example, the 12,000 Chinese technicians working in Silicon Valley computer firms and the large numbers of wealthy Iranians in Beverly Hills (Clark, 1997). There are those in the United States today who would ban all immigration. The practicalities are, however, that there is a labor shortage in the U.S. The U.S. Department of Labor projects that in the decade between 1998 and 2008, the increase in jobs will number 20 million, while the increase in workers will be only 17 million. "As baby boomers begin to retire, U.S. companies are facing a certain worker shortage that will force them to look outside the country if they want to stay afloat" (DeGroat, 2006). The U.S. now needs 500,000 new workers every year (Incognito, Feb, 2007). Closing the gates is not an option. The options are who and how many to admit.

U.S. immigration patterns reflect U.S. immigration policy and its changes over time. At times it sought to restrict racial/ethnic groups, such as the Asian exclusion laws of the late nineteenth century, and at other times encourage groups, such as the Hmong tribesmen from Laos, Philippine nurses, and Mexican farm workers. In 1965, racist/nationality preferences were eliminated. Immigration policy "now involves three different sets of rules: those for legal immigration, those for humanitarian admissions, and those that affect illegal entry. These three sets of rules have generated three distinct immigration themes" (Friedman & DiTomaso, 1996).

---

 **Points of Law**

U.S. immigration has separate rules for

- Legal immigration
- Humanitarian admission
- Illegal entry

*Immigration and Nationality Act http://www.immigration-usa.com/ina_96.html*

---

## Documented vs. Undocumented

The turmoil over immigration today stems largely from a huge influx of illegal immigrants ("illegals"), estimated to be between 11 and 12 million and comprising about 29 percent of the total foreign-born population in the U.S. Since 2000, an estimated 850,000 illegals arrive every year (Gardner, 2007), not all of whom sneak in over U.S. borders. Some arrive on work or student visas and fail to leave when they expire. The voracious demand for labor, changing immigration policies, and a confusion of court rulings have produced a two-tier system of legal and illegal immigrants with unprecedented numbers of undocumented workers (illegals)—workers who serve the U.S. economy's needs, but who are often very badly served by this economy. The growing backlash against the undocumented workers "is the same reaction seen in this country each time a new immigrant group reaches critical mass" (Frankel, 2006).

## THE TRANSITION PROCESS

### Acceptance

Once through the gates, the process of assimilation of immigrants into the host culture begins—a process that throughout U.S. history has been fraught with hostility, scapegoating, stereotyping, prejudice, and discrimination to the detriment of host and newcomer alike. More than 200 years ago, for instance, Benjamin Franklin pronounced judgment on recent arrivals from Germany as "the most stupid in the nation. Few of their children speak English, and through their indiscretion or ours, or both, great disorders may one day arise among us" (Masci, 2001). The discrimination suffered by every past immigrant stream into the U.S is no different for today's immigrants.

---

 **Points of Law**

… the Immigration Reform and Control Act of 1986 makes it illegal to employ illegal aliens and punishes employers who knowing do so … with fines and even jail time for repeat offenders.

*(Masci, 2001).*

---

Transition into another culture is a slow process at best and one requiring adaptation by both parties. Newcomers are interlopers in an established social scene and when they seek the company of others like themselves, host country prejudices are fueled by fears of loss of cultural and employment. Backlash erupts when newcomer numbers reach critical mass and the perceived foreign cultural encroachment triggers smoldering resentment building into resistance and discrimination. Historically, "many immigrants faced discrimination in employment and housing by society at large and violence at the hands of hate groups" (Brown, 2006). In 2005 more than 600 active racist hate groups (groups such as the Minutemen, Neo-Nazis, white supremacists, and militiamen) were identified (Brown, 2006). By 2006 that number had grown to over 800 (Ressner, 2006).

In the U.S. today the smoothest transitions are probably made by the educated and skilled elite. They are recognized as important additions to the nation's social capital and as vital to keeping the country competitive in the global marketplace. They come to the U.S bringing education and skills gained at someone else's expense. Often they arrive with jobs waiting.

Even top layer immigrants and visitors do not necessarily find the transition road a smooth one, however. Scientific, artistic, technical, or academic acceptance does not mean *social* acceptance even in high-tech industry and university workplaces where skills are valued. Immigrants, especially those without home country support groups, are often "loners."

Suro (2000) observes that some immigrants are better off than the average American, while others are worse off and "as such, immigrants elicit both envy and distain."

Acceptance of newcomers varies by community, particularly so for the undocumented. The *New York Times* reports that the rising backlash against illegal immigrants led every state legislature to consider immigration issues in 2007. According to the National Conference of State Legislatures, "a total of 1,404 measures were considered with 41 states enacting a total of 170" (Preston, 2007). The American Civil Liberties Union reports that dozens of local communities also passed immigration ordinances in 2007 (Bazar, 2007; Broder, 2007). These laws and proposed ordinances not only targeted employers hiring illegal immigrants, but companies doing business with the government, landlords renting to illegals, and even taco stands. Some proposed using highway patrol officers as immigration law enforcers. Some made it more difficult for illegals to obtain state identification documents like driver's licenses and still others barred illegals from collecting unemployment and other public benefits (Preston, 2007).

Some of these laws have been struck down by the courts (the federal government has jurisdiction over immigration) and some have produced ironic results. In Colorado for example, strict documentation requirements led documented and undocumented workers alike to avoid the state thereby resulting in such a severe labor shortage on farms that officials are now forced to turn to prison labor (Guillen, 2007).

Not all states and communities seek to exclude illegal immigrants, however. Some states enacted legislation to extend education and health care to immigrant children and 15 adopted laws to punish immigrant smugglers "especially if the victims were foreigners coerced into prostitution or other sexual commerce" (Preston, 2007). For example, five years ago Tennessee became the first state to permit noncitizens to apply for state driver's licenses, and Utah provides a 'driving privilege card' for applicants who do not have Social Security numbers (Cole, 2006). New Haven, Connecticut, is a city that openly welcomes immigrants. Police there are prohibited from asking about immigration status and the city has begun a program to provide illegal aliens with ID cards "to help them open bank accounts and access many city services." Some companies, too, have instituted practices, such as English language classes, financial literacy information, and networking programs to aid foreign-born workers (Kim, 2006).

The reception accorded all immigrants seems to depend in large part on whether they are perceived as competition to, or complementary to, the local economy.

---

 **Points of Law**

"It is unlawful to threaten to report, or to report a worker to INS because a worker opposed unlawful discrimination or participated in a proceeding under the antidiscrimination laws ...If an unauthorized worker is retaliated against, that worker is entitled to damages without regard to his or her work status".

(EEOC, 1999)

*http://www.eeoc.gov/policy/docs/qanda-ndoc.html*

## The Workplace

The highly trained are sought by universities and industries. The untrained (documented and undocumented), however, are sought by employers to provide cheap labor. They tend to work in factories, restaurants, agriculture, construction, hospitality, and service industries. "About half of current undocumented workers are in the informal 'sector' as gardeners, day laborers, domestic workers, nannies, dishwashers, and other service workers. "Others work for subcontractors who ply their wares in the garment trade and other manufacturing industries…" (Fine, 2004). Seasonal migratory workers traditionally cross the southern U.S. border to pick crops, while Europeans—particularly eastern Europeans—work in Maine resorts each summer at jobs that Americans shun (AP, Worcester Sunday Telegram, 2007, July 1). Unskilled immigrants are more often found in dangerous and undesirable jobs than are natives of comparable skill and they are frequently viewed with scorn and disdain.

---

 **Points of Law**

"The federal employment discrimination laws protect all employees in this country who work for an employer with 15 or more employees, including those who are not authorized to work."

(EEOC, 1999, October 29; NELP, n.d.)

---

## Exploitation

The 11 to 12 million illegals account for about 5 percent of the total U.S workforce (Visconti & Peacock, 2006). In the marketplace, normal business practices are altered when they (and even low skill documented immigrants) are employed. Conditions often deteriorate into long hours, low pay, uncompensated workplace injuries, lack of health benefits, failure to be paid, union smashing, and evasion of basic rights and labor laws. Undocumenteds, in particular, are at the mercy of their employers. "The federal employment discrimination laws protect all employees in this country who work for an employer with 15 or more employees, including those who are not authorized to work" (EEOC, 1999). Most are afraid to stand up for their basic rights, however, for they find themselves blacklisted or fired if they do.

---

The most common protections denied undocumented workers include

- The right to receive the promised wage and/or at least the minimum wage and overtime pay for work actually performed
- The right to healthy and safe conditions on the job
- The right to receive workers' compensation benefits for injuries on the job
- The right to be free from discrimination based on sex, color, race, religion, and national origin, age and disabilities.

Workplace Fairness (2007)

Employer arguments that illegals take jobs that no native citizen will take are countered by those of displaced native workers saying that the presence of the illegals allows management to reduce working conditions and wages so low that natives won't take the jobs. Employers contend that they must hire cheap immigrant labor to remain competitive in local and international markets and not hiring these workers means downsizing or sending work overseas, where labor is cheap. Displaced native workers and unions lobby for decreased immigration saying natives will take the jobs if decent wages and working conditions are present.

The Immigration Reform and Control Act of 1986 makes it illegal to employ undocumented aliens and punishes employers who knowingly do so … with fines and even jail time for repeat offenders. Until 2006, this was rarely enforced (Masci, 2001). The situation changed in May 2006, when the INS began sweeping raids aimed at rounding up "fugitive aliens" for deportation. By the end of January 2007, over 13,000 illegals were arrested. Families were separated, children were stranded, hearings were slow, and the illegals were held at detention centers in conditions that frequently violated federal standards, including overcrowding and health and safety violations. "Most [immigrants] had no criminal records and less than 20% had previous deportation orders." According to ICE reports, 190,000 migrants were deported in 2006 (Carlsen, 2007). In 2007, INS began prosecuting those who employed them.

The deportation of thousands of illegals and the fines levied on those that hired them leave employers in limbo — they face laying off thousands of workers — especially in agriculture and low-wage industries, a situation that will likely discriminate against Hispanic workers who are heavily concentrated in these jobs (Preston, 2007, August 8).

## IMPACT: WHAT DO THEY BRING AND WHAT DO THEY COST?

Computing the costs and contributions of the foreign-born is complicated. Measurement is not easy and immigrant groups vary considerably in the form of their impact. Arguments are made about their value on a number of different fronts.

### The Economy

Opinion varies widely on how much immigrants add to the U.S. economy. Estimates range from little or none — "the gains from immigration seem much too small, and could even be outweighed by the costs of providing increased social services" (Borjas, 1996, p. 20) — to estimates of billions each year, not counting the contribution of immigrant-owned businesses or the impact of highly skilled immigrants on overall productivity (Incognito, 2007).

Economist Giovanni Peri points out that during the past decade, with its heavily foreign-born labor force, "…the gross domestic product has grown from the result of immigration, leading to billions of dollars in economic output" (Kim, 2006).

> Immigrants (undocumented and documented) bring an estimated benefit of $330 billion back into the economy, a figure surmised by adding their yearly estimated earnings ($240 billion) and what they pay in taxes ($90 billion), according to Urban Institute, a nonpartisan research organization, and American Studies. (Kim, 2006).

Assessments of the impact of illegal immigrants varies. "Undocumented immigrants cost the taxpayers $45 billion annually, according to an estimate by the

Immigration and Naturalization Service (INS)" (Kim, 2006). In contrast, supporters point out that illegal aliens pay taxes and by their cheap labor, reduce the costs of services to consumers. Further, "in some places the local economy is largely supported by the labor of illegal aliens ...one estimate: one out of every three businesses in Atlanta employs undocumented workers" (Masci, 2001). Ironically, "The ICE (Immigration and Customs Enforcement) reports that even the U.S. military employs illegal migrant labor" (Carlsen, 2007).

## Entrepreneurship

"Immigrants are more likely to start businesses—from corner grocery stores to giant computer companies—than native-born Americans are "...one out of every four new businesses in Silicon Valley is founded by an entrepreneur of Indian or Chinese origin" (Masci, 2001). A Duke University study reports that "immigrants started 25 percent of the new U.S. technology and engineering companies over the past decade" (Mass High Tech, 2007, v. 25, no. 26, June 27-28).

The benefit the immigrants bring to the economy increases when the estimated value of these immigrant-based companies is included. "As of 2005...immigrant-founded companies generated $52 billion in annual sales and created 450,000 jobs nationwide" (Williams, 2007; Incognito, 2007). "Twenty-six percent of the biotech companies founded in New England have at least one foreign-born founder...These companies generated 7.6 billion in sales and employed 4,300 workers across the region" (MHT, 2007, v 25, p. 29).

## Employment/Productivity

Detractors accuse immigrants of causing low wages (Incognito, 2007) and assert that mass hiring of less skilled workers has harmed the economic opportunities of less skilled natives whose jobs are now at risk (Borjas, 1996). Proponents of immigration, arguing that immigrants do not take away jobs from natives, point to a Pew study that reports that "In parts of the country with few immigrants, 'low-wage jobs still get done, and by native-born people' " (Masci, 2001). They argue further that "skilled native workers...have much to gain when less skilled workers enter the United States. Skilled workers can then 'devote all their efforts to jobs that use their skills effectively while immigrants provide cheap labor for service jobs' " (Borjas, 1996).

## Service and Consumer Products

Proponents of immigrants report that "Our work shows that cities with more diversity—more immigrants—in the workforce exhibit higher productivity than the American-born employees" (Kim, 2006) and that "without immigrants working these lower-wage jobs, the service sector and consumer products would balloon in price" (Kim, 2006). They argue too, that immigrant labor does not automatically lower wage levels. In the trades, for example, immigrants have a higher percentage of union membership than U.S.–born workers (Incognito, 2007).

## Taxes

"Immigrants pay between $90 billion and $140 billion a year in federal, state and local taxes, according to the National Immigration Forum and the Social Security

Administration" (Kim, 2006). Undocumented immigrants often "use fake social security numbers and though they don't get any benefits, they still have income tax taken out of their pay checks" (Kim, 2006). "A New York Times story in 2005 reported that an 'estimated 7 million or so illegal immigrant workers in the United States are now providing the Social Security system with a subsidy of as much as $7 billion a year'" (Porter, 2005).

## Social Services

Immigrants settle in specific areas of the U.S., which can create problems for these communities. While the national economy may benefit from their arrival, it is these local economies that bear the costs of the social and educational services they need. According to Stephen Moore, "…in areas with high concentrations of low-skilled, low-paid immigrants they impose net costs on U.S.–born workers" (Suro, 2000). The burdens they place on courts, police, jails, health facilities, housing, and schools, as well as the administrative problems of dealing with a population of non–English speakers, and the economic dislocations that can be caused by a steady influx of new immigrant workers can be overwhelming to local economies (Suro, 2000). One community of 40,000 residents, for example, reported that more than 30 languages are spoken by students in the school system (Worcester Telegram and Gazette, 2007, June 13).

An often overlooked factor in immigration assessment and policy is the *age* of the immigrant population. Age figures strongly in projections of productivity and of costs to society (Suro, 2000). At least half of the new immigrants are low-cost, young, single adults between the ages of 18 and 34 years, in their most productive years and at the stage of life when they contribute to society while making few demands on it. Once they start families, this changes. Their children (and elderly relatives who may join them) are mostly nonproducers who draw heavily upon community services.

The U.S. today has a growing "mature immigrant population." The heavy influx of the 1990s means that many of those young immigrants are now at the age when they have families. The heavy immigration of the past 30 years, particularly the last 10, means that a large portion of those immigrants are now drawing upon community resources. The situation is not quite the same for the illegal immigrants as they are denied access to social services in most communities.

## Neighborhoods

The impact of high concentrations of immigrants in neighborhoods brings both blame and praise. In some cases they are blamed for *blighted* properties and neighborhoods. They run afoul of local laws governing housing—in particular, laws that prohibit overcrowding. Small single family houses turn into rooming houses with whole families living in each bedroom and more people sleeping on mattresses in the basements. In other communities, however, immigrants are praised for *revitalizing* decaying neighborhoods by creating businesses there and thus generating employment and income. The maturing immigrant population is expected to have a beneficial impact on the sagging housing market itself. Immigrants "both legal and illegal—and their native-born children are forecast to provide the bulk of coming years' growth in home-buying demand, nudging the market back up and aiding the broader economy" (Jewell, 2007).

Neighborhood crime is another area of disagreement. Illegals are blamed for raising crime rates. In the words of one city mayor, they "brought drugs, crime and gangs to the city...they are destroying the city and driving up crime" (Rubinkham, 2007). Other observers, however, find that immigrants help to keep crime down (Dale, 2007, June 30), reporting that the vast majority tend to work very hard to better themselves and are not involved in crime. Finally, there is the complaint that "high immigration levels are overcrowding the United States, especially in urban areas" (Masci, 2001); the population is too large now—more immigrants means more overcrowding.

## Assimilation

Arguments are put forth to slow down (or cease) immigration to provide time to "Americanize" current immigrants and let schools and governing institutions catch up (Masci, 2001). "The way we're going now we won't turn these people into Americans, and without assimilation we will increasingly be beset by ethnic conflicts," says John O'Sullivan (Masci, 2001). The large number of immigrants in the "two-tier" system "impedes our country's ability to integrate documented and undocumented newcomers into our society" (Visconti & Peacock, 2006).

Opponents are quick to counter that people who migrate to the U.S. *want to be Americans* (Masci, 2001). Indeed, many Americans, like Alan Greenspan, consider that it is the immigrant work ethic and motivation "makes them cornerstones of America's economic prosperity" (Masci, 2001). Perhaps the most cogent response to charges that we need to "Americanize" our immigrants comes from Barbara Frankel (2006):

> Yet the very essence of American culture is its ability to change and grow and build on the heritages of both its established citizens and its newest occupants.

## IMMIGRATION POLICY

The exploration of immigration policy and reform is a volatile and complicated issue socially, politically, and legally—and one that goes beyond the scope of this article. The questions of how to deal with the aging (mature) immigrant population and with the huge population of undocumented immigrants now in the United States, however, must be added to the basic questions of who and how many to admit.

## LESSONS FROM HISTORY

### What Might History Say About Immigration?

Sowell's eloquent account of cultural transfer would argue that immigration provides an excellent avenue of cultural transmission directly through the different concepts, information, products, and technologies it introduces, and indirectly through the enrichment of the host country's social capital—providing skills and knowledge resources for future advances. Former Intel chairman Andrew S. Grove voices similar thoughts: "Immigration keeps this country attractive stating that without inclusion and diversity of new workers and people, the United States would stop moving forward as a progressive nation" (Kim, 2006). Peter Ortiz (2006) puts the case in even stronger terms: "What would happen to the economy of the United States if the immigrants, legal and not, stopped coming? It would fall apart." (Ortiz, 2006).

What might history say about the fear that floods of immigrants are overwhelming the United States and chipping away at American culture? Other than the native Indians, the United States *is a nation composed completely of immigrants*—something that later generations tend to forget. The global scope of all the cultural advances Sowell outlines vividly portrays how much of American culture has come from other cultures and, further, that cultures existing in isolation do not advance nearly so much as those with doors open to other cultures:

> …many great thinkers of the past…[labored] to advance the human race. Their legacies…belong to all people—and all people need to claim that legacy, not seal themselves off in a dead-end of tribalism or in an emotional orgy of cultural vanity.

> [Cultures] are "living, changing ways of doing all the things that have to be done in life. …Every culture discards over time the things which do not do the job as well as things borrowed from other cultures"… (p. 36, 37)

What might history say about immigration policies and state and local laws restricting immigration? Sowell contends that it is not possible for governments or laws to stop the infusion of new ideas and ways of doing things. Historically,

> Individuals have decided for themselves how much of the old they wished to retain, how much of the new they found useful in their own lives. … In this way, cultures have enriched each other in all the great civilizations of the world. (p. 36)

## DISCUSSION QUESTIONS

1. Research today's *legal* immigrants. From which countries do they originate? What are their educational and skill levels? Specifically, what jobs do they take? Where do they relocate geographically?

2. Research today's *illegal* immigrants. From which countries do they originate? What are their educational and skill levels? Specifically, what jobs do they take? Where do they relocate geographically?

3. Research current immigration laws as they pertain to the workplace, i.e., what rights do undocumented immigrants have?

4. Considering the three types of immigration law—legal, humanitarian, and illegal—what kind of immigration policies do you think the United States should pursue in the future? Why?

## BIBLIOGRAPHY

Anderson, C. (2007, July 20-26). A call for congress to act now on high-skills immigration reform. MHT (*Mass Highech*), p. 26.

Bazar, E. (2007, July 11). States target illegal hiring. Immigration laws focus on bosses. *USA Today,* 1A.

Borjas, G. (2000). The new economics of immigration. Affluent Americans gain; poor Americans lose. *Debating Points.*

Broder, D.S. (2007, July 9). Congress has failed in its duty regarding immigration reform. *Worcester Telegram and Gazette,* A7.

Brown, C. (2006, April). The history of hate. *DiversityInc.* pp. 62-66.

Carlsen, L. (2007, March 4). Migrants, globalization's junk mail. PressTV. Retrieved March 13, 2007, from http://www.presstv.ir/detail.aspx?id=1413&sectionid=3510303.

Clark, C. (1977, June 24). The new immigrants. *Annual Editions,* Article 10, pp. 51-71. Guildford, CT: McGraw-Hill/Dushkin.

Cole, D. (2003). Five myths about immigration: the new know-nothings. In Plous, S. (Ed) *Understanding prejudice and discrimination.* Boston: McGraw Hill.

Cole, Y. (2006, April). Creating wealth and strife in Tennessee. *DiversityInc.,* pp. 36-43.

Christophersen, J. (2007, July 25). How northeast cities chart diverging paths for illegals. *Worcester Telegram and Gazette,* p. A4.

Dale, M. (2007, June 30). Some say immigrants help keep crime down, higher immigration rates linked with less homicide, experts note. *Worcester Telegram and Gazette,* A11.

DeGroat, T.J. (2006, April). A nation of immigrants, a cultue of nativism. *DiversityInc.,* pp. 44-51.

EEOC. (1999, October 29). Questions and answers. Enforcement guidance on remedies available to undocumented workers under federal employment discrimination laws. Retrieved on July 28 from http://www.eeoc.gov/policy/docs/qanda-udoc.html.

Fine, J. (2004, January 11). Bush plan's 3 flaws. *Boston Globe.* Retrieved March 26, 2007, from http://www.commondreams.org/views04/0111-04.htm.

Frankel, B. (2006, April). Us vs them doesn't work. *DiversityInc Editor's letter,* p. 14.

Friedman, J., & DiTomaso, H. (1996, Summer.) Myths about diversity: What managers need to know about changes in the U.S. labor force. *California Management Review. v. 38. no. 4.*

Gardner, A. (2007, March 13). Undocumented immigrants' childbirth is top emergency Medicaid expense. *Washington Post.* Retrieved March 13, 2007, from http://www. washingtonpost.com/wp-dyn/content/article/2007/03/13/AR2007031300555.html.

Gilgoff, D. (2006, April 10). Border war, immigration reform is frought with political peril. When it's over plenty of people are going to be angry. *U.S. News & World Report,* p 25.

Guillen, R. (2007, March 12). Replacing immigrants with convict slaves. *Texas Civil Rights Review.* Retrieved July 15, 2007, from http://texascivilrightsreview.org/phpnuke/modules.php?name=News&file=article&sid=872.

Incognito, L. (2007). The human being is illegal. *Peoples Weekly World* newspaper online. Retrieved July 23, 2007, from http://www.pww.org/index.php/article/articleview/10597/1/359.

Jewell, M. (2007, July 31). New country, new homes. *Worcester Telegram & Gazette,* p. D2.

Kim, W. (2006, April). The rising value of immigration. *DiversityInc.,* pp 53-56.

Masci, D. (2001). Debate over immigration. The issues. In Kromkowski, J. (Ed). *Race and ethnic relations,* 11th ed. 2001-2002. McGraw-Hill/Dushkin Guilford, CT.

McFarlane, C. (2007, August 15). Immigrants may hold security key. *Worcester Telegram and Gazette,* p. B1.

MHT. (2007, June 22-28). Immigrants come to study, leave to be entrepreneurs. *Mass High Tech, v. 25 issue 26.*

Nakamura, L. (2000). "Where do you want to go today?" Cybernetic tourism, the Internet and transnationality. From Dines, G. and Humez, J. (eds.) *Gender, race and class in media text reader,* (2nd ed. Thousand Oaks, CA: Sage 2002, p. 684-687.

NELP (n.d.). Immigrant worker project. Workplace rights. *National Employment Law Project.* Retrieved July 29, 2007, from http://www.nelp.org/iwp/rights/index.cfm.

Ortiz, P. (2006, April). Immigration: America's lifeline. *DiversityInc.,* pp 24-25.

Porter, E. (2005, April 5). Illegal immigrants are bolstering social security with billions. *The New York Times,* business and financial, section A, col. 1, p. 1. http://www.nytimes.com

Preston, J. (2007, August 6). Surge in immigration laws around U.S. Retrieved August 8, 2007, from New York Times: http://www. nytimes.com.

Preston, J. (2007, August 8). Toughening stance. New rules aim at illegal employment. *Worcester Telegram & Gazette,* p. A2.

Reagan, M. (2006, August 28). English language lost under the stampede of immigration. *Worcester Telegram and Gazette*, A7.

Ressner, J. (2006, June 5). Rousing the zealots. *Time*.

Sowell, T. (2005). A world view of cultural diversity. From *Understanding and Managing Diversity Readings, Cases and Exercises*, 3rd ed. Upper Saddle River, New Jersey: Prentice Hall.

Suro, R. (2000). Watching Americas door. The immigration backlash and the new policy debate. In Tischler, H. (Ed*). Debating points: race and ethnic relations*. Upper Saddle River, NJ: Prentice Hall.

The Associated Press. (2007, July 1). Europeans fill Maine seasonal jobs. *Worcester Sunday Telegram and Gazette*, p. A4.

The Chronicle of Higher Education. (2007, July 13). Foreign students still face hurdles. p. A31.

Viscarolasaga, E. (2007, August 3-9). Stunting growth. Fast-growing companies find it harder to fill key posts. *MassHighTech*, p. 1, 20.

Visconti, L. & Peacock, F. (2006, April). Learning from history: The business case for immigration. *DiversityInc. Publishers Letter*, p. 17.

Williams, C. (2007, June 1-7). New England immigrants play a growing role in tech entrepreneurship. *Mass High Tech*, pp. 1, 28.

Worcester Telegram and Gazette. (2007, June 13). Marlboro immigrants upset over proposal. pp. A1, A6.

Workplace Fairness. (2007). Undocumented workers. Retrieved March 26, 2007, from http://www.workplacefairness.org/sc/undocumentedworkers.php.

---

### Diversity on the Web

Visit the site below to learn about U.S. citizens traveling out of the country, and visitors and immigrants to the United States Research the four questions below.

*http//tinet.ita.doc.gov/research*

**Travel**

1. How many visitors came to the United States last year? What were their countries of origin? Where did they visit in the United States?
2. How many U.S. citizens traveled out of the United States? Where did they go?
3. There are 300 million United States citizens and over 32 million (legal and illegal) immigrants. Considering a) the number of United States citizens who traveled outside the United States last year (and their destinations) and b) the number and origin of foreign visitors traveling to the United States, what cultural changes might you predict by the year 2030?

**Trade**

4. Examine the amounts and patterns of world and U.S. trade figures. What does this say about the transmission of products among cultures?

Canadian Note: Web site listed also contains Canadian information.

# Negotiating:

## The Top Ten Ways That Culture Can Effect Your Negotiation

### Jeswald W. Salacuse

When Enron was still—and only—a pipeline company, it lost a major contract in India because local authorities felt that it was pushing negotiations too fast. In fact, the loss of the contract underlines the important role that cultural differences play in international negotiation. For one country's negotiators, time is money; for another's, the slower the negotiations, the better and more trust in the other side. This author's advice will help negotiators bridge the cultural differences in international negotiation.

International business deals not only cross borders, they also cross cultures. Culture profoundly influences how people think, communicate, and behave. It also affects the kinds of transactions they make and the way they negotiate them. Differences in culture between business executives—for example, between a Chinese public sector plant manager in Shanghai and a Canadian division head of a family company in Toronto—can create barriers that impede or completely stymie the negotiating process.

The great diversity of the world's cultures makes it impossible for any negotiator, no matter how skilled and experienced, to understand fully all the cultures that may be encountered. How then should an executive prepare to cope with culture in making deals in Singapore this week and Seoul the next? In researching my book *The Global Negotiator: Making, Managing, and Mending Deals Around the World in the Twenty-First Century* (Palgrave Macmillan, 2003), I found that ten particular elements consistently arise to complicate intercultural negotiations. These "top ten" elements of negotiating behavior constitute a basic framework for identifying cultural differences that may arise during the negotiation process. Applying this framework in your international One time permission to reproduce granted by Ivey Management Services. business negotiations may enable you to understand your counterpart better and to anticipate possible misunderstandings. This article discusses this framework and how to apply it.

1. **Negotiating Goal: Contract or Relationship?**
   Negotiators from different cultures may tend to view the purpose of a negotiation differently. For deal makers from some cultures, the goal of a business

negotiation, first and foremost, is a signed contract between the parties. Other cultures tend to consider that the goal of a negotiation is not a signed contract but rather the creation of a relationship between the two sides. Although the written contact expresses the relationship, the essence of the deal is the relationship itself. For example in my survey of over 400 persons from twelve nationalities, reported fully in *The Global Negotiator,* I found that whereas 74 percent of the Spanish respondents claimed their goal in a negotiation was a contract, only 33 percent of the Indian executives had a similar view. The difference in approach may explain why certain Asian negotiators, whose negotiating goal is often the creation of a relationship, tend to give more time and effort to negotiation preliminaries, while North Americans often want to rush through this first phase of deal making. The preliminaries of negotiation, in which the parties seek to get to know one another thoroughly, are a crucial foundation for a good business relationship. They may seem less important when the goal is merely a contract.

It is therefore important to determine how your counterparts view the purpose of your negotiation. If relationship negotiators sit on the other side of the table, merely convincing them of your ability to deliver on a low-cost contract may not be enough to land you the deal. You may also have to persuade them, from the very first meeting, that your two organizations have the potential to build a rewarding relationship over the long term. On the other hand, if the other side is basically a contract deal maker, trying to build a relationship may be a waste of time and energy.

2. **Negotiating Attitude: Win-Lose or Win-Win?**
Because of differences in culture, personality, or both, business persons appear to approach deal making with one of two basic attitudes: that a negotiation is either a process in which both can gain (win-win) or a struggle in which, of necessity, one side wins and the other side loses (win-lose). Win-win negotiators see deal making as a collaborative, problem-solving process; win-lose negotiators view it as confrontational. As you enter negotiations, it is important to know which type of negotiator is sitting across the table from you. Here too, my survey revealed significant differences among cultures. For example, whereas 100 percent of the Japanese respondents claimed that they approached negotiations as a win-win process, only 33% of the Spanish executives took that view.

3. **Personal Style: Informal or Formal?**
Personal style concerns the way a negotiator talks to others, uses titles, dresses, speaks, and interacts with other persons. Culture strongly influences the personal style of negotiators. It has been observed, for example, that Germans have a more formal style than Americans. A negotiator with a formal style insists on addressing counterparts by their titles, avoids personal anecdotes, and refrains from questions touching on the private or family life of members of the other negotiating team. A negotiator with an informal style tries to start the discussion on a first-name basis, quickly seeks to develop a personal, friendly relationship with the other team, and may take off his jacket and roll up his sleeves when deal making begins in earnest. Each culture has its own formalities with their own special meanings. They are another means of communication among the persons sharing that culture, another form of adhesive that binds them together as a community.

For an American, calling someone by the first name is an act of friendship and therefore a good thing. For a Japanese, the use of the first name at a first meeting is an act of disrespect and therefore bad.

Negotiators in foreign cultures must respect appropriate formalities. As a general rule, it is always safer to adopt a formal posture and move to an informal stance, if the situation warrants it, than to assume an informal style too quickly.

4. **Communication: Direct or Indirect?**

Methods of communication vary among cultures. Some emphasize direct and simple methods of communication; others rely heavily on indirect and complex methods. The latter may use circumlocutions, figurative forms of speech, facial expressions, gestures and other kinds of body language. In a culture that values directness, such as the American or the Israeli, you can expect to receive a clear and definite response to your proposals and questions. In cultures that rely on indirect communication, such as the Japanese, reaction to your proposals may be gained by interpreting seemingly vague comments, gestures, and other signs. What you will not receive at a first meeting is a definite commitment or rejection.

The confrontation of these styles of communication in the same negotiation can lead to friction. For example, the indirect ways Japanese negotiators express disapproval have often led foreign business executives to believe that their proposals were still under consideration when in fact the Japanese side had rejected them. In the Camp David negotiations that led to a peace treaty between Egypt and Israel, the Israeli preference for direct forms of communication and the Egyptian tendency to favor indirect forms sometimes exacerbated relations between the two sides. The Egyptians interpreted Israeli directness as aggressiveness and, therefore, an insult. The Israelis viewed Egyptian indirectness with impatience and suspected them of insincerity, of not saying what they meant.

5. **Sensitivity to Time: High or Low?**

Discussions of national negotiating styles invariably treat a particular culture's attitudes toward time. It is said that Germans are always punctual, Latins are habitually late, Japanese negotiate slowly, and Americans are quick to make a deal. Commentators sometimes claim that some cultures value time more than others, but this observation may not be an accurate characterization of the situation. Rather, negotiators may value differently the amount of time devoted to and measured against the goal pursued. For Americans, the deal is a signed contract and time is money, so they want to make a deal quickly. Americans therefore try to reduce formalities to a minimum and get down to business quickly. Japanese and other Asians, whose goal is to create a relationship rather than simply sign a contract, need to invest time in the negotiating process so that the parties can get to know one another well and determine whether they wish to embark on a long-term relationship. They may consider aggressive attempts to shorten the negotiating time as efforts to hide something. For example, in one case that received significant media attention in the mid-1990s, a long-term electricity supply contract between an ENRON subsidiary, the Dabhol Power Company, and the Maharashtra state government in India, was subject to significant challenge and was ultimately cancelled on the grounds that it was concluded in "unseemly haste" and had been subject to "fast track procedures" that circumvented established practice for developing such projects in the past. Important segments of the Indian public automatically assumed that the government had failed to protect the public interest because the negotiations were so quick. In the company's defense, Rebecca Mark, chairman and CEO of Enron International, pointed out to the press: "We were extremely concerned with time, because time is money for us." (Enron's Rebecca Mark: 'You Have to be Pushy and Aggressive,' *Business Week,* February 24, 1997, http://www.businessweek.com/ 1997/08/b351586.htm.)

This difference between the Indian and U.S. attitudes toward time was clearly revealed in my survey. Among the twelve nationalities surveyed, the Indians had the largest percentage of persons who considered themselves to have a low sensitivity to time.

6. **Emotionalism: High or Low?**
Accounts of negotiating behavior in other cultures almost always point to a particular group's tendency to act emotionally. According to the stereotype, Latin Americans show their emotions at the negotiating table, while the Japanese and many other Asians hide their feelings. Obviously, individual personality plays a role here. There are passive Latins and hot-headed Japanese. Nonetheless, various cultures have different rules as to the appropriateness and form of displaying emotions, and these rules are brought to the negotiating table as well. Deal makers should seek to learn them.

In the author's survey, Latin Americans and the Spanish were the cultural groups that ranked themselves highest with respect to emotionalism in a clearly statistically significant fashion. Among Europeans, the Germans and English ranked as least emotional, while among Asians the Japanese held that position, but to a lesser degree.

7. **Form of Agreement: General or Specific?**
Whether a negotiator's goal is a contract or a relationship, the negotiated transaction in almost all cases will be encapsulated in some sort of written agreement. Cultural factors influence the form of the written agreement that the parties make. Generally, Americans prefer very detailed contracts that attempt to anticipate all possible circumstances and eventualities, no matter how unlikely. Why? Because the deal is the contract itself, and one must refer to the contract to handle new situations that may arise. Other cultures, such as the Chinese, prefer a contract in the form of general principles rather than detailed rules. Why? Because, it is claimed, that the essence of the deal is the relationship between the parties. If unexpected circumstances arise, the parties should look primarily to their relationship, not the contract, to solve the problem. So, in some cases, a Chinese negotiator may interpret the American drive to stipulate all contingencies as evidence of a lack of confidence in the stability of the underlying relationship.

Among all respondents in my survey, 78 percent preferred specific agreements, while only 22 percent preferred general agreements. On the other hand, the degree of intensity of responses on the question varied considerably among cultural groups. While only 11 percent of the English favored general agreements, 45.5 percent of the Japanese and of the Germans claimed to do so. Some experienced executives argue that differences over the form of an agreement are caused more by unequal bargaining power between the parties than by culture. In a situation of unequal bargaining power, the stronger party always seeks a detailed agreement to "lock up the deal" in all its possible dimensions, while the weaker party prefers a general agreement to give it room to "wiggle out" of adverse circumstances that are bound to occur. According to this view, it is context, not culture that determines this negotiating trait.

8. **Building an Agreement: Bottom Up or Top Down?**
   Related to the form of the agreement is the question of whether negotiating a business deal is an inductive or a deductive process. Does it start from an agreement on general principles and proceed to specific items, or does it begin with an agreement on specifics, such as price, delivery date, and product quality, the sum total of which becomes the contract? Different cultures tend to emphasize one approach over the other. Some observers believe that the French prefer to begin with agreement on general principles, while Americans tend to seek agreement first on specifics. For Americans, negotiating a deal is basically making a series of compromises and trade-offs on a long list of particulars. For the French, the essence is to agree on basic principles that will guide and indeed determine the negotiation process afterward. The agreed-upon general principles become the framework, the skeleton, upon which the contract is built.

   My survey of negotiating styles found that the French, the Argentineans, and the Indians tended to view deal making as a top down (deductive process); while the Japanese, the Mexicans and the Brazilians tended to see it as a bottom up (inductive) process. A further difference in negotiating style is seen in the dichotomy between the "building-down" approach and the "building-up" approach. In the building-down approach, the negotiator begins by presenting the maximum deal if the other side accepts all the stated conditions. In the building-up approach, one side begins by proposing a minimum deal that can be broadened and increased as the other party accepts additional conditions. According to many observers, Americans tend to favor the building-down approach, while the Japanese tend to prefer the building-up style of negotiating a contract.

9. **Team Organization: One Leader or Group Consensus?**
   In any negotiation, it is important to know how the other side is organized, who has the authority to make commitments, and how decisions are made. Culture is one important factor that affects how executives organize themselves to negotiate a deal. Some cultures emphasize the individual while others stress the group. These values may influence the organization of each side in a negotiation.

   One extreme is the negotiating team with a supreme leader who has complete authority to decide all matters. Many American teams tend to follow this approach. Other cultures, notably the Japanese and the Chinese, stress team negotiation and consensus decision making. When you negotiate with such a team, it may not be apparent who the leader is and who has the authority to commit the side. In the first type, the negotiating team is usually small; in the second it is often large. For example, in negotiations in China on a major deal, it would not be uncommon for the Americans to arrive at the table with three people and for the Chinese to show up with ten. Similarly, the one-leader team is usually prepared to make commitments more quickly than a negotiating team organized on the basis of consensus. As a result, the consensus type of organization usually takes more time to negotiate a deal.

Among all respondents in my survey, 59 percent tended to prefer one leader while 41 percent preferred a more consensual form of organization. On the other hand, the various cultural groups showed a wide variety of preferences on the question of team organization. The group with the strongest preference for consensus organization was the French. Many studies have noted French individualism. (Edward T. Hall and M. Reed Hall, *Understanding Cultural Dfference,* Yarmouth, Maine: Intercultural Press, 1990.)

Perhaps a consensual arrangement in the individual French person's eyes is the best way to protect that individualism. Despite the Japanese reputation for consensus arrangements, only 45 percent of the Japanese respondents claimed to prefer a negotiating team based on consensus. The Brazilians, the Chinese, and the Mexicans to a far greater degree than any other groups preferred one-person leadership, a reflection perhaps of the political traditions of those countries.

10. **Risk Taking: High or Low?**

Research supports the conclusion that certain cultures are more risk averse than others. (Geert Hofstede, *Culture's Consequences: International Differences in Work-related Values.* Newbury Park, CA: Sage Publications, 1980)

In deal making, the negotiators' cultures can affect the willingness of one side to take risks— to divulge information, try new approaches, and tolerate uncertainties in a proposed course of action. The Japanese, with their emphasis on requiring large amounts of information and their intricate group decision-making process, tend to be risk averse. Americans, by comparison, are risk takers.

Among all respondents in the author's survey, approximately 70 percent claimed a tendency toward risk taking while only 30 percent characterized themselves as low risk takers. Among cultures, the responses to this question showed significant variations. The Japanese are said to be highly risk averse in negotiations, and this tendency was affirmed by the survey which found Japanese respondents to be the most risk averse of the twelve cultures. Americans in the survey, by comparison, considered themselves to be risk takers, but an even higher percentage of the French, the British, and the Indians claimed to be risk takers.

---

Faced with a risk-averse counterpart, how should a deal maker proceed? The following are a few steps to consider:

1. Don't rush the negotiating process. A negotiation that is moving too fast for one of the parties only heightens that person's perception of the risks in the proposed deal.
2. Devote attention to proposing rules and mechanisms that will reduce the apparent risks in the deal for the other side.
3. Make sure that your counterpart has sufficient information about you, your company, and the proposed deal.
4. Focus your efforts on building a relationship and fostering trust between the parties.
5. Consider restructuring the deal so that the deal proceeds step by step in a series of increments, rather than all at once.

Negotiating styles, like personalities, have a wide range of variation. The ten negotiating traits discussed above can be placed on a spectrum or continuum, as illustrated in the chart below. Its purpose is to identify specific negotiating traits affected by culture and to show the possible variation that each trait or factor may take. With this knowledge, you may be better able to understand the negotiating styles and approaches of counterparts from other cultures. Equally important, it may help you to determine how your own negotiating style appears to those same counterparts.

### The Impact of Culture on Negotiation

*Negotiation Factors*

| | | | |
|---|---|---|---|
| **Goal** | Contract | ←——→ | Relationship |
| **Attitudes** | Win/Lose | ←——→ | Win/Win |
| **Personal Styles** | Informal | ←——→ | Formal |
| **Communications** | Direct | ←——→ | Indirect |
| **Time Sensitivity** | High | ←——→ | Low |
| **Emotionalism** | High | ←——→ | Low |
| **Agreement Form** | Specific | ←——→ | General |
| **Agreement Building** | Bottom Up | ←——→ | Top Down |
| **Team Organization** | One Leader | ←——→ | Consensus |
| **Risk Taking** | High | ←——→ | Low |

## DISCUSSION QUESTIONS

1. To conduct successful negotiations, why does the author think that business people need to know more than the cultural tendencies of specific cultures?

2. If you are trying to negotiate a contract in another culture, why is it advantageous for you to understand how the other party may view your approach?

3. a. Write an original short business case that illustrates how a lack of knowledge of several of these dimensions could cause misunderstandings in a contract negotiation for leasing office space in another country.
   b. Rewrite the case with the culture appropriate dialogue. Compare the two cases. How did the second version improve the chances of a successful outcome for the negotiators?

# Negotiations—BWA Discovers the Indonesian Way

## M.E. (Pete) Murphy
### *Assumption College*

Jared Campbell, a project manager for BWA, sat down at his desk and wondered where he should begin to fix the problems at the building site. BWA was a Canadian/American firm that had a $200 contract to design, supply, and construct a power plant for the National Electric Company (NEC) in Indonesia. This project was part of a World Bank–financed power development initiative with a value of near $1 billion U.S. dollars. Many piling casings—steel pipes that are the first step in a building's foundation—were defective and needed to be replaced. This setback would add a six-month or longer delay to the project schedule. Besides having to reschedule materials and labor, Jared would have to calculate the cost impact and extend his family's planned three-year stay.

Although Jared was an experienced U.S. project manager who had managed other projects of equal size and complexity, this was his first international assignment. He expected that the Asian location would add additional problems, particularly in terms of communication, but he felt these could be resolved with frequent progress meetings and good record keeping. To prepare for the assignment, Jared talked with other experienced BWA project managers, who had already completed complex foreign assignments. He learned that delays were common, particularly in obtaining payments and communication could be problematic.

## THE ISSUES

When Jared arrived in Indonesia, some of the equipment was already at the job site. Other materials were still in the process of being shipped by sea and more was in fabrication in shops around the world. Special construction machinery and skilled workers from Japan were poised to travel to the site. Now, everything would have to be changed and rescheduled. Such delays create the need to store materials and escalate construction costs. Cash flow is interrupted and a cost of working capital is incurred.

Jared needed to estimate these cost increases and prepare a contract claim with a price increase for the buyer, NEC. Since payments to BWA were based on percent of actual project work completed, this meant that payments for construction and site progress would be delayed six months. Key personnel would have to remain on the project longer and site costs added another $600 thousand. Construction personnel and equipment costs and specific storage costs, when added to the personnel and site costs, made the cost of delay $5 million. Jared calculated an estimated $45 million in delayed payments. The BWA standard cost of capital (18% of $45÷2 million) was $4.5 million. In the U.S., Jared would have prepared his claim calculation, submitted it with an invoice, and met with the client to discuss and negotiate a financial resolution.

Jared wasn't as sure how to proceed in Asia, so the following week, during the regular project meeting with NEC and their engineering firm MEC, he raised the problem of the delay and the costs it would create. The NEC engineers seemed surprised and uncomfortable when Jared explained that the delay would have a cost. They asked no questions, not even what these costs would be. Instead, they told Jared that projects have delays, this one is not significant and his company should have expected and considered them. They then moved on to other topics. Jared decided not press this issue further at this meeting.

Back at his office, Jared called Anwar, who worked for the local sales service company, PT Fagar. In Indonesia, local sales agents provide access to decision makers and help to influence the buying decision. Anwar was responsible for sales to NEC under a commission agreement. PT Fagar sold the current project and was expected to provide support. Anwar advised Jared that getting more money for the delay would be difficult, because such delays are common and expected in his country. Anwar knew that NEC had little additional funding for the project and they would not be very receptive to a big claim. This would probably be a very contentious issue, difficult to present, and difficult to resolve. If Jared must pursue the claim, then the best way would be to first meet informally and learn what might be done. Anwar agreed to arrange a lunch meeting with several of the NEC and MEC project engineers.

**Project Structure and Contract Hierarchy**

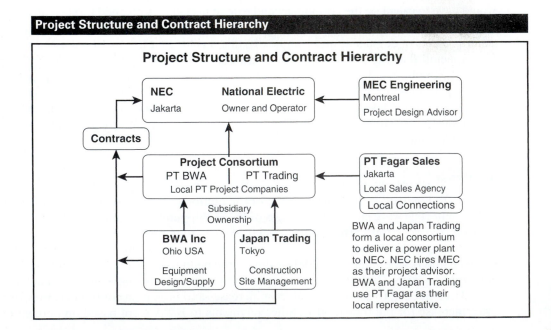

# THE INFORMAL CAMPAIGN—ASIAN STYLE

At lunch, Anwar raised the issue of the project delay during conversation about the project. He explained that extra costs would occur and asked if the engineers could help find a way to cover some of these costs. He talked about the commitment from BWA and PTF to work together with NEC and make this a successful project. He said any help they could provide would be welcome. Although he explained the additional costs in detail, he never mentioned the $5 million estimate. The engineers listened and indicated that they understood the problem. The lunch conversation went on to other topics and at the end, Anwar thanked the engineers for coming.

A week later, Jared happened to meet some of the same engineers at a party. While discussing the project, Jared asked about delay costs. The engineers said that it was a very difficult problem, but they had been discussing it internally. They said it might take some time to find an answer. They offered nothing else and Jared thanked them for their efforts.

When Jared called Anwar to tell him about his conversation at the party, Anwar said he would investigate. Another week went by before Anwar called back to say that the engineers from NEC had suggested a meeting with their boss, the senior manager of the project, Hasan Madjid. Anwar explained that this should be an informal meeting to hear the offer that NEC would propose. He told Jared the meeting should be handled by the president of the PTF, Abdul Hasan. President Hasan knew the senior manager Madjid well and was the right person to open this discussion. Jared and Anwar met with Hasan, the president of PTF and Anwar's boss. They explained the delay problem and the costs it created. Jared gave Hasan the estimate of $5 million. They told him about the preliminary discussions, the response, and asked him to please speak to Madjid of NEC about the problem of the delay. Hasan agreed to meet informally and explore how much NEC would be willing to pay to compensate for the delay.

Hasan called Madjid and arranged to visit him several days later in the evening at his home. Hasan presented the estimate of $5 million and discussed the reasons for the estimate. Madjid said he was surprised and that NEC could not afford such a payment. He agreed that the costs to cover the additional personnel, equipment storage, and increased labor rates were reasonable, but he did not agree to the 18% for the cost of capital or to any interest charges. In any case, he said that the company could not afford to pay more than a maximum offer of $1 million. Hasan indicated that he understood and would do his best to resolve the matter on this basis.

Jared and Anwar met with Hasan to hear the results of the meeting with Madjid. When Hasan explained the offer of $1 million, he advised Jared to redo his cost estimate based on specific, expected cost increases in material and labor, storage, and personnel. No cash flow or interest cost could be included, since these would not be accepted. The total cost in the estimate should be close to the $1 million limit suggested. This revised estimate should remain informal for the time being, and should be given without a formal cover letter. Hasan would then meet informally again with Madjid of NEC to confirm an agreement. After this informal confirmation, Jared could include the claim as an agenda item for the next regular project meeting and formally present the estimate. NEC would then formally accept the claim and Jared could submit an invoice.

## A DIFFERENT APPROACH

After hearing these recommendations, Jared needed to update his boss and obtain approval to continue to proceed on this basis. So, Jared prepared a report, sent it back to his boss, Malcolm Johns, the vice president of project management in Ohio, with the original calculation of the cost of delay, and reported the results from the many informal meetings. Jared recommended that his company accept the $1 million in delay payments tentatively offered, and seek other ways to minimize the cost of the delay. Jared felt that he handled the matter well, even though the offer was well below the estimate, it was probably all they could expect to get.

Within a week, Jared received a fax directly from his division vice president, Alex Stewart. He was told that the $1 million was not enough and that he should prepare and present an invoice for the full $5 million claim. When Jared called Alex and tried to explain the situation and the reason for his recommendation, Alex said this approach was wrong. There was no need for all of these informal discussions. Anwar and his local company, PTF, were just a sales group and knew nothing about managing construction projects and delay claims. The contract was quite clear. NEC must pay all reasonable costs since they were responsible for the delay and the calculation of the costs were based on long-time industry standards.

He ordered Jared to meet directly with NEC and to negotiate a better deal. Alex also told Jared that he was sending Malcolm, Jared's boss, to assist in the negotiation of the claim because Malcolm had a lot of useful experience in these types of claims. Jared was told to set up a meeting with Madjid at NEC for early next week. Malcolm would fly in the day before, meet with Madjid for the first time, present the invoice, and negotiate the additional payment. Jared hung up the phone in shock. Jared tried calling Malcolm to promote the acceptance of the $1 million settlement, but Malcolm seemed confident he could make a better deal in the meeting next week.

## THE MEETING, AMERICAN STYLE

When he arrived, Malcolm spent some time reviewing the delay cost calculations with Jared, but made no changes. The following day Jared and Malcolm met with two engineers who had been involved informally and two other NEC managers. After introductions and the exchange of business cards, Malcolm went directly to the topic. He passed out the delay cost calculation and an invoice for $5 million. He discussed the details of the claim calculation and pointed out that a standard industry format was used in the calculation. He concluded by stating that the delay costs were justified and amounted to $5 million U.S. dollars, which NEC was obligated to pay under the terms of the contract. When he finished his explanation, there was silence. Finally, Madjid quietly said, "We reject your claim for delay costs. You will not be paid. There is no point to discuss the matter further." Then he stood, as did the others in the room, and left. Malcolm looked at Jared and asked, "What just happened?"

## DISCUSSION QUESTIONS

1. What reaction did Jared get the first time he raised the delay cost with NEC? In terms of hierarchy and uncertainty, what was happening?

2. Why did Jared consult Anwar? Why did Anwar take the approach that he did? Why didn't Anwar handle the problem himself?

3. Did Jared make any mistakes in getting the $1 million offer? Did he get the best deal for his company? Should he have handled things differently? How? What were the cultural issues in terms of relationship, harmony, and time?

4. Why did things go so wrong with Jared's managers in Ohio? What should he have done differently? Could Jared have better prepared the way as a link between cultures?

5. After Jared was instructed by his vice president to present the original claim, was it too late to save the situation? Why or why not? What other actions could have been taken by Anwar? By Jared?

6. What really happened in the meeting with NEC? What were NEC's expectations? Why did they do what they did? How could Jared have done a better job? Considering relationships, hierarchy, and harmony issues, what should he tell his boss, Malcolm?

7. Will Jared now be able to get any money for the delay? Explain.

8. What is a contract? Why were there different views of a contract? Is one view right and the other wrong? At this point should Jared's company sue?

9. American businesses often use the phrase "Time is money." What is the issue with this expression in terms of the interest and time value of money? How are these issues viewed in different cultures?

10. What is the model for resolving problems in Asia? Do American managers have to follow this model when working in Asia? What are the alternatives?

11. There are some very successful economies in Asia and a lot of business is getting done. So, how does this happen if every time you go to a business meeting you can't discuss the important issues and you can't suggest any solutions?

# EPILOGUE

No one from NEC was ever willing to discuss the delay claim again, formally or informally, either with Anwar or representatives of PTF. Jared began to have other project problems, particularly the processing of any invoices for payment. Unpaid invoices piled up and Jared received very little cooperation from anyone in NEC in resolving any problems. The project became increasingly difficult to manage.

Some months later at the end of Ramadan, the Moslem holy month, Anwar called Jared and suggested a solution. The last two days of Ramadan are holy days and days of atonement known as Idul Fitri. Atonement means that forgiveness can be asked, and if asked, it should be given. Anwar suggested going to Madjid at NEC during these days and asking for forgiveness.

Madjid did see them, Jared asked for forgiveness for any wrongs he or his company had committed in the past year. Madjid expressed his appreciation and assured Jared that they would work together in the coming year. No mention was made of any specific project problems or claims. Jared did not get to discuss the delay claim again and no payment was ever made, but other problems simply disappeared. Other invoices got paid, problems got resolved, and the project working relationship improved enormously.

The $1 million payment offered was never mentioned again. The contract terms could have supported a delay claim payment, but BWA would probably have to file a suit in local courts, an unwise choice for a foreign firm. The delay costs were minimized in other ways.

## BIBLIOGRAPHY

Ferraro, G. P. (2006). *The cultural dimension of international business*. (5th ed.). Upper Saddle River: Prentice Hall.

Hall, E.T. (1976). *Beyond culture*. New York: Doubleday.

Hofstede, G. (1980). *Culture's consequences: international differences in work-related values*. London: Sage.

Kluckhohn, F., & Strodtbeck, F. L. (1961). *Variations in value orientations*. New York: Harper & Row.

Salacuse, J W. (2004, September/October). Negotiating: The top ten ways that culture can effect your negotiation. *Ivey Business Journal*, 1–6.

---

**Diversity on the Web**

**Briefing Paper**

## M. June Allard

*Assumption College*
*Worcester State College Professor Emerita*

You have been assigned the task of preparing a briefing paper for teams departing for an extended overseas assignment in one of the countries listed below. The briefing paper will present, in very concise form, important information about the country and its people—information that will aid the visitors in understanding and in living in the country. Assume that the team members know very little about the country to which they are being sent and assume further that many will have their families with them.

| | |
|---|---|
| **General Country Information** | Include information such as geographic location, climate, type of government, currency, religion, ethnicity/ethnic groups, relationships, class structure, sources of national pride, ratings on Hofstede's dimensions (Hofstede ratings may be included under Business Customs and Behaviors instead), etc. |
| **Social Customs and Manners** | Include information on greetings, forms of proper address, dress code, tipping, gift-giving, |

**Business Customs and Behaviors**

attitudes toward foreigners, general etiquette and manners, etc.

Include information such as greetings, business card usage, gift-giving, dress code, religious significance, communication and negotiation style, attitude toward women workers, attitude toward older workers, etc.

## Countries

| Asia | Latin America and Mexico |
|------|--------------------------|
| CHINA | ARGENTINA |
| HONG KONG | CHILE |
| JAPAN | COLOMBIA |
| MALAYSIA | ECUADOR |
| RUSSIA | MEXICO |
| SOUTH KOREA | VENEZUELA |

## SUGGESTED INTERNET SOURCES

http://globaledge.msu.edu
http://globaledge.msu.edu/ibrd/busresmain.asp?ResourceCategoryID=17
http://www.state.gov/www/regions/background_info_countries.html
http://getcustoms.com
http://cyborlink.com
http://cyborlink.com/besite/hofstede.htm
http://cyborlink.com/default.htm
http://memory.loc.gov/frd/cs/cshome.html
http://dir.yahoo.com/Society_and_Culture/Cultures_and_Groups/Cultures/
http://www.itim.org

## *Writing Assignment*

Countries and cultures are not homogeneous. Although each culture and each country has distinctive social and business customs, the members of each culture vary considerably from each other. In addition, when individuals migrate to another culture, they make changes in their social and business behavior as they adapt and integrate into the new culture.

Research members of the country you selected for your Briefing Paper who now reside in the United States. Write a two or three page explanation of how different their social and business are customs from those of their country of origin.

# Interpreting Intercultural Communication at a Business Meeting

Arthur Shriberg

*Xavier University*

Richa Kumari

*Aurora, Illinois*

The reality of today's global workplace is that technological tools such as e-mail, conference calls, video conferencing, and the Internet have made it very likely that individuals in one country will interact directly with colleagues, customers, and suppliers in other countries and cultures. Globalization and technology have created unique communication challenges as people find that although geographic disconnects can be overcome with relative ease, the more subtle disconnectedness created by different value systems and internalized assumptions is harder to diagnose and, therefore, harder to overcome. Adding to the complication is the fact that globalization is not a static concept, but rather a dynamic one, affecting groups differently and being affected by seemingly discrete forces, such as national or regional events and lifestyles.

## INTRODUCTION TO THE EXERCISE

The simulation that follows is an example of how a virtual business meeting of culturally unaware managers can quickly become ineffective. The point of some of the seeming exaggerations is to showcase the importance of cultural understanding. It is also important to clarify that the cultural characteristics of countries depicted herein should not be used to stereotype people that belong to that country. Every individual is a product of many different factors, one of which is culture. In a virtual gathering, the race, ethnicity, and other visual cues may be missing and increase the possibility of participants assuming some basic level of homogeneity. In addition to culture, things like gender, age and, most importantly, personalities, influence people's interactions with each other.

However, for simplicity, this simulation focuses only on the cultural aspects, because the aim of this exercise is to demonstrate different cultural dynamics and how they can affect routine communications.

## CULTURAL BARRIERS TO BUSINESS COMMUNICATION

Culture is often defined, historically and anthropologically, as a shared pattern of beliefs, values, norms, attitudes, and behaviors that are transferred from generation to generation. However, it is increasingly being recognized that culture refers to commonalities that have developed and continue to evolve in the context of the sociopolitical environment based on various dimensions including race, ethnicity, sexuality, gender, religion, etc. In the United States, the attributes that form the dominant culture are white skin, Christianity, physical and economic ability, heterosexuality, and English as a primary language. The population that has one or more of the dominant characteristics also enjoys privilege and access, which means, among other things, that they do not have to acknowledge their culture as the norm, and that they have greater access to resources, connections, and status. In the United States, most business leaders are likely to fit this profile and, more often than not, are male. However, global companies often have leaders in their business units that differ from their American counterparts in terms of one or more of these attributes. Privilege for the dominant group obviously creates a potential for the dynamics of domination. Behaviorally, this translates into instances like using colloquialisms or sports terminology where the member of the 'dominant' group assumes that everyone else understands what is meant.

Hofstede (2001) has measured the dominant values of more than 50 countries on five dimensions that can affect people's behaviors in fairly predictable ways. The dimensions are as follows:

*Power Distance:* the extent to which less powerful members of organizations and institutions accept and expect that power is distributed unequally.

*Uncertainty Avoidance:* the extent to which a culture programs its members to feel either uncomfortable or comfortable in unstructured situations (degree to which society tries to control the uncontrollable).

*Individualism/Collectivism:* the degree to which individuals are supposed to look after themselves or remain integrated into groups, usually around family.

*Masculinity/Femininity:* the distribution of emotional roles between genders (tough—masculine, caring—feminine societies).

*Long Term/Short Term Orientation:* the extent to which a culture programs its members to accept delayed gratification of their material, social, emotional needs.

These and other values of global managers can influence their styles of communications greatly. While Hofstede's model has its limitations and detractors, it is still one of the predominant models for predicting cultural differences.

In real life, a situation as extreme as this, where every team member is from a different culture and all the differences are so clearly manifested, may not occur. However, even one team member's cultural distance from the rest of the team is likely to have a detrimental impact on communication and group effectiveness and create misunderstandings.

Ethnocentrism is another significant barrier to successful intercultural business communication. Ethnocentrism is defined as an "exaggerated tendency to think that the characteristics of one's own group or race are superior to those of other groups or races" (Drever, 1952, p. 86). The practical implication of this is that members of the different group are likely to draw conclusions about others based on what they think is 'appropriate' behavior in their own cultural context. For instance, someone who was acculturated to believing that unwavering eye contact is a sign of sincerity may mistakenly jump to the assumption of dishonesty when confronted with someone from a country like many Arab countries or India, where lowering of eyes is a sign of respect for superiors.

Even when people do make attempts to be sensitive to these differences, cultural misinformation can pose a significant problem. Cultural misinformation is the act of applying historical information about a group of people as generalizations to individuals belonging to that group. Examples would include statements like "Women are more nurturing than men," "Indians value large families," "Men have better mechanical ability than women," and the like. Such generalizations close the door to understanding individual differences. Culturally misinformed individuals are likely to reinforce stereotypes about a group by generalizing the commonly held assumptions, but individualizing the deviations from those assumptions. For instance, if they were to meet a woman with very sound mechanical skills, they would say something like "unlike other women, she has excellent mechanical ability," instead of recognizing that there may be other women out there that may have similar or better mechanical skills than some men. Such generalizations are also often used to prescribe how most people of a group *should* behave. Cultural misinformation feeds into stereotyping, which is the act of labeling others based only on their membership in one group and then labeling others who are like them in one characteristic as if they are similar in all characteristics. Stereotyping is a part of normal psychological processes, but, under relevant conditions, can lead to inaccurate assumptions and generalizations about individuals based on hearsay, opinions, and distorted, preconceived ideas.

## BECOMING CULTURALLY SENSITIVE

Ackbar Abbas (1997) refers to an effect created by globalization that he calls "dislocation" of culture. He speaks of the confusion created as a result of abstract and imploding cultures and the fact that it is becoming harder to predict what a culture might be given that surface appearances may not be an accurate reflection of reality. Every individual is a product of his or her own unique cultural experiences. These experiences result in assumptions about the individual's own reference group (be it race, gender, ethnicity, or any other) as well as other groups. With no intervention in one direction or the other, the manifestation of these assumptions may be positive or negative. However, a lot can be achieved in terms of productivity and efficiency if a conscious effort is made to understand the impact of cultural differences.

While most people are aware of the technical tools available to them that facilitate interactions across geographic barriers, they tend to ignore the cognitive tools that serve the same purpose. People often overlook the fact that the technologies that are used to bridge physical barriers between people can be used effectively to become better acquainted with the cultures, values, and assumptions of the diverse groups they do or are likely to deal with. There is a wealth of information available in the public domain on different countries, their values, business etiquette, and cultures that can be easily accessed and used to understand behaviors.

The cultural differences that members bring to a cross-cultural team can be leveraged in a variety of ways. For an effective change in behavior to occur, four essential components must be present: intent, awareness, knowledge, and skill (Abbas, p. 428).

## THE SIMULATION

Four leaders of a global organization
American leader ............................................................. Jamie Hyder
Brazilian leader ............................................................. Ana Barbosa
Indian leader ............................................................. Dr. K. D. Niraj
Swedish leader ............................................................. Bjorn Svenson

Since the simulation involves four very different countries, the following box characterizing each of the countries in terms of Hofstede's dimensions will aid in understanding the dynamics of the conversation. The higher the value in a box, the stronger the country is on that dimension.

Your instructor will provide instructions and scripts for the simulation.

| | Power Distance | Individualism | Uncertainty Avoidance | Masculinity | Long Term Orientation |
|---|---|---|---|---|---|
| Brazil | 69 | 38 | 76 | 49 | 65 |
| India | 77 | 48 | 40 | 56 | 61 |
| Sweden | 31 | 71 | 29 | 5 | |
| U.S.A. | 40 | 91 | 46 | 62 | 29 |

## DISCUSSION GUIDE

A. Would the barriers be reduced if all participants could see each other? If so how?

B. Can you think of anything that might make the situation more complicated if everyone were physically present?

C. Would Jamie and Dr. Niraj's gender make a difference? Why or why not?

D. How could each participant have prepared better for the meeting?

E. Have you experienced anything that supports or contradicts material presented here?

## BIBLIOGRAPHY

Abbas, A. (1997). *Hong Kong: Culture and the politics of disappearance*. Minneapolis: University of Minnesota Press.

Drever, J. (1952). *A dictionary of psychology*. Harmondsworth, Middlesex: Penguin.

Held, D. & McGrew, A. (2000). *The global transformations reader: An introduction to the globalization debate* (pp. 1–46). Cambridge: Polity Press.

Hofstede, G. (2001). *Cultures and consequences: Comparing values, behaviors, institutions, and organizations across nations*. California: Sage Publications.

# How Canada Promotes Workplace Diversity

Marc S. Mentzer

*University of Saskatchewan*

It is easy to fall into the trap of treating Canada as merely a colder version of the United States. Although outwardly similar to the United States, Canada has its own unique history and traditions. The differences between Canada and the United States are deep, yet not immediately visible to the visitor.

To appreciate the differences between the two countries, one must go back to the time of the American Revolution. The American revolutionaries expected that present-day Canada would join them in the fight against the English king, but the area that makes up present-day Canada stayed loyal to the king and continued under British rule until Canada became independent in 1867. As a result, Canadians have a faith in government that is very different than the usual skepticism and suspicion toward government that one sees in the United States.

Another key difference is that the Canadian federal government has less power than the U.S. government, especially where employment regulation is concerned. On employment issues, laws of the Canadian federal government affect only those industries that are federally regulated according to the Canadian constitution: broadcasting, telecommunications, banking, railroads, airlines, shipping, other transport across provincial boundaries, uranium mining, and crown corporations. (A crown corporation is a company in which the government owns all the stock, such as the Canadian Broadcasting Corporation.)

All other businesses are beyond the jurisdiction of the Canadian government, and are affected only by laws passed by the province in which they operate. As an example, consider Sears, the department store chain. In the United States, Sears must obey U.S. federal law regarding nondiscrimination, minimum wage, and so on. Each state has its own laws, but with some exceptions, a company as large as Sears can ignore the state laws because state laws are overridden by U.S. federal law.

In Canada, Sears also has stores throughout the country, but retailing is not federally regulated under the Canadian constitution. Therefore, Sears in Canada must obey the laws of each province in which it operates. A Sears store in Ontario must obey Ontario laws; a store in Quebec must obey Quebec laws, and so on, which complicates the numerous burdens on Sears executives in Canada.

# THE CANADIAN HUMAN RIGHTS ACT

In 1977, Parliament passed the Canadian Human Rights Act, which forbids discrimination by federally regulated employers on the basis of race, gender, and certain other grounds. This act prohibits systemic (indirect) discrimination, e.g., when an employer asks an applicant about her childbearing plans or engages in sexual harassment, as well as direct discrimination, e.g., when an employer says women applicants will not be considered. Instead of complaints being heard in court, as in the United States, discrimination complaints are made to the Canadian Human Rights Commission. This allows victims to have a hearing without having to hire a lawyer, although monetary damages tend to be much lower than they would be in a U.S. court. In severe cases of discrimination, the Commission has the power to impose a hiring quota for women or minorities, but this power is rarely used.

Another feature of the Canadian Human Rights Act is that it requires comparable worth in compensation, which in Canada is known as pay equity. Every covered employer must ensure that predominantly female occupations are paid the same as predominantly male occupations of equal importance or difficulty in the same organization. For example, secretaries working for a railroad might claim that their job is of equal importance or difficulty as that of a track maintenance worker, and thus could demand that their pay be the same. Pay equity or comparable worth is a type of law that does not exist in the United States at the federal level, because it is seen as interfering with market forces, but it is a fact of life for organizations under the jurisdiction of the Canadian federal government. At the provincial level, Ontario and Quebec also have pay equity laws that cover both public- and private-sector employers. Most other provinces have pay equity laws limited to public-sector organizations, such as universities and hospitals.

# EMPLOYMENT EQUITY LEGISLATION

Initially it was hoped that the Canadian Human Rights Act would be sufficient to break down the barriers that prevent the economic progress of women and minorities. However, it became apparent that simply forbidding discrimination was not enough. In 1984 a parliamentary commission recommended legislation that would push employers to take proactive or aggressive measures to increase the numbers of women and minority employees (Canada, 1984). This commission noted that in the United States, affirmative action has been divisive because it pits men against women and whites against minorities. Thus, to avoid the ill will surrounding the term affirmative action, a new term, employment equity, was created to cover such proactive measures as targeted recruiting, providing child care facilities, accommodating the needs of people with disabilities, and so on.

The resulting legislation, the Canadian Employment Equity Act of 1986, was mainly symbolic, relying on persuasion and embarrassment so that employers would be more serious about creating workplaces that value diversity. Covered employers submit their data to the federal government, which then assigns grades (A, B, etc.) to each employer. A later version of the law, the Canadian Employment Equity Act of 1995, put in place modest fines up to $50,000 for employers not meeting their targets. In practice, these fines are rarely imposed (Agocs, 2002).

## THE FOUR PROTECTED GROUPS

In the United States, initially, the main thrust of civil rights legislation was to end discrimination against blacks. This has never been a burning issue in Canada because blacks make up only 2 percent of the Canadian population, versus 13 percent in the United States. Similarly, Hispanics constitute only 1 percent of the Canadian population, compared with 14 percent in the United States Therefore, when Canada introduced employment equity legislation, there was a question about which groups should be chosen for special protection. In the end, the government designated four protected groups:

1. **Women**
   As in the United States, Canadian women lag behind men in income and representation in high-paying jobs.

2. **Aboriginal Peoples**
   This group includes Indians, Inuit (the aboriginal people of the Arctic regions), and Métis (those of mixed French–Indian ancestry in western Canada). Aboriginal people constitute 3 percent of the Canadian population, compared with 1 percent in the United States. The low Canadian percentage is deceptive, because there are large regions of Canada where aboriginal people are the majority. Aboriginal people frequently overcome barriers to gain education and achieve success in Canadian society, but there are many who have difficulty entering the economic mainstream.

3. **People with Disabilities**
   Both Canada and the United States define disabilities to include psychological conditions as well as physical conditions.

4. **Visible Minorities**
   This is the most interesting, and most controversial, protected group under Canadian law and it has no exact equivalent in U.S. law. "Visible minorities" refers to those of black, Asian, Arab, Pacific Islander, or Latin American ancestry. Chinese Canadians, comprising 3 percent of the Canadian population, are the largest of the ethnic groups in this category. The visible minority category

includes some groups, such as Japanese Canadians, that have very high income levels today, but had historically been targets of discrimination. "Visible minorities" includes other groups, such as Pacific Islander Canadians or Southeast Asian Canadians, who are relatively recent arrivals in Canada, with high unemployment rates and very low incomes on average. The category of visible minorities, which constitute 13 percent of the Canadian population, is an assortment of ethnic groups that have little in common with one another (Hum & Simpson, 2000).

Other minorities sought to be included as protected groups under the Employment Equity Act, but were excluded, although their rights are protected elsewhere under Canadian law. For example, note that lesbians and gays are not a protected group. Also, French-speaking people in predominantly English-speaking areas wanted to be treated as a protected group, but were not included. One fourth of the population speaks French as their first language, and in some areas they feel they are at a disadvantage in an English-language-dominated society. Because the Human Rights Act covers these minority groups, it is still illegal to discriminate against people on the basis of their sexual orientation or whether they learned French before English. However, employers are not required to engage in proactive or aggressive actions to increase their representation in the workforce.

There have been some glitches in the implementation of employment equity (Mentzer, 2002). An employee cannot be counted as a member of a minority group unless he or she identifies as such on a questionnaire administered by the employer. If some minority employees don't complete the questionnaire due to a desire to blend in and not draw attention, then the employer cannot count them in employment equity statistics. Another dilemma is that people of Arab or west Asian (for example, Turkish) descent often don't realize that the government defines them as being in the visible minority category, so the resulting statistics are likely to undercount visible minority employees.

In the United States, some white individuals have won lawsuits claiming reverse discrimination, causing the unravelling of some of the U.S. affirmative action initiatives. A claim of reverse discrimination cannot be made in the Canadian legal system. Section 15 of the Charter of Rights and Freedoms, which is part of the Canadian constitution, states that discrimination is illegal. It then goes on to state that policies that improve the situation of disadvantaged groups are an allowable exception to the antidiscrimination clause. This key difference between the U.S. and Canadian constitutions has far-ranging implications for affirmative action and employment equity policies.

## EMPLOYMENT EQUITY IN ACTION

Employment equity, when properly implemented, goes far beyond merely increasing the number of women and minority employees. Instead, the focus of employment equity should be to encourage flexibility and create a workplace in which people of all backgrounds feel comfortable.

For example, Pelmorex, which owns specialized cable channels, regularly does employee recruiting at aboriginal events and in campus offices for students with disabilities. Pelmorex also conducts special Employer Outreach Sessions for people who are blind and are interested in applying for employment. Another example of Pelmorex's commitment to diversity is providing office space to be used as prayer rooms (Weather Network, 2006).

Another success story in employment equity is Cameco, a uranium company operating in northern Saskatchewan, where aboriginal people make up four-fifths of the local population. When hiring miners, Cameco gives preference to local residents. A local community college provides training at Cameco's expense, to prepare aboriginal people for mining careers. In addition, Cameco provides courses for employees to improve their literacy skills, on company time and at company expense (Cameco, 2006, communication from company).

One of Canada's largest banks is BMO, formerly known as Bank of Montreal. BMO has an internship program for aboriginal and visible minority university students. Also, BMO asks some of its aboriginal employees to speak at aboriginal schools about career opportunities in banking. For those balancing work with family responsibilities, BMO has a flexible work arrangements policy and offers a 24-hour hotline for emergency child care (BMO, 2004).

The previous few examples show how Canadian employers creatively reach out to those in the four protected groups under employment equity legislation. When properly implemented, employment equity changes an organization's internal culture to one that welcomes diversity in all its forms, and where all employees can reach their full potential.

## CANADA'S PROVINCES AND TERRITORIES

Canada is divided into ten provinces and three territories, which, generally speaking, have more power than U.S. state governments. Each of the ten provinces and three territories has its own human rights laws forbidding discrimination. With a few exceptions, these laws also include provisions for imposing hiring quotas on employers who are chronic offenders, similar to the features of the Canadian Human Rights Act, although the provisions for punitive hiring quotas are rarely used. While every province and territory forbids discrimination, none of them have laws requiring employers to engage in proactive measures in the spirit of employment equity or affirmative action.

The result is that only those employers in federally regulated industries are required by legislation to have employment equity programs. Such household names as Wal-Mart, McDonald's, or General Motors are not in federally regulated industries, and therefore are not covered by the Canadian Employment Equity Act, although they may create *voluntary* employment equity plans if they wish. However, such companies must obey the antidiscrimination laws of the provinces and territories in which they operate.

Lastly, provincially regulated companies that sell goods or services to the federal government are required to have employment equity programs or else risk losing their federal contracts.

Executives of companies operating in both the United States and Canada face a special challenge, because they must be knowledgeable about the laws of two countries, and in many instances the laws of Canada's ten provinces and three territories as well. Frequently, a human resource policy that is legal in the United States will be illegal in Canada, or vice versa, and such companies have to obey the laws of the jurisdiction in which they operate. Two countries, similar in so many ways, have entirely different legal structures to address the issue of increasing diversity in the workplace.

## DISCUSSION QUESTIONS

1. How does the power of the Canadian federal government differ in relation to the provinces, from the power of the United States federal government in relation to the states?

2. a. If a U.S.–based retail chain has stores throughout Canada, which laws apply—those of the United States, those of the Canadian federal government, or those of each province?
   b. If a Canadian chain has stores throughout the United States, which laws apply—those of the United States, those of the Canadian federal government, or those of the province in which it is based?

3. What is the difference between employment equity and pay equity?

4. How does the Canadian constitution affect affirmative action–type programs?

5. a. Make an argument that it is easier for employers to comply with diversity legislation in Canada than it is in the United States.
   b. Make an argument that it is *not* easier for employers to comply with diversity legislation in Canada than in the United States.

## BIBLIOGRAPHY

Agocs, C. (2002). Canada's employment equity legislation and policy, 1987–2000. *International Journal of Manpower, 23*, 256–276.

BMO Financial Group (2004). 2004 Employment Equity Narrative Report. Retrieved September 2006, from http://www.bmo.com

Canada. Minister of Supply and Services (1984). *Report of the Commission on Equality in Employment.* Judge Rosalie Silberman Abella, Commissioner. Ottawa, Canada.

Hum, D., & Simpson, W. (2000). Not all visible minorities face labour market discrimination. *Policy Options/Options Politiques, 21*(10), 45–48.

Mentzer, M. S. (2002) The Canadian experience with employment equity legislation. *International Journal of Value-Based Management, 15*, 35–50.

Weather Network [Pelmorex] (2006). Careers at TWN: Diversity. Retrieved September 2006, from http://www.theweathernetwork.com/twn/careers/diversity.htm

## NOTE

U.S. statistics are from the 2005 National Population Estimates, as reported by the U.S. Census Bureau. Retrieved September 2006 from http://www.census.gov
Canadian statistics are from the 2001 census, as reported by Statistics Canada Retrieved September 2006 from http://www.statcan.ca

# WEBSITES

**Canadian (Federal) Human Rights Commission**
For employers that are directly regulated by the federal government, this agency enforces employment equity legislation as well as other antidiscrimination legislation:
*http://www.chrc-ccdp.ca*

**Ontario Human Rights Commission**
This agency enforces human rights in Ontario, which is the most populous of the provinces (Toronto is the capital):
*http://www.ohrc.on.ca*

**Ontario Pay Equity Commission**
Also, of all the provinces, Ontario has the strictest pay equity (comparable worth) laws:
*http://www.payequity.gov.on.ca/*

**Quebec: Commission des droits de la personne et des droits de la jeunesse**
This agency enforces human rights in Quebec, which is the only predominantly French-speaking province. For this Web site, French is the default language, but there is a link that can be clicked on to get the English version.
*http://cdpdj.qc.ca*

**Assembly of First Nations**
This organization represents the aboriginal Indians of Canada.
*http://www.afn.ca*

**Inuit Tapiriit Kanatami**
This organization represents the Inuit, who are the aboriginal people of the Arctic.
*http://www.itk.ca*

┌─ **Diversity on the Web** ──────────────────────────────────┐

1. The aboriginal people of Canada are often referred to as "First Nations." The term carries symbolic meaning, reminding us that organized societies existed in Canada before the arrival of white people.

   Go to http://en.wikipedia.org/wiki/First_Nations_of_Canada and choose three aboriginal groups from different regions of Canada. For each group you chose, in which province or territory are they concentrated? What is distinctive about each group you chose? Summarize any information about each group's current economic situation, if available.

2. Choose a Canadian bank, and look at its Web site to see what is presented regarding employment equity or diversity. Next, choose a U.S. bank and look at what its Web site says regarding diversity. To what extent do differences between the two Web sites relate to differences between Canada and the United States? In some cases, it will be necessary to do a Web search within the bank's Web site for the keywords "diversity" or "employment equity."

   To get started, here are some Web sites of Canadian banks:
   http://www. rbc.com       http://www.td.com           http://www.cibc.com
   http://www. nbc.ca        http:// www.scotiabank.com   http://www.bmo.com/

3. Choose one province or territory, look up the Web site of its human rights commission, and discuss what sort of cases or complaints dominate the work of that organization. In some instances, there will be a section of the Web site labeled "Decisions." Are the issues addressed by your chosen organization different than one would expect from a similar enforcement agency in the United States? The following Web sites are particularly well designed:

   | | |
   |---|---|
   | **British Columbia:** | *http://www.bchrt.bc.ca* |
   | **Newfoundland and Labrador:** | *http://www.justice.gov.nl.ca/hrc/* |
   | **Ontario:** | *http://www.ohrc.on.ca* |
   | **Quebec (clickable link converts** | |
   | **the webpage into English):** | *http://www.cdpdj.qc.ca* |
   | **Saskatchewan:** | *http://www.shrc.gov.sk.ca* |
   | **Yukon:** | *http://www.yhrc.yk.ca* |

└─────────────────────────────────────────────────────────────┘

# Women in the Workforce:
## How Far Have They Come?

**Gina Colavecchio**

*FirstComp Insurance*

---

*Mark each item as T (True) or F (False)*

_____ 1. In the United States, the 200 highest paid CEOs are all male.

_____ 2. United Airlines board of directors includes two women.

_____ 3. It will take 270 years for an equal number of women and men to be represented in top management at businesses in the United States.

_____ 4. AOL Time Warner has 24 top executives. None of these are women.

_____ 5. Ten (10) percent of CEOs at Fortune 500 companies are women; 90 percent are men.

_____ 6. Median weekly earnings for a woman working full time in 2003 were $522. This is 80 percent of the average for men ($695).

_____ 7. Women with an average age of 35, earned ¾ of what their male colleagues earned in 2004.

_____ 8. Women in the age bracket of 18–24 years earned the same pay as their male counterparts in 2003.

_____ 9. Since the 1970s, women's wages have increased by 34 percent.

_____ 10. Women account for 30 percent of all MBA slots at top schools in the United States.

# Women in Leadership Positions

Deborah L. Larsen

*Bank of America*

**O**ften, women leaders find themselves in a "no-win" situation. Mired by stereotypes that persist, perceptions of women as incompetent leaders, and the centuries-old practice of gender inequality, professional women are left questioning how much progress really has been made over the years.

Why are today's women still suffering penalties for failing to live up to gender role expectations? *Gender,* is a socially constructed characteristic consisting of behaviors and attitudes considered proper for males and females. Gender varies from one culture to another and serves as a significant way in which society controls its members. Many societies set up barriers to provide unequal access to power, property, and prestige on the basis of sex. "Privilege exists when one group has something of value that is denied to others simply because of the groups they belong to, rather than because of anything they've done or failed to do" (Minas, 1993).

---

**Examples of gender privilege are:**

- Men can generally assume that when they go out in public, they won't be sexually harassed or assaulted, and if they are victimized, they won't be asked to explain what they were doing there or why they were out alone.
- Most men can assume that their gender won't be used to determine whether they'll fit in at work or whether teammates will feel comfortable working with them.
- Men don't find themselves slotted into a limited range of occupations identified with their gender like women are slotted into human resources, social work, teaching, nursing, and secretarial positions.

---

Gender inequality exists in terms of wealth, income, and status and occurs in the workplace, family, and educational systems. In addition, everyday life provides demonstrations of the generalized devaluation of women and feminine traits. If a football team isn't playing well, a coach might tell his boys that they are playing like a bunch of

■ 120 ■

girls and the assumption communicated to the boys is that nothing is worse. A baseball player making a poor throw might be told, "You threw that one like a girl."

"It's a man's world" is an expression pointing to the male-dominated character of society that places most power in the hands of men. It is still common to use masculine pronouns to refer to people in general, or to use *man* to name the entire species as in "mankind." The idea of "brotherhood" carries powerful meaning about human connection, as in the line from *America the Beautiful*, "And crown thy good with brotherhood from sea to shining sea" (Bates, 1893).

Men are the cultural standard for humanity. If a woman is being celebrated in the office and her coworkers sing, "For she's a jolly good fellow," no one objects because in a male-identified society, it's an honor to be considered "one of the guys" but to reverse this would certainly be an issue. Male identification is evident in every aspect of everyday life. Most respected occupations are organized around qualities associated with masculinity, such as assertiveness and competitiveness, where women are identified with such qualities as cooperativeness and nurturing. If a woman is identified as cooperative and nurturing, she is likely to be seen as not having what it takes to get the job done or as unable to make "tough" decisions. On the other hand if she shows that she can be assertive and competitive, she may be described as being "cold" or a "bitch." In addition, if a woman changes her behavior to be more accepted by her male coworkers, her female coworkers may see her as a traitor.

## A HISTORY OF PATRIARCHY

A society is patriarchal to the degree that it is male-dominated and male-identified. Political, economic, legal, religious, educational, and military positions of authority are generally reserved for men. Heads of state, corporate chief executive officers, corporate board members, religious leaders, members of legislatures at all levels of government, senior law partners, generals, etc., tend to be mostly males under patriarchy. When women find themselves in these positions, people tend to think of them as exceptions to the general rule. Consequently, male dominance creates power differences between men and women and promotes the idea of male superiority. If men occupy more powerful positions, then viewing men as superior is not a stretch. If presidents, generals, legislators, priests, popes, and corporate CEOs are mostly men with a few women as exceptions to the rule, then men as a group become identified with superiority even though most men are not powerful in their individual lives.

In patriarchal societies core ideas about what is desirable or normal are associated with men. The idea of a high-level career with its implicit 60-plus-hour workweeks assumes the worker has a wife at home to provide support with child care, laundry, and the creation of a relaxing environment when the work day is finally over. Since a woman is more likely to not have a caregiver at home, she might begin her day making lunches, planning dinner, and doing laundry before she sets off to work. It is difficult for women to compete on this unequal playing field. Men with stay-at-home wives go home to dinner on the table, while many working women begin cooking dinner when they eventually get home from their long workday.

Some women—such as Condoleezza Rice, the United States secretary of state; Sandra Day O'Connor, retired United States Supreme Court justice; Hillary Rodham Clinton, United States senator; Ruth Bader Ginsburg, United States Supreme Court justice; and Wu Yi, China's vice premier and minister of health—do make it to positions of power today. Each powerful woman is surrounded with powerful men and none of these women could hold her position without accepting at some level the society's core patriarchal values.

## THE WOMEN'S RIGHTS MOVEMENT AND WOMEN'S LEGAL RIGHTS

In early U.S. society, the second-class status of women was taken for granted. A husband and wife were legally one person: him. Women could not serve on juries, vote, make legal contracts, or hold property in their own names. Because men tenaciously held onto their privileges and used social institutions to maintain their positions, basic rights for women came only through a prolonged struggle.

In 1848 a group of women led by Elizabeth Cady Stanton used the Declaration of Independence as the framework for writing the "Declaration of Sentiments." Among the many inequalities it sought to correct are the following:

- Women were not allowed to vote.
- Married women had no property rights.
- Husbands had legal power over, and responsibility for, their wives to the extent that they could imprison or beat them with impunity.
- Women had to pay property taxes although they had no representation in the levying of these taxes.
- Most occupations were closed to women and when women did work they were paid only a fraction of what men earned.
- Women were not allowed to enter professions such as medicine or law.
- Women had no means to gain an education, since no college or university would accept female students.

Women finally won the right to vote in 1920. During this time, the birth control education issue was gaining momentum. In 1936, a Supreme Court decision declassified birth control information previously judged to be obscene. It was not until 1965 that married couples in all states could legally obtain contraceptives.

In 1963 President Kennedy convened a commission on the status of women, naming Eleanor Roosevelt as its chair. The report documented discrimination against women in virtually every area of American life. That same year, Betty Friedan published *The Feminine Mystique,* a book acknowledging the oppression that middle-class, educated women experienced because of their limited life options.

Title VII of the 1964 Civil Rights Act prohibited employment discrimination on the basis of sex as well as race, religion, ethnicity, and national origin. The Equal Employment Opportunity Commission was established to investigate discrimination complaints and women filed 50,000 discrimination claims within the first five years. Since many women felt that the commission was not very interested in pursuing these complaints, members of various state commissions on the status of women and other feminists united to form a civil rights organization—the National Organization for Women (NOW)—in 1966.

With the inclusion of Title IX in the Education Codes of 1972, equal access to higher education, professional schools, and high school and college sports teams became the law. The number of female doctors, lawyers, engineers, and other professionals grew substantially. Sports participation by women and girls also rose as a result of Title IX.

Another area with dramatic change has been women's financial independence. Twenty-five years ago, a married woman could not get a credit card in her own name or a loan without a male cosigner. Help wanted ads were segregated into "Help wanted—women" and "Help wanted—men."

The Equal Rights Amendment, after languishing in Congress for almost fifty years, was finally passed in 1972 and sent to the states for ratification. The wording was simple: "Equality of rights under the law shall not be denied or abridged by the United States or any state on account of sex." When the deadline for ratification came in 1982, the ERA was three states short of the 38 needed to write it into the U.S. constitution. Despite the large majority of the population supporting the ERA, it was considered by many politicians to be too controversial and was never passed.

While many women today may be hesitant to be thought of as "feminist" for fear of being criticized, few would give up the personal freedoms and opportunities that feminists have won for them over the last 150 years. Whatever choices women make in their own lives, most envision a world for their daughters and granddaughters where all females will have the opportunity to develop their unique skills and talents.

## INEQUALITIES IN THE EDUCATION SYSTEM

Gender inequality in education often is not readily apparent.

> More women than men go to college, and they earn 56 percent of all bachelor's degrees and 57 percent of all master's degrees. A closer look however, reveals gender tracking, which reinforces male–female distinctions: Men earn 83 percent of bachelor's degrees in the "masculine" field of engineering, while women are awarded 88 percent of bachelor's degrees in the "feminine" field of library science. Because socialization gives men and women different orientations to life, they enter college with gender-linked aspirations. It is their socialization, not some innate characteristics that channels men and women into different educational paths (Henslin, 2005, p. 264–265).

In the summer of 2006, the U.S. Department of Education scheduled in-depth investigations of how colleges and universities treat women and men students and faculty in their science and mathematics departments. The current push to apply Title IX to academic departments stems in part from a July 2004 study by the Government Accountability Office, which found Title IX compliance reviews in the sciences to "have largely been neglected." The compliance reviews of university math and science programs look for polices that may result in women "feeling unwelcome in pursuing advanced degrees or tenured positions," according to Stephanie Monroe, assistant secretary for civil rights (Feminist Majority Foundation, 2006). The National Science Foundation is working with the U.S. Department of Education to create the review process, focusing in part on whether engineering and computer science departments offer as much support to women students as to men.

"Women face discrimination from academic institutions in science and technology fields." The report finds that women's lack of participation within science and technology fields in academia can be attributed to gender bias and barriers within hiring and promotion practices in research institutions. Emphasized in the report is the important role that women scientists play in keeping the United States competitive in science and engineering. To decrease gender bias, the report suggests that an interinstitutional organization be established to monitor academic institutions and set guidelines for hiring and promotion practices (National Academy of Science, 2006).

## INEQUALITIES IN THE PAY SYSTEM

Equal pay has been the law since 1963, when President Kennedy signed the Equal Pay Act into law as an amendment to the Wages and Hours Act that prohibits discrimination based on sex resulting in unequal pay for equal work. Despite more women moving into higher positions, pay between the sexes remains unequal.

Economists Rex Fuller and Richard Schoenberg studied the starting salaries of the business majors at the University of Wisconsin in 1991 where 47 percent of the graduates were women. They found that starting salaries for the women averaged 11 percent ($1,737) less than those of the men. Reviewing college records, the economists found that women had higher grades and more internship hours. Even with equal or better qualifications, women were offered lower salaries. Checking five years later, Fuller and Schoenberg found that instead of narrowing, the pay gap had grown even wider with women earning 14 percent ($3,615) less than men (Henslin, 2006).

In 2005, women continued to earn only 77 cents on the dollars of their male counterparts. Many people believe that the earnings gap between men and women is disappearing, but statistics show that the gender pay gap has persisted over the past half century with little evidence of narrowing (U.S. Census Bureau, 2005).

Several factors explain such differences. Women sometimes choose different and often lower paying careers than men. This was especially true in the sixties when today's older women entered the workforce. Through the seventies, women married and had children earlier than today's women. These choices usually moved them off the fast track, while their husbands kept advancing. When these women finally returned to work, they could not match the experience or the seniority of their male counterparts. These factors still operate today although less often than in the past. New mothers still drop out of the workforce more often than new fathers do and women often choose jobs with flexible hours or even part-time positions that don't pay as well.

Whether it is done knowingly or not, discrimination maintains a system of privilege. Giving preference to the son of a Harvard or Yale graduate is a form of discrimination because it favors the children of privileged parents over others, regardless of their qualifications. President George W. Bush, an average student, attended prep school at Andover Academy because his father was an alumnus. He didn't get good grades at Andover, but got into Yale because the Bushes were alumni there as well. Direct ancestors James Bush, Samuel Bush, Prescott Bush, and his father, George H. W. Bush, all attended Yale University. George W. Bush would later attend Harvard, where he earned his MBA. He was admitted to Harvard despite earning only a C average while at Yale.

> His high school record was ordinary and his SAT scores were 566 verbal and 640 math. They may not have had an explicit point system at Yale in 1964 but Bush clearly got into Yale because of affirmative action for the son and grandson of alumni and being a member of a politically influential family (Kinsley, 2003).

These forms of affirmative action still go on today. The *Wall Street Journal* reported in January 2003 that Harvard accepts 40 percent of its applicants who are children of alumni, but only 11 percent of its applicants generally (Golden, 2003).

The effects of white male privilege show up in the workplace, where glass ceilings keep educated women from reaching the management and executive ranks. While the gender gap in income has shrunk somewhat over the past several decades, progress has been at a snail's pace.

> In 2004, a typical college-educated woman working full time earned $31,223 a year, compared to $40,798 for a college-educated man—a difference of $9,575. College-educated women 25 and older earned 75 percent of what their male peers earned. This pay gap appears within the first year after college, even when women are working full time in the same fields as men, and widens in the first ten years in the workforce (U.S. Census Bureau, 2005).

Corporate America is not alone in gender discrimination. A study of the 1972–1975 University of Michigan Law School graduates found first year salaries to be similar, but fifteen years out of law school the story was different, with men earning 40 percent more than women. In addition, only a little over half the women graduating in the 1980s reach the level of partner after ten years of experience. Today only about 12 percent of law firm partners are women, and a much smaller number can be found in top management roles (Wood, Corcoran, & Courant, 1993).

Similar findings hold true in education, with an often significant gap between male and female professors. In April of 1999 both MIT and the University of Texas released information confirming what many female professors suspected all along. MIT's report "documented a pattern of discrimination which grew more evident as women faculty members progressed through the university's hierarchy." The University of Texas report quoted committee co-chair Janet Staiger, a professor in UT's Department of Communications as saying, "All the efforts to take affirmative measures to get people into the upper echelons of teaching positions have been unsuccessful" (Barnett, 1999).

Former Harvard President Larry Summers publicly remarked that innate differences between men and women might explain why men tend to dominate science and engineering. The furor that followed his remarks led many colleges to reexamine the standing of women in the sciences and eventually contributed to Mr. Summers's resignation.

At a 1999 roundtable discussion on equal pay, Hillary Clinton cited a report issued by MIT stating that tenured women faculty in the School of Science were discriminated against in areas such as hiring, awards, promotions, committee assignments, and the allocation of resources, such as lab space and research dollars. "The report showed that even women who supposedly break through the glass ceiling and reach the highest echelons of their professions still find themselves bumping up against some gender discrimination" (The White House Office of the Press Secretary, April 1999).

## INEQUITIES ON THE CORPORATE LADDER: THE GLASS CEILING

Inequality exists in the opportunity for advancement in professions. Many women have paid their dues—even a premium—for a chance at a top position, only to find a glass ceiling, the barrier keeping women from advancing higher *because they are women*. "There are still pervasive stereotypes that women don't want the top job, that women don't want to relocate, and that they don't want to travel," reports Paulette Gerkovich, senior director of research at Catalyst (2004). Meanwhile, men in traditionally female jobs such as teaching find themselves riding a "glass escalator" to the top of the organization.

Proof that discrimination still exists today can be found in the numerous lawsuits citing gender discrimination that cost corporate America millions. Consider the following examples:

---

*June 2002:*

A federal judge gave final approval to a $31 million settlement by ***American Express Co***. of an age and sex discrimination lawsuit. Three women who filed a complaint with the EEOC in October 1999 were later joined by 14 more in what became a class-action law suit alleging they were unfairly denied promotions and pay. The women said the financial services giant created a "glass ceiling" for female financial advisers by favoring men in training, mentoring, and promotion. *(http://www.miller-obrien.com/amex.html)*

*August 2004:*

A ***Costco*** assistant warehouse manager filed a national sex discrimination class-action suit in San Francisco which charged that ***Costco*** imposes a "glass ceiling" denying women promotions to high paying assistant and general store manager positions. ***Costco*** has no job posting or application procedure for assistant manager and general manager positions, nor any written promotion standards or criteria for these jobs.
*(https://genderclassactionagainstcostco.com)*

*May 1998:*

A sex discrimination suit filed by eight female employees of ***Merrill Lynch*** in February 1997 was settled. The plaintiff charged that they were systematically deprived of training, support staff, and other resources because of their sex. They also alleged that many women had returned from maternity leave to find their positions either eliminated or themselves demoted.
*(http://www.msmagazine.com/news/uswirestory.asp?id=3610)*

---

Successful women business leaders differ from their male counterparts in another fundamental way. Throughout their careers, they had to operate with multiple levels of pressure: the pressure of the job itself, the pioneer pressure of breaking new ground on the job, and the strain of their family obligations that made their advancement harder and that much more remarkable.

From the many studies describing gender differences in leadership styles, a number of important themes emerge. Companies trying hard to promote women into leadership report the following observations:

- Overall, women are less prepared to enter the upper ranks, based on time in the pipeline and years of experience.

- Women often have time constraints as a result of family obligations.
- Women tend to focus more on being good at what they do rather than on gaining a strong and broad circle of influence.
- Women's leadership styles often differ from men's. The consensus style of leadership observed in many women differs from those in senior management and consequently, prevents promotion.

Sometimes the challenge is in convincing others in management to promote women, work with them, or adapt to the positive elements of their different style:

- Men have less experience working with women in leadership roles and have to learn how to adjust.
- Men have more informal networks than women and are not adequately motivated to change the way these networks function.
- While many men are pleased with the more "family friendly" work environment appreciated by women, the corporate norm for rising executives still places tremendous time burdens on men and women.
- One reason women have difficulty moving up the corporate ladder is that in the United States most CEOs come from marketing, sales, finance, and engineering positions within the corporation, but women tend more towards jobs in public relations and human resources. Another reason is a serious lack of mentors for young professional women. These particular networks develop so much more naturally for men, and teach them the many informal rules that women also need to understand to get ahead.

## WHAT'S HOLDING WOMEN BACK?

Forbes' power list of women includes activists, queens, businesswomen, and Oprah. Number one on the list for the second straight year is United States Secretary of State Condoleezza Rice. Power, as defined by Forbes, requires influence in the global marketplace as well as economic and cultural clout. Forbes ranks these individuals based on global visibility and economic impact, as well as the size of the economic area over which they have influence.

While this may sound very encouraging, the percentage of high-powered women in the world remains diminutive compared with their male counterparts. "Several years into the new millennium, women make up more than half of the managerial and professional labor pool but account for just over 1 percent of all Fortune 500 chief executives." (Wellington, Kropt, & Gerkovich, 2003.)

Catalyst is a nonprofit research and advisory organization working to advance women in business that is consistently ranked by the American Institute of Philanthropy as the highest rated nonprofit in the United States focused on women's issues. Part of their research work is to track the representation of women in Fortune 500 corporate officer positions. According to their annual census, women held just 8.7 percent of Fortune 500 corporate officer positions in 1995. By 2002, the percentage had nearly doubled to 15.7 percent. While this is an increase it still represents a very small number of positions. For example,

...In 2002, although women comprise 39% of the overall financial services industry population, they comprise 79% of staff positions and 17% of line positions. These proportions are virtually unchanged from 2000.

Looking at the data another way, of the 6,002 women in the financial services industry included in the study, 72 % (4,299) hold staff positions while 28% (1,073) of women hold line positions. By comparison, of the 9,198 men in the financial services industry, 87% (8,036) hold line positions and 13% (1,162) hold staff positions.

(Catalyst, 2002, p. 8).
(http://www.catalyst.org/files/full/WCM2002.pdf)

In 2003, Catalyst surveyed Fortune 1000 CEOs and women executives at the vice presidential level and above. Asked about the challenges women face in advancing to the highest levels of corporate leadership, most everyone agreed that the lack of general management or line experience was the primary obstacle. CEOs consistently reported that when they sought successors for chairman and CEO slots, they looked for people with high level profit and loss experience. Since men still hold a large majority of these positions, they thereby dominate the long-term pool available for the next generation of business leaders. Some women do not rise to top leadership positions because they do not know these positions are available, while others may be discouraged from pursuing these roles by colleagues or superiors who don't feel that women can perform well at this level.

Women cited a number of other factors that may block their advancement, including exclusion from informal networks, stereotyping, lack of mentoring, a shortage of role models, commitment to family responsibilities, and little accountability for top management to promote diversity.

## THE MYTH OF HAVING IT ALL

Anyone who believes that women in the United States can have high-powered careers and families should consider these sobering statistics from economist Sylvia Ann Hewlett's 2002 survey:

- 49% of ultra-achieving career women (earning more than $100,000) aged 41–55 are childless.
- By contrast, the more successful a man is, the more likely he has a spouse and children. Only 19% of ultra-achieving men are childless and 17% are unmarried.

The statistics make it clear that women do not have it all. The demands of ambitious careers, the lack of balance within male-female relationships, and later life childbearing difficulties conspire against executive women who want to have children. These realties take a personal toll on women who must decide whether they will pursue an ambitious career or leave the full-time workforce to stay at home and raise their families. Either choice is a difficult one and involves giving up something important to a woman. "Companies and the economy also pay a price as industry cannot really afford to have 25 percent of the female talent pool forced out of their jobs when they have children. During a significant labor crunch in 2000, 22 percent of the women with professional degrees were not working" (Hewlett, 2002).

In order to avoid the waste of educated talent, business leaders and the federal government need to establish new policies to support working parents and assist in improved work-life balance. For professional women, it's unusual not to step off the career fast track at least once. With children to raise, elderly parents to care for, and other family demands, many women feel they have little choice but to give up their demanding careers. Companies can assist in this area by offering reduced hours, job sharing, flexible workdays, and removal of the stigma that takes place when a woman takes an extended leave and then tries to return to work.

## CONCLUSION

There can be no denying that women have made progress over the last twenty-five years. Women now sit on the Supreme Court and fight in combat as part of the war on terror. Overt sexual behavior in the workplace is less tolerated and a small percentage of women have successfully entered corporate management. Concern exists however, that the publicity around these successes leads to an illusion that issues of inequality based on gender no longer exist.

Today, blatant cases of gender discrimination are rare. They have been wiped out by laws and by increased organizational awareness that there is nothing to gain and a whole lot to lose, by keeping women out of positions of authority. That doesn't mean that gender inequity has vanished. It has just gone underground and become more subtle. Most organizations have been created by and for men and are based on the male experience. Even though women entered the workforce by the thousands in the last twenty years and added great value to their organizations, the definitions of leadership are still associated with traits more associated with men, such as toughness, aggressiveness, and decisiveness. Although many families have both parents working, most organizations still act as if women have the primary responsibility for the home and children.

The challenge society faces is that gender discrimination has existed for thousands of years. With a large number of the population sitting on the sidelines and not seeing themselves as part of either the problem or the solution, their silence allows the problem to continue. The greatest obstacle to change is that dominant groups hardly ever see the issues of the subordinate groups as theirs. Diversity is the engine that drives originality and creativeness and gender is part of that diversity. To be effective in today's global marketplace, business organizations must fully utilize their talent pool and commit to advancing all groups of employees.

## DISCUSSION QUESTIONS

1. This article states: "women tend to focus more on being good at what they do rather than on gaining a strong and broad circle of influence." If you were the manager of a talented female employee who does this, what could you do to mentor her in terms of career development?

2. If women face difficulty in climbing the corporate ladder in part due to a "serious lack of mentors for young professional women"
   a. What could the women themselves do to correct this situation?
   b. What role can organizations play in facilitating mentoring?

3. This article states that women as a group tend to have a more collaborative style of management.
   a. What are the advantages and disadvantages of this style for women in today's business world?
   b. What can happen if a woman has what is considered to be a more "masculine" management style?

## BIBLIOGRAPHY

Barnett, E. (May, 1999). Academic angst. *The Austin Chronicle*. Retrieved February 24, 2007, from http://weeklywire.com/ww/05-03-99/austin_pols_feature1.html

Bartlett, K. (1997). *Women in the legal profession: the good news and the bad*. Durham, N.C.: Duke University. Retrieved February 22, 2007, from http://gos.sbc.edu/b/bartlett.html

Bates, K. (1893, 1904, 1913). *America the beautiful*. Verses contributed by R. Fitzpatrick, the Falmouth Historical Society. Retrieved February 22, 2007, from http://www.fuzzylu.com/falmouth/bates/america.html

Committee on Maximizing the Potential of Women in Academic Science and Engineering. (2006). Beyond bias and barriers: Fulfilling the potential of women in academic science and engineering. *National Academy of Sciences, National Academy of Engineering, and Institute of Medicine*. Washington, DC: The National Academies Press.

*Costco Gender Discrimination Class Action Lawsuit*. (August 17, 2004). Retrieved February 22, 2007, from the Costco Class Web site https://genderclassactionagainstcostco. com

Catalyst. Report to women in capital markets: Benchmarking 2002. Retrieved February 23, 2007, from http://www.catalyst.org/files/full/WCM2002.pdf

*Explaining trends in the gender wage gap, a report by the council of economic advisors*. (June 26, 1998). Washington, DC. Retrieved February 23, 2007, from http://clinton4. nara.gov/ WH/EOP/CEA/html/gendergap. html

Feminist Majority Foundation. Postsecondary Science and Math Programs Face Title IX Review. *Inside Higher Education March 27, 2006. Feminist Daily News Wire, April 3, 2006.*

Retrieved February 22, 2007, from http://www.womenandpolicing.org/article.asp?id=9596

Friedan, B. (1963). *The feminine mystique.* NY: Dell Publishing.

Golden, D. (2003, Jan 15). Admissions preferences given to alumni children draw fire. (Jan. 15, 2003). *Wall Street Journal*. Retrieved February 22, 2007, from http://online.wsj. com/public/resources/documents/golden3. htm

Henslin, J. *Essentials of sociology*, 5th ed. (2005). NY: Allyn and Bacon.

Hewlett, S. *Executive women and the myth of having it all*. (April, 2002). Boston: Harvard Business Review. 80, p. 1.

Kinsley, M. (2003). *How affirmative action helped George W.* quoted in Discriminations posted by John Rosenberg, Jan 20, 2003. *Kinsley's Invidious Ubiquitous Non Sequitur*. Retrieved February 22, 2007, from http://www.discriminations.us/2003/01/kinsleys _invidious_ubiquitous.html

Merrill Lynch settles sex discrimination suit. (May 5, 1998). *Feminist organization news*. Retrieved February 22, 2007, from http://www.msmagazine.com/news/uswirestory. asp?id=3610

Miller-Obrien. (2002). *Judge approves $31 million payment to women at Amex*. Retrieved February 22, 2007, from http://www. miller-obrien.com/amex.html

Minas, A. (1993). *Gender basics: feminist perspectives on women and men*. Belmont, CA: Wadsworth.

*Remarks of the president and first lady at roundtable on equal pay* (April 7, 1999). The White House Office of the Press Secretary. Retrieved February 22, 2007, from http:// clinton3.nara.gov/WH/EOP/First_lady/html/ generalspeeches/1999

U.S. Census Bureau. (2005). Income, poverty, and health insurance coverage in the United States 2005. U.S. Government Printing Office, Washington, DC. Retrieved Dec. 20, 2006, from http://www.census.gov/prod/2006pubs/p60-231.pdf.

Wellington, S., Kropt, M., & Gerkovich, P. (2003). What's holding women back?

*Harvard Business Review.* 81 p. 6, 19. Boston: Harvard Business School Publishing Corporation.

Wood, R., Corcoran, M., & Courant, P. (July 1993). *Pay differences among the highly paid: the male-female earnings gap in lawyers' salaries. Journal of Labor Economics, 11,* No. 3, pp. 417–441.

---

### Diversity on the Web

Because of the issues facing women in organizations today, many women are choosing to start their own businesses. In 1972 women owned less than 5 percent of all U.S. businesses. In 2004, nearly half of all U.S. businesses were at least 50 percent owned by women.

Visit the following Web site of the Center for Women in Enterprise, http://www.cweonline.org. Why was this organization founded, and what do they do that relates to some of the issues explained in this article?

# The Power of Talk: Who Gets Heard and Why

## Deborah Tannen

The head of a large division of a multinational corporation was running a meeting devoted to performance assessment. Each senior manager stood up, reviewed the individuals in his group, and evaluated them for promotion. Although there were women in every group, not one of them made the cut. One after another, each manager declared, in effect, that every woman in his group did not have the self-confidence needed to be promoted. The division head began to doubt his ears. How could it be that all the talented women in the division suffered from a lack of self-confidence?

In all likelihood, they didn't. Consider the many women who have left large corporations to start their own businesses, obviously exhibiting enough confidence to succeed on their own. Judgments about confidence can be inferred only from the way people present themselves, and much of that presentation is in the form of talk. The CEO of a major corporation told me that he often has to make decisions in 5 minutes about matters on which others may have worked 5 months. He said he uses this rule: If the person making the proposal seems confident, the CEO approves it. If not, he says no. This might seem like a reasonable approach, but my field of research, sociolinguistics, suggests otherwise. The CEO obviously thinks he knows what a confident person sounds like. But his judgment, which may be dead right for some people, may be dead wrong for others.

Communication isn't as simple as saying what you mean. How you say what you mean is crucial, and differs from one person to the next, because using language is learned social behavior: How we talk and listen are deeply influenced by cultural experience. Although we might think that our ways of saying what we mean are natural, we can run into trouble if we interpret and evaluate others as if they necessarily felt the same way we'd feel if we spoke the way they did.

Since 1974, I have been researching the influence of linguistic style on conversations and human relationships. In the past 4 years, I have extended that research to the workplace, where I have observed how ways of speaking learned in childhood affect judgments of competence and confidence, as well as who gets heard, who gets credit, and what gets done.

The division head who was dumbfounded to hear that all the talented women in his organization lacked confidence was probably right to be skeptical. The senior managers were judging the women in their groups by their own linguistic norms, but women—like people who have grown up in a different culture—have often learned different styles of speaking than men, which can make them seem less competent and self-assured than they are.

## WHAT'S LINGUISTIC STYLE?

Everything that is said must be said in a certain way—in a certain tone of voice, at a certain rate of speed, and with a certain degree of loudness. Whereas often we consciously consider what to say before speaking, we rarely think about how to say it, unless the situation is obviously loaded—for example, a job interview or a tricky performance review. Linguistic style refers to a person's characteristic speaking pattern. It includes such features as directness or indirectness, pacing and pausing, word choice, and the use of such elements as jokes, figures of speech, stories, questions, and apologies. In other words, linguistic style is a set of culturally learned signals by which we not only communicate what we mean but also interpret others' meaning and evaluate one another as people.

Consider turn taking, one element of linguistic style. Conversation is an enterprise in which people take turns: One person speaks, then the other responds. However, this apparently simple exchange requires a subtle negotiation of signals so that you know when the other person is finished and it's your turn to begin. Cultural factors such as country or region of origin and ethnic background influence how long a pause seems natural. When Bob, who is from Detroit, has a conversation with his colleague Joe, from New York City, it's hard for him to get a word in edgewise because he expects a slightly longer pause between turns than Joe does. A pause of that length never comes because, before it has a chance to, Joe senses an uncomfortable silence, which he fills with more talk of his own.

Both men fail to realize that differences in conversational style are getting in their way. Bob thinks that Joe is pushy and uninterested in what he has to say, and Joe thinks that Bob doesn't have much to contribute. Similarly, when Sally relocated from Texas to Washington, D.C., she kept searching for the right time to break in during staff meetings—and never found it. Although in Texas she was considered outgoing and confident, in Washington she was perceived as shy and retiring. Her boss even suggested she take an assertiveness training course. Thus, slight differences in conversational style—in these cases, a few seconds of pause—can have a surprising impact on who gets heard and on the judgments, including psychological ones, that are made about people and their abilities.

Every utterance functions on two levels. We're all familiar with the first one: Language communicates ideas. The second level is mostly invisible to us, but it plays a powerful role in communication. As a form of social behavior, language also negotiates relationships. Through ways of speaking, we signal—and create—the relative status of speakers and their level of rapport. If you say, "Sit down!" you are signaling that you have higher status than the person you are addressing, that you are so close to each other that you can drop all pleasantries, or that you are angry. If you say, "I would be honored if you would sit down," you are signaling great respect—or great sarcasm, depending on your tone of voice, the situation, and what you both know about how close you really are. If you say, "Your must be so tired—why don't you sit down," you are communicating either closeness and concerns or condescension. Each of these ways of saying the same thing—telling someone to sit down—can have a vastly different meaning.

In every community known to linguists, the patterns that constitute linguistic style are relatively different for men and women. What's "natural" for most men speaking a given language is, in some cases, different from what's "natural" for most women. That is because we learn ways of speaking as children growing up, especially from peers, and children tend to play with other children of the same sex. The research of sociologists, anthropologists, and psychologists observing American children at play has shown that, although both girls and boys find ways of creating rapport and negotiating status, girls tend to learn conversational rituals that focus on the rapport dimension of relationships whereas boys tend to learn rituals that focus on the status dimension.

Girls tend to play with a single best friend or in small groups, and they spend a lot of time talking. They use language to negotiate how close they are; for example, the girl you tell your secrets to becomes your best friend. Girls learn to downplay ways in which one is better than the others and to emphasize ways in which they are all the same. From childhood, most girls learn that sounding too sure of themselves will make them unpopular with their peers—although nobody really takes such modesty literally. A group of girls will ostracize a girls who calls attention to her own superiority and criticize her by saying, "She thinks she's something"; and a girl who tells others what to do is called "bossy." Thus, girls learn to talk in ways that balance their own needs with those of others—to save face for one another in the broadest sense of the term.

Boys tend to play very differently. They usually play in larger groups in which more boys can be included, but not everyone is treated as an equal. Boys with high status in their group are expected to emphasize rather than downplay their status, and usually one or several boys will be seen as the leader or leaders. Boys generally don't accuse one another of being bossy, because the leader is expected to tell lower-status boys what to do. Boys learn to use language to negotiate their status in the group by displaying their abilities and knowledge, and by challenging others and resisting challenges. Giving orders is one way of getting and keeping the high-status role. Another is taking center stage by telling stories or jokes.

This is not to say that all boys and girls grow up this way or feel comfortable in these groups or are equally successful at negotiating within these norms. But, for the most part, these childhood play groups are where boys and girls learn their conversational styles. In this sense, they grow up in different worlds. The result is that women and men tend to have different habitual ways of saying what they mean, and conversations between them can be like cross-cultural communication: You can't assume that the other person means what you would mean if you said the same thing in the same way.

My research in companies across the United States shows that the lessons learned in childhood carry over into the workplace. Consider the following example: A focus group was organized at a major multinational company to evaluate a recently implemented flextime policy. The participants sat in a circle and discussed the new system. The group concluded that it was excellent, but they also agreed on ways to improve it. The meeting went well and was deemed a success by all, according to my own observations and everyone's comments to me. But the next day, I was in for a surprise.

I had left the meeting with the impression that Phil had been responsible for most of the suggestions adopted by the group. But as I typed up my notes, I noticed that Cheryl had made almost all those suggestions. I had thought that the key ideas came from Phil because he had picked up Cheryl's points and supported them, speaking at greater length in doing so than she had in raising them.

It would be easy to regard Phil as having stolen Cheryl's ideas and her thunder. But that would be inaccurate. Phil never claimed Cheryl's ideas as his own. Cheryl herself told me later that she left the meeting confident that she had contributed significantly and that she appreciated Phil's support. She volunteered, with a laugh, "It was not one of those times when a woman says something and it's ignored, then a man says it and it's picked up." In other words, Cheryl and Phil worked well as a team, the group fulfilled its charge, and the company got what it needed. So what was the problem?

I went back and asked all the participants who they thought had been the most influential group member, the one most responsible for the ideas that had been adopted. The pattern of answers was revealing. The two other women in the group named Cheryl. Two of the three men named Phil. Of the men, only Phil named Cheryl. In other words, in this instance, the women evaluated the contribution of another woman more accurately than the men did.

Meetings like this take place daily in companies around the country. Unless managers are unusually good at listening closely to how people say what they mean, the talents of someone like Cheryl may well be undervalued and underutilized.

## ONE UP, ONE DOWN

Individual speakers vary in how sensitive they are to the social dynamics of language — in other words, to the subtle nuances of what others say to them. Men tend to be sensitive to the power dynamics of interaction, speaking in ways that position themselves as one up and resisting being put in a one-down position by others. Women tend to react more strongly to the rapport dynamic, speaking in ways that save face for others and buffering statements that could be seen as putting others in a one-down position: These linguistic patterns are pervasive; you can hear them in hundreds of exchanges in the workplace every day. And, as in the case of Cheryl and Phil, they affect who gets heard and who gets credit.

## GETTING CREDIT

Even so small a linguistic strategy as the choice of pronoun can affect who gets credit. In my research in the workplace, I heard men say "I" in situations where I heard women say "we." For example, one publishing company executive said, "I'm hiring a new manager. I'm going to put him in charge of my marketing division, as if he owned the corporation." In stark contrast, I recorded women saying "we" when referring to work they alone had done. One woman explained that it would sound too self-promoting to claim credit in an obvious way by saying, "I did this." Yet she expected—sometimes vainly—that others would know it was her work and would give her the credit she did not claim for herself.

Managers might leap to the conclusion that women who do not take credit for what they've done should be taught to do so. But that solution is problematic because we associate ways of speaking with moral qualities: The way we speak is who we are and who we want to be.

Veronica, a senior researcher in a high-tech company, had an observant boss. He noticed that many of the ideas coming out of the group were hers but that often someone else trumpeted them around the office and got credit for them. He advised her to "own" her ideas and make sure she got the credit. But Veronica found she simply didn't enjoy her work if she had to approach it as what seemed to her an unattractive and unappealing "grabbing game." It was her dislike of such behavior that had led her to avoid it in the first place. Whatever the motivation, women are less likely than men to have learned to blow their own horn. And they are more likely than men to believe that if they do so, they won't be liked.

Many have argued that the growing trend of assigning work to teams may be especially congenial to women, but it may also create complications for performance evaluation. When ideas are generated and work is accomplished in the privacy of the team, the outcome of the team's effort may become associated with the person most vocal about reporting results. There are many women and men—but probably relatively more women—who are reluctant to put themselves forward in this way and who consequently risk not getting credit for their contributions.

## CONFIDENCE AND BOASTING

The CEO who based his decisions on the confidence level of speakers was articulating a value that is widely shared in U.S. businesses: One way to judge confidence is by an individual's behavior, especially verbal behavior. Here again, many women are at a disadvantage.

Studies show that women are more likely to downplay their certainty, and men are more likely to minimize their doubts. Psychologist Laurie Heatherington and her colleagues devised an ingenious experiment, which they reported in the journal *Sex Roles* (Volume 29, 1993). They asked hundreds of incoming college students to predict what grades they would get in their first year. Some subjects were asked to make their predictions privately by writing them down and placing them in an envelope; others were asked to make their predictions publicly, in the presence of a researcher. The results showed that more women than men predicted lower grades for themselves if they made their predictions publicly. If they made their predictions privately, the predictions were the same as those of the men—and the same as their actual grades. This study provides evidence that what comes across as lack of confidence—predicting lower grades for oneself—may reflect not one's actual level of confidence but the desire not to seem boastful.

These habits with regard to appearing humble or confident result from the socialization of boys and girls by their peers in childhood play. As adults, both women and men find these behaviors reinforced by the positive responses they get from friends and relatives who share the same norms. But the norms of behavior in the U.S. business world are based on the style of interaction that is more common among men—at least, among American men.

## ASKING QUESTIONS

Although asking the right questions is one of the hallmarks of a good manager, how and when questions are asked can send unintended signals about competence and power. In a group, if only one person asks questions, he or she risks being seen as the only ignorant one. Furthermore, we judge others not only by how they speak but also by how they are spoken to. The person who asks questions may end up being lectured to and looking like a novice under a schoolmaster's tutelage. The way boys are socialized makes them more likely to be aware of the underlying power dynamic by which a question asker can be seen in a one-down position.

One practicing physician learned the hard way that any exchange of information can become the basis for judgments—or misjudgments—about competence. During her training, she received a negative evaluation that she thought was unfair, so she asked her supervising physician for an explanation. He said that she knew less than her peers. Amazed at his answer, she asked how he had reached that conclusion. He said, "You ask more questions."

Along with cultural influences and individual personality, gender seems to play a role in whether and when people ask questions. For example, of all the observations I've made in lectures and books, the one that sparks the most enthusiastic flash of recognition is that men are less likely than women to stop and ask for directions when they are lost. I explain that men often resist asking for directions because they are aware that it puts them in a one-down position and because they value the independence that comes with finding their way by themselves. Asking for directions while driving is only one instance—along with many others that researchers have examined—in which men seem less likely than women to ask questions. I believe this is because they are more attuned than women to the potential face-losing aspect of asking questions. And men who believe that asking questions might reflect negatively on them may, in turn, be likely to form a negative opinion of others who ask questions in situations where they would not.

## CONVERSATIONAL RITUALS

Conversation is fundamentally ritual in the sense that we speak in ways our culture has conventionalized and expect certain types of responses. Take greetings, for example. I have heard visitors to the United States complain that Americans are hypocritical because they ask how you are but aren't interested in the answer. To Americans, "How are you?" is obviously a ritualized way to start a conversation rather than a literal request for information. In other parts of the world, including the Philippines, people ask each other "Where are you going?" when they meet. The question seems intrusive to Americans, who do not realize that it, too, is a ritual query to which the only expected reply is a vague "Over there."

It's easy and entertaining to observe different rituals in foreign countries. But we don't expect differences, and are far less likely to recognize the ritualized nature of our conversations, when we are with our compatriots at work. Our differing rituals can be even more problematic when we think we're all speaking the same language.

## APOLOGIES

Consider the simple phrase *I'm sorry*.

> CATHERINE:  How did that big presentation go?
>
> BOB:  Oh, not very well. I got a lot of flak from the VP for finance, and I didn't have the numbers at my fingertips.
>
> CATHERINE:  Oh, I'm sorry. I know how hard you worked on that.

In this case, *I'm sorry* probably means "I'm sorry that happened," not "I apologize," unless it was Catherine's responsibility to supply Bob with the numbers for the presentation. Women tend to say *I'm sorry* more frequently than men, and often they intend it in this way—as a ritualized means of expressing concern. It's one of many learned elements of conversational style that girls often use to establish rapport. Ritual apologies—like other conversational rituals—work well when both parties share the same assumptions about their use. But people who utter frequent ritual apologies may end up appearing weaker, less confident, and literally more blameworthy than people who don't.

Apologies tend to be regarded differently by men, who are more likely to focus on the status implications of exchanges. Many men avoid apologies because they see them as putting the speaker in a one-down position. I observed with some amazement an encounter among several lawyers engaged in a negotiation on a speakerphone. At one point, the lawyer in whose office I was sitting accidentally elbowed the telephone and cut off the call. When his secretary got the parties back on again, I expected him to say what I would have said: "Sorry about that. I knocked the phone with my elbow." Instead, he said, "Hey, what happened? One minute you were there; the next minute you were gone." This lawyer seemed to have an automatic impulse not to admit fault if he didn't have to. For me, it was one of those pivotal moments when you realize that the world you live in is not the one everyone lives in and that the way you assume is the way to talk is really only one of many.

Those who caution managers not to undermine their authority by apologizing are approaching interaction from the perspective of the power dynamic. In many cases, this strategy is effective. On the other hand, when I asked people what frustrated them in their jobs, one frequently voiced complaint was working with or for someone who refuses to apologize or admit fault. In other words, accepting responsibility for errors and admitting mistakes may be an equally effective or superior strategy in some settings.

## FEEDBACK

Styles of giving feedback contain a ritual element that often is the cause for misunderstanding. Consider the following exchange: A manager had to tell her marketing director to rewrite a report. She began this potentially awkward task by citing the report's strengths and weaknesses and then moved to the main point: the weaknesses that needed to be remedied. The marketing director seemed to understand and accept his supervisor's comments, but his revision contained only minor changes and failed to address the major weaknesses. When the manager told him of her dissatisfaction, he accused her of misleading him: "You told me it was fine."

The impasse resulted from different linguistic styles. To the manager, it was natural to buffer the criticism by beginning with praise. Telling her subordinate that his report is inadequate and has to be rewritten puts him in a one-down position. Praising him for the parts that are good is a ritualized way of saving face for him. But the marketing director did not share his supervisor's assumption about how feedback should be given. Instead, he assumed that what she mentioned first was the main point and that what she brought up later was an afterthought.

Those who expect feedback to come in the way the manager presented it would appreciate her tact and would regard a more blunt approach as unnecessarily callous. But those who share the marketing director's assumptions would regard the blunt approach as honest and no-nonsense, and the manager's as obfuscating. Because each one's assumptions seemed self-evident, each blamed the other: The manager thought the marketing director was not listening, and he thought she had not communicated clearly or had changed her mind. This is significant because it illustrates that incidents labeled vaguely as "poor communication" may be the result of different linguistic styles.

## COMPLIMENTS

Exchanging compliments is a common ritual, especially among women. A mismatch in expectations about this ritual left Susan, a manager in the human resources field, in a one-down position. She and her colleague Bill had both given presentations at a national conference. On the airplane home, Susan told Bill, "That was a great talk!" "Thank you," he said. Then she asked, "What did you think of mine?" He responded with a lengthy and detailed critique as she listened uncomfortably. An unpleasant feeling of having been put down came over her. Somehow she had been positioned as the novice in need of his expert advice. Even worse, she had only herself to blame, since she had, after all, asked Bill what he thought of her talk.

But had Susan asked for the response she received? When she asked Bill what he thought about her talk, she expected to hear not a critique but a compliment. In fact, her question had been an attempt to repair a ritual gone awry. Susan's initial compliment to Bill was the kind of automatic recognition she felt was more or less required after a colleague gives a presentation, and she expected Bill to respond with a matching compliment. She was just talking automatically, but he either sincerely misunderstood the ritual or simply took the opportunity to bask in the one-up position of critic. Whatever his motivation, it was Susan's attempt to spark an exchange of compliments that gave him the opening.

Although this exchange could have occurred between two men, it does not seem coincidental that it happened between a man and a woman. Linguist Janet Holmes discovered that women pay more compliments than men (*Anthropological Linguistics,* Volume 28, 1986). And, as I have observed, fewer men are likely to ask, "What did you think of my talk?" precisely because the question might invite an unwanted critique.

In the social structure of the peer groups in which they grow up, boys are indeed looking for opportunities to put others down and take the one-up position for themselves. In contrast, one of the rituals girls learn is taking the one-down position but assuming that the other person will recognize the ritual nature of self-denigration and pull them back up.

The exchange between Susan and Bill also suggests how women's and men's characteristic styles may put women at a disadvantage in the workplace. If one person is trying to minimize status differences, maintain an appearance that everyone is equal, and save face for the others while another person is trying to maintain the one-up position and avoid being positioned as one down, the person seeking the one-up position is likely to get it. At the same time, the person who has not been expending any effort to avoid the one-down position is likely to end up in it. Because women are more likely to take (or accept) the role of advice seeker, men are more inclined to interpret a ritual question from a woman as a request for advice.

## RITUAL OPPOSITION

Apologizing, mitigating criticism with praise, and exchanging compliments are rituals common among women that men often take literally. A ritual common among men that women often take literally is ritual opposition.

A woman in communications told me she watched with distaste and distress as her office mate argued heatedly with another colleague about whose division should suffer budget cuts. She was even more surprised, however, that a short time later they were as friendly as ever. "How can you pretend that fight never happened?" she asked. "Who's pretending it never happened?" he responded, as puzzled by her question as she had been by his behavior. "It happened," he said, "and it's over." What she took as literal fighting to him was a routine part of daily negotiation: a ritual fight.

Many Americans expect the discussion of ideas to be a ritual fight—that is, an exploration through verbal opposition. They present their own ideas in the most certain and absolute form they can and wait to see if they are challenged. Being forced to defend an idea provides an opportunity to test it. In the same spirit, they may play devil's advocate in challenging their colleagues' ideas—trying to poke holes and find weaknesses—as a way of helping them explore and test their ideas.

This style can work well if everyone shares it, but those unaccustomed to it are likely to miss its ritual nature. They may give up an idea that is challenged, taking the objections as an indication that the idea was a poor one. Worse, they may take the opposition as a personal attack and may find it impossible to do their best in a contentious environment. People unaccustomed to this style may hedge when stating their ideas in order to fend off potential attacks. Ironically, this posture makes their arguments appear weak and is more likely to invite attack from pugnacious colleagues than to fend it off.

Ritual opposition can even play a role in who gets hired. Some consulting firms that recruit graduates from the top business schools use a confrontational interviewing technique. They challenge the candidate to "crack a case" in real time. A partner at one firm told me, "Women tend to do less well in this kind of interaction, and it certainly affects who gets hired. But, in fact, many women who don't 'test well' turn out to be good consultants. They're often smarter than some of the men who looked like analytic powerhouses under pressure."

The level of verbal opposition varies from one company's culture to the next, but I saw instances of it in all the organizations I studied. Anyone who is uncomfortable with this linguistic style—and that includes some men as well as many women—risks appearing insecure about his or her ideas.

## NEGOTIATING AUTHORITY

In organizations, formal authority comes from the position one holds, but actual authority has to be negotiated day to day. The effectiveness of individual managers depends in part on their skill in negotiating authority and on whether others reinforce or undercut their efforts. The way linguistic style reflects status plays a subtle role in placing individuals within a hierarchy.

## MANAGING UP AND DOWN

In all the companies I researched, I heard from women who knew they were doing a superior job and knew that their coworkers (and sometimes their immediate bosses) knew it as well, but believed that the higher-ups did not. They frequently told me that something outside themselves was holding them back and found it frustrating because they thought that all that should be necessary for success was to do a great job, that superior performance should be recognized and rewarded. In contrast, men often told me that if women weren't promoted it was because they simply weren't up to snuff. Looking around, however, I saw evidence that men more often than women behaved in ways likely to get them recognized by those with the power to determine their advancement.

In all the companies I visited, I observed what happened at lunchtime. I saw young men who regularly ate lunch with their boss, and senior men who ate with the big boss. I noticed far fewer women who sought out the highest-level person they could eat with. But one is more likely to get recognition for work done if one talks about it to those higher up, and it is easier to do so if the lines of communication are already open. Furthermore, given the opportunity for a conversation with superiors, men and women are likely to have different ways of talking about their accomplishments because of the different ways in which they were socialized as children. Boys are rewarded by their peers if they talk up their achievements, whereas girls are rewarded if they play theirs down. Linguistic styles common among men may tend to give them some advantages when it comes to managing up.

All speakers are aware of the status of the person they are talking to and adjust accordingly. Everyone speaks differently when talking to a boss than when talking to a subordinate. But, surprisingly, the ways in which they adjust their talk may be different and thus may project different images of themselves.

Communications researchers Karen Tracy and Eric Eisenberg studied how relative status affects the way people give criticism. They devised a business letter that contained some errors and asked 13 male and 11 female college students to role-play delivering criticism under two scenarios. In the first, the speaker was a boss talking to a subordinate; in the second, the speaker was a subordinate talking to his or her boss. The researchers measured how hard the speakers tried to avoid hurting the feelings of the person they were criticizing.

One might expect people to be more careful about how they deliver criticism when they are in a subordinate position. Tracy and Eisenberg found that hypothesis to be true for the men in their study but not for the women. As they reported in *Research on Language and Social Interaction* (Volume 24, 1990/1991), the women showed more concern about the other person's feelings when they were playing the role of superior.

In other words, the women were more careful to save face for the other person when they were managing down than when they were managing up. This pattern recalls the way girls are socialized: Those who are in some way superior are expected to downplay rather than flaunt their superiority.

In my own recordings of workplace communication, I observed women talking in similar ways. For example, when a manager had to correct a mistake made by her secretary, she did so by acknowledging that there were mitigating circumstances. She said laughing, "You know, it's hard to do things around here, isn't it, with all these people coming in!" The manager was saving face for her subordinate, just like the female students role-playing in the Tracy and Eisenberg study.

Is this an effective way to communicate? One must ask, effective for what? The manager in question established a positive environment in her group, and the work was done effectively. On the other hand, numerous women in many different fields told me that their bosses say they don't project the proper authority.

## INDIRECTNESS

Another linguistic signal that varies with power and status is indirectness—the tendency to say what we mean without spelling it out in so many words. Despite the widespread belief in the United States that it's always best to say exactly what we mean, indirectness is a fundamental and pervasive element in human communication. It also is one of the elements that vary most from one culture to another, and it can cause enormous misunderstanding when speakers have different habits and expectations about how it is used. It's often said that American women are more indirect than American men, but in fact everyone tends to be indirect in some situations and in different ways. Allowing for cultural, ethnic, regional, and individual differences, women are especially likely to be indirect when it comes to telling others what to do, which is not surprising, considering girls' readiness to brand other girls as bossy. On the other hand, men are especially likely to be indirect when it comes to admitting fault or weakness, which also is not surprising, considering boys' readiness to push around boys who assume the one-down position.

At first glance, it would seem that only the powerful can get away with bald commands such as "Have that report on my desk by noon." But power in an organization also can lead to requests so indirect that they don't sound like requests at all. A boss who says, "Do we have the sales data by product line for each region?" would be surprised and frustrated if a subordinate responded, "We probably do" rather than "I'll get it for you." Examples such as these notwithstanding, many researchers have claimed that those in subordinate positions are more likely to speak indirectly, and that is surely accurate in some situations. For example, linguist Charlotte Linde, in a study published in *Language in Society* (Volume 17, 1988), examined the black-box conversations that took place between pilots and copilots before airplane crashes. In one particularly tragic instance, an Air Florida plane crashed into the Potomac River immediately after attempting take-off from National Airport in Washington, D.C., killing all but 5 of the 74 people on board. The pilot, it turned out, had little experience flying in icy weather. The copilot had a bit more, and it became heartbreakingly clear on analysis that he had tried to warn the pilot but had done so indirectly. Alerted by Linde's observation, I examined the transcript of the conversations and found evidence of her hypothesis. The copilot repeatedly called attention to the bad weather and to ice buildup on other planes:

> COPILOT: Look how the ice is just hanging on his, ah, back there, see that? See all those icicles on the back there and everything?
>
> PILOT: Yeah.
>
> [The copilot also expressed concern about the long waiting time since deicing.]
>
> COPILOT: Boy, this is a, this is a losing battle here on trying to decide those things; it [gives] you a false feeling of security, that's all that does. [Just before they took off, the copilot expressed another concern— about abnormal instrument readings—but again he didn't press the matter when it wasn't picked up by the pilot.]
>
> COPILOT: That don't seem right, does it? [3-second pause]. Ah, that's not right. Well—
>
> PILOT: Yes it is, there's 80.
>
> COPILOT: Naw, I don't think that's right. [7-second pause] Ah, maybe it is.

Shortly thereafter, the plane took off, with tragic results. In other instances as well as this one, Linde observed that copilots, who are second in command, are more likely to express themselves indirectly or otherwise mitigate, or soften, their communication when they are suggesting courses of action to the pilot. In an effort to avert similar disasters, some airlines now offer training for copilots to express themselves in more assertive ways.

This solution seems self-evidently appropriate to most Americans. But when I assigned Linde's article in a graduate seminar I taught, a Japanese student pointed out that it would be just as effective to train pilots to pick up on hints. This approach reflects assumptions about communication that typify Japanese culture, which places great value on the ability of people to understand one another without putting everything into words. Either directness or indirectness can be a successful means of communication as long as the linguistic style is understood by the participants.

In the world of work, however, there is more at stake than whether the communication is understood. People in powerful positions are likely to reward styles similar to their own, because we all tend to take as self-evident the logic of our own styles. Accordingly, there is evidence that in the U.S. workplace, where instructions from a superior are expected to be voiced in a relatively direct manner, those who tend to be indirect when telling subordinates what to do may be perceived as lacking in confidence.

Consider the case of the manager at a national magazine who was responsible for giving assignments to reporters. She tended to phrase her assignments as questions. For example, she asked, "How would you like to do the X project with Y?" or said, "I was thinking of putting you on the X project. Is that okay?" This worked extremely well with her staff; they liked working for her, and the work got done in an efficient and orderly manner. But when she had her midyear evaluation with her own boss, he criticized her for not assuming the proper demeanor with her staff.

In any work environment, the higher ranking person has the power to enforce his or her view of appropriate demeanor, created in part by linguistic style. In most U.S. contexts, that view is likely to assume that the person in authority has the right to be relatively direct rather than to mitigate orders. There also are cases, however, in which the higher ranking person assumes a more indirect style. The owner of a retail operation told her subordinate, a store manager, to do something. He said he would do it, but a week later he still hadn't. They were able to trace the difficulty to the following conversation: She had said, "The bookkeeper needs help with the billing. How would you feel about helping her out?" He had said, "Fine." This conversation had seemed to be clear and flawless at the time, but it turned out that they had interpreted this simple exchange in very different ways. She thought he meant, "Fine, I'll help the bookkeeper out." He thought he meant, "Fine, I'll think about how I would feel about helping the bookkeeper out." He did think about it and came to the conclusion that he had more important things to do and couldn't spare the time.

To the owner, "How would you feel about helping the bookkeeper out?" was an obviously appropriate way to give the order "Help the bookkeeper out with the billing." Those who expect orders to be given as bold imperatives may find such locutions annoying or even misleading. But those for whom this style is natural do not think they are being indirect. They believe they are being clear in a polite or respectful way.

What is atypical in this example is that the person with the more indirect style was the boss, so the store manager was motivated to adapt to her style. She still gives orders the same way, but the store manager now understands how she means what she says. It's more common in U.S. business contexts for the highest-ranking people to take a more direct style, with the result that many women in authority risk being judged by their superiors as lacking the appropriate demeanor—and, consequently, lacking confidence.

## WHAT TO DO?

I am often asked, what is the best way to give criticism or what is the best way to give orders? In other words, what is the best way to communicate? The answer is that there is no one best way. The results of a given way of speaking will vary depending on the situation, the culture of the company, the relative rank of speakers, their linguistic styles, and how those styles interact with one another. Because of all those influences, any way of speaking could be perfect for communicating with one person in one situation and disastrous with someone else in another. The critical skill for managers is to become aware of the workings and power of linguistic style, to make sure that people with something valuable to contribute get heard.

It may seem, for example, that running a meeting in an unstructured way gives equal opportunity to all. But awareness of the differences in conversational style makes it easy to see the potential for unequal access. Those who are comfortable speaking up in groups, who need little or no silence before raising their hands, or who speak out easily without waiting to be recognized are far more likely to get heard at meetings. Those who refrain from talking until it's clear that the previous speaker is finished, who wait to be recognized, and who are inclined to link their comments to those of others will do fine at a meeting where everyone else is following the same rules but will have a hard time getting heard in a meeting with people whose styles are more like the first pattern. Given the socialization typical of boys and girls, men are more likely to have learned the first style and women the second, making meetings more congenial for men than for women. It's common to observe women who participate actively in one-on-one discussions or in all-female groups but who are seldom heard in meetings with a large proportion of men. On the other hand, there are women who share the style more common among men, and they run a different risk—of being seen as too aggressive.

A manager aware of those dynamics might devise any number of ways of ensuring that everyone's ideas are heard and credited. Although no single solution will fit all contexts, managers who understand the dynamics of linguistic style can develop more adaptive and flexible approaches to running or participating in meetings, mentoring or advancing the careers of others, evaluating performance, and so on. Talk is the lifeblood of managerial work, and understanding that different people have different ways of saying what they mean will make it possible to take advantage of the talents of people with a broad range of linguistic styles. As the workplace becomes more culturally diverse and business becomes more global, managers will need to become even better at reading interactions and more flexible in adjusting their own styles to the people with whom they interact.

## DISCUSSION QUESTIONS

1. What evidence have you seen to support or refute Tannen's article in either students' behaviors in this class or at work?

2. What is the relationship between American corporate culture and the idea that women's learned conversation styles work against them in the workplace while men's conversation styles are an advantage?

3. Why does merely adding women to a team not necessarily result in women's points of views being equally represented in a discussion?

4. What is the relationship between conversational styles and sexual harassment in the workplace?

# Is This Sexual Harassment?

## Carol P. Harvey
### *Assumption College*

## INSTRUCTIONS

Given the legal guidelines in the following Points of Law box, which of the following incidents are examples of sexual harassment? Explain your reasons for your answers.

1. While teaching Gary how to run the new spreadsheet program on the computer, Lois, his supervisor, puts her hand on his shoulder.

2. Julie, the new secretary to the vice president of manufacturing, frequently has to go out into the plant as part of her job. Several of the machinists have been whistling at her and shouting off-color remarks as she passes through the shop. One of the other women in the company found Julie crying in the ladies' room after such an incident.

3. Paul and Cynthia, two sales reps, are both married. However, it is well known that they are dating each other outside of the office.

4. Jeanne's boss, Tom, frequently asks her out for drinks after work. She goes because both are single and she enjoys his company. On one of these occasions, he asks her out to dinner for the following Saturday evening.

5. Steve's boss, Cathy, frequently makes suggestive comments to him and has even suggested that they meet outside of the office. Although at first he ignored these

remarks, recently he made it clear to her that he had a steady girlfriend and was not available. When she gave him his performance appraisal, much to his surprise, she cited him for not being a team player.

6. Jackie received a call at work that her father died suddenly. When she went to tell her boss that she had to leave, she burst into tears. He put his arms around her and let her cry on his shoulder.

7. Marge's coworker, Jerry, frequently tells her that what she is wearing is very attractive.

8. While being hired as a secretary, Amanda is told that she may occasionally be expected to accompany managers on important overnight business trips to handle the clerical duties at these meetings.

9. Joe, an elderly maintenance man, often makes suggestive comments to the young females in the office. His behavior has been reported to his supervisor several times, but it is dismissed as, "Don't be so sensitive, old Joe doesn't mean any harm."

10. Jennifer frequently wears revealing blouses to the office. Several times she has caught male employees staring at her.

 ## Points of Law

The Equal Employment Opportunity Commission's Guidelines defines sexual harassment as . . . Unwelcome sexual advances, requests for sexual favors, and other physical and verbal contact of a sexual nature when it affects the terms of employment under one or more of the following conditions: such an activity is a condition for employment: such an activity is a condition of employment consequences such as promotion, dismissal, or salary increases; such an activity creates a hostile working environment.

# The Negative Consequences of Male Privilege

## Steven Farough
### *Assumption College*

This piece argues that despite the privileges men receive from dominant masculinity, it is in their interest to work against it. As an entryway into this seemingly audacious claim, consider the following statements:

- "Do you want to fight?"
- "You throw like a girl!"
- "What are you, a fag?"
- "Be a *real* man."
- "Men are just more competitive and aggressive than women."

How often have we all heard such declarations? How often have we seen men use these challenges and declarations to other men and women? When men are confronted by such statements, they realize that their *manhood* is on the line—that if they back down they will be seen as weak or feminine. Although this is only one part of masculinity and need not be the way masculinity is practiced, such comments are representative of a dominant form of masculinity in the United States that is defined as being tough, domineering, in control, and not feminine or gay (Connell, 1995). We are all familiar with this pervasive type of masculinity. We see it performed in the mass media and in our everyday lives. We might be scared by it. We might enjoy it, but we are surely aware of its centrality in our lives. However, what we are perhaps less familiar with is the proposition that men would greatly benefit from rejecting this dominant form of masculinity.

## DOMINANT MASCULINITY

The previous statements regarding the dominant culture of masculinity are by no means exhaustive, nor do they reflect the varieties of masculinities in the United States, other nations, or across history. The word "dominant" is intended to suggest that although there are a variety of masculinities in every culture, some are more pervasive and powerful than others. In this case, dominant masculinity in the United States embodies the following characteristics:

- Men are expected to be physically powerful.
- Men are obliged to hide their emotions.
- Men are supposed to excel at competition.
- Men are to be in control of their lives and the situations they inhabit.
- Men are expected to earn income to support their families comfortably.
- Men are not to act feminine.
- Men should not be gay. (Kimmel, 2004; Messner, 1997; Connell, 1995)

What is particularly striking about dominant masculinity is that it is defined in part by what it is *not*. To be part of dominant masculinity means that one must not act in ways that are seen as feminine or gay; to be a "man" within the ideology of dominant masculinity is to be straight and unfeminine. It is also defined in a way that is associated with some of the key strategies for success in American enterprise: competition, control, and withholding of emotions are all practices that many in the business world expect of their employees. The outcome of this widespread use of masculinity results in the gendering of work, where the key jobs and strategies for success are deeply linked to masculinity (Anderson, 2003; Pierce, 1995). For instance, to achieve financial and professional success, lawyers are expected to be intimidating and aggressive (Pierce, 1995). Bill collectors are expected to deflate the status of truant clients through intimidation (Hochschild, 1983). Car salesmen are supposed to use their wits to get customers to purchase an automobile for more than it is really worth. Stockbrokers' confident and assertive sales pitches to clients are imbued with a culture of dominant masculinity. Indeed, this dominant form of masculinity has provided untold wealth, power, and prestige for men as a group at the expense of women as a group. Dominant masculinity may be a stereotype, but a very powerful and successful one.

## PRIVILEGES OF DOMINANT MASCULINITY

Before addressing the seemingly bold claim that it is in the interests of men to work against dominant forms of masculinity, attention should be given to the obvious benefits men receive from it, even if not all men share equally in the privileges of dominant masculinity. Of course, many have heard about men being the victims of "reverse discrimination" from affirmative action or how they have become the "new minority." Critiques against "political correctness" are pervasive as well, suggesting that men are consistently portrayed as the "bad guys" in the public sphere. Despite the public criticism of men, this has not prevented men—particularly white men—from maintaining disproportionate access to power and resources. Men continue to earn more than women in virtually every occupational category (U.S. Department of Labor, 2001). Even with high school degrees men earn almost as much as women with bachelor's degrees (U.S. Bureau of the Census, 1999).

Men are also overrepresented in the decision-making processes of business and government. White men constitute 95 percent of senior managers, 90 percent of newspaper editors, and 80 percent of the wealthiest Americans (Rhode, 1997). The same holds true with elected officials. In 1997 men comprised 67.5 percent of all elected politicians (Hurst, 2001). The data clearly demonstrate that men continue to be disproportionately represented in key positions of power. Still, these generalized patterns tell us nothing about *why* men are overrepresented in such positions. To answer this, further attention must be given to the structural mechanisms that provide men as a group greater access to economic and political power in the United States.

Upon closer look at these generalized patterns, the data unequivocally demonstrate that white men in particular possess a whole set of advantages when compared with equally qualified white women and people of color. Research shows that people will rate a resume or work performance more critically if they think it belongs to a woman (Rhode, 1997). Men experience greater upward mobility than women in their occupations (Andersen, 2003; Lorber, 1994). Men have greater access to and control of networks for employment (Lorber, 1994). Men also receive greater access to mentoring relationships in business (Lorber, 1994). Mentoring and networking are key ways one moves up into better paying and more prestigious jobs. Federal government data on employment discrimination note that white men are the least likely to experience discrimination in the workplace (Reskin, 1998). Men rarely face sexual harassment or other types of unwanted behaviors that make work a psychologically exhausting and painful experience (Andersen, 2003). In higher education, where it is noted that women now earn the majority of bachelor's degrees, men continue to earn more after graduation (U.S. Department of Labor, 2001).

In part, this has to do with the structure of the American family and sex segregation in the workplace (Andersen, 2003; Rhode, 1997). Although changing, men's family roles continue to place them in positions of the primary income earner, whereas women continue to be forced into work that is more compatible with family life (Rhode, 1997). This contributes to the gender segregation of the workforce. For instance, men constitute 72.1 percent of physicians, 70.4 percent of lawyers, and 91.9 percent of engineers (U.S. Department of Labor, 2001). In more "family friendly" occupations like elementary teachers, nurses, and secretaries, women constitute over 80 percent of those employed (U.S. Department of Labor, 2001). In fact, the occupational structure is so segregated that in order to desegregate work, between 60 and 70 percent of men and women would have to change jobs (Lorber, 1994).

Women have made significant inroads into the work world, but they still run into the glass ceiling. This results in greater difficulty in gaining access to higher paying jobs dominated by men (Glass Ceiling Commission, 1995). Women in male-dominated occupations often experience sexual harassment (Andersen, 2003). Also, it is more difficult for women to move up into higher positions due to an alienating "male culture," because of the lack of network contacts, and/or fewer mentoring relationships (Lorber, 1994; Pierce, 1995). Women can face the "mommy track" as well: the practice of not hiring or promoting women during their childbearing years (Lorber, 1994). In these existing forms of discrimination and family obligations, women continue to be the primary caregivers of children, making it more difficult for women to move up the occupational ladder than men.

> Even with passage of the 1993 Family and Medical Leave Act legislation designed to allow workers to take unpaid time away from work, only full-time employees working for organizations with more than 100 employees are covered. Ironically, more men are capable of taking advantage of this legislation because they are more often in full-time positions. Still, only between one and seven percent of eligible men take advantage of the legislation (Rhode, 1997). Even in occupations where women are the majority, men are often pushed up into better paying administrative jobs
>
> (Williams, 2004).

Some might argue that men and women freely choose family roles and occupations. However, the choices men and women make are the *result* of gender inequality, not a *cause*. Despite the significant gains by women over the past thirty years, discriminatory practices and structural constraints limit their chances for upward mobility and occupational choice. As one prominent philosopher said, "[People] make history, but they do not make it just as they please" (Marx, 1999/1882: 42). Such data also fly in the face of Affirmative Action critics who claim white men are the "new minority" and experience "reverse discrimination." Even though there is variation in terms of race, class, and sexuality, when it comes to access to power and resources, men continue to do very well when compared to women. They are not the "new minority" and experiences of reverse discrimination are extraordinarily rare, although highly publicized (Reskin, 1998). Despite the gains of the civil rights and women's movements, white men continue to be a privileged group in the United States.

## NEGATIVE CONSEQUENCES OF DOMINANT MASCULINITY

Given the advantages of masculinity already mentioned, some men might ask themselves why on earth they would want to give up such a wide range of advantages. These structural benefits are no doubt seductive to many men. High status jobs, respect and deference from others, disproportionate influence, and accumulating wealth are but a few of the advantages of dominant masculinity and the infrastructure of privilege that supports it. Why give all this up?

Accompanying these advantages comes a range of negative consequences for men who invest in dominant masculinity. Public health data clearly show some of the noticeable disadvantages. The average life span for men is 71.3 years, but for women it is 78.3 years (Sabo, 2004). Men are more likely to develop heart disease, have accidents, and be a victim of violent crime and homicide than women (Sabo, 2004). There are multiple reasons for this, but one key factor is the investment in dominant masculinity. Men who buy into it must engage in elaborate techniques of withholding their feelings and engage in behavior that puts them at greater physical risk (Sabo, 2004). To be a "man" is to deny physical pain, which can result in a failure to notify doctors of potentially life-threatening aliments. If one desires to be a "real man," one should be prepared for an early death.

Men who withhold their feelings suffer psychologically. They experience higher rates of depression and suicide than women (Sabo, 2004). They also have more emotionally shallow relationships with families and friends. Men who cannot fit into dominant masculinity also suffer. Often denied access to living wages or control over their environment, working class men, men of color, and gay men often cannot fit fully into dominant masculinity, leaving them subject to critiques of their self-worth. Dominant masculinity works as the underlying rationale for men bullying other men who do not conform to this norm. This leaves significant numbers of men marginalized from and scarred by the dominant masculinity, which is often white, middle class, and straight. Dominant masculinity makes it more difficult to have a variety of legitimate masculinities in our society. Because dominant masculinity is defined as being superior to femininity (Connell, 1995), men who invest in it suffer from being unable to have more egalitarian and emotionally open relationships with women. It also can result in creating discriminatory work environments. Dominant masculinity can even undermine meritocracy. Because men receive unearned advantages for being men in the workplace and political life, it is more difficult for equally qualified women and people of color to be rewarded for their hard work. Clearly, dominant masculinity has negative consequences, leaving men with shorter lives, higher rates of physical aliments, less emotionally fulfilling experiences, and contributes to the undermining of democratic principles. Greater access to power and resources may seem attractive, but when compared with the negative consequences, dominant masculinity becomes more problematic and undesirable.

## WHERE DO WE GO FROM HERE?
## THE FEMINIST/SOCIOLOGICAL PERSPECTIVE

If men are both privileged by and suffer from dominant masculinity, we need a perspective that allows men (and women) to realize that it is in their interest to work against it. This way of thinking is what I call the feminist/sociological perspective. The feminist/sociological perspective shifts our thinking away from looking at dominant masculinity as solely a personality characteristic or biological disposition to focusing on how dominant masculinity is a *social construction,* or a powerful stereotype created by social relations. For instance, consider again how some of the key elements of the dominant masculinity are deeply associated with success in American enterprise as previously mentioned. As a result of this association, the business world is deeply linked to the dominant masculinity. If we can consciously realize how gendered American business is, it then becomes possible to work toward de-gendering the occupational structure. For instance, some of the key strategies of success in American business, such as competition and aggressiveness, may be important, but they need not be associated only with masculinity! Both men and women can be competitive and aggressive. De-gendering such strategies would free talented women to move up the occupational ladder more fairly.

However, seeing dominant masculinity as a social construction includes seeing it as part of a broader social system of gender that privileges men who conform to it and marginalizes women and men that fail to participate in its performance. In other words *gender should be viewed as a central institution in society.* As a social system or institution we can also see how gender organizes virtually every aspect of our lives including the economy, family, politics, and the nation-state to name but a few. We can then also see how the institution gives men and women varying access to power. In order to alleviate these inequalities, the feminist/sociological perspective helps those in American businesses to focus on these structural inequities as well as stereotypes. This means focusing on strategies and social policy designed to eliminate the glass ceiling, concentrating on how unequal family obligations lead to gender inequality, and recognizing that occupations are unfairly sex segregated.

Any discussion of gender inequality and identity would be severely limited without considering how *gender interacts with race, class, and sexual institutions,* the third key area of the perspective. Although women are often in subordinate positions in American business, race, class, and sexual institutions can vary the amount of oppression and privilege. In that same vein, despite men often possessing more social power in business, the institutions of class, race, and sexuality can temper or thwart such privileges in certain contexts. In our quest for gender equity, it is imperative to consider how these factors affect one's opportunities as well.

The feminist/sociological perspective's attention to these aspects allows both men and women to see the constraints and benefits of the system. Although men who are sexist, or those who resist transforming gender inequality, should be held accountable for their actions, this perspective does not focus blame on individual men, but rather on a social system. With its attention to the unequal distribution of power, the feminist/sociological perspective invites us to rally around one of the most foundational principles of the United States: democracy. If we see dominant masculinity as a standpoint in a broader social system of gender that unfairly benefits men, both men and women can fight against it for the sake of further developing a meritocratic system. The feminist/sociological perspective is an invitation for men to work with women to overcome these constraints. And as already pointed out, by noting the benefits and disadvantages of dominant masculinity, men can also see how this social system negatively affects men as well. Men can take pride in working to undermine it and refuse it. This can be achieved by highlighting the anti-meritocratic aspects of dominant masculinity and its negative effects to men as a group. The feminist/sociological perspective is nothing less than a call for men to join with women to overcome the negative effects of dominant masculinity.

## DISCUSSION QUESTIONS

1.  How do the key characteristics of dominant masculinity privilege men? How do these characteristics hurt men?

2.  What other characteristics could be included in dominant masculinity?

3.  If dominant masculinity is defined through such characteristics as physical strength, competition, control, and emotional distance, what does this say about femininity?

4.  How do the key elements of the feminist/sociological perspective encourage men and women to work together against sexism?

5.  Do you agree that the feminist/sociological perspective will help men and women work together to overcome sexism? Why or why not?

6.  If the structure of the traditional family contributes to gender inequality, what can American businesses do so that women have the same chances for upward mobility as men?

7.  How could the feminist/sociological perspective be implemented in American businesses?

8.  What can be done to reduce the glass ceiling in American business?

## BIBLIOGRAPHY

Andersen, M. (2003). *Thinking about women: Sociological perspectives on sex and gender.* Boston: Allyn & Bacon.

Connell, R.W. (1995). *Masculinities.* Berkeley: University of California Press.

Glass Ceiling Commission. (1995). *Good for business: Making full use of the nation's human capital.* Washington, D.C.: U.S. Government Printing Office.

Hurst, C. (2001). *Social inequality: Forms, causes, and consequences.* Boston: Allyn & Bacon.

Kimmel, M. (2004). *The gendered Society.* 2nd ed. New York: Oxford University Press.

Lorber, J. (1994). *The paradoxes of gender.* New Haven, CT: Yale University Press.

Marx, K. (1999/1852). "The eighteenth Brumaire of Louis Bonaparte," In Lemert, C. (Ed.) *Social theory: The multicultural & classic readings.* pp. 41–49. Westview Press.

Messner, M. (1997). *Politics of masculinities: Men in movements.* Thousand Oaks, CA: Sage Publications, Inc.

Pierce, J. (1995). *Gender trails.* Berkeley: University of California Press.

Reskin, B. (1998). *The realities of affirmative action.* Washington, D.C.: American Sociological Association.

Rhode, D. (1997). *Speaking of sex: The denial of gender inequality.* Cambridge, MA: Harvard University Press.

Sabo, D. (2004). "Masculinities and men's health: Moving toward post-superman era prevention." In Kimmel, M. (ed.) *The gendered society reader.* pp. 327–343. New York: Oxford University Press.

U.S. Bureau of the Census. (1999). *Statistical abstract of the United States.* Washington, D.C.: U.S. Government Printing Office.

U.S. Department of Labor. (2001). *Employment and earnings 2000.* Washington, D.C.: U.S. Department of Labor.

Williams, C. (2004). "The glass escalator: Hidden advantages for men in the 'female' professions" In Kimmel, M, & Messner, M. (Eds.) *Men's lives.* 6th edition. Boston: Allyn & Bacon.

# Does Social Class Make a Difference?

Carol P. Harvey

*Assumption College*

**S**ocial class, which is usually determined by a combination of one's income, education, and occupation, may be less visible than other types of difference. However, in many countries where individualism is valued, it is common to believe that all people are created equal and that the same opportunities are available to everyone who has the innate talent and is willing to put in the effort. However, this position ignores the challenge of overcoming the social, educational, and networking resources of class origins. For example, the U.S. General Accounting Office reported that suburban school districts spend up to 10 times more on their public school systems than urban districts (U.S. GAO, 1997).

This exercise is designed to help you to understand how social class *could* affect a person's life experience due to differences in access and resources. Although social class in childhood does *not* necessarily determine status across one's life span, it may limit educational and career options. This may make it more difficult for a person to achieve his or her career and personal goals. Of course, individuals within a social class can have very different experiences, due to a variety of factors.

## DIRECTIONS

Complete the following two columns by thinking about what is apt to be the more common experience of a child growing up in Justin's or Clark's situation. Considering that Justin represents a child born into the lower socioeconomic class and Clark represents one born into the upper middle class, your answers should reflect what is likely to be the more common experiences for children born into these situations.

**Justin** was born to a 16-year-old single mother who lived with her family in an inner-city housing project. When he was born, she dropped out of high school to care for him. After he started school, she took a job cleaning rooms in a local hospital. She is currently studying nights to get her General Equivalency Diploma (GED), so that she can get a better job.

**Clark** was born to a suburban couple in their mid-thirties. His mother has an MBA, and his father is a lawyer. Clark's mother quit her job when he was born. She returned to a managerial position when his younger sibling was in junior high.

| | *Justin* | *Clark* |
|---|---|---|
| How might this child spend his time before he attends kindergarten? | | |
| Why does this matter? | | |
| When he goes to kindergarten, he is diagnosed with a learning disability. What types of help is he most likely to receive? | | |
| Why might these resources be somewhat different for these two boys? | | |
| During grammar school, how is he likely to spend his school vacations? | | |
| Why does this matter? | | |
| In what types of after-school activities is he likely to participate? | | |
| What difference could this make in their lives? | | |
| What role may sports play in his life? | | |
| Why may these roles be quite different for these boys? | | |
| As a teenager, who are most apt to be his role models? | | |
| He needs help with math in high school. What types of resources are most apt to be available to him? | | |
| Where can he learn about technology and develop computer expertise? | | |
| If his college board scores aren't too high, what resources may be available to help him raise his scores? | | |
| What are his three most likely life choices after high school? | | |
| Why may these differ? Who has a better chance of graduating from high school? Why? | | |
| If he goes to college, how are his expenses paid? | | |
| How could this affect his grades or experiences in college? | | . |
| If he needs an internship in college, who can help him secure one? | | |
| Given the differences of growing up in different social classes, what job-related life and career skills may he have that give him workplace advantages or disadvantages? | | |

# DISCUSSION QUESTIONS

1. In terms of the workplace, how does social class matter?

2. Is social class *really* an invisible difference or are there ways that people often deduce other's social class origins? What can be the effect of this in job interviews, work-related social situations, etc.?

3. Do you think that the concept of "privilege" as explored in Peggy McIntosh's "White Privilege and Male Privilege . . ." article also apply to social class privilege? Why or why not?

4. What role does the media play in perpetuating both positive and negative social class stereotypes? Support your answer with examples.

5. In this exercise, both people were male and no specific race was suggested. Which of your answers might have been different, if the examples were female or nonwhite? Why?

## *Writing Assignments*

1. There are many programs and organizations such as Head Start, the Nativity Schools, Big Brothers and Big Sisters, Boys and Girl's Clubs, Girls Inc., etc., that attempt to help individuals to overcome some of the effects of social class. Research and visit one of these organizations to better understand their mission and the roles that they play in providing access and opportunity. Specifically, how can these organizations change the life experiences and access to resources for children from lower classes?

2. Spend a day in a school that is the opposite from your own grammar or high school experience. If you attended a private school, arrange to visit an inner-city school. If you attended a school that was predominately lower or working class, arrange to visit a private school. Analyze any differences that you observe in terms of student body, dress, the academic experience, faculty, physical plant, athletic, and after-school activities. Try to interview students and faculty about their perceptions of the total educational experience at the school. How does what you learned from this visit relate to this exercise? How does it translate into "privileges" in the workplace?

## BIBLIOGRAPHY

Anyton, J. (2003). Inner cities, affluent suburbs, and unequal educational opportunity. In J.A. Banks & C.A. McGee Banks (Eds.), *Multicultural education: Issues and perspectives* (pp. 85–102). New York: Wiley.

Mantsios, G. (1998). Media magic: Making class invisible. In P. Rothenberg (Ed.), *Race, class, and gender in the United States: An integrated study* (pp. 563–571). New York: St. Martin's Press.

U.S. General Accounting Office (GAO) (1997). *School finance: State efforts to reduce funding gaps between poor and wealthy districts.* Washington, DC: U.S. Government Printing Office.

# Social Class Diversity

Colleen A. Fahy

*Assumption College*

**O**prah Winfrey, the nation's wealthiest African American, overcame impoverished beginnings in rural Mississippi to accumulate an estimated net worth of $1.4 billion.[1] High school friends Steve Jobs and Steve Wozniak founded the Apple Computer Company in Job's garage with $1300 in start-up money.[2] Political heavyweights Rudy Giuliani and John Edwards rose from working class backgrounds to become presidential contenders. Such stories of self-made men and women help fuel the perception of America as the land of opportunity, a place where anyone can achieve almost anything with a combination of hard work, intelligence, and determination.

Do you believe that anyone, regardless of the family and community into which he or she was born, *could* be where you are today? If you are like most, your answer is yes. In a *New York Times* poll, 80 percent of Americans answered "yes" to the question, "Is it possible to start out poor, work hard, and become rich?"[3] A *Chronicle of Higher Education* (2006) poll found that 78.6 percent of college freshman agree that "through hard work, everybody can succeed in American society."

The U.S. economic system is commonly viewed as a "meritocracy" where rewards are bestowed upon those who have earned them. If individuals face equality of opportunity, then one's social class position becomes a reflection of his or her personal qualities. Those who have achieved success must have earned it somehow, and those who have failed to climb the social ladder must simply have not tried hard enough. This common perspective leads to negative stereotyping and discrimination of individuals from lower social classes or "classism."

Classism, like many other "isms," results from prejudices based on false assumptions. Despite widely held perceptions, social class mobility in the United States is far from fluid. Those born with few resources face serious obstacles in their efforts to achieve a higher economic and social status. Those born into privilege are given a head start in life with many extra boosts along the way. Once it is recognized that merit has only a small role in determining one's place on the social ladder, the foundation of classism crumbles.

## SOCIAL CLASS MEASUREMENT

The most popular measures of social class are income and wealth. Persons, households or families can be ranked according to their income or wealth and then divided into groups. For example, in 2005, the highest 20 percent of U.S. households had an income exceeding $91,705—while the income of households in the lowest quintile fell below $19,178.[4] Because of its cumulative nature, wealth is unevenly distributed among the U.S. population, with the top 10 percent of families having an estimated median net worth of $1.4 million and the bottom 25 percent having a median net worth of $1700. The top 10 percent of families own an estimated 70 percent of the total net worth in the United States.[5]

Social class is also measured by educational achievement and occupational pres-tige. A National Opinion Research Center survey ranked 447 jobs in terms of their prestige level. Doctors come in first, accountants 35th, elementary school teachers 45th, retail salespersons 366th, and housekeepers 440th.[6] A *New York Times* interactive site allows individuals to enter their occupation, education, income, and wealth in order to determine where they fall in the social class hierarchy. A housekeeper with an eighth grade education making $20,000 per year and holding $5000 in net worth is in the 17th percentile of total social class. A surgeon making $300,000 per year, with $1 million net worth is in the 98th percentile.[7]

## CLASS IN THE WORKPLACE

The frequency of workplace interaction between persons of different social classes will vary by occupation and industry. For example, in occupations such as construction and education, workers are less likely to have frequent interactions with coworkers from sig-nificantly different social classes. In other settings, particularly when there is a hierar-chical structure, individuals are more likely to work closely with those from other social classes. In hospitals, for example, doctors, nurses, LNAs, and maintenance workers come into frequent contact with one another (Scully & Blake-Beard, 2006, p. 442).

Defining class in the workplace is complicated by its multidimensional nature. While income, wealth, education, and occupation are undoubtedly correlated, associa-tions are not always perfect. A carpenter may never have finished high school or he may be a college graduate. A retail salesperson may be a single mother working as the sole breadwinner for her family or a college-educated, married mother working for extra income.

In a meritocracy, those higher on the social ladder have done something to deserve their place and are therefore somehow "better" than those below them. The resulting sense of status can undoubtedly lead to friction in the workplace. According to Bullock (2004),

> In the United States, individualistic explanations for poverty (e.g., lack of thrift, laziness) and wealth (e.g., hard work, ability) tend to be favored over structural or societal attribution for poverty (e.g., failure of society to provide strong schools, discrimination) and wealth (e.g., inheritance, political influence, and 'pull') (p. 232).

Bullock further argues that these beliefs lead to "classism" including negative stereotypes such as "lazy, uninterested in self-improvement, and lacking in initiative and intelligence" and discrimination that includes "behaviors that distance, avoid, and/or exclude poor and working class people" (p. 232).

Thus classism is rooted in the ultimate faith in America as a meritocracy. Economic and social outcomes are a function of merit because individuals face equal-ity of opportunity. Level playing fields promote social class mobility. Unfortunately, this is an idealistic view that fails to stand up under scrutiny. Social class mobility is very much constrained by existing economic and social systems. The movement of individuals from one social class to another is the exception, rather than the rule. Much of where you end up depends on where you begin.

## SOCIAL MOBILITY IN THE UNITED STATES

In contrast to popular opinion, a number of studies have concluded that (1) social class is actually quite sticky, (2) class mobility has not increased in recent decades (and may even have decreased)[8] and (3) the United States has a relatively low level of social mobility compared with other developed nations. For example,

> * 53.3 percent of the families who were in the *lowest* income quintile in 1988 were still there in 1998. Only 10.7 percent of these families made it into the top two quintiles (Bradbury and Katz, 2002).
> * 53.2 percent of the families who were in the *highest* income quintile in 1988 were still there in 1998. Only 8.7 percent had fallen to the lowest two quintiles (Bradbury and Katz, 2002).
> * An intergenerational study found that children from low income families had only a 1 percent chance of reaching the top 5 of the income distribution. They had a 65.5 percent chance of staying in the bottom two quintiles (Hertz, 2006).
> * The same intergenerational study found that while 32.3 percent of white children born into the poorest income quintile were there as adults, this number jumps to 62.9 percent for blacks.
> * The odds of reaching the top 5 percent of income earners is less than 2 percent for anyone starting out in the bottom 3 quintiles (Hertz, 2006).
> * Parental income is highly correlated with the future income of children in the United States. The intergenerational elasticity of earnings is estimated to be .47 indicating that a 10 percent change in parental earnings is predicted to have a 4.7 percent change in the expected future earning of the child (Hertz, 2006).
> * In a comparison of nine high income countries, the United States was second to last in terms of intergenerational mobility (Hertz, 2006).

These studies paint a picture of a country where class mobility is significantly less fluid than most people would like to believe. The correlation between parent and child income and the low probability of moving up the income ladder seem to indicate that "making it" must not be as simple as setting a goal and working hard to achieve it. Of course, some parent–child correlation is expected. Sawhill and McLanahan (2006) write "the attributes that contribute to success in both generations—ability, motivation, and health—are at least partially inherited" (p. 5). However, such a high level of intergenerational correlation indicates that there is more than genetics at work.

If the playing field were truly level we would see significantly more movement between classes. Many more of those born into poverty would work their way up the ladder and many more of those born rich would find themselves sliding down.

# EDUCATION

Equality of education is often cited as the key to social mobility. If our educational system ensured equal access and opportunities for all, regardless of social class, then the playing field would be significantly leveled. Unfortunately, socioeconomic status has a great deal of influence on what students bring to, as well as what they take from, the classroom. In summarizing sixteen recently published works on educational opportunity, McPherson and Schapiro (2006) conclude, "Educational opportunity in the United States is simply spectacularly unequal" (p. 6). Children's academic achievements are heavily dependent on the income, education, and race of their parents.

## Elementary and Secondary Schools

Measures of math, reading, and social skills show significant differences among socioeconomic groups as early as kindergarten.[9] Possible explanations for this gap include differences in birth weight, health, parental skills, and the effect of stress on neurocognitive development.[10] While high quality preschool programs can offset some of the disadvantages faced by lower-income children, access to such programs is extremely limited (Barnett and Belfield, 2006).

The disadvantages that individual poor children face become compounded in the aggregate. The primary source of funds for public elementary and secondary schools is property taxes. Thus, wealthier communities with higher housing values have greater sources of revenue. In many states, this disparity is offset somewhat by additional state funds going to poorer communities. However, poorer districts tend to have higher costs due to a greater proportion of special education and higher need children, as well as higher wage costs. The same dollar simply doesn't go as far in a poorer neighborhood school.

Even if resources were equalized, children from poorer communities face additional obstacles. Academic expectations from parents, neighbors, and teachers may be lower for children from poorer backgrounds. There is a good deal of evidence from experimental studies that show students will achieve more if more is expected of them (Rouse and Barrow, 2006). Unfortunately, teachers are not impervious to stereotyping and discrimination. One study found that given children with equal academic abilities, teachers were more likely to recommend the children with "high status" names to a gifted and talented program (Figlio, 2005).

## Post Secondary Education

A college education improves social class rank in many ways. Education level itself is a measure of social class, occupations that require a college education tend to be more prestigious and a college education usually leads to higher income. In 1979, college graduates made 75 percent more than high school graduates. In 2003 the income premium stood at 230 percent (Rouse and Barrow, 2006). This relationship between a college education and social class is amplified by the tendency of college graduates to marry one another. For example, a college-educated married couple each making the median income for his or her gender would have a household income of almost $89,000 (in 2005), while for a single, high school–educated woman, the median income is just over $21,000.[11]

While 91 percent of all 10th grade students aspire to a college education,[12] this dream is particularly difficult to achieve for students from low income families. While financial constraints are an obvious factor, other issues play an important role as well.

**Knowledge**  The first hurdle faced by less privileged high school students is the general lack of knowledge about the "college education game." Selecting potential colleges, understanding and applying for financial aid, putting the right materials together, all of these are more difficult for families who are unfamiliar with the process. In fact only one-third of inner-city students take the SATs by October of their senior year, compared with 97 percent of suburban students (Haveman and Smeeding, 2006).

**Preparedness**  Bowen (2006) argues that, in contrast to ability to pay, "more consequential factors include college preparedness in all of its dimensions such as health, attitudes at home, motivation, the availability of information, the quality of elementary and secondary education, out-of-school enrichment opportunities, and residential and social segregation" (p. 25). Quantifiable results support this argument. SAT scores are directly and positively correlated with family income. In 2004 students with a family income of less than $10,000 per year had an average combined SAT score of 884, while those whose families made more than $100,000 had an average combined score of 1119.[13] Hill and Winston (2006) find that only 13 percent of the students from the bottom two income quintiles would qualify for admission to the nation's most selective colleges and universities.

**Affordability**  There are three general categories of postsecondary education: a state system including community colleges, private four-year colleges, and the elite college or university. For generations, state schools have been a means for lower income students to gain access to higher education. Unfortunately, the recent trend has been for a decrease in state support for such institutions. In many states, public funding has decreased and tuition has risen sharply. Because the increased tuition has not made up for falling state expenditures, per pupil expenditure and faculty salaries are beginning to lag (Kane, Orszag and Gunter, 2003).

A majority of private, four-year colleges have academic standards that are not out of reach for students of low income backgrounds. Unfortunately, these institutions tend to have lower endowments and are therefore heavily tuition dependent. There has been a growing tendency for such institutions to increase the emphasis on "merit" as a criterion for financial aid and to decrease the emphasis on "need" (McPherson & Schapiro, 2006). The source of this shift is a topic for debate, but many feel that it is driven by publications such as *U.S. News and World Report,* whose college rankings are determined, in part, by the academic credentials of students. This shift in emphasis toward merit and away from need is doubly hurtful to economically disadvantaged kids who don't have the cash for tuition or the high SAT scores the colleges want.

The final category of postsecondary education is the elite college or university. Such schools have plenty of endowment money and can afford to meet any economic need a family might face. The problem is a lack of qualified students. Of those students who score 1420 or better on the SAT, 3.7 percent of are from the lowest income quintile while 45.9 percent are from the highest income quintile (Hill & Winston, 2006).

A lack of information, academic preparedness, and financial means constitute a significant obstacle for poorer children in achieving a college education. In 2004, 49.6 percent of high school graduates from the lowest income quintile began college right away. For the highest income quintile this figure was 79.3 percent.[14] Differences in enrollment patterns are exacerbated by differences in graduation rates. Of those who enrolled in a four-year institution in 1995, 41.4 percent of the lowest quartile income graduated within 5 years while 66.2 percent of the highest quartile did.[15] Thus, students from lower income classes are less likely to enroll in college and once there are less likely to graduate.

The education of children begins at birth. The income and education of their parents; the quality of their neighborhood, peers, and school; and the opportunities for outside enrichment will all have an effect on the intellectual growth of children. The education of children begins at birth. Children born into privilege are read to more and taken to museums and libraries. Their parents attend more school functions. Their families have the time and money for extracurricular activities, enriching not only their educational experience, but their odds of gaining admittance to the college of their choice. In school, they are surrounded by high-achieving peers and teachers with high expectations. If trouble arises, tutors can be hired. A high quality college education is both achievable and affordable. While it is certainly not impossible for children from lower socioeconomic groups to achieve the goal of a college education, it is clearly a more daunting task.

## SOCIAL AND CULTURAL CAPITAL

In their book *The Meritocracy Myth,* Stephen McNamee and Robert Miller, Jr., explain the importance of social and cultural capital in gaining access to quality educational and employment opportunities. They argue that social capital or "who you know" is critical in developing "academic aspirations" and is therefore directly related to a child's academic success. More directly, personal connections are very helpful in job placement and advancement. Those from lower socioeconomic groups are disadvantaged in terms of social capital as they "tend to be members in resource-poor networks that share a relatively restricted variety of information and influence" (p. 78).

Cultural capital or "fitting in" is also critical to upward mobility. Belonging to a group means knowing about the things they know. Cultural capital is accumulated from birth. The things a person knows about, the things he values, and the way he dresses and speaks will have much to do with the environment in which he is raised. McNamee and Miller argue that the accumulation of cultural capital is not perfectly correlated with socioeconomic status, as some lower income parents may emphasize cultural knowledge or young adults may seek it on their own. However, such information is "often esoteric, specialized, costly, and time-consuming to accumulate" (McNamee and Miller, p. 71). Because such knowledge is easier to pick up along the way than to consciously learn, there is a strong tendency for those born into a particular group to acquire the cultural capital necessary to "fit in" with that group.

Scully and Blake-Beard (2006) emphasize the importance of cultural capital in the identification of social class in the workplace. Dress, speech patterns, accents, manners, and reasoning styles are all used to distinguish those of different classes. The player must fit the part and "people from privileged backgrounds often enter organizations with this kind of style already in hand" (p. 441). In competition for jobs and promotions, the sheer number of equally qualified applicants can make style, in all its forms, the "tie-breaker."

## Homeownership and Neighborhood Effects

The probability of owning one's own home increases significantly with income and wealth. Home ownership, in turn, is associated with numerous personal and social benefits. To begin with, a house is a primary source of wealth. This accumulation of wealth has an intergenerational effect, as home equity can be used to finance a child's education or can be passed down as an inheritance. Additionally, studies have found multiple positive effects on children whose families own their own home. Holding family characteristics constant, home ownership leads to improvements in home environment (physical condition of the house itself, the presence of educational materials, self esteem, mental and physical health). When families own their homes, their kids do better in school, receiving higher test scores and getting into less trouble. (Again, this is holding other family characteristics constant.) The improvement in educational outcomes may be due to the improvements in home environment, as well as an increased probability of remaining in the same school for a longer period of time (Haurin, 2003).

There are spillover effects of home ownership as well. Owners have a stake in the capital gains on their homes. They have a greater incentive to maintain their homes and push for better community resources, including safety and quality schools. Better public services increase property values and thus the wealth of the individuals living in the community.

While neighborhood quality is dependent on the values of the families residing therein, the reverse may also be true. We have seen that residents of affluent neighborhoods have access to higher quality schools and superior social and cultural capital. Incorporated into the concept of social capital is the broader notion of neighborhood effects. The general question is whether individuals are affected by the behavior of those around them. It seems intuitive that people are social and therefore not immune to the values of those with whom they associate. The empirical literature on family and peer influences on economic and social outcomes is extensive. While it is generally accepted that families play the largest role, the role of the neighborhood is more controversial with some studies finding significant effects and others dismissing these effects as inseparable from the role of the family.

In any discussion of socioeconomic outcomes there is a difficulty in separating out the effect of race. Home ownership rates are much lower for minorities than for whites, with 75 percent of whites owning their own homes, as opposed to 46 percent of blacks and 48 percent of Hispanics (Ohlemacher, 2006). Much of this difference is simply due to the lower average income of minorities. In fact, one study found that, holding income and wealth constant, minorities were no less likely to own their homes than whites (Di & Liu, 2005).

However, in terms of neighborhoods, the United States is highly segregated by race. It has been estimated that 65 percent of blacks would need to relocate in order to achieve full geographical integration (Friedman, 2006). Some of this clustering is explained by economics, as minorities are more likely to be poor and neighborhoods tend to be homogenous in terms of income. However, McNamee and Miller (2004) argue that only 20–25 percent of black segregation is explained by economic factors. They go on to say that, in general, blacks do want integrated neighborhoods, but whites do not. It is estimated that more than 60 percent of blacks face housing discrimination. Samantha Friedman (2006) reports that blacks—regardless of whether they are urban or suburban—face poorer neighborhood conditions, including trash, abandoned buildings, bars on the windows, and more "social disorder."

Once again, we see the self-perpetuating nature of social class. Those born with less are less likely to live in their own homes. The result is a lower quality of life for parents and children alike. Educational quality suffers as children change schools more often. Families lose out on an important source of wealth, one that could be used as a source of financing for investments in their children's future. Residents of poor neighborhoods suffer from a lack of funding for public goods, including safety and education. Such neighborhoods lack quality social networks, peers, and role models. These problems are exacerbated for minorities, who face housing discrimination and neighborhood segregation.

## RACE AND GENDER

Issues of race, gender, and class often intersect, making it difficult to isolate individual sources of stereotyping and discrimination. Minorities have lower average values for commonly used measures of social class status. While 18 percent of whites are in the lowest income quintile, the figure is 34 percent for blacks and 25 percent for Hispanics (See Note 4). While 27.6 percent of adult whites have at least a bachelor's degree, only 17.3 percent of blacks and 11.4 percent of Hispanics have achieved this level of education.[16] Finally, occupational prestige is significantly lower for blacks than whites, although the gap does appear to be shrinking (Kim & Tamborini, 2006).

Tom Hertz (2006) completed an extensive study of social mobility and found that among those born into the poorest income quartile, blacks are twice as likely as whites to remain poor and only one quarter as likely to move to the highest quartile. He also finds that a significant portion of the income gap between blacks and whites is due to factors other than parental attributes, such as education, occupation, attitudes, and behavior.

Gender and social class are also intrinsically linked. Women make approximately 75 cents on the dollar compared with men (Bergmann, 2005). While women have made significant headway in terms of education (according to the NCES, 57 percent of bachelor's degrees in 2004 were awarded to women), there is still significant segregation by occupation. Pay and prestige vary by occupation. For example, chemical engineers—86 percent of which are men—have a prestige ranking of 6th and an average annual income of approximately $81,600. Nursing, on the other hand is a predominantly female occupation (92 percent) and has a prestige rank of 31 and an average annual income of $59,700.[17]

Workers without a college degree are often segregated into blue collar and pink collar occupations. Again the prestige (given in parentheses) and pay vary by field. Women are a vast majority of the workers in such fields as secretarial (186), hairdressing (313), and child care workers (335). Men represent a strong majority in such fields as firefighting (111), electricians (135), and auto mechanics (278). An interesting example is teaching, where 98 percent of preschool and kindergarten teachers are women and the occupational prestige ranking is 100. For secondary school teachers, women's representation falls to 57 percent and the prestige rank increases to 34.

The relationship between occupational pay/prestige and gender has a certain chicken-and-the-egg quality. Do women's occupations pay less because they are women's occupations or are women somehow steered into these occupations? Is prestige a function of gender representation or vice versa? Such questions are important, but whatever the cause, the result is the same. Many low-paying, low-prestige jobs are filled by women. Forty-three percent of women working full time in 2005 earned less than $30,000—while the figure for men was 29 percent.[18]

Because social class is intrinsically linked to gender and race, issues of classism, sexism, and racism are often intertwined. The disadvantages faced by poor black women are more than merely the sum of the disadvantages faced by each particular group. It is also wrong to assume that some "isms" are merely mistaken for others. While women and minorities are overrepresented among the poor, it is incorrect to say that racism and sexism are simply classism in disguise or vice versa.

Social class diversity undoubtedly deserves its own seat at the table. As Jim Vander Putten (2001) argues, Bill Gates and an Appalachian coal miner are quite different, even though they are both white men. In fact, when a group of experts were asked which they would choose at birth if they could—race, class, or gender—the vast majority picked class (Sawhill & McLanahan, 2006). The relevance of social class should not, however, minimize the importance of race and gender as each "will have a great deal to do with the resources (social as well as financial) that are available to us as individuals, the reactions that we will face from other individuals and our self image" (Albelda, Drago, & Shulman, 2004, p. 129).

Scully and Blake-Beard argue that not only is it inappropriate to emphasize class at the expense of race and gender, it may be dangerous to do so. "A potential blind spot of class analyses can be a stance that class trumps all other dimensions of identity as it is the most fundamental, economically situated identity. This stance does not help for building alliances across members of different social identity groups committed to working on diversity and justice" (p. 448).

## CLASS IN THE WORKPLACE REVISITED

Workplace attitudes toward social class are certainly a reflection of the attitudes of the greater society. An appreciation of the difficulties facing individuals from less privileged backgrounds is a good first step in diminishing biases held by those working within an organization. However, the categorization of social class as something determined outside of an organization can make things worse.

Scully and Blake-Beard argue that many organizations view social class identity as something that is determined before the employee walks through the door. What these businesses fail to see is that their own practices often reinforce preexisting social class stratification. One example of such a reinforcing policy is the rise in credentialism. The precise qualifications of a potential employee are often difficult to measure, especially when the application process is still in the paper stages. In order to efficiently rank applicants, employers often use educational achievement as a sorting mechanism. When the ability to do the job is not dependent on an academic degree, social class stratification becomes unjustly reinforced.

Businesses create positions and put their own values on them. They decide what the pay level will be and what the "perks" will be (office space, restrooms, lunch rooms, leave policies, educational benefits). Thus, as Scully and Blake-Beard argue, "organizations are where social class is constructed and enacted" (p. 446). Any organization attempting to break the psychology of class-based discrimination must look not only at society at large, but also within their own walls.

## A MULTI-LAYERED APPROACH TO CHANGE

The social class structure within an organization both reflects and reinforces attitudes toward class held by society at large. Stereotypes justified by a meritocratic myth must be challenged at all levels, from national economic policies to business-specific diversity training. At all levels, the measurement of merit and existing institutional reward systems must be called into question.

At the national level, while the stickiness of social class has remained fairly constant over time, relative income positions have widened. This is due to a dramatic increase in income inequality in the United States. According to Bernstein (2006), "Since the late 1970s, the real after-tax income of those at the top of the income scale grew by 200 percent . . . and those at the bottom, 9 percent" (p. 84). The average American has been treading water for some time, while the rich have gotten significantly richer. Possible explanations for this change are many. However, one quick statistic is illuminating. In 2006 the federal minimum wage was $5.15 per hour. In real terms (inflation adjusted) the value of the minimum wage in 1968 was $9.27 per hour. As the range of incomes has spread, the difference between rich and poor has become more pronounced. A full-time minimum-wage worker earns $10,300 annually, while the average S&P 500 CEO pulls in $8.3 million (Simon, 2007). As this relative reward system changes, so does the implicit value of the work being done.

There are signs that Americans are becoming uncomfortable with the current obstacles facing the poor. There has been a surge in support for higher minimum wages, and as of 2006, 23 states had adopted a minimum wage greater than the federal minimum. After the 2006 election, the federal government followed suit and increased the federal minimum wage by $2.15 (in increments over two years). There has also been an increased role for the federal government in education policy (No Child Left Behind) and a building momentum for some type of universal health care coverage. However, given the widespread belief in a meritocratic system, government policy will probably play only a small role in minimizing the benefits associated with class and in aiding the mobility of those at the bottom. Institutional changes are also needed.

A glaring example of the disconnect between rewards and merit is the unequal access to higher education. This is a particularly important issue because a college education is linked to higher income, wealth, and occupational prestige, as well as numerous positive effects on future children. Admissions policies that emphasize standardized test scores and ability to pay reward existing class privilege. SATs, which many argue are a relatively poor predictor of college success, are heavily weighted in admissions decisions and are highly correlated with economic resources. Fortunately, the trend toward SAT prep courses, admissions coaches, and merit-based aid is beginning to produce a backlash of sorts. A number of colleges are implementing plans to increase the number of students from economically disadvantaged backgrounds. Universities such as Princeton, Harvard, and Brown have replaced loans with grants for low-income students. The University of Virginia and the University of North Carolina have gone one step further in improving recruitment efforts from lower income groups (Tebbs & Turner, 2006). Improved access to higher education by members of lower economic classes will carry many of the same benefits as greater representation of racial minorities. A diverse student body (in all aspects) promotes understanding of differing world views and helps to diminish negative stereotyping.

While many of the components of social class are determined outside of the workplace, it is a serious mistake to assume class is simply exogenous to an organization. Businesses themselves must realize that social class is reinforced within their own walls. Are qualified persons from all social classes considered for job openings? Is everyone given equal access to opportunities once employed, or are outward symbols of social class, such as dress and speech patterns, weighed in these decisions? Are academic credentials being used as appropriate placement tools or are they being used to unjustly eliminate people from consideration?

Businesses should also take a hard look at wages and benefits. Are only some employees given access to paid leave and educational opportunities? If so, are these differences justified? Are symbols of class apparent in the work environment, executive washrooms, and lunchrooms, for example? According to Bullock (2004), changes in workplace policies will meet with resistance, "Creating a more just workplace requires middle-class managers and others in positions of authority to examine the implications of 'business as usual' and take personal responsibility for the classist policies and practices within their own organization. For those who unquestioningly accept their class privilege as earned, this will likely be a difficult process" (p. 241).

Because social class is commonly viewed as something that is changeable, resulting inequities are often seen as deserved. But like racism and sexism, classism is based on false assumptions about underlying differences between groups. Structures and systems create a set of rewards that typically reinforce the status quo. Americans need to take a hard look at the way the system really works, how merit is measured and rewarded. Only then will conceptions of the personal qualities of those of lower status be questioned and discrimination redu.

## NOTES

1. *Forbes* list of billionaires 2006. Retrieved July 31, 2007, from *http://www.forbes.com/lists/2006/10/O0ZT.html*

2. Shiny Apple. (1979, November 5). *Time.* Retrieved July 30, 2007, from *http://www.time.com/time/magazine/article/0,9171,912528,00.html*

3. Class Matters: A Special Section. *New York Times.* Retrieved June 24, 2007, from *http://www.nytimes.com/packages/html/national/20050515_CLASS_GRAPHIC/index_04.html?adxnnl=1&adxnnlx=1182864457-HIF4kzqfFaXW0qu7fLgACA*

4. U.S. Census Bureau, Current Population Survey. (2006) *Annual Social and Economic Supplement.* Table HINC05. Retrieved July 30, 2007, from *http://pubdb3.census.gov/macro/032006/hhinc/new05_000.htm*

5. Net worth Data is for 2004 and is taken from table 3 in Bucks, Kennickell, & Moore (2006).

6. As reported on the *New York Times* interactive site. (See Note 3 for Web address).

7. See Note 3 for Web address.

8. Ever higher society, ever harder to ascend - Meritocracy in America. (2005, January 1). *The Economist*, 374, p. 23. Retrieved July 30, 2007, from *InfoTrac OneFile*.

9. See Denton & West (2002).

10. See *Future of Children* (2005) Vol 15(1) for a number of articles on these issues.

11. U.S. Census Bureau, Current Population Survey. (2006) Table PINC03. Retrieved July 30, 2007, from
   *http://pubdb3.census.gov/macro/032006/perinc/new03_253.htm* (for women) and *http://pubdb3.census.gov/macro/032006/perinc/new03_127.htm* (for men).

12. Author's calculation from the National Center for Education Statistics. (2005). *Youth Indicator* Table 18. Retrieved July 30, 2007, from
   *http://nces.ed.gov/pubs2005/2005050.pdf*

13. Author's calculation from the National Center for Education Statistics. (2005). *Digest of Education Statistics* Table 128. Retrieved July 30, 2007, from *http://nces.ed.gov/programs/digest/d05/tables/dt05_128.asp*

14. National Center for Education Statistics. (2006). *Condition of Education* Table 29–1. Retrieved July 30, 2007, from *http://nces.ed.gov/pubs2006/2006071_App1.pdf*

15. National Center for Education Statistics. (2004). *College Persistence on the Rise: Changes in 5-Year Degree Completion and Postsecondary Persistence Rates Between 1994 and 2000.* Retrieved July 30, 2007, from *http://nces.ed.gov/pubs2005/2005156.pdf*

16. Author's calculations from U.S. Census Bureau. (2006). *Educational Attainment* Table 10. Retrieved July 30, 2007, from *http://www.census.gov/population/www/socdemo/education/cps2006.html*

17. The percentage in each occupation by gender is taken from table A1 of Bergmann (2005). The occupational prestige is taken from the *New York Times* Web site, (see note 3). Data for wages is the mean for 2006 found in the Bureau of Labor Statistics. (2006). *Occupational Employment Survey by Occupation.* Table 1. Retrieved July 30, 2007, from *http://www.bls.gov/news.release/pdf/ocwage.pdf*

18. Author's calculations from U.S. Census Bureau, Current Population Survey. (2006). *Annual Social and Economic Supplement.* Table PINC10. Retrieved July 30, 2007, from *http://pubdb3.census.gov/macro/032006/perinc/new10_000.htm*

## DISCUSSION QUESTIONS

1. In your own success in achieving a college education, consider the following four factors: (1) your parents' attitude toward education, (2) your parents' financial resources, (3) the quality of your elementary and secondary schools, and (4) your own hard work and determination. (a) Rank these factors in terms of their importance in your experience. (b) Choose any three combinations of two factors (e.g., school quality and student work ethic), and explain why they are likely to be correlated.

2. Suppose a financial services company offered tuition reimbursement to their employees who work as financial advisors, but not to the administrative assistants. Why might a company do this? How do policies such as this reduce class mobility? Do you believe such policies are fair?

3. After reading the article, do you agree with the statement: "through hard work, everybody can succeed in American society?" If so, try to counter the arguments given in the article. If not, what do you believe is the biggest obstacle? If you believe that change is needed, give an example of a government or organizational policy that needs to be altered to help reduce classism.

## BIBLIOGRAPHY

Albelda, R., Drago, R.W., & Shulman, S. (2004). *Unlevel playing fields: understanding wage inequality and discrimination*. MA: Economic Affairs Bureau, Inc.

Attitudes and characteristics of freshman. (2006, August 2). *The Chronicle of Higher Education, 53*(1), 19.

Barnett, W.S., & Belfield, C.R. (2002). Early childhood development and social mobility. *Future of Children, 16*(2), 73–98. Retrieved July 30, 2007, from http://www.futureofchildren.org/usr_doc/05_5563_barnett-belfield.pdf

Bergmann, B.R. (2005). *The economic emergence of women*. New York: Palgrave Macmillan

Bowen, W.G. (2006). Extending opportunity: What is to be done? In M.S. McPherson, & M.O. Schapiro (Eds.). *College access: opportunity or privilege?* (pp. 19–34). The College Board.

Bradbury, K., & Katz, J. (2002). Are lifetime incomes growing more unequal? Looking at the new evidence on family income mobility. *Regional Review, 12*(4), 3–5. Retrieved July 30, 2007, from http://www.bos.frb.org/economic/nerr/rr2002/q4/issues.pdf

Bucks, B.K., Kennickell, A.B., & Moore, K.B. (2006, March 22). Recent changes in U.S. family finances: Evidence from the 2001 and 2004 survey of consumer finances. *Federal Reserve Bulletin*. Retrieved July 30, 2007, from http://www.federalreserve.gov/pubs/oss/oss2/2004/bull0206.pdf

Bullock, H.E. (2004). Class diversity in the workplace. In M.S. Stockdale & F.J. Crosby (Eds.), *The psychology and management of workplace diversity* (pp. 224–242). MA: Blackwell.

Denton, K., & West, J. (2002). Children's reading and mathematics achievements in kindergarten and first grade. *National Center for Education Statistics Report 2002125.*

Retrieved July 30, 2007, from http://nces.ed.gov/pubs2002/2002125.pdf

Di, Z.X., & Liu, X. (2005). The importance of wealth and income in the transition to homeownership. *Joint Center for Housing Studies, Harvard University Working Paper W05-6.* Retrieved July 30, 2007, from http://www.jchs.harvard.edu/publications/homeownership/w05-6.pdf

Figlio, D. (2005). Names, expectations and the black-white test score gap. *National Bureau of Economic Research Working Paper 11195.* Retrieved July 30, 2007, from http://www.nber.org/papers/w11195

Friedman, S. (2006) Not in my neighborhood: numbers show Americans still cluster in segregated communities. *Northeastern University Alumni Magazine, 32*(1), 24–25.

Haurin, D.R. (2003) *The private and social benefits of homeownership*. Transcript from Habitat for Humanity University Lecture Series, December 11, 2003. Retrieved June 24, 2007, from Habitat for Humanity Web site: http://elearning.hfhu.org/hfhu/documents/haurinshow.pdf

Haveman, R., & Smeeding, T. (2006). The role of higher education in social mobility. *Future of Children, 16*(2), 125–150. Retrieved July 30, 2007, from http://www.futureofchildren.org/usr_doc/07_5563_haveman-smeeding.pdf

Hertz, T. (2006). *Understanding mobility in America*. Retrieved June 24, 2007, from the Center for American Progress Web site: http://www.americanprogress.org/kf/hertz_mobility_analysis.pdf

Hill, C.B., & Winston, G.C. (2006) How scarce are high-ability, low-income students? In M.S. McPherson , & M.O. Schapiro (Eds.). *College access: opportunity or privilege?* (pp. 75–102) The College Board.

Kane, T.J., Orszag, P.R., & Gunter, D.L. (2003). State fiscal constraints and higher education spending. *Urban-Brookings Tax Policy Center Discussion Paper No. 11.* Retrieved July 30, 2007, from http://www.urban.org/UploadedPDF/310787_TPC_DP11.pdf

Kim, C., & Tamborini, C. (2006). The continuing significance of race in the occupational attainment of whites and blacks: a segmented labor market analysis. *Sociological Inquiry, 76*(1), 23–51.

Mazumder, B. (2004). Sibling similarities, differences and economic inequality. *Federal Reserve Bank of Chicago Working Paper 2004–13.* Retrieved July 31, 2007, from http://www.chicagofed.org/publications/workingpapers/wp2004_13.pdf

McNamee, S.J., & Miller, R. K. Jr. (2004). *The meritocracy myth.* Lanham: Rowman & Littlefield.

McPherson, M.S, & Schapiro, M.O. (Eds.). (2006). *College access: opportunity or privilege?* The College Board.

Ohlemacher, S. (2006, November 14). Persistent race disparities found: Minorities still lag in income, education, census data show. *The Washington Post.* Retrieved July 31, 2007, http://www.washingtonpost.com/wp-dyn/content/article/2006/11/13/AR2006111301114.html?referrer=emailarticle

Rouse, C.E., & Barrow, L. (2006). U.S. elementary and secondary schools: equalizing opportunity or replicating the status quo?

*Future of Children, 16*(2), 99–123. Retrieved July 31, 2007, from http://www.futureofchildren.org/usr_doc/05_5563_barnett-belfield.pdf

Sacks, P. (2007, January 12). How colleges perpetuate inequality. *The Chronicle of Higher Education, 53*(19), B9-B10.

Sawhill I., & McLanahan, S. (2006). Introducing the issue. *Future of Children, 16*(2), 3–17. Retrieved July 31, 2007, from http://www.futureofchildren.org/usr_doc/01_5563_intro.pdf

Scully, M.A., & Blake-Beard, S. (2006). Locating class in organizational diversity work: class as structure, style and process. In A.M. Konrad, P. Pushkala, & J.K. Pringle (Eds.), *Handbook of workplace diversity* (pp. 431–454). London: Sage.

Simon, E. (2007, June 11). Half of S&P 500 CEOs topped $8.3 million. *Washington Post.* Retrieved July 31, 2007, from http://www.washingtonpost.com/wp-dyn/content/article/2007/06/11/AR2007061100798.html

Tebbs, J., & Turner, S. (2006). The challenge of improving the representation of low-income students at flagship universities. In M.S. McPherson, & M.O. Schapiro (Eds.). *College access: opportunity or privilege?* (pp. 103–115). The College Board.

Vander Putten, J. (2001). Bringing social class to the diversity challenge. *About Campus, 6*(5), 14–19.

---

**Diversity on the Web**

Visit the following site and determine your social "class percentile," using answers that represent where you expect to be in 10 years.

If you are currently employed full time, use your current information or information 10 years forward.

*http://www.nytimes.com/packages/html/national/20050515_CLASS_GRAPHIC/index_04.html?adxnnl=1&adxnnlx=1182864457HIF4kzqfFaXW0qu7fLgACA*

# Generational Diversity Scenarios in the For-Profit and Nonprofit Sectors

Diane M. Holtzman
Evonne J. Kruger
Charles D. Srock
*The Richard Stockton College of New Jersey*

For the first time in history, four distinctively diverse generations are employed in our workforce: Veterans, Baby Boomers, Gen Xers, and Millennials. These generations frequently collide in today's workplace, creating environments characterized by individual and generational enmity, where attitudes of "Us vs. Them" and "every man and woman for himself and herself" surface (Zemke, Raines, & Filipczak, 2000, p. 5). The adversarial atmosphere impedes the energies, productivity, teamwork, and collaborative problem solving required by complex and competitive global markets. To foster organizational environments that are positive and productive, employers must be aware of the strengths and assets that each generation brings to the organization and become skilled in dealing with multiple generations as both subordinates and supervisors.

As a group, each generation tends to have different attitudes about work ethic, career development, work/life balance, job expectations, communication styles, training and development, adaptation to and use of electronic technology, money, rewards, and compensation (Center for Generational Studies, 2006). According to Lancaster and Stillman (2002), ". . . different generations of employees won't become more alike with age. They will carry their 'generational personalities' with them throughout their lives. In fact, when hard times hit, the generations are likely to entrench themselves even more deeply into the attitudes and behaviors that have been ingrained in them" (p. 8).

Demographers agree about the overall profiles of the distinct cohorts in the workforce, but disagree on the years of birth and cohort names. The oldest workers, those 44.2 million born between 1922 and 1943 are termed "veterans," the "swing generation," or the "great generation" depending on the social observer. Those born between 1900 and 1945 tend to be called "traditionalists." The baby boomer generation—approximately 77 million people—has been defined both as those born between 1943 and 1960 and those with births spanning the years 1946 through 1964. The 52.4 million generation Xers have been defined as being both born between 1965 and 1980, as well as between 1960 and 1980. The Generation Y cohort is also termed the Millennials and Generation Nexters. At 77.6 million, they are now the largest generation. Some place their births between 1980 and 2000, others between 1981 and 1999 (Lancaster & Stillman, 2002; Zemke, Raines, & Filipczak, 2000). Those born within a year or two of the start of a new generation are called "cuspers," because they "stand in the gap between the two sides . . . [and] become naturals at mediating, translating, and mentoring" between generations (Lancaster & Stillman, 2002, p. 39).

The four generations will continue to be in the workforce for quite some time. In an article in *Business Week,* Coy (2005) found that starting in the mid-eighties, older Americans chose to keep working. This can be attributed to improved physical and mental health, the desire to stay useful, and the need of organizations to hold on to experience. Even executives are making career switches rather than retiring. They are primarily motivated by boredom with retirement, a sense of productivity, and intellectual challenge (San Jose Business Journal, Report, 2007).

Each generation evidences unique perspectives and values about work and the work environment. In traditional hierarchical organizations, generations used to be more segregated, as individuals rose to higher positions with experience. In general, older employees tended to be in upper and upper-middle management, middle-aged employees in middle management and occasionally in upper management, and younger employees in lower-to-middle levels. However, as organizations flatten into more horizontal structures, a "mixing" of generations occurs that profoundly influences organizational processes. As teamwork increases, intergenerational differences spark interpersonal conflict, creating issues surrounding collaborative problem solving, motivation, communication, training, and supervision. Thus, *diversity of generations* must be added to traditional discussions of diversity in the workplace and its impact on organizational effectiveness.

The nomenclature and the time frames for the cohorts that follow are those presented by Ron Zemke, Claire Raines, and Bob Filipczak (2000) and Raines (2002).

# GENERATIONS IN THE WORKPLACE

## The Profile for Veterans:
## Born between 1922 and 1943

**The Core Values of Veterans** include dedication, discipline, sacrifice, hard work, duty before pleasure, delayed rewards, conformity, consistency and uniformity, sense of history, and an orientation toward the past; respect for authority, adherence to the rules, preference for hierarchy; patience; conservative spending; and a deep sense of personal, organizational, and national honor.

**Veterans Were Influenced** by world events that included the 1929 stock market crash, the Dust Bowl, and the Great Depression in the 1930s; Franklin Roosevelt's presidency—particularly his optimism and the New Deal that brought Social Security and other social programs; the rise of Hitler and fall of Europe; Pearl Harbor and the United States at war, victory in Europe and Japan; and the Korean War.

**Assets of Having Veterans in the Workplace** include their stability, orientation to detail, thoroughness, loyalty, and consistent hard work. Their liabilities include their difficulty coping with ambiguity and change, reluctance to buck the system, discomfort with conflict, and reticence to disagree with those in positions of authority.

**Messages That Motivate Veterans** include, "Your experience is respected here; it's valuable to the rest of us to hear what has, and hasn't, worked in the past." When communicating with Veterans, employers should use inclusive language, written or face-to-face communication, and more formal language.

**In Their Leadership Style** Veterans are directive, use command-and-control leadership, and practice executive decision making. They want to take charge and delegate, but make the bulk of the decisions themselves (Aldisert, 2002, p. 25; Zemke, Raines, and Filipczak, 2000, pp. 29–32).

## The Profile for Baby Boomers: Born between 1943 and 1960

**The Core Values of Baby Boomers** include optimism, team orientation, personal gratification, health and wellness, personal growth, youth, hard work, and involvement.

**Boomers Were Influenced** by the McCarthy hearings in 1954; victories over polio and tuberculosis; the struggle for Civil Rights, from Rosa Parks through school integration; Martin Luther King, Jr.; the involvement of students in voter registration, bomb shelters, and nuclear power; easily accessible birth control; John F. Kennedy's presidency, including the establishment of the Peace Corps; the Cuban missile crisis; astronauts in space; the assassinations of JFK, Martin Luther King, Jr., and Robert Kennedy; the Vietnam War and student protests that culminated in the Kent State University shootings; the founding of the National Organization for Women; and the resignation of Richard M. Nixon.

**Assets of Having Boomers in the Workplace** include their service orientation, willingness to "go the extra mile," ability to establish and maintain good working relationships, desire to please, and their team spirit. Liabilities include frequent lack of budget orientation, discomfort with conflict to the point of conflict avoidance, reluctance to disagree with peers for fear of harming working relationships, comfort with process frequently overshadowing the need for goal attainment, being overly sensitive to feedback, being judgmental of those who see things differently, and self-centeredness.

**Messages That Motivate Boomers** include, "You're valued here," "We need you," "I approve of you," and "Your contributions are unique and important." When communicating with Boomers employers should use an open, direct style; answer questions thoroughly; avoid controlling, manipulative language; use face-to-face or electronic communication; and convey flexibility.

**In Their Leadership Style** Boomers are collegial and consensual, but sometimes authoritarian. They are passionate and concerned about participation, spirit, humanity in the workplace, and creating a fair and level playing field for all. Because Boomers grew up with conservative parents and worked in their early careers for command-and-control supervisors, they often slip into that style when collegiality fails. Many Boomer managers lack sophisticated communication, motivation, supervision, and delegation skills (Aldisert, 2002, pp. 25–26; Zemke, Raines, & Filipczak, 2000, pp. 63–91).

## The Profile for the Gen Xers: Born between 1960 and 1980

**The Core Values of the Gen Xers** include appreciation of diversity, ability to think globally, the balance of work and home life, techno-literacy, espousing the idea that work should be fun, having a casual approach to authority, self-reliance and independence, and pragmatism.

**The Gen Xers Were Influenced** by the following events: the struggle for women's liberation and gay rights, the Watergate scandal, the energy crisis, personal computers, the Three Mile Island meltdown, disenchantment with nuclear power, successive recessions accompanied by massive layoffs, the Iran hostages episode, erosion of America's world dominance and respect, the Challenger disaster, the Exxon Valdez oil spill, AIDS, Operation Desert Storm, and the fall of communism.

**Assets of Having Xers in the Workplace** include that they are adaptable, techno-literate, independent, not intimidated by authority, voracious learners, financially savvy, multitask oriented, experienced team members, and creative. Liabilities include that they are impatient, have poor people skills, are cynical, have low expectations about job security, are less willing to make personal sacrifices at work, and resist being micromanaged.

**Messages That Motivate Gen Xers** include, "Do it your way," "We've got the newest hardware and software," and "There are not a lot of rules around here." When communicating with Gen Xers, employers should use e-mail as the primary tool. They should also use short sound bytes, present facts, ask for feedback, share information immediately, use an informal style, and listen.

**In Their Leadership Styles** Xers are uncomfortable with bureaucratic rules and procedures and traditional chain-of-command systems. They know that sophisticated and demanding customers expect their needs to be met immediately. The Gen X leader is skilled at supporting and developing a responsive, competent team who can change direction, or projects, quickly. They are egalitarian and not hierarchical in their thinking. In addition, they are adept at accessing information on the Internet, via e-mail, and through the organization's information systems (Aldisert, 2002, p. 26; Zemke, Raines, & Filipczak, 2000, pp. 92–126).

## The Profile for the Millennials: Born between 1980 and 2000

**The Core Values for the Millennials** include a sense of civic duty, confidence, optimism, achievement, sociability, morality, collaboration, open-mindedness, "street smarts," an appreciation of diversity, respect for community and authority, and desire to stay connected to others and the world through communication technology.

**The Millennials' Sphere of Seminal Events** and trends includes violence such as the terrorism of September 11th, the school yard shootings, Columbine, and the Oklahoma City bombing; the increased use of technology in schools and in the home; busy lives; the Clinton and Lewinsky scandal; and years of service learning throughout elementary and secondary school.

**Assets of Having Millennials in the Workplace** include their optimism, tenacity, heroic spirit, multitasking capabilities, technological know-how, collaborative skills, and goal orientation. Liabilities include their need for supervision, mentoring, and structure; inexperience in handling difficult interpersonal issues; need for constant feedback and praise; distaste for menial work; lack of skills for dealing with difficult people; impatience; and overconfidence.

**Messages That Motivate Millennials** include, "You'll be working with other bright creative people," "You and your colleagues can help turn this company around," "Your boss is in his (or her) sixties," "Your schedule will be flexible." When communicating with Millennials, employers should use descriptive language and action verbs; not talk down, show respect; use e-mail, voicemail, and visual communication to motivate; seek constant feedback; use humor; and be encouraging.

## Summary of Generational Differences

|  | *Veterans* (1922–1943) | *Baby Boomers* (1944–1964) | *Generation X* (1965–1980) | *Generation Y* (1981–1999) |
|---|---|---|---|---|
| **Core Values** | Discipline, sacrifice, dedication | Optimism, team orientation, health and wellness, hard work | Global perspective, work-life balance, self-reliance, technology | Community, civic duty, confidence technology |
| **Historical Influences** | World War II, the Great Depression, stock market collapse, New Deal | The civil rights movement, nuclear power, space exploration, Cuban missile crisis, Vietnam War | Women's and gay rights, energy crisis, AIDS, fall of communism | September 11th, terrorism, school shootings, service to community |
| **Assets** | Stable, thorough, hardworking | Desire to please, willing to go the extra mile | Independent, team players, technologically savvy, adaptable | Multitaskers, collaborative, technological |
| **Liabilities** | Difficulties coping with change and ambiguity, avoid conflict, reluctant to buck the system and disagree with authority | Focus more on process than goals, self-centered, judgmental | Poor people skills, cynical, don't expect job security, resist management | Need constant feedback and praise, over-confident impatient |

**In Their Leadership Style** Millennials combine the teamwork ethic of the Boomers with the can-do attitude of the Veterans and the technological savvy of the Xers. Resiliency is one of their strongest traits. They are very comfortable dealing with Boomers. Their learning preferences include teamwork, technology, structure, entertainment and excitement, and experiential activities (Aldisert, 2002, pp. 27–29; Zemke, Raines, & Filipczak, 2000, pp. 127–150; Raines, 2002; Zust (nd)).

# SCENARIO EXERCISES

The two scenarios presented here depict generational differences arising in for-profit and nonprofit work settings. After reading the scenarios, be prepared to answer the discussion questions at the end of the scenarios.

## Scenario: Boom-X

Stan, age 55, is vice president for Customer Services at the Davis Employment Agency. Stan started working for the company 33 years ago, right out of college, and advanced to a position under the mentorship of the founder, Benjamin Davis. Benjamin's son, Connor, 33, is now in charge of the agency. Upon retiring, Benjamin announced, "I leave the company under the capable direction of my son and the sound management of Stan, who we all know is knowledgeable about the 'Davis Way.' Stan, known for loyalty, commitment, and dedication to the company, is valued and respected by many in the agency."

Recently billings have begun to decline noticeably, even though industry billings are up. In response, Connor has hired several new employees to provide new and creative ways to meet clients' needs. One of the new employees is Alex, a 32-year-old assistant vice president for Customer Services, who works under Stan. Alex manages the office and deals with clients, but has only been at Davis four months out of a six-month probationary period. He is having difficulty adapting to his coworkers, many of whom have been at the company for more than 10 years, and who are familiar with Stan's management style. Alex has many good ideas, but is not empowered to enact any significant changes. This is frustrating to him because he believes incorporating these ideas would bring the company "into the technological era." Alex cannot convince Stan these ideas would enhance efficiency and more effectively meet clients' needs.

Some of the office employees say that "Stan's Way" may seem antiquated by today's office procedures and technological advances, but he is very competent, and on top of everything, he knows operations and each client's history. However, Stan's need to follow procedures creates confusion with newer employees, who find them cumbersome and often overlapping. They do not appreciate all memos and correspondence being done on paper versus electronic messaging, and the endless number of informational meetings. They prefer charts and aggregated data to long, detailed memos and keeping each other informed via e-mail, as opposed to face-to-face meetings.

Stan sees the procedures as time proven and cannot understand why Alex does not value going through channels, following the company procedures manually documenting details, and articulating the "big picture" before proceeding. Alex believes in getting things done efficiently, using technology to enhance productivity, finding short-cuts, and avoiding wasted time by being overly cautious.

When Alex tries to explain how procedures could be improved or done more efficiently, Stan listens politely, expresses a look of frustration, and tells Alex to "Do it my way." Alex sighs and leaves the office, mumbling.

One week Alex was working under a lot of pressure on projects Stan had assigned with tight deadlines. Alex took charge, completed the assignments in a style to which Stan was not accustomed. Alex did not ask to have Stan approve each step. "Surely Stan will appreciate me now," thought Alex. One night when Alex was working late, Connor stopped by the office and Alex explained the sophisticated charting of one project and how the data was presented in an easy-to-follow manner using spreadsheets created on Excel. Connor was interested and commented about finally being able to communicate with clients on their wavelengths. The next morning when Stan asked Alex how the projects were progressing, Alex stated that they were all done and on the way to clients. Stan's temper flared and a heated dialogue ensued.

Stan wrote a disciplinary letter to Alex citing insubordination. In addition, Stan wanted to start documenting Alex's performance in order to terminate him eventually. Alex has requested a formal grievance hearing regarding the disciplinary letter. The grievance hearing committee is composed of three HR members:

Lou, age 56, Vice President for Human Resources

Fran, age 37, Assistant Vice President for Human Resources

Jordan, age 23, Human Resources Specialist

Both Stan and Alex have been asked to come in individually to meet with the grievance hearing committee.

## DISCUSSION QUESTIONS ON SCENARIO BOOM-X

1. What should the grievance committee recommend? How do you think this recommendation would be accepted by the two managers?

2. Do you think the grievance committee members will be in agreement in their decision? Why or why not?

3. What generational issues are involved in this case?

4. What do you think will actually happen? Why?

## SCENARIO: THE FUTURE OF NONPROFITS: FROM GENERATION TO GENERATION

Bay Street Friends, a community nonprofit organization dedicated to preserving the unique character of a suburb of a large eastern city, has been in existence for over 24 years. Bay Street Friends has a membership of about 950 families. It is governed by an elected board and executive committee. Its budget is met via dues, contributions, and small fundraisers.

Active members tend to be older, retired residents with histories of supporting their community. Several are women who have devoted years to supporting civic causes. While they may not have ever worked for pay, they have run nonprofit boards, organized successful fundraising events, and have a wealth of knowledge about how community nonprofits work. Over the years, the retired members of the Bay Street Friends board have raised millions for the major nonprofit organizations in the city: the world renowned orchestra, the opera, theaters, major teaching hospitals, and universities. The board also includes several members in their fifties, mostly working professionals, and a few younger professionals in their thirties and forties.

Bay Street Friends has been responsible for many community improvements, such as better street lighting and signs, a Web page for those considering moving into the community, articles for the region's papers about the unique nature of the community, playground improvements in the parks, volunteer clean-up projects, and public space in one of the neighborhood shopping areas.

One of the events planned for the 25th year anniversary of Bay Street Friends is a major fundraiser. The goal is to raise over a million dollars to obtain a permanent home on the grounds of a large park containing an art center and the music school. Participation by younger members in their thirties and forties is eagerly sought to ensure the future of the Bay Street Friends, while older community members in their fifties through eighties are encouraged to stay active and solicited because they have the discretionary money and often make sizable gifts.

The fundraiser involves a day-long event and a community ad book of individual and business donors. A task force has been formed, co-chaired by three board members: Molly, who is over 80 and has a history of devoting time and effort to making fundraising ventures successful, Barbara, who is in her late fifties and has worked as a professional fundraiser and been active in the community's organizations, and Rick, a forty-year-old lawyer who wants to make a difference in the community. Other members include the president of the Friends, who is in her fifties and a close friend and contemporary of Molly, a couple of retired professionals in their mid-sixties, four professionals in their fifties, and five younger men and women in their thirties and forties. The younger members include a lawyer and two marketing managers.

## The Meetings

Over the last six months the task force has held 15 meetings to plan the event and discuss how to personally contact and persuade members to support the ad book. The three co-chairs alternate in leading the meetings. All three send e-mail messages about the meetings' agendas and periodic updates on the ad book. When Rick conducts a meeting he tends to stand, and the members sit in a circle around him. He starts by stating how long he thinks the meeting should last and reinforces how busy he is and that this is all the time he has. He does not allow time on the agenda for lengthy discussion of agenda items. While he tries to control meetings tightly by dominating the agenda, the older members tend to ignore him and take as long as they need to discuss the issues. At times it appears that Rick is impatient or has a schedule that is too busy to allow for additional discussion to take place at the meetings.

During one meeting Rick and Barbara carried on a conversation during the entire meeting working at the blackboard trying to lay out a schedule for the concluding event. Meanwhile, Molly circulated among the members and spoke with selected long-term members about who should be invited to major donor meetings. The rest of the group, new members and those in their thirties and forties, just sat and chatted. They were ignored by Rick, Barbara, and Molly.

Whenever Molly chairs a meeting, it is clear that member input could be solicited by e-mail or that longer items could have been e-mailed prior to the meeting rather than discussed in person at the meeting. Her style is to present each item for discussion, even if it is only for information, and solicit contributions from the members. Frequently, conversation is tangential to the topic, wanders, and goes off on the histories of individuals to be targeted and how similar events have been run in other organizations.

Those members in their fifties and above leave these meetings feeling stimulated and rewarded. Younger members leave angry and frustrated that valuable time has been wasted. They feel it is unnecessary to encourage others to make comments and recount the history of other successful fundraising events. These younger members believe that rehashing old successes will not advance the current fundraising efforts. Their understanding of fundraising is that if you present a rational worthy case, funds will be given. They tend to focus on the content of telephone scripts, printed material, and prepared presentations. Older members are not as interested in discussing the content of solicitation messages as they are in individual personalities, who knows whom, and histories of giving and community participation. Their experience has shown them that their generation gives not so much based on the worthiness of the cause, although that certainly is important, but because of the individual relationship forged with the institution requesting funds and/or with those doing the soliciting.

When Barbara leads a meeting, like Molly, she sits as part of the circle, and actively solicits participation. She tries to stay on topic, although because of the individual nature of the fundraising component of the project, there are lengthy discussions of individual community members and how to best approach them. She attends all of the meetings with Molly, and works well with both Molly and Rick.

## Marketing to Donors

For one of the major projects designed to inform potential donors about the fundraising event, the two marketing managers and Rick worked with an outside public relations agency to design an impressive—and costly—brochure aimed at the largest potential givers. Because of the busy schedules of the consultants and Rick, the brochures were barely produced on time. The task force then voted on a smaller promotional brochure for the rest of the Friends and other targeted members of the community that would be both mailed and used for personal solicitations. The older task force members explained that, from their past experiences, the Friends—who tended to be in their fifties and older—were important potential donors and it was vital to keep them informed about the fundraiser.

The three men voiced the opinion that the additional promotional brochure was not needed. In the opinion of the two consultants and Rick, sufficient information had gone out via post cards. It would be a waste of money to develop a brochure for these members, because they would toss the brochure in the trash with other unsolicited mail. The task force voted to go ahead and develop and send the smaller promotional piece. A date for delivery of the smaller brochure was agreed upon by the three men who were responsible for overseeing the brochure's development and production.

The date came and went with no brochures. When the task force asked Rick about the status of the brochures, he replied that the public relations firm was running a few days late, or that the brochures were at the printer, or that the brochures were at the mailing firm, or in the mail. This went on for four weeks and time was running out for the arrival of the brochures. When the brochures finally arrived they were eye-catching and complete. Since the fundraising event was about two weeks away, several members called to complain about receiving their brochures so late. The members explained that they might not be able to attend the event on such short notice and that their donations might not be as substantial as in past years, since it appeared they were only an afterthought. They would have preferred being notified eight weeks prior to the fundraising event, as in previous years.

As the event drew near, Rick and the younger members were barely participating in the Bay Street Friends' meetings or activities. Rick was passed over for an officer position. In lieu of a task force member in her forties, Barbara was made an officer. Rick and the younger members all resigned from the organization. Molly—who knows that her future in the organization is limited, given her age—wanted to mentor Rick. She was hurt and angry.

## DISCUSSION QUESTIONS ON THE NONPROFIT SCENARIO

1.  What happened between Rick and Molly?

2.  How could generational differences have influenced decision making in this nonprofit organization?

3.  What could have been avoided in this case and how?

4.  What should Molly have done to help Rick?

5.  What should Rick have considered when taking a leadership role in the organization?

6.  Are the generational issues in nonprofit volunteer organizations different than those in the for-profit sector? If so, why/how?

7.  Have you experienced a generational conflict that you could share? Explain how you believe different generational viewpoints created the conflict.

8.  Can intergenerational conflict be caused by one group of members having too many activities and the other group having time they want to fill by socializing with other members at meetings? If you answered yes, how would you help reduce these conflicts between people's needs?

## GENERAL DISCUSSION QUESTIONS

In answering these questions, be sure to include specific information about the generational issues. Remember to support your statements using information from your experiences or from the information presented in this text on diversity issues. For written assignments, research the topic using additional books and journals.

1. Compare and contrast the generational issues in the two scenarios. In responding to this question, discuss how individuals frame issues in terms of their generational cohort and how generational issues can influence decisions in resolving intergenerational conflicts.

2. Identify issues surrounding the ability of older individuals to adapt to changing technologies, as well as whether the organization has any responsibility to older, loyal employees or members and what that "responsibility" encompasses.

3. How might any of the following affect decision making for retention of employees: employee's age, length of employment, organizational position, and the individual's ability to change?

4. Write a reflective essay on your generational viewpoints about the scenario issues and discuss how your answers to the questions in the scenario may have been based on your own generational framing.

5. What are the ethical and legal implications involved with generational issues that involve terminating employees in the Baby Boomer generation? Research legal cases and age discrimination legislation to support your viewpoints.

6. What additional generational issues should be considered when working with volunteer nonprofit groups?

## BIBLIOGRAPHY

Aldisert, L. M. (2002). *Valuing people: How human capital can be your strongest asset.* Chicago: Dearborn Trade Publishing.

Center for Generational Studies. (2006). Frequently asked questions about generational differences. Retrieved on May 3, 2007, from http://www.gentrends.com/faq.html

Coy, P. (2005, June 27). Old.Smart.Productive. Surprise! *Business Week,* 78–84.

Lancaster, L.C., & Stillman, D. (2002). *When generations collide: Who they are. Why they clash. How to solve the generational puzzle at work.* New York: Harper Collins.

Raines, C. (2002). Managing millennials. Retrieved on May 3, 2007, from http://www.generationsatwork.com/articles/millenials.htm

Report: Baby boomer execs are making late career switches (2007, March 29). *San Jose Business Journal.* Retrieved on July 8, 2007, from http://milwaukee.bizjournals.com/sanjose/stories/2007/03/26/daily58.html

Zemke, R., Raines, C., & Filipczak, B. (2000). *Generations at work: Managing the clash of veterans, boomers, Xers, and nexters in your workplace.* New York: AmRickan Management Association.

Zust, C. W. (nd). Baby boomer leaders face challenges communicating across generations. *Emerging Leader.Com.* Retrieved on June 6, 2007, from http://www.emergingleader.com/article16.shtml

## ADDITIONAL RESOURCES

Center for Applied Research (2004).
"Educating the net gen: Strategies that
work", November 3, 2004, from the Starlinks
Broadcast. Faribault Campus of South
Central Technical College: Minnesota, MN.

Generations at work: The online home of
Claire Raines Associates. Retrieved on June
5, 2007, from http://www.generationsatwork.
com/

---

### Diversity on the Web

1. Go to the following site and read the article *Generation X and The Millennials: What You Need to Know About Mentoring the New Generations* by Diane Thielfoldt and Devon Scheef.

   a. What suggestions do the authors give for mentoring different generations?
   b. What recommendations can you make to Molly about mentoring Rick based on your reading of the article?

   *http://www.abanet.org/lpm/lpt/articles/mgt08044.html*

2. Go to the following site and read the article, *Choosing Appropriate Outreach Techniques for Different Generations* by the Corporation for National and Community Service.

   Based on the article, what advice can you give Molly about recruiting new members in different generations for Bay Street Friends?

   *http://nationalserviceresources.org/epicenter/practices/index.php?ep_action=view ep_id=1057*

# Organizational Innovations for Older Workers

Carol P. Harvey

*Assumption College*

One of the most dramatic demographic and economic changes is and will continue to be the aging of the American workforce. In 2012 approximately 20 percent of the U. S. labor force will be 55 or older. As recently as 2000, this figure was 13 percent (Toossi, 2004). The annual growth rate of workers aged 55 and older is 4.1 percent, which is four times the rate of the overall workforce (Toossi, 2005). Approximately "10,000 Baby Boomers are turning 50 every day and this trend is expected to continue for the next decade" (Gardner, 2007, p. 13). If workers continue to retire at the traditional ages, the United States will face a shortage of skilled, experienced, and educated labor, particularly in industries such as health care, education, and engineering as the "baby bust," generation Y, moves into middle and upper management.

"By the year 2020, there will be 27.7 individuals aged 65 and older for every 100 working adults: this ratio will represent a 28% increase in just two decades" (Challenger, 2005). With more people living longer, 79–83 years for men and 83–86 years for women (DeLong & Associates, 2006), but fewer workers contributing to the Social Security and Medicaid programs, these demographics could place an enormous economic strain both on the federal budget and the growth of American business.

While it would seem advantageous, in terms of the economy and the business case for diversity, to develop programs such as telecommuting and flexible work options, to keep older workers employed and contributing to Social Security longer, several factors account for the failure of many businesses to capitalize on the talents of this segment of the workforce. In a survey of middle- to large-sized employers, the Watson Wyatt consulting firm, found that only 16 percent of the organizations surveyed had some type of flexible program for older workers and 70 percent had simply not seen the need for such programs (Watson Wyatt Worldwide, 2004). In addition, negative perceptions and stereotypes about older workers—such as their being inflexible, less productive, hard to manage, more costly, and lacking and/or unwilling to learn new technology—still prevail. Other employers may try to avoid hiring older employees because of a fear of age discrimination lawsuits.

Current federal regulations regarding pension benefits and contributions under ERISA legislation (Employment Retirement Income Security Act) and the IRS are outdated and may complicate adopting these innovative programs. According to an Employment Policy Foundation study, 65 percent of the employers surveyed said that they didn't offer phased retirement employment programs because of government regulations (Fetterman, 2005). "Pensions pose some of the biggest challenges for companies that want to keep older employees. The Internal Revenue Service prohibits employers from distributing pension payments to workers still on the job" (Cullen, 2006).

## REDEFINING RETIREMENT

Traditionally, retirement meant "cliff retirement," i.e., leaving one's job completely and relying on defined benefit pension plans and Social Security for support. Soaring health care costs; increased longevity; more reliance on self-managed, defined-contribution retirement plans, instead of guaranteed income streams; low savings rates; and a desire to try a new occupation or self-employment has changed this concept for older workers.

Today, retirement in stages, called "working retirement," is gaining in popularity (Cahill, Giandrea, & Quinn, 2006). In a recent survey, the American Association of Retired Persons (AARP), found that 70 percent of workers over forty-five plan to seek part-time work or flexible schedules or to never retire at all (AARP, 2007). A survey commissioned by MetLife revealed that the primary reasons for older workers to continue employment are that they either need the money (60 percent), or want to stay active (45 percent). However, motivators and needs varied among older workers depending upon their life stages. While workers 60–65 years old value job design and flexible work schedules, workers aged 66–70 are more interested in meeting their needs for social interaction and mental stimulation (DeLong & Associates, 2006).

## FLEXIBLE WORK ARRANGEMENTS, PHASED RETIREMENT, AND BRIDGE JOBS

Research conducted by the University of Minnesota's Vital Aging Network indicates that, "all of the industrialized countries are confronted with an aging and shrinking workforce with labor shortages projected for the future" (Vital Aging Network, 2006). Due to the shift from physically demanding manufacturing jobs to increased service sector and knowledge-based jobs, physical ability and strength may not be as crucial as experience, organizational loyalty, and skills. Some organizations have developed successful programs that capitalize on the strengths and advantages that older workers can bring to the workplace and that can serve as models.

**Flexible Work Arrangements** are often sought by older workers because of their desire to have more time for travel, volunteer work, hobbies, or their need to care for grandchildren and/or spouses. However, a 2001 study by the United States General Accounting Office found that

Though they exist, flexible employment arrangements are not yet widespread in the private sector. According to our interviews with experts, consultants and employers, in many instances, these arrangements or programs are provided on an ad hoc basis and to limited groups of employees. The employees involved in these arrangements tend to be skilled workers with an expertise for which an employer has a special need (25).

Since skilled employees in the health care industry—particularly nurses—are in short supply, Mercy Health System, located in Janesville, Wisconsin, provides an example of an organization that has linked its mission and needs to the flexible utilization of older workers. They offer such innovative schedules as a Weekender Program—work only weekend shifts, and a Traveler Options—work on a 6- to 13-week assignment (AARP, 2006). However, a MetLife survey found that

Less than 12% of people age 66–70 are employed by organizations with over 1,000 employees. Large organizations in particular need to institute strategies that will attract older workers for the long term. Currently, older workers are gravitating towards self-employment or working for small businesses (2006, 19).

---

# FLEXIBLE WORK ARRANGEMENTS— THE VITA NEEDLE COMPANY

A notable example of a small business that has developed very flexible work arrangements for older workers is the Vita Needle company. Located in a former theater in Needham, MA, this organization supplies over 1,000 customers, in 50 industries ranging from fiber optics to athletic equipment to medicine with high quality reusable needles and fabricated stainless steel products. Vita Needle was founded in 1934 and is a fourth-generation family business that employs 35 workers, 95 percent of them part-time senior citizens. Their ages range from 39 to 89, with an average age of 74.

To compete successfully with global manufacturing competition, the Vita Needle company must produce a high quality product while keeping its manufacturing costs low. While President Fred Hartman says that, "it is this dedicated low-tech workforce that is behind Vita Needle's high-tech success" (Employees inject vitality, n.d.), his willingness to meet the needs of his older employees is also a key factor. Research indicates that older workers, as a group, tend to bring a hard-work ethic, loyalty, and sense of responsibility to the workplace (Vital Aging Network, 2006: MetLife, 2006).

For older workers, flexible scheduling is one of their most important motivators (AARP, 2007). What makes Vita Needle unique is that the management has structured the work around the employees' needs and lifestyles, which Hartman describes as the "ultimate flex-time." Each worker has a key to the building and can come and leave according to their needs.

In turn, the employees produce such a high quality product that there is no longer a need for quality control procedures. Costs are kept low because most employees receive their health care through Medicare and wages are slightly above minimum wage. "Just because you hire senior citizens, it doesn't mean that you can't compete in the marketplace. We advertise that we are the low-cost producer and we can beat anybody's price in the marketplace"(Shea & Haasen, 2006). Hartman says that "there is a huge benefit to be gained from the experience, values, loyalty, and the dedication to quality that senior citizens can bring to the workplace. . . . We profit from it and so do our customers" (Employees inject vitality, n.d.).

Because of its unique utilization of older workers, the Vita Needle company has been featured on German and Dutch television programs and on *60 Minutes*, the *Today Show*, and *NBC Nightly News*. In 2003, Vita Needle was honored as an Outstanding Employer of Older Workers by Experience Works.

**Phased retirement** is a workplace plan that allows workers of a specified age to gradually reduce the hours that they work for their current employer. This option allows employers to maintain a trained workforce while employees can have more free time and a gradual transition to full retirement. Phased retirement works best when it ties to an organization's mission and objectives. For example, meeting the specific labor force needs for increased staffing during seasonal peaks, or to complete project-based work, etc., is a win-win situation in terms of the business case for diversity and for older workers. The company gets knowledgeable trained workers who already know the culture and procedures of the organization and the older workers are able to work fewer hours. L.L. Bean, the clothing and sports equipment retailer based in Freeport, Maine, encourages its 861 retirees to return to work when seasonal orders peak (AARP, 2006). Since 1991, Monsanto has maintained a database of retired workers who want to work part time, full time, or on special assignments. Currently, 66 percent, (200) of them have work assignments (Fetterman, 2005).

## THE AEROSPACE CORPORATION—PHASED RETIREMENT

Founded in El Segundo, California, in 1960, The Aerospace Corporation conducts federally funded research and provides advisory services to national defense space systems for the United States Air Force. As an independent, nonprofit organization, The Aerospace Corporation's mission requires the development and retention of skilled engineers and scientists with high level security clearances, who are at the leading edge of technology. "We don't manufacture anything. Our greatest asset is the technical expertise of our people" (The Aerospace Corporation, 2007).

With nearly 51 percent of The Aerospace Corporation's 3,400 full-time employees over 50, retention of these highly educated workers is a major issue. The "Retirement Transition Program" allows the corporation to employ scientists and engineers past traditional retirement age by offering four options for phased retirement: pre-retirement leaves of absence, part-time status in preparation for retirement, post-retirement employment on a consulting basis, and the most popular program—post retirement employment on a "casual" basis. In the latter category, employees can work up to 999 hours per year and still retain full pension benefits. Currently, there are about 250 retirees utilizing these programs at any one time.

Adapted from www.aero.org

**Bridge jobs** provide a transition into retirement that follows a career job and usually involves taking a position with a new organization that was not one's career employer. Many of these positions are part time or temporary. A study by the Boston College Center for Aging and Work revealed that approximately 60 percent of full-time workers are employed in some type of bridge job after leaving full-time employment (Cahill, Quinn, and Giandrea, 2007).

Additionally, a Merrill Lynch survey of baby boomers indicated that 13 percent desired to bridge into retirement by starting their own businesses (Merrill Lynch, 2005). For example, in 2007, faced with narrowing profit margins and a need to decrease its highly educated and older workforce, "IBM launched a $2 million program that will pay for tuition, licensing, and interim salaries for employees who want to bridge into new careers as math and science teachers (Cullen, 2006).

While research indicates that bridge jobs benefit the employees by providing structure and continued activity, a more flexible work schedule, less stress about retiring from one's career position, and an improved sense of self-worth (Feldman & Kim, 2000), they also benefit the organization by providing skilled employees often at lower salary and benefits costs. Marriott, Staples, H&R Block, and REI are examples of employers who intentionally seek to hire older workers for bridge jobs (Gardner, 2007).

## CVS PHARMACIES—BRIDGE JOBS AND THE SNOWBIRD PROGRAM

Filling over a billion prescriptions a year in 2006 with 6,200 stores and $43.8 billion in sales, CVS Caremark is the nation's largest pharmacy chain (Gentry, 2007). Headquartered in Woonsocket, RI, CVS/pharmacy employs over 176,000 people. In the early 1990s, motivated by a desire to have employees match its customer base, to improve customer service and to reduce turnover, CVS began a campaign to recruit older workers through networks of seniors and by contact with church groups. By offering the flexible schedules that retirees often seek and health care benefits for working over 30 hours a week, CVS/pharmacy increased its over-50 staff from 7 percent to 18 percent.

However, many older workers were torn between their desire and/or need to work and spending their winters in warmer climates. Because the demand for pharmacy and store personnel is greater in the winter months in warmer climates, CVS developed a unique seasonal "Snowbird" program, which allows employees to transfer from stores in colder climates to the south and southwest during the winter months and then back to their original locations in the spring. Currently over 1,000 employees, mostly over the age of 50, take advantage of this option.

In addition to its "snowbird" program, CVS/pharmacy has established a Senior Pharmacy Legacy Mentoring Program in which working and retired senior pharmacists mentor pharmacy technicians and high school students who are contemplating pharmacy careers.

In March 2007, CVS/pharmacy received the American Society on Aging's large business award for rethinking how older workers can contribute to business success.

While these companies provide innovative examples of the effective utilization of older workers, they are the exceptions, not the norm. In a culture that values youth, older workers still face considerable discrimination and prejudice in the workplace. By 2025, it is estimated that one out of every five United States workers will be over age 55.

> Companies need to be more proactive in anticipating the changing needs, motivators and interests as employees move into their sixties. If firms don't provide more creative, flexible opportunities for older workers, they are going to continue to lose their most loyal, highly-skilled and experienced performers at a time when the competition for talent is becoming increasingly intense (MetLife, 2006)

## BIBLIOGRAPHY

Abelson, J. (2006). Snowbirds at work. *The Boston Globe*, March 1, 2006.

AARP. (2006). Winning strategies, 2006. Retrieved on June 24, 2007, from http://www. aarp. org/money/careers/employerresource-center/ bestemployers/winners/mercy_health_ system. html.

AARP. (2006). Winning strategies 2006. Retrieved on June 21, 2007, from http://www.aarp.org/ money/careers/employerresourcecenter/best employers/winners/ll_bean.html.

AARP. (2007).Workforce tends. Retrieved from on June 20, 2007 http://www.aarp.org/ money/careers/ employerresourcecenter/ trends/a2004-04-20-olderworkers.html.

Cahill, K., Giandrea, M., & Quinn, J. (2006). Retirement patterns from career employment, *The Gerontologist 46*(4), 514–523.

Cahill, K., Quinn, J., and Giandrea, M. (2007). Down shifting: the role of bridge jobs after career employment. *The Boston College Center for Aging & Work*: Chestnut Hill, MA.

Challenger, J. (2005). 24 trends reshaping the workplace (part I). *Managing Diversity*, March, 2005, 14, #6, pp. 1, 6 & 8.

Cullen, L. (2006). Not quite ready to retire. *Time*, February 19, 2006. Retrieved on June 22, 2007, from http://www.time. com/time/ magazine/ article/0,9171,1161224,00.html.

DeLong, D., & Associates. (2006). Findings from a national survey of aging workers who remain in-or return to-the workplace, how they fare and why. *MetLife Mature Market Institute*. Retrieved from on June 20, 2007, http://www.metlife.com/WPSAssets/11091110 421147725122V1FLivingLonger.pdf.

Employees inject vitality into needle production [Electronic version]. (n.d.). *Thomas Register's Trendletter*, 108, 1–2.

Fetterman, M. (2005). Retirees back at work, with flexibility. *USA Today*, June 9, 5B–6C.

Feldman, Daniel C., & Kim, Seongsu. (March, 2000). Bridge employment during retirement: a field study of individual and organizational experiences with post-retirement employment.(University of California)(Statistical Data Included). In *Human Resource Planning*, 23, p. 14. Retrieved June 21, 2007, from Expanded Academic ASAP via Thomson Gale: http://find.galegroup.com/itx/infomark.do?&contentSet=IAC-Documents&type=retrieve&tabID=T002&prodId=EAIM&docId=A63025949&source=gale&userGroupName=mlin_c_assumpt&version=1.0

Gardner, M. (2006). One firm, two locations adds up to a healthy work arrangement for a handful of seniors. *The Christian Science Monitor,* February 8, 2006. Retrieved on June 22, 2007, from http://www.csmonitor.com/2006/0208/p13s02-lifp.html.

Gardner, M. (2007). Age friendly workplaces on the rise. *The Christian Science Monitor,* May 7, 13.

General Accounting Office. (2001). Demographic trends pose challenges for employers and workers. Unites States General Accounting Office. Retrieved June 21, 2007, from http://www.gao.gov/new.items/d0285.pdf.

Gentry, C. (2007). Diamonds in the rough. *Chain Store Age*, June, 2007, 29–32.

Merrill Lynch. (2005). The Merrill Lynch new retirement survey. Retrieved June 21, 2007, from www.totalmerrill.com/retirement.

Shea, G.F., & Haasen A. (2006). Excerpt from the older worker advantage: making the most of the aging workforce. Praeger Publishers: Westport, CT. Retrieved on December 7, 2006, from http://www.vitaneedle.com/pages/older_worker.htm.

The Aerospace Corporation Web site (2007). Retrieved June 21, 2007, from http://www.aero.org/corporation.

Towers-Perrin. (2005). The business case for workers over 50+. Retrieved on June 20, 2007, from http://assets.aarp.org/rgcenter/econ/ workers_fifty_plus_1.pdf.

Toossi, M. (2004). Labor force projections to 2012: the graying of the American workforce. *Monthly Labor Review*, February, 2004.

Toossi, M. (2005). Labor force projections to 2014: retiring boomers. *Monthly Labor Review*, November, p. 25–44. Retrieved on 6/20/07 from http://www.bls.gov/opub/mlr/2005/11/art3full.pdf.

Vital Aging Network. (2006). Working beyond the traditional retirement age. University of Minnesota. Retrieved on June 20, 2007, from http://www.van.umn.edu/options/2b6_workbeyond.asp.

Watson Wyatt Worldwide. (2004). Phased retirement: aligning employer programs with worker preferences. Washington, D.C: Watson Wyatt.

## DISCUSSION QUESTIONS

1. In spite of people living longer and healthier lives, stereotypes about older workers being hard to manage and slow to adapt to new technologies still persist. How does the media contribute to and reinforce these perceptions?

2. The three organizations profiled in this article (the Vita Needle company, CVS, and The Aerospace Corporation) are quite different and represent a successful small business, a huge corporation, and a not-for-profit government contractor. What might they all have in common that has enabled them to be innovative about their programs for older workers?

3. Will the development of Internet technologies and the capability to telecommute, etc., provide more viable new work opportunities for older workers? Why or why not?

---

**Diversity on the Web**

Each year the American Association of Retired Persons honors organizations that support the utilization of older workers. Visit the AARP Web site and review this year's list of "Winning Strategies" organizations.

Select one that you consider to be innovative. What does it do that benefits the organization's mission <u>and</u> meets the needs of the older workers?

http://www.aarp.org

---

 **Points of Law**

The Age Discrimination in Employment Act of 1967 was an expansion of Title VII of the Civil Rights Act. The provisions apply to federal, state, and local governments and organizations with twenty or more employees. This law protects job applicants and employees over forty years of age from employment discrimination based on age in terms of hiring, firing, promotion, layoffs, benefits, compensation, job assignments, and/or training. In addition, the ADEA forbids retaliation against those who file charges, testify, or participate in investigations, proceedings, and litigation under the ADAE.

http://www.eeoc.gov/types/age.html

# Religion, Culture, and Management in the New Millennium

## Asha Rao

*Spirituality could be the ultimate competitive advantage.*
— Ian Mitroff, *A Spiritual Audit of Corporate America*

*Across the country, major-league executives are meeting for prayer breakfasts and spiritual conferences. In Minneapolis, 150 business chiefs lunch monthly at a private ivy-draped club to hear chief executives such as Medtronic Inc's William George and Carlson Co's Marilyn Carlson Nelson draw business solutions from the Bible. In Silicon Valley, a group of high-powered, high-tech Hindus—including Suhas Patil, founder of Cirrus Logic, Desh Despande, founder of Cascade Communications, and Krishna Kalra, founder of BioGenex—are part of a movement to connect technology to spirituality.*

— Business Week, Nov. 1999

As we end a millennium and move into the twenty-first century, the world of business and management is turbulent and evolving faster than it has in the past. We live and work in "Internet time" where firms form, go public, and disband before decision trees and 5-year plans can be developed (Conlin, 1999). In this time of rapid change, there seems to be a renewed interest in old traditions: spirituality and religion in business. American CEOs and executives are drawing on the Bible, Bhagvad Gita, Talmud, and other scriptures for inspiration (Brahm, 1999; Conlin, 1999; Leigh, 1997).

The trend is not limited to the United States; Asian leaders have espoused the role of "Asian values" derived from Confucianism in the rapid economic development of the ASEAN region (*The Economist,* 1992; Hofstede and Bond, 1988). In countries ranging from India to Burma to France, religion has played a part in management processes and economic development (or the lack thereof). At an individual level, we now truly live in a global village where more people than ever are internationally mobile or work in cross-cultural environments in global teams, which are often temporary or even virtual teams (Adler, 1997; Conlin, 1999). Consequently, people are directly affected by the cultural beliefs, religious norms, and practices of others.

This article examines the role of religion or faith in culturally derived values, beliefs, and management practices across the globe and discusses the implications for international managers. It focuses on work issues raised by major religions or faiths such as Christianity, Confucianism, Hinduism, Islam, and Judaism to examine their impact on management today, and potentially for the future. Although some of these religions directly affect the behavior of people at work, others have a more subtle effect through ethnic culture.

## CONCEPTUAL FRAMEWORK

The statistics indicate that 95 percent of Americans say that they believe in God or a religious faith, and 48 percent bring religion into the workplace (Conlin, 1999). Our future global leaders, the presidential candidates in the current U.S. elections, report turning to the Bible for advice on a range of their decisions (*New York Times,* 2000). United State's attendance rates at religious services are among the highest in the world (Gannon, 1994). Recent reports suggest that top executives from a range of firms believe that faith has an impact on the bottom line (Conlin, 1999). Indeed, Ian Mitroff states that in the new millennium, spirituality could be the ultimate competitive advantage by raising productivity in the workplace (Mitroff, 1999).

The impact of religion is not always blatant or intentional. It can have an indirect, more subtle impact through national or ethnic culture. For instance, the concept of the 5-day workweek in the West is firmly rooted in Christianity, but most Christians or even Americans see this as an accepted business practice rather than a religious one. To understand the subtle impact of religion on business today, one needs to understand national or ethnic cultures.

## CULTURE

Three critical mechanisms explain the origins of different cultures. They are religion, language, and geographical proximity (Ronen and Shenkar, 1985). Because religion is only one of three determinants of culture, it is clear that cultures sharing religious roots can differ because of variations in the latter two mechanisms. This explains the differences in cultures between the Latin American cluster and the Anglo cluster. The power of religion is evident in the similarities of culture in the Islamic nations and in the overseas Chinese. Cultural bonds, or the collective programming, is usually difficult to break even later in adulthood. We maintain culturally derived values, beliefs, and behavior in the workplace and even when traveling across cultures as demonstrated by much research in the field of cross-cultural management (Adler, 1997).

Cultures have several layers, as depicted in Figure 1. Elements in layer one change with time. These include language, clothing, or appearance and behavior. These elements are based on the deeper levels of culture. At the next level lie attitudes and rituals—key among them being the attitude toward women in the workplace. These too can change with time, but they adapt at a much slower pace. At the core of the culture, in the third layer, lie values and beliefs that are stable, often across generations, and relatively impermeable to the passage of time. Religious

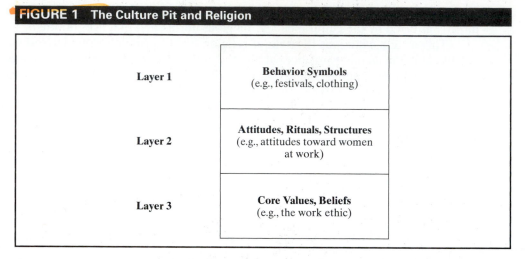

**FIGURE 1  The Culture Pit and Religion**

| Layer 1 | **Behavior Symbols** (e.g., festivals, clothing) |
| Layer 2 | **Attitudes, Rituals, Structures** (e.g., attitudes toward women at work) |
| Layer 3 | **Core Values, Beliefs** (e.g., the work ethic) |

beliefs and practices can be linked to each layer of culture. The following discussion begins with the bottom layer and draws upon it in examining the upper layers of culture.

## RELIGION AND CULTURAL VALUES

The impact of religion at the level of core values and beliefs is strong. Take for instance the meaning of work in different cultures, cultural assumptions, and ethics. Religions differ in their emphasis on the role of work in life. Much has been written about the Protestant Work Ethnic, which helps explain the criticality of work in the United States. Succinctly, the ethic holds that a good Protestant will work hard on earth and be successful in order to reap rewards later in heaven. A person's work, or their calling, comes from God. In working hard, people make evident their worth to both God and themselves. In the United States, the Protestant ethic was joined by Social Darwinism, as so well expressed by Russell Conwell, a Methodist minister and the first president of Temple University (Burr, 1917). He extolled his followers, "I say you ought to be rich; you have no right to be poor . . . I must say that you ought to spend some time getting rich." He went on to conclude that it was absurd to believe that people should not want wealth, because wealth enables people to truly accomplish something of value on earth (Gannon, 1991). In this fashion, the work value is united with both drive and a high need for achievement in the United States.

Other religions also speak of the value of work. The book of Islam, the Quran, indicates that work is an obligation. Indeed, the prophet Muhammad was a trader by profession. But Islam also breeds an element of fatalism in the workplace, letting employees off the hook, because destiny is in the hand of God, who is the ultimate creator of wealth (Rice, 1999). Hindu philosophy offers *dharma* (duty) as one of the four means to salvation. This aspect of Hindu religion espoused in the *Bhagvad Gita* as *karma,* which represents work or duty without an attachment towards immediate rewards. Kalra, founder and CEO of BioGenex laboratories says, "The *Bhagvad Gita* teaches that I have rights on action, but no rights on the fruits of action, nor should I be attached to inaction as a result. So I have the right to be the best CEO but no right to how much money I can earn ... As a result of this, I have no fear of failure, and I can take risks," (Brahm, 1999).

Work helps the Hindu earn a living, satisfy worldly interests, gain power and status, and take care of the family (Gannon, 1994). But, Hinduism dictates that the role of work changes during different stages in life. The role of work is strongest in the second stage of life, where the *grahasta* is obliged to work and fulfil his duty to society. At later stages, the Hindu needs to withdraw from worldly accomplishments such as work to focus on the search for the truth.

Differences in power relations can also be traced back to religions. For instance, Confucius declared that the stability of society is based on unequal relationships and listed five basic and unequal relationships as follows: father–son, husband–wife, ruler–subject, older brother–younger brother, older friend–younger friend. This philosophy helps explain the power differentials between men and women, bosses and subordinates, and the relevance of seniority in cultures such as China, Japan, and Korea. Also, these relationships are held together by mutual and complementary obligations, which helps explain the power of *guanxi* in Chinese business (Leong and Tung, 1998).

Religion and culture have been linked to economic development. In one analysis, cultures where long-term values of persistence, ordered relationships, thrift, and a sense of shame were dominant tended to experience rapid economic growth. Cultures that clung to short-term Confucian values of personal steadiness, face, tradition, and reciprocity of favors tended to be slow developers (Hofstede and Bond, 1988). Taking this a level higher, the rulers of South Korea and Singapore have long used Confucian principles as a means of societal change and control.

## Religion and Ethics

Religious values and management interface in discussions of ethics and social responsibility but surface in different forms in different cultures (Laczniak, 1999; Rice, 1999; Vogel, 1992). U.S. firms today are formulating codes of ethical conduct for their employees worldwide. In trying to explain why the level of public interest in business ethics in the United States exceeds that in the rest of the world, Vogel (1992) draws upon America's Protestant heritage, which makes the creation of wealth "God's work"; it raises people's expectations of the moral behavior of businesspeople. Most Americans also believe that these ethics are or should be universal, compared with Eastern cultures that allow for situational or contextual variations (Trompenaars, 1993).

In discussing Islamic ethics, Rice (1999) states that Islam requires the free-market system to be complemented by a moral filter so that scarce resources are equitably distributed in society. The religion stresses brotherhood, equality, and socioeconomic justice for all. In the Gulf countries, oil has brought amazing wealth to a few, but interestingly that wealth has also trickled down to the masses through social welfare programs. *Zakat,* or alms tax, is one of the five pillars of Islam.[1] According to Rice, the Quranic injunction "there is no compulsion in religion" leads people to follow a strong moral code.

Jewish business ethics also acknowledge the centrality of the community (Pava, 1998) as reflected in three talmudic principles. First is the recognition of different levels of responsibility for charity; second, the *Kofin* principles "formalize a minimum standard. If B's situation can improve at no cost to A, A should willingly waive legal rights." Third, *lifnim mishurat hadin* calls for ethical conduct beyond meeting legal norms. The emphasis on community over wealth is apparent in Brahm's (1999) account of Arron Feuerstein's (President/CEO, Malden Mills Industries) decision to keep his mill open and his employees on the payroll even after the mill burned down. Feuerstein drew on the teachings of the Talmud, which stress that money is not as crucial as taking care of others and acquiring a good name, which is "the greatest treasure a man can acquire." Feuerstein paid his employees for the next few months and was rewarded with his employees' motivation and loyalty.

These contrasting approaches show that global religions focus on different aspects of ethics. It is interesting to note that in the United States the focus is on creating ethical codes of conduct to control managerial behavior such as bribery and the misuse of resources, whereas Islamic societies focus on the welfare of all, that is, socioeconomic issues.

## ATTITUDES, SOCIAL STRUCTURES AND THE CONCEPT OF TIME

The concepts discussed in this section are based on the values and core assumptions described in the previous one, but these include rituals or artifacts that are observable as well as discernable attitudes that are based on core values. Some of the key concepts include attitudes such as those towards women and work, and structures such as the Hindu caste system, Islamic banking, and ethical codes such as Catholic Social Teaching (Laczniak, 1999).

### Women in Management

Sadly, most religions can be held accountable for the lower status of women in the workforce. Christianity, Islam, Hinduism, Judaism, and Confucianism all assign women to nurturing, family primary roles, allowing for power differentials between men and women. In the United States, the Southern Baptist Convention recently declared that wives should be submissive to their husbands (*New York Times*, 2000). Fundamentalist leaders in different cultures have used religion to drastically limit the ability of women to acquire an education and to participate in the workforce (for example, the Taliban in Afghanistan).

The beliefs on the appropriate role of women in society affect state policy. For instance, until 1977 the Federal Republic of Germany had laws that gave husbands the right to prevent their wives from working outside the home. In South Africa, a husband could control his wife's right to negotiate and undertake contracts until 1984 (Adler and Israeli, 1988). In a more indirect fashion, the family primary role advocated for women legitimizes the social limits to their career choices along with business practices such as unequal pay for equal work prevalent in most cultures (Adler and Israeli, 1988).

### Social Hierarchies and Business Codes

Although educated Indians deem caste a medieval degeneration, it has been a basic feature of Hindu society. The caste system mandated a religious division of labor into four castes of priests (*brahamans*), warriors (*kshatryias*), businessfolk (*vaishyas*) and workers (*sudras*). The discriminatory negative consequences of this inherited division of labor are well known. Yet, much of Indian enterprise, in India and overseas, can be traced to the business families belonging to the *viashya* clans (Saha, 1993). The knowledge that it was their mandated role in society and centuries of specialization helped the *vaishya* business houses develop their skills.

In Islamic countries such as Saudi Arabia, business law is derived from the Quran and the Hadith. The fact that the prophet Mohammad prohibited *riba*, or unearned profit, has lead to the development of systems of Islamic banking where banks invest in business or enter into partnership so that the lender and borrower share the same risk and reward rather than profit from another's work.

# SURFACE CULTURE

Values, core assumptions, attitudes, and rituals are manifested in the surface culture. This layer is paradoxically the most evident, yet the most mutable layer of culture. Some evident manifestations of the cultural layers include schedules and calendars, festivals, and the concept of the workweek.

## Calendars, Schedules, and the Workweek

Although the 5-day workweek is common in many countries, it is most accepted in Christian ones. In 1992 when merchants in Montreal sought to overturn legislation that kept stores closed on Sunday, people raised the issue that even God rested on Sunday after creating the world and so should Quebec residents. The president of YKK (North America) found this to be a point of conflict between American and Japanese employees. The former hated working over weekends, which was a common practice for Japanese expatriates. He traced the difference to differences in faith or religion because the Japanese picked up the workweek concept from the Americans after World War II, and didn't take it too seriously (Ishino, 1994). Sunday has no religious significance for much of the world. In the Islamic world, the weekend begins on Thursday. In predominantly Hindu India, the workweek is 5-1/2 days.

Devout Christians go to church on Sunday, a holiday in the Western world, but Jews and Muslims have to make adjustments to manage the clash between their religious rituals and work. Given that Orthodox Jews cannot operate machines (such as cars) from Friday sundown to Saturday sundown, it poses a challenge for people who are asked to work late on Fridays. Prayer is one of the five pillars of Islam, and a devout Muslim must pray five times a day. A colleague in Princeton keeps a prayer mat rolled up in his drawer at work and schedules his prayer times between meetings.

Religious days for many groups including the Hindus and Muslims are determined by the lunar calendar and change from year to year. This is important for the modern business traveler because, across the globe, most mandated holidays are religious ones. Mapping them has become a business necessity and enterprise. Work slows down in the Muslim world during the month of Ramadan (the ninth month in the Islamic calendar) when people generally fast from sunrise to sunset and focus on prayer. A similar phenomenon occurs around Christmas in the United States and Diwali in India. In an interesting development in international negotiations, South Americans realized that U.S. businesspeople were tempted to make concessions and close deals so that they could return home for Christmas. They then scheduled negotiations around the holidays to gain an advantage (Adler, 1997).

Finally, religious norms often dictate dress in the workplace. In Islamic cultures where modesty is a virtue, women wear loose-fitting clothing in public. Women often wear the veil, which represents honor, dignity, chastity, purity, and integrity, to work. Devout Muslim men often have beards and wear skull caps. Jewish men, too, may wear skullcaps to work. In both religions, the cap is viewed as a symbol of subservience to their God.

## Causes

The popular press suggests many motives for the current interest in religion and spirituality in the workplace. For one, the changing nature of business, especially in the high-technology area, leads managers into uncharted territory. Although the formal attendance rates at churches in the United States is high, the number usually increases during periods of crisis (Gannon, 1994). A potential explanation for the interest in religion is that the pace of change in the business environment, and the stress of working in this environment, creates an internal crisis that draws people to their religion.

## Consequences

In sum, the impact of religion on management is widespread through its impact on culture. However, what we see happening today is a more direct application of religion and spirituality in the workforce by executives, rather than the incidental application through culture. The current belief is that this is conducive to the workplace because it spurs the development of employee programs such as on-site day care and flextime, enhances motivation, and increases productivity (Mitroff, 1999). But what of its consequence in a global economy? To some extent, it is positive because managers can theoretically schedule work to take advantage of religious differences—such as having non-Christians work over Christmas, and non-Muslims over Ramadan. But, on another level, it is bound to create conflict when different religious practices and beliefs collide. Conflicts that emerge from differences in beliefs and values are usually difficult to resolve because people become committed to positions based on principles and will not compromise (Lewicki, Litterer, and Saunders, 1988). Managers need to consider the implications of these trends and consider ways to deal with the negative consequences. Because religion and culture have many layers, some are more critical to people than others. Mapping the similarities and differences of dominant religions will help managers reduce conflict and build on universal norms. Unlike other management trends, religion is a personal issue at the core of most people's values. The inappropriate application of religious principles can have potentially dangerous consequences.

## DISCUSSION QUESTIONS

1. Identify a belief, value, or attitude of yours that you can attribute to your religion. Examine its impact on your work and career.

2. How could your religion affect your role and performance in a multicultural workplace?

3. In small-group discussions, map some of the similarities and differences in religious beliefs, attitudes, and behavior of people following different world religions and faiths. Present your findings to the class.

## BIBLIOGRAPHY

Adler, N.J. (1997). *International dimensions of organizational behavior*. Ohio: South Western.

Adler, N.J., and Israeli, D.N. (1988). *Woman in management worldwide*. Armonk, NY: Sharpe.

Alexandrin, G. (1993). Elements of buddhist economies. *International Journal of Social Economics*, *20*(2), pp. 3–11.

Ananth, S. (1998). *Vaastu: The classical Indian science of architecture and design.* India: Penguin.

Brahm, J. (1999). The spiritual side. *Industry Week*, *248*(3), pp. 48–56.

Burr, Agnes Rush. (1917). *Russell H. Conwell and his work, one man's interpretation of life.* Philadelphia: John C. Winston Company.

"Motorola's Cultural Sensitivity Pays Off from Hong Kong to Texas." *Business Week*, 1991.

Conlin, M. (1999). Religion in the workplace: The growing presence of spirituality in corporate America. *Business Week*, Nov. 1, pp. 151–159.

Copeland, L., and Griggs, L. (1985). *Going International.* New York: Random House.

Digh, P. Religion in the workplace: Make a good-faith effort to accommodate. *HR Magazine*, *43*(13), pp. 84–91.

Ferraro, G.P. (1994). *The cultural dimensions of international business*. Upper Saddle River, N.J.: Prentice Hall.

Flynn, G. (1988). Accomodating religion on the job: Few rules, lots of common sense. *Workforce*, *77*(9), pp. 94–97.

Gannon, M. (1994). *Understanding global cultures: Metaphorical journeys through 17 countries.* Thousand Oaks, CA: Sage.

Hofstede, G. (1980). *Cultures consequences: International differences in work related values.* Beverly Hills: Sage.

Hofstede, Geert, and Bond, M.H. The Confucius connection: From cultural roots to economic growth. *Organizational Dynamics*, Spring 1988, *16*(4), pp. 4–22.

Ishino, Y. "Religion in Management," presented at McGill University, 1994.

Laczniak, G.R. (1999). Distributive justice, catholic social teaching, and the moral responsibility of marketeers. *18*(1), pp. 125–129.

Leigh, P. (1997). The new spirit at work. *Training and Development*, *51*(3), pp. 26–33.

Lloyd, B. and Trompenaars, F. (1993). Culture and change: conflict or consensus? *Leadership and Organizational Journal*, *14*(6), p. 17.

Mitroff, I. (1999). *A spiritual audit of corporate america.* San Francisco: Jossey-Bass.

Pava, M.I. (1998). The substance of Jewish business ethics. *Journal of Business Ethics*, *17*(6), pp. 603–617.

Rice, G. (1999). Islamic ethics and the implications for business. *Journal of Business Ethics*, *18*(4), pp. 345–358.

Ronen, S., and Shenkar, O. (1985). Clustering countries on attitudinal dimensions: A review and synthesis. *Academy of Management Review*, *19*(3), pp. 435–54.

Saha, A. (1993). The caste system in india and its consequences. *International Journal of Sociology and Social Policy*, *13*(3), pp. 1–76.

Teaching New Values. *The Economist*, Nov. 28, 1992, *325*(7787), p. 31.

The 2000 Campaign: Al Gore's Journey. *The New York Times*, October 22, 2000, p. 20.

Vogel, D. (1992). The globalization of business ethics: Why America remains distinctive. *California Management Review*, *35*(1).

Yeung, I., and Tung, R. (1996). Achieving business success in confucian societies: The importance of guanxi. *Organizational Dynamics*, *25*(2), pp. 54–65.

## ENDNOTE

1. The other four pillars are the belief in one God, *salat* or prayer, the observance of *ramadan*, and pilgrimage to Mecca in one's lifetime.

┌─ **Diversity on the Web** ──────────────────────────────────

Select a religion (other than your own) and research the following: 1) A brief history of the religion, 2) The religion's major beliefs and practices that could have an impact in the workplace, such as holy days; dress; diet; and attitudes about women, racial minorities and gays, etc., 3) Specific past or current workplace issues that have been raised with respect to this religion and/or its practices and 4) Examples of specific workplace legal cases related to this religion.

**Suggested Web sites:**

America religious identification survey from The Graduate Center at The City University of New York:
*http://www.gc.cuny.edu/studies/aris_index.htm*

The Anti-Defamation League:
*http://www.adl.org/issue_religious_freedom/religious_ac/accommodation_QA.asp*

Title VII of the Civil Rights Act of 1964:
*http://www.eeoc.gov/laws/vii.html*

The Pluralism Project at Harvard University:
*http://www.pluralism.org/resources/links/index.php*
*http://religions.rutgers.edu/vri/*

Virtual Religion Index, maintained by the Religion Department at Rutgers University:
*http://www.virtualreligion.net*

University of Wyoming Program of Religious Studies:
*http://www.uwacadweb.uwyo.edu/religionet/er/DEFAULT.HTM*

The Wabash Center: Guide to Internet Resources for Teaching and Learning in Theology and Religion:
*http://www.wabashcenter.wabash.edu/*

Adapted from "Exploring Religious Diversity" by Pamela Sherer, in C. Harvey & M. J. Allard's *Understanding and Managing Diversity: Readings. Cases and Exercises,* 3rd edition, Prentice Hall, 2005.

# Religion and Work

## Carol P. Harvey
### *Assumption College*

In today's global society, it is useful to learn more about the religions that may be practiced by coworkers. Without some knowledge, individuals may attribute incorrect meanings to others' behaviors. In addition, organizations may have policies and practices that inadvertently conflict with their employees' religious beliefs. For example, some organizations do not allow vacation time to be accrued, thus preventing pilgrimages that may require a month of leave. Others require all workers to take Christian holidays and do not capitalize on the opportunity to have non-Christians work on days that have no significance to them. Jewish employees, for example, may choose to work on Christmas Eve in exchange for having Yom Kippur off with pay. Because many individuals may be reluctant to discuss their religion or to explain its practices in a work setting, misunderstandings of behavior can result.

The following scenarios depict workplace incidents in which others are not aware of the religious basis for the individual's behavior. In each case, the employee is put in the limelight because of his/her religion. The supervisor or coworker, who has little or no knowledge of the religious practices that are at the root of these actions, may attribute an incorrect reason for the behavior that they see. These scenarios illustrate that lack of knowledge can lead to conflict, decreased productivity, and diminished motivation for workers as well as managers.

## DIRECTIONS

Each scenario illustrates the intersection between religion and the workplace. Form small groups and through the sharing of information (or if given as a research assignment, through library and Web sources) answer the following questions.

A. Using only the information provided in the scenario, list the *possible* attributions (i.e., explanations of why this person is behaving as he/she is without knowing the real reasons behind the behavior) that coworkers and managers in the case could use to explain the person's behavior.

B. Discuss the negative and/or positive effects of these attributions on the work organization.

C. Explain what a manager should do in this situation.

D. If someone in your group has some knowledge about religions, ask him/her to explain the religious significance of this worker's behavior. **(Note: It is important to this exercise that this is the last step in the discussion.)**

### Scenario 1

Mary Ellen comes to work with a dark spot on her forehead. Several times during the day, coworkers tease her about forgetting to wash her face and suggest that she visit the ladies room.

### Scenario 2

David sits with his coworkers at a luncheon provided during a meeting. Chicken, with a creamy sauce, salad, and rice are served but he declines to eat and only sips water. People at the table ask him if he is feeling well. He keeps assuring them that he is fine.

### Scenario 3

Kaleen never attends any company informal or formal social events (drinks after work, trips to a nearby casino, holiday parties, etc.). In addition, in an organization where "open doors" are a strong cultural norm, his door is often closed for short periods of time. During his performance appraisal, his boss tells Kaleen that he needs to become more sociable and accessible if he expects to move into a management position.

### Scenario 4

Tyler works full time as an assistant manager in a large retail chain store that is open 12 hours a day, 7 days a week. It is company policy that all managers must rotate working on weekends. Tyler has been using many different excuses to avoid working on Saturdays. Although Tyler is a good worker, his boss no longer believes Tyler's stories and will be noting this behavior in his next performance review.

┌─ **Diversity on the Web** ─────────────────────────────────

1. Using the Internet, research a religion that you are unfamiliar with and write an original scenario like those in this exercise, in which an employee's work behavior, based on religious beliefs and practices, is misunderstood by a boss or coworker.

2. Conduct research through the Internet into the history, beliefs, dietary practices, ethical standards, and implications for workplace behavior of a religion with which you are *totally* unfamiliar. Ideas include: Assemblies of God, Buddhism, Shintoism, Confucianism, Eastern Rite Catholicism, Taoism, Sikhism, Hinduism, Seventh-day Adventists, Mennonite/Amish, Roman Catholicism, Quaker (Religious Society of Friends), Hassidic Judaism, Bahai, and Native American/First Nation, beliefs, etc.

---

# *Writing Assignment*

1. Plan to attend a service at the temple, church, or meeting place of the religion you have researched under instruction number 2 in Diversity on the Web. You should contact the priest, minister, rabbi, or leader to ask permission, check on the time of the service, and inquire about any dress codes that may be necessary to observe. Be prompt, dress appropriately, and be able and willing to stay for the entire service.

2. Write a 5- to 6-page double-spaced paper that explains what a manager should know about this religion to better understand his/her workers who practice this faith. What did you learn about those who practice this religion from attending the service? Emphasis should be placed on understanding the cultural and historic roots of the faith, discussion of the behavioral and work-related implications of the values, ethical beliefs, and practices of the religion.

Information and links to many additional resources on the major religions of the world can be found at http://www.religioustolerance.org. An excellent book on the subject of religious practices is *How to Be a Perfect Stranger* (2003), 3rd edition, by Stuart M. Matlins and Arthur J. Magida, Skylight Paths Publishing: Woodstock Vermont.

# Musical Chairs

M. June Allard

*Assumption College*
*Worcester State College Professor Emerita*

The goal of this exercise is to provide an experience in how it feels to be physically challenged; in this case, how it feels to be unable to communicate with people in the traditional way.

## INSTRUCTIONS

1. Form a group of four to six members and arrange your chairs in a circle.

2. Read the following passage to yourself:

---

Fifty students reported for a class that had 35 student desk-chairs: 30 RH (Right Hand) and five LH (Left Hand). Fifteen RH students then volunteered to transfer to an honors section down the hall, thereby leaving everyone in the original class seated.

After class, six RH students and one LH student reported their chairs were broken and needed replacing. Later that afternoon the honors instructor called saying that eight of the transfer students were not eligible for the honors class and were, therefore, returning to the original class.

How many additional RH and LH desk-chairs did the original instructor need for his class?

---

3. **Working as a group,** come to a consensus on the answer to the question posed in the box.

4. Your instructor will provide further instructions on how your group will conduct the exercise.

┌─────────────────────────────────────────────────────────────────┐

**Diversity on the Web**

## Accommodating Challenges

Under the ADA (Americans with Disabilities Act), employers may not discriminate in the hiring of persons with disabilities. Further, employers are required to provide reasonable accommodations to enable individuals with disabilities to perform their jobs and communicate effectively.

Note that tax incentives are provided for "qualified architectural and transportation barrier removal expenses." The employer is not required, however, to provide accommodations primarily for personal use, such as hearing aids and wheelchairs.

### Directions

1. Search the Internet for job ads and select two ads for jobs. Make them as different as possible: different types of jobs, different levels, different qualification.

2. Try to select jobs for which you have some familiarity.

3. Your instructor will assign a physical challenge for each of your jobs. Research those disabilities, noting how many Americans are afflicted.

4. Assume that someone with the physical challenge assigned to each of your jobs is by far the best-qualified candidate.

5. Devise workplace accommodations appropriate for the challenge.

### Sources

*http://www.monster.com*               *http://www.careerbuilder.com*
*http://www.usa.jobs.gov*               *http://www.hotjobs.yahoo.com*
option: *google* employment opportunities

The office of Disability Employment Policy, part of the U.S. Department of Labor, maintains JAN (Job Accommodation Network), a valuable resource on work site accommodations:

http://www.jan.wvu.edu/soar/disabilities.html

└─────────────────────────────────────────────────────────────────┘

# The Employee Who Couldn't...

## Michael M. Harris
### *University of Missouri, St. Louis*

---

**Customer Service Representative** wanted for automobile service center. Duties include light cleaning of showroom/waiting areas/cars, driving customers to work, and other tasks as assigned. Qualified candidates should be reliable, have at least one year of customer service experience, and possess a safe driving record. Send resume to Lauren Morris, service manager, Lennon Motors....

---

Two months ago, Lauren Morris placed this ad for a customer service employee in the local newspaper. Much to her surprise she received only three resumes. During each interview, Lauren carefully reviewed the job description with applicants, emphasizing certain issues that had been problematic with previous employees: regular attendance, the need for an excellent driving record, and especially the requirement to keep the showroom clean during the day. Although the night crew did most of the heavy cleaning, the floors could become quite dirty during heavy traffic periods. This was a serious concern because the previous employee in this job often complained about doing this task.

After interviewing the three candidates, Lauren selected Brian Cutler for the position. During the interview, Brian assured Lauren that he would have no problem with any of these jobs. At the conclusion of the interview, Brian told her that he had a medical condition called lupus, but that it would not interfere with his performance and that he could perform all of these functions.

Next, Lauren checked into Brian's work and personal history. His last employer, at a local high school, gave him an excellent reference. The supervisor at a previous bank job simply confirmed that Brian worked there for four years. Lauren was unable to contact the third reference, the director of a nonprofit organization where Brian volunteered. A check on Brian's driving record indicated that he was a very good driver. The preemployment drug test, which the dealership requires of all new employees, was delayed due to a mix-up. The general manager said that it was alright to hire Brian, because so few applicants test positive (i.e., are shown to be drug users). Although Lauren had her concerns, she was under pressure to hire someone soon and the other applicants were not as acceptable (e.g., looked unkempt, were job hoppers, and/or had criminal records).

Needing someone immediately for the job, Lauren agreed to hire Brian. On his third day of employment, the problems began. Brian told Lauren that due to his medical condition, lupus, he would be unable to mop the showroom floor. The chemicals used in the cleaning fluid aggravated his medical condition. Lauren consulted the general manager, who said he would assign this responsibility to someone else.

The next week, Brian informed Lauren that because of his medical condition, he would need to sit down for a 10-minute break every two hours. After discussing this new issue with her boss, Lauren refused the request, telling Brian that he could have the standard break, just like the other employees.

When the drug test results finally came back, they showed that Brian was taking a prescription drug for his lupus. According to the doctor that Lauren consulted, Brian should not be driving a car while taking this medication. When Lauren went into the waiting room to talk to Brian, she heard him telling a customer that this dealership discriminates against people with disabilities.

## DISCUSSION QUESTIONS

1. What should the supervisor do now? What could she have done differently at each step in the hiring process? Be specific in your answers.

2. What should Lauren do to avoid this situation with future hires?

3. The last sentence of this case reads, "When Lauren went into the waiting room to talk to Brian, she heard him telling a customer that this dealership discriminates against people with disabilities." What should be done to resolve this issue?

4. Further information on retaliation can be found at (www.eeoc.gov/policy/docs/retal.html). Note especially section "8-II Elements of a Retaliation Claim."

---

### Diversity on the Web

Make a list of fifteen questions you think an employer can ask a job applicant and another list of questions you think an employer cannot ask.

Visit the following Web site and check your list:

http://www.eeoc.gov/facts/jobapplicant.html

# Progress and Backlash: Making Sense of Lesbian, Gay, Bisexual, and Transgender Issues in the Workplace

Gerald Hunt

*Ryerson University, Toronto, Canada*

---

- Colleagues of a Colorado police officer refuse her calls for back-up help when they learn she is a lesbian.
- A Maine manufacturing company informs a manager that he will be fired if rumors that he is gay are true—the manager quits rather than face dismissal.
- In early 2000, American Airlines expands their equal opportunities statement to include transgendered people.

---

**T**hese stories illustrate the contradictions and mixed messages surrounding lesbians, gays, bisexuals, and transgendered (LGBT) issues in the workplace. On the one hand, there have been important and supportive shifts in the legal environment and in public opinion. Many workplaces are sensitive to issues raised by sexual and gender minorities. LGBT characters have become a common and accepted part of mainstream television programs and Hollywood films. Some organizations fully embrace issues related to sexual and gender diversity, and have removed as many discriminatory policies and procedures as possible. Influential organizations, such as General Motors, AT&T and IBM, offer same-sex partner benefits; Disney holds an annual "gay day" in Orlando.

At the same time, many institutions continue to openly discriminate. There is antigay bias in law, housing, and the media. Some churches are very vocal in their opposition to what they term "the gay lifestyle." Some conservatives declare that homosexuals are "sick" and "perverse," not worthy of support of any kind. The American military continues to proclaim that no openly gay man or lesbian should ever be allowed to serve in the defense of his/her country. The American Boy Scouts legally exclude gay men from their midst. In many settings, discrimination and hate are still harsh facts of life if you are lesbian, gay, or bisexual, and especially if you are trans-gendered (dressing and/or behaving differently to the norms associated with one's birth sex). To the casual observer, it must be a bit confusing. Have LGBT minorities come a long way, just a little way, or no way at all? Are organizations legally and/or morally required to accommodate sexual and gender identity diversity? Is it okay to hate and despise this minority group?

## LGBT ISSUES AT WORK

In the late 1940s, in his pioneering work on human sexuality, Kinsey (1948) found upwards of 10 percent of the American population to be engaged in homosexual activity. Recent American and Canadian studies report 5–6 percent of the population to be predominately homosexual, identifying exclusively as gay or lesbian. That percentage rises to as high as 13–15 percent when bisexuals and transgendered people are included (Bagley and Tremblay 1998). These figures mean that the LGBT population is larger than the number of Asian Americans (3.6 percent in the 2000 census) and greater than the number of Jewish people living in the United States (estimated at 3 percent). Unlike most minority groups; however, LGBT people are not readily visible. Many have chosen to remain invisible, especially at work, because they fear the negative consequences that might result from revealing their identity. As the murder of Matthew Shepard illustrated, being openly and visibly gay can still cost your life. Matthew was an openly gay 21-year-old student at the University of Wyoming who was savagely murdered to make the point that homosexuals deserve to die. Throughout history there are many examples of organizations harassing and dismissing employees when they learned—or just suspected—that they were homosexual.

In spite of the very real risks, in recent years, more and more LGBT people have come out to fight for equal rights. They find living in the closet too demeaning a price to pay for "protection" from discrimination. As a result, equality for LGBT people is now an issue of concern and an important rallying point for all people (straight and gay) who are concerned about equity and fairness at work.

Spokespersons offer a clear message: the gay, lesbian, bisexual, transgender community is discriminated against and treated inequitably at work. Change is demanded in human resources policies and practices concerned with recruiting, hiring, promotion, discipline, and benefits. Activists call for organizational leaders to foster and promote an environment that is positive and supportive of **all** human difference and diversity.

These demands closely parallel those made by women and Blacks, and in some ways the LGBT movement has only now caught up with other human rights movements. All of these groups desire equal treatment—not special or exceptional treatment—and want the social and institutional barriers that prevent them from getting it removed.

The overwhelming difference between sexual orientation and gender identity and other types of diversity issues is that for some people sexual diversity at work is more controversial. Homosexuality and gender nonconformity make some people extremely uncomfortable and/or angry. Some conservative thinkers portray the LGBT minority as immoral and degenerate. Others feel that homosexuality is a "private" issue and should not be exposed in the public domain, even though heterosexuality is never reduced to being merely a bedroom activity. Some, guided by Christian teachings, quote from the Bible to defend their views (Leviticus 18:22 states that homosexuality is an abomination). These people fail to note that Leviticus 10:10 also indicates that eating shellfish is an abomination and that Exodus 35:2 clearly states that a neighbor who insists on working on the Sabbath should be put to death.

The polarization around homosexuality creates work situations characterized by a lack of consensus regarding the merit of appeals for equal treatment and justice being made by the LGBT community, thus resulting in a range of organizational responses. Some organizations have made extensive efforts to ensure that policies and benefits are equal for everyone and value their LGBT employees equally with other workers. In other settings, little if any accommodation exists. A few employers go so far as to dismiss these minorities if their identity becomes known.

## SOCIAL, LEGAL AND ECONOMIC DEVELOPMENTS

In spite of controversies and differing perspectives, more and more LGBT people are open about their identities and vocal about their desire for change. This, when combined with a changing social, legal, and economic environment, has convinced more and more organizations to rethink and overhaul policies and practices in order to accommodate LGBT employees.

### Social Forces

With each passing year, the LGBT community has acquired a higher and more positive public profile. Yeager (1999) estimated there were 124 openly gay and lesbian elected officials serving at the federal, state, and municipal levels. These people ranged from Congressman Barney Frank to Margo Frasier, an elected sheriff in Austin, Texas, to Tim Mains, who serves on the Rochester City Council. Perhaps the greatest change though, is from the devastating impact of AIDS, which has given the LGBT community a much stronger presence and voice in society.

Public opinion polls show a steadily increasing tolerance toward homosexuals in general, and their workplace rights in particular. Wilcox and Wolpert (2000:28), in a summary of polling data from throughout the 1990s, found that attitudes have moved in a positive direction since 1992, even though there remains a minority "voicing strongly negative reactions, often rooted in basic emotional reactions." Research conducted in 1998 (Yang 1999) found that a majority of Americans supported the idea of gays and lesbians having equality in employment (84%), housing (81%), inheritance rights (62%), social security benefits (57%), and the military (66%).

Since then, public opinion has shifted steadily toward even more acceptance. A May 2006 Gallup poll found that 89 percent of Americans believed gays and lesbians should have equal rights in job opportunities (Bowman and Foster, 2006). A May 2005 Gallup poll found that 76 percent of Americans thought homosexuals should be allowed in the armed forces, and 62 percent believed they should be hired as high school teachers (Bowman and Foster, 2006). In other words, while there may not be widespread public involvement in the fight for LGBT rights, and some people continue to be extremely vocal in their opposition, there is less basis for believing that the majority of citizens in the United States support either overt or covert discrimination in the workplace on the basis of sexual orientation.

## Legal Change

The increased visibility of LGBT people, combined with more assertive demands for equal rights, has generated considerable legal action. For the past decade, federal, state, and municipal legislators debated changes in legislation that would affect LGBT minorities in almost every aspect of their lives, including violence and harassment, employment and housing discrimination, adoption and child care, domestic partner benefits, and the freedom to marry. In some jurisdictions, the legal changes are widespread; in others there has been little or no change.

At one time, all states had laws regulating and criminalizing consensual sexual activity between adults of the same sex. The beginning of 2003 found "sodomy" laws still on the books in 13 states. However, in a landmark case in June 2003, the Supreme Court struck down the sodomy law in Texas, effectively eliminating discriminatory sodomy laws throughout the country.

Increasing numbers of governments have passed bills to include sexual orientation as a protected class, particularly in employment and housing. By the year 2007, seventeen states (California, Connecticut, Hawaii, Illinois, Maryland, Maine, Massachusetts, Minnesota, Nevada, New Hampshire, New Jersey, New Mexico, New York, Rhode Island, Vermont, Washington, and Wisconsin), as well as the District of Columbia, had civil rights laws prohibiting employment discrimination based on sexual orientation. Laws protecting gender nonconformity in the workplace are less widespread. Minnesota and Rhode Island are the only states specifically including gender identity in their antidiscrimination laws, but courts have ruled that transgendered people are protected under existing discrimination laws in Connecticut, Massachusetts, New Jersey, and New York. As well, a growing number of cities, such as Boulder, Atlanta, Dallas and Houston, prohibit employment discrimination based on gender identity (HRC, 2006a).

In December 1999, Vermont made history by becoming the first American jurisdiction to equalize benefits for all people. Lesbians and gays who enter civil unions are eligible to receive the same protections and benefits that Vermont currently provides to married couples. Vermont was a logical place for this to happen, since it was the first state to offer domestic partner benefits to state workers and one of the first to approve same-sex adoptions and prohibit discrimination on the basis of sexual orientation. To date, few states have mirrored Vermont's progressive initiatives, although some cities now have a mechanism for partner registration.

A very dramatic development also occurred in San Francisco. In 1997, the city passed an Equal Benefits Ordinance Law requiring any company doing business with the city or county of San Francisco to offer the same benefits to the domestic partners of its employees as it offers to the legal spouses of employees. In response to San Francisco's law, many organizations, such as Shell and United Airlines, implemented domestic partner benefits. Other companies, such as FedEx, did so only after losing court challenges.

Even more dramatically, in 2003, the Massachusetts Supreme Court ruled that the prohibition of gay marriage was in violation of the state's constitution. As a result, Massachusetts became the first state to allow same-sex marriages, beginning in May 2004. Similarly, in 2006, the New Jersey Superior Court ruled that the state had to expand their definition of marriage to include same-sex couples, and that any "civil union" recognition had to be "equivalent" to marriage. No other American jurisdictions allow same-sex marriage, but a growing number allow some form of civil union registration.

## Labor Union Activity

Although initially unsupportive, some labor organizations now support LGBT rights (Bielski, 2005; Krupat and McCreery, 2001; Bain, 1999; Frank, 1999). This support ranges from formal nondiscrimination clauses that include sexual orientation to the formation of subcommittees and caucuses focusing on issues of concern to LGBT workers. In 1997, the AFL-CIO (American Federation of Labor and Congress of Industrial Organizations) approved "Pride at Work" as a funded constituency group, and many state and local labor councils have adopted similar measures. Bielski (2005) found that teachers' unions, along with the largest public sector union (American Federation of State, County, and Municipal Employees—AFSCME), the Service Employees International Union (SIEU), the United Auto Workers (UAW), and the Communication Workers (CWA), had gone the furthest in representing their sexual minority members.

At the same time, Bielski found that other unions had taken only a few initiatives. Among these were the United Food and Commercial Workers (UFCW), the International Association of Machinists (IAM), the Teamsters (IBT), the steelworkers (USWA), and the electrical workers (IBEW).

One of the most dramatic examples of union activity is with the UAW. For a number of years, the issue of LGBT rights had been the subject of some of the most divisive debates in the union's history. A 1997 *New Yorker* article profiled the story of Ron Woods, a UAW worker at Chrysler's Trenton, Michigan, plant (Stewart, 1997). In the early 1990s, Ron helped to organize a caucus with the goal of pressuring the union to take on LGBT issues. He also became involved in picketing a Cracker Barrel restaurant (a chain that openly fired suspected gay and lesbian workers). After a newspaper photo of him in the picket line appeared in a Detroit paper, he began to experience very serious homophobic harassment, including physical assault, from his coworkers.

Initially, the union's response was unsupportive, but by 1998, the UAW pressured General Motors and Ford to adopt a nondiscrimination policy that included sexual orientation. Chrysler continued to refuse to take this step. By August 2000, the "Big Three" had all agreed not only to an inclusive nondiscrimination policy, but also to medical, dental, and prescription coverage for same-sex partners, covering about 466,000 workers throughout the United States.

## Economic Forces

The LGBT community represents an important market segment and a group with considerable clout if it decides to boycott a product, service, or organization. Badgett (2001) argues that gays and lesbians are not as affluent as many believe, and on average earn no more than heterosexuals. However, this is a group (especially gay men) that is less likely to have children, probably making discretionary income levels higher than average, and spending with more political sensitivity than most others. Buford (2000) points out that advertising for these so called "gay dollars" in the media generally and the "gay media" in particular, is big business. Like Badgett, he argues that what matters about this group from a marketing point of view, is not affluence, but slightly higher discretionary income, combined with more free time and desire to buy from LGBT-positive companies.

Activists affect the bottom line of anti-LGBT corporations in a variety of ways. They wage proxy contests against homophobic companies, urge public institutions to buy the shares of companies that prohibit antigay discrimination and to sell the shares of companies that do not. Boycotts of homophobic corporations, such as Cracker Barrel restaurants and Coors beer in the 1990s, for example, provide indications that activists have a direct impact on company policy. Cracker Barrel finally added sexual orientation to its written nondiscrimination policy in 2002.

In the early 1980s, the Coors organization went so far as to require lie detector tests to screen out prospective employees identified as gay or lesbian. This prompted countrywide boycotts, leading to a significant reduction in the company's market share. Since then, Coors has taken steps to position itself as a more LGBT-positive company. Wal-Mart's addition of sexual orientation to its nondiscrimination policy in July 2003, after years of pressure from activists, is an important milestone, especially since Wal-Mart is the nation's largest employer, with over one million workers.

## ORGANIZATIONAL RESPONSE

### Corporate Sector

More and more organizations are responding positively to the concerns about discrimination raised by the LGBT community. Many large cities hold an annual Pride Day, with events that are often partially sponsored by high-profile corporations, such as breweries and clothing manufacturers. Increasing numbers of organizations have adopted antidiscrimination policies and instituted domestic partner benefit packages inclusive of same-sex partners. According to one survey, fewer than 24 employers offered same-sex, domestic partner benefits at the beginning of the 1990s, but this number rose to nearly 10,000 by the year 2007 (HRC, 2006a).

During the 1990s, the information technology sector led the way in implementing inclusive benefits, by the end of the decade, oil companies, major banks, hospitality, airlines, and accounting firms were leading the pack. Many of the private-sector employers that now have LGBT-friendly policies, are among the most prestigious and prosperous organizations in the United States. Companies offering domestic partner health benefits include Ford; eBay, Inc.; AT&T; Boeing; Home Depot, Inc.; Walt Disney; McDonald's Corp.; Xerox; Eastman Kodak; Gap, Inc.; Nike; Verizon Communications, Inc; and Starbucks Corp.

### Public Sector

State and local governments, colleges, and universities were among the first organizations to institute nondiscrimination policies and offer benefits packages that included same-sex partners (see Table 1). In 1998, President Clinton signed an executive order banning discrimination based on sexual orientation throughout the federal civil service. Even though most of the federal government does not yet offer same-sex benefits, all

| TABLE 1  Employers with LGBT-friendly policies (2006) |
|---|

A) Employers with nondiscrimination policies that include sexual orientation
- 430  *Fortune* 500 companies
- 1625  Other private companies, nonprofit organizations, and unions
- 562  Colleges and universities
- 300  State and local governments

B) Employers with domestic partner benefits that include same-sex partners
- 263  *Fortune* 500 companies
- 8594  Other private companies, nonprofit organizations, and unions
- 299  Colleges and universities

C) Employers with nondiscrimination policies that include gender identity
- 118  *Fortune* 500 companies
- 143  Other private companies, nonprofit organizations, and unions
- 75  Colleges and universities

D) Organizations with formal gay, lesbian, bisexual, and transgender employee groups
- 306  All organizations

(Source: http://www.hrc.org/worknet) Used with permission HRC Worknet, the Workplace Project Campaign Foundation

cabinet-level departments and 24 independent agencies have nondiscrimination policies. If the Employment Non-Discrimination Act currently before Congress moves forward, it will grant the same benefits currently available to legal spouses to all domestic partners, including same-sex couples. However, such a move seems unlikely at the current time.

Business schools, long thought to be holdouts in developing LGBT-friendly environments for students and staff, are beginning to catch up. A 2002 survey of the top 20 business schools found that 100 percent had antidiscrimination policies based on sexual orientation, 86 percent had same-sex partner benefits, 86 percent had LGBT student groups, and 57 percent had at least one "out" professor (Aplomb Consulting, 2002). Table 1 provides an overview of employers with LGBT-friendly policies.

## Corporate Equity Index

The corporate equality index (CEI) is a set of standards and benchmarks established by the Human Rights Campaign Foundation Workplace Project, that examines and evaluates corporate policies affecting LGBT employees throughout the country (HRC, 2006b). Among the items measured by the CEI are

- Official recognition of a LGBT group
- Sexual orientation nondiscrimination policy
- Health and other benefits for domestic and same-sex partners
- Training aimed at increasing the understanding of sexual orientation and/or gender identity
- Level of coverage for domestic partner health insurance, transgender wellness benefits, and/or other domestic partner benefits, unrelated to health

Many companies now realize that a positive CEI score is a good idea. It often equates to a more inclusive work environment overall since it sends a strong message about valuing diversity in all its forms. In 2006, a total of 138 rated companies received the top CEI rating of 100 percent, representing a tenfold increase from the initial findings in 2002, when only 13 companies received the highest rating. This significant jump can be attributed to the double-digit increase of companies adhering to CEI criteria and a domino effect, whereby an initial company institutes standards and others within the industry realize they need to catch up. Some of the well-known companies that scored 100 percent in 2006 were Ford Motor Co., Gap, Inc, Google, Inc., Sun Microsystems, Inc., and US Airways Group, Inc. (HRC, 2006b).

## NetworkQ

Another interesting development is NetworkQ, a nonprofit organization with over 1,000 members that offers services to the LGBT business school community. It holds an annual conference chronicling the advances of LGBT issues within business. It also maintains an online database of LGBT individuals, listing their skills and/or industry expertise, provides information to prospective business students, and prepares a calendar of worldwide LGBT events. NetworkQ members represent business schools such as MIT, Harvard, Stanford, Columbia, Wharton, Kellogg, Stern, UCLA, University of Toronto, and 200 other business schools from around the world.

## LGBT Employee Network Groups

Many organizations now have groups or caucuses dealing with sexual orientation and gender identity issues. These groups provide a forum for LGBT people to meet each other and socialize, and at the same time create a vehicle for pressuring their organizations to adopt LGBT-friendly policies and procedures. Some of these groups merged with race, gender, and disability activists to become "rainbow alliances." Nearly 300 organizations are known to have LGBT employee groups, or gay-straight alliances, including 3M, American Express, AT&T, Federal Government, Levi Strauss, Kaiser Permanente, McKinsey and Co., Microsoft, NBC, and Warner-Lambert.

## Gender Identity and Transgender Issues

In recent years, workplace issues related to transgenderism and gender identity have developed a much higher profile. Transgenderism is an umbrella term referring to a person who does not conform to traditional gender norms. It includes those who cross-dress, are intersexed, and/or live substantial portions of their lives as other than their birth gender (HRC, 2006a). Transgendered and transgendering people pose a number of unique accommodation issues in the workplace, ranging from restroom use to dress codes. The response to these issues ranges from extreme hostility to full acceptance. American Airlines, for example, was one the first organizations to expand its equal opportunities statement to include gender identity, with policies and guidelines specifically addressing transgendered issues. Employees must use restrooms appropriate to their current gender, but have the right to access different restrooms if they alter their gender identity. American's policy stipulates that the attire of a transitioning employee should reflect the appropriate dress codes of the job they hold and the office where they work, underscoring that all employees are held to the same uniform appearance standards within their gender identity status.

## BACKLASH: THE SPECTRE OF DISCRIMINATION CONTINUES

Not all people and organizations are committed to confronting sexual orientation discrimination. Some conservatives feel such gains have happened too quickly, gone too far, and represent a threat to their sense of identity and well-being. In fact, the shifts in attitudes, policies, and legislation related to LGBT people have generated a considerable backlash of opposition. In 1996, Congress passed the "Defense of Marriage Act," which, among other things, defined marriage as between one man and one woman, and allowed states to refuse to honor same-sex marriages performed in another state. By 2007, twenty-six jurisdictions had enacted constitutional amendments to define marriage as between a man and a woman, and twenty states had enacted statutory "defense of marriage" acts. States such as Florida, Texas, and Ohio now go so far as to ban all forms of same-sex partner recognition, including marriage, civil unions, and domestic partnerships.

A number of religious and conservative groups have emerged whose primary mission is to resist what they term "the gay agenda." The Web site for "Concerned Women for America," for instance, indicates the following: "many of the largest corporations in America have bought into the 'homosexual agenda' . . . Americans should work to roll back these ill-advised policies" (Knight, 2006, Web).

Some corporations steadfastly refuse to alter their human resources polices and practices to accommodate LGBT minorities. Other companies have even rescinded such protections and benefits after mergers and changes in ownership. In 1998, for example, Perot Systems Corporation became the first major American company to end its policy of offering domestic partner benefits to its gay and lesbian employees once Ross Perot returned to the CEO position after his unsuccessful presidential bid.

Similarly, when Phillips Petroleum merged with Conoco in 2002, the new company rescinded Conoco's nondiscrimination policy covering sexual orientation. Prior to the merger of Mobile Oil and Exxon, Mobile had a nondiscrimination policy and offered domestic partner benefits, whereas Exxon did not. After the merger, a policy was put in place to allow same-sex partners of former Mobile employees to continue receiving benefits, but excluding former employees of Exxon or new employees of ExxonMobile from the same perks.

Another organization that fights to retain homophobic policies is the Boy Scouts of America. The Supreme Court ruled in July 2000 that the Boy Scouts could maintain a policy excluding gay men from joining the organization. Several organizations, such as Levi Strauss and the United Way, discontinued contributions to the Boy Scouts as a form of protest, and several churches, such as the United Methodists, have condemned the policy, but the Boy Scouts remain adamant. In contrast, the Girl Scouts has reaffirmed its inclusive nondiscrimination policy.

## DEVELOPMENTS IN CANADA

The situation for LGBT people has undergone spectacular change in many other parts of the world. This is particularly true in Canada, which now ranks among the most favorable places in the world for sexual minorities (along with Belgium, Denmark, and the Netherlands). The Charter of Rights and Freedoms, roughly equivalent to the American constitution, is interpreted to include sexual orientation and all human rights codes as protected grounds in housing and employment. Most provinces recognize same-sex relationships in family law, including the right to adopt children. In June 2005, Canada became the third jurisdiction in the world to allow same-sex marriages in all provinces and territories (the Netherlands and Belgium were the first).

These legislative changes followed initiatives already underway in many Canadian organizations. As early as the mid-1980s, some unions such as the Canadian Auto Workers and the Canadian Union of Public Employees were fighting for nondiscrimination policies and negotiating same-sex benefit packages in collective agreements (Hunt 1999; 2002). By the time they were legislatively mandated to do so, most universities, colleges, and public sector organizations, as well as many in the private sector, had already moved toward inclusive policies and practices.

One measure of the speed and depth of change is the Canadian military. Until the early 1990s, the armed forces could dismiss members found to be gay or lesbian. By 1998, they were advertising the same benefits, opportunities, and protections to all members and their families, regardless of sexual orientation—but only for those sufficiently brave to be open in what many believe is still an unwelcoming organizational culture in relation to sexual diversity.

However, the Canadian situation highlights the fact that access to a legal system does not necessarily change a culture of exclusion and exclusivity. If organizational leaders and the culture remain opposed to LGBT equality, then bias and subtle discrimination are likely to remain in force. People committed to diversity initiatives within Canada tend to focus their efforts on education in an effort to address the values and attitudes that support prejudice.

## CONCLUSIONS

Of all the diversity challenges an organization faces, accommodation to sexuality issues appears to be the most contentious. Although there has been considerable accommodation to the LGBT minority in American organizations over the past decade, this progress has also produced a backlash by people and organizations that do not endorse these changes. As a result, we see contradictions and mixed messages in the response LGBT people receive to their demands for equity, that result in significant variation among states, local authorities, cities, and organizations.

On the one hand, significant change has occurred. The overwhelming majority of Americans support equal workplace rights for LGBT minorities and a number of states and local governments prohibit employment discrimination. Increasingly, organizations are taking steps to curb heterosexual bias in their HR policies and practices, with some going out of their way to provide a welcoming environment for their LGBT workers.

On the other hand, in some settings, there has been no change at all. It is still legally possible to fire someone on the basis of sexual orientation or gender nonconformity in a number of jurisdictions. Some organizations fight assertively for the right to fire LGBT people who might slip through their discriminatory firewalls. Others passively comply with legal changes, but make no effort to create a safe and welcoming environment for LGBT minorities. A few organizations exist whose mission is to overturn advances made by sexual minorities in general and corporations in particular. Such organizations attempt to organize boycotts of corporations who offer a supportive environment to their LGBT employees, and lobby politically to prevent change.

The legal situation in Canada is more supportive than in the United States, but there are organizations that implement change only when forced to do so.

In many ways, accommodating sexual diversity in the workplace acts as a litmus test for an organization's acceptance of diversity more generally. An organization that recognizes and acknowledges its sexual minorities is almost certain to do the same for its other minorities. Benchmark organizations with a broad-based commitment to diversity accept the challenges and opportunities associated with their LGBT employees. They discontinue discriminatory practices and alter HR and benefit polices to ensure that they are equal and fair for everyone. They include sexual diversity in training programs and recruitment strategies. Progressive, pro-diversity organizations make clear through their disciplinary policies and cultural messages that anti-LGBT behavior will not be tolerated any more than will sexist or racist behavior.

## DISCUSSION QUESTIONS

1. Why have some states and local governments introduced protections for LGBT people and other states and local governments have not?

2. Why have some employers introduced protections for LGBT people and other employers have not?

3. You are the CEO of a large retail store. You have just completed a meeting with a delegation of religious leaders from the community who have indicated that they will recommend a boycott of your store to their parishioners if you go ahead with plans to offer same-sex benefits to your employees. What factors should you consider? How will you deal with this situation?

---

*Writing Assignment*

You are working in the human resources department of a large manufacturing organization that likes to think it has excellent HR policies. You have been assigned the task of preparing a diversity-training module on LGBT issues in the workplace. The module will be about two hours in length, and is to be part of a longer course on diversity. This will be the first time that LGBT topics have been included in the course. Outline the topics that you will include in the module and describe your approach to teaching this topic.

---

## BIBLIOGRAPHY

Aplomb Consulting. (2003). *Report on the LGBT-friendliness of the nation's top business schools.* Aplomb Consulting. (Available online at www.aplomb.com)

Bagley, C., and Tremblay, P. (1998). On the prevalence of homosexuality and bisexuality, in a random community survey of 750 men aged 18–27. *Journal of Homosexuality, Vol. 36*(2).

Bain, C. (1999). A short history of lesbian and gay labor activism in the United States" in Hunt, G. *Laboring for Rights: Unions and*

*Sexual Diversity Across Nations,* Philadelphia: Temple University Press.

Badgett, L. (2001). *Money, myths and change: The economic lives of lesbians and gay men.* Chicago: University of Chicago Press.

Bielski, M. (2005). *Identity at work: U.S. labor union effort to address sexual diversity through policy and practice.* Unpublished Ph.D. dissertation. Rutgers, The State University of New Jersey.

Bowman, K., and Foster, A. (2006). *Attitudes about homosexuality and gay marriage.* Washington, DC: American Enterprise Institute.

Buford, H. (2000). Understanding gay consumers. *The Gay and Lesbian Review, Vol VII (2)*, Spring, pp. 26–27.

Frank, M. (1999). Lesbian and gay caucuses in the U.S. labor movement. In Hunt, G. *Laboring for rights: Unions and sexual diversity across nations*, Philadelphia: Temple University Press.

HRC. (2006a). *The state of the workplace for Lesbian, gay, bisexual and transgender Americans 2005–2006.* Washington, DC: Human Rights Campaign Foundation.

HRC. (2006b). *Corporate equity index 2006: A report card on gay, lesbian, bisexual and transgender equality in corporate America.* Washington, DC: Human Rights Campaign Foundation.

Hunt, G. (2002). Organized labour and sexual diversity union activism in Canada. In F. Colgan and S. Ledwith (eds.). *Gender, Diversity and Trade Unions International Perspectives.* London: Routledge.

Hunt, G. (1999). No longer outsiders: Labor's response to sexual diversity in Canada. In Hunt, G. *Laboring for Rights: Unions and Sexual Diversity Across Nations,* Philadelphia: Temple University Press.

Kinsey, A., et al. (1948). *Sexual Behaviour in the Human Male.* New York: Saunders.

Knight, R. (2006). The corporate curtain. (Retrieved December 2006 from Concerned Women of America Web site: http://www.cwfa.org)

Krupat, K., and McCreery, P. (2001). *Out at work: building a gay-labor alliance.* Minneapolis: University of Minnesota Press.

Plant, R. (1986). *The pink triangle: The nazi war against homosexuals.* NY: Henry Holt.

Stewart, J. (1997). Coming out at Chrysler. *The New Yorker* (21 July):38–49.

Wilcox, C., and Wolpert, R. (2000). Gay rights in the public sphere: Public opinion *gay rights.* Chicago: The University of Chicago Press.

Yang, A. (1999) *From wrongs to rights, 1973–1999: Public opinion on gay and lesbian Americans moves toward equality.* Washington, DC: Policy Institute of the National Gay and Lesbian Task Force.

Yeager, K. (1999). *Trailblazers: Profiles of America's gay and lesbian elected officials.* NY: The Hawthorn Press.

---

┌─ **Diversity on the Web** ──────────────────────────────

Read about lesbian, gay, bisexual, and transgender issues at IBM at the following Web site, and answer these questions:

1. Why do you think IBM employs such a person?
2. What would a job like this involve?
3. Do you think other organizations should have a position designated for GLBT issues? Why or why not?

http://www-03.ibm.com/employment/ca/en/people_brad.html
└─────────────────────────────────────────

# The Cracker Barrel Restaurants

## John Howard
### *King's College, London*

**D**iscrimination against lesbians and gays is common in the workplace. Sole proprietors, managing partners, and corporate personnel officers can and often do make hiring, promoting, and firing decisions based on an individual's real or perceived sexual orientation. Lesbian and gay job applicants are turned down and lesbian and gay employees are passed over for promotion or even fired by employers who view homosexuality as somehow detrimental to job performance or harmful to the company's public profile. Such discrimination frequently results from the personal biases of individual decision makers. It is rarely written into company policy and thus is difficult to trace. However, in January 1991, Cracker Barrel Old Country Store, Inc., a chain of family restaurants, became the first and only major American corporation in recent memory to expressly prohibit the employment of lesbians and gays in its operating units. A nationally publicized boycott followed, with demonstrations in dozens of cities and towns. The controversy would not be resolved until a decade later. In the interim, Cracker Barrel would also face several charges of racism from both its employees and customers—suggesting that corporate bias against one cultural group may prove a useful predictor of bias against others.

## THE COMPANY: A BRIEF HISTORY OF CRACKER BARREL

Dan Evins founded Cracker Barrel in 1969 in his hometown of Lebanon, Tennessee, 40 miles east of Nashville. Evins, a 34-year-old ex-Marine sergeant and oil jobber, decided to take advantage of the traffic on the nearby interstate highway and open a gas station with a restaurant and gift shop. Specializing in down-home cooking at low prices, the restaurant was immediately profitable.

Evins began building Cracker Barrel stores throughout the region, gradually phasing out gasoline sales. By 1974, he owned a dozen restaurants. Within five years of going public in 1981, Cracker Barrel doubled its number of stores and quadrupled its revenues: In 1986, there were 47 Cracker Barrel restaurants with net sales of $81 million. Continuing to expand aggressively, the chain again grew to twice its size and nearly quadrupled its revenues during the next five years.

By the end of the fiscal year, August 2, 1991, Cracker Barrel operated over 100 stores, almost all located along the interstate highways of the Southeast and, increasingly, the Midwest. Revenues exceeded $300 million. Employing roughly 10,000 nonunionized workers, Cracker Barrel ranked well behind such mammoth family chains as Denny's and Big Boy in total sales, but led all U.S. family chains in sales per operating unit for both 1990 and 1991.

As of 1991, Cracker Barrel was a well-recognized corporate success story, known for its effective, centralized, but authoritarian leadership. From its headquarters, Cracker Barrel maintained uniformity in its store designs, menu offerings, and operating procedures. Travelers and local customers dining at any Cracker Barrel restaurant knew to expect a spacious, homey atmosphere; an inexpensive, country-style meal; and a friendly, efficient staff. All were guaranteed by Dan Evins, who remained as president, chief executive officer, and chairman of the board.

## THE POLICY: NO LESBIAN OR GAY EMPLOYEES

In early January 1991, managers in the roughly 100 Cracker Barrel operating units received a communiqué from the home office in Lebanon. The personnel policy memorandum from William Bridges, vice president of human resources, declared that Cracker Barrel was "founded upon a concept of traditional American values." As such, it was deemed "inconsistent with our concept and values and . . . with those of our customer base, to continue to employ individuals . . . whose sexual preferences fail to demonstrate normal heterosexual values, which have been the foundation of families in our society."

Throughout the chain, individual store managers, acting on orders of corporate officials, began conducting brief, one-on-one interviews with their employees to see if any were in violation of the new policy. Cheryl Summerville, a cook in the Douglasville, Georgia, store for three-and-a-half years, asked if she were a lesbian, knew she had to answer truthfully. She felt she owed that to her partner of 10 years. Despite a history of consistently high performance evaluations, Summerville was fired on the spot, without warning and without severance pay. Her official separation notice, filled out by the manager and filed with the state department of labor, clearly indicated the reason for her dismissal: "This employee is being terminated due to violation of company policy. The employee is gay."

Cracker Barrel fired as many as 16 other employees across several states in the following months. These workers, mostly waiters, were left without any legal recourse. Lesbian and gay antidiscrimination statutes were in effect in Massachusetts and Wisconsin and in roughly 80 U.S. cities and counties, but none of the firings occurred in those jurisdictions. Federal civil rights laws, the employees learned, did not cover discrimination based on sexual orientation.

Under pressure from a variety of groups, the company issued a statement in late February 1991. In it, Cracker Barrel management said, "We have re-visited our thinking on the subject and feel it only makes good business sense to continue to employ those folks who will provide the quality service our customers have come to expect." The recent personnel policy had been a "well-intentioned over-reaction." Cracker Barrel pledged to deal with any future disruptions in its units "on a store-by-store basis." Activists charged that the statement did not represent a retraction of the policy, as some company officials claimed. None of the fired employees had been rehired, activists noted, and none had been offered severance pay. Moreover, on February 27, just days after the statement, Dan Evins reiterated the company's antagonism toward nonheterosexual employees in a rare interview with a Nashville newspaper. Lesbians and gays, he said, would not be employed in more rural Cracker Barrel locations if their presence was viewed to cause problems in those communities.

## THE BOYCOTT: QUEER NATIONALS VERSUS GOOD OL' BOYS

The next day, when news of Cracker Barrel employment policies appeared in the *Wall Street Journal, New York Times,* and *Los Angeles Times*, investment analysts expressed surprise. "I look on [Cracker Barrel executives] as pretty prudent business people," said one market watcher. "These guys are not fire-breathing good ol' boys." Unconvinced, lesbian and gay activists called for a nationwide boycott of Cracker Barrel restaurants and began a series of demonstrations that attracted extensive media coverage.

The protest movement was coordinated by the Atlanta chapter of Queer Nation, which Cheryl Summerville joined as co-chair with Lynn Cothren, an official with the Martin Luther King, Jr., Center for Nonviolent Social Change. Committed to nonviolent civil disobedience, lesbian and gay activists and supporters staged pickets and sit-ins at various Cracker Barrel locations, often occupying an entire restaurant during peak lunch hours, ordering only coffee.

Protesters were further angered and spurred on by news in June from Mobile, Alabama. A 16-year-old Cracker Barrel employee had been fired for effeminate mannerisms and subsequently was thrown out of his home by his father. Demonstrations continued throughout the summer of 1991, spreading from the Southeast to the Midwest stores. Arrests were made at demonstrations in the Detroit area; Cothren and Summerville were among several people arrested for criminal trespass at both the Lithonia and Union City, Georgia, stores. Reporters and politicians dubbed Summerville the "Rosa Parks of the movement," after the civil rights figure whose arrest sparked the Montgomery, Alabama, Bus Boycott of 1955–1956.

Support for the Cracker Barrel boycott grew, as organizers further charged the company with racism and sexism. Restaurant gift shops, they pointed out, sold Confederate flags, black mammy dolls, and other offensive items. The Cracker Barrel board of directors, they said, was indeed a good ol' boy network, made up exclusively of middle-aged and older white men. In addition, there was only one female in the ranks of upper management. Among the numerous groups that joined in support of the protests were the National Organization for Women (NOW); Jobs with Justice, a coalition of labor unions; the National Rainbow Coalition, founded by Reverend Jesse Jackson; and the American Association of Public Health Workers. By early 1992, Summerville and Cothren had appeared on the television talk shows *Larry King Live* and *The Oprah Winfrey Show*. The two were also featured in a segment on ABC's *20/20*, after which Barbara Walters declared that she would refuse to eat at Cracker Barrel restaurants.

## THE RESOLUTION: NEW YORK ATTEMPTS TO FORCE CHANGE

Meanwhile, New York City comptroller, Elizabeth Holtzman, and finance commissioner, Carol O'Cleiracain, at the urging of the National Gay and Lesbian Task Force, wrote a letter to Dan Evins, dated March 12, 1991. As trustees of various city pension funds, which owned about $3 million in Cracker Barrel stock, they were "concerned about the potential negative impact on the company's sales and earnings which could result from adverse public reaction." They asked for a "clear statement" of the company's policy regarding employment and sexual orientation, as well as a description of "what remedial steps, if any, [had] been taken by the company respecting the employees dismissed."

Evins replied in a letter of March 19 that the policy had been rescinded and that there had been "no negative impact on the company's sales." Unsatisfied, the City of New York officials wrote back, again inquiring as to the status of the fired workers. They also asked that the company put forth a policy that "would provide unequivocally" that discrimination based on sexual orientation was prohibited. Evins never responded.

Shortly thereafter, Queer Nation launched a "buy one" campaign. Hoping to gain additional leverage in company decision making, activists became stockholders by purchasing single shares of Cracker Barrel common stock. At the least, they reasoned, the company would suffer from the relative expense of mailing and processing numerous one-cent quarterly dividend checks. More importantly, they could attend the annual stockholders meeting in Lebanon, Tennessee.

In November 1991, company officials successfully prevented the new shareholders from participating in the annual meeting, and they used a court injunction to block protests at the corporate complex. Nonetheless, demonstrators lined the street, while inside, a representative of the New York City comptroller's office announced the submission of a resolution "banning employment discrimination against gay and lesbian men and women," to be voted on at the next year's meeting. The resolution was endorsed by the Philadelphia Municipal Retirement System, another major stockholder. Cracker Barrel refused any further public comment on the issue.

## THE EFFECT: NO DECLINE IN CORPORATE GROWTH

The impact of the boycott on the corporate bottom line was negligible. Trade magazines reiterated the company's claim that neither sales nor stock price had been negatively affected. Indeed, net sales remained strong, up 33 percent at fiscal year-end 1992 to $400 million, owing in good part to continued expansion: There were now 127 restaurants in the chain. Though the increase in same-store sales was not as great as the previous year, Cracker Barrel at least could boast growth, whereas other chains blamed flat sales on the recession. Cracker Barrel stock, trading on the NASDAQ exchange, appreciated 18 percent during the first month after news of the scandal broke, and the stock remained strong throughout the next fiscal year, splitting three-for-two in the third quarter.

Dan Evins had good reason to believe that the firings and the boycott had not adversely affected profitability. One market analyst said that "the feedback they get from their customers might be in favor of not hiring homosexuals." Another even ventured that "it's plausible . . . the majority of Cracker Barrel's local users support an explicit discriminatory policy." Such speculation was bolstered by social science surveys indicating that respondents from the South and from rural areas in particular tended to be less tolerant of homosexuality than were other Americans.

Queer Nationals looked to other measures of success, claiming at least partial victory in the battle. Many customers they met at picket lines and inside restaurants vowed to eat elsewhere. Coalitions were formed with a variety of civil rights, women's, labor, and peace and justice organizations. Most importantly, the media attention greatly heightened national awareness of the lack of protections for lesbians and gays on the job. As the boycott continued, increasing numbers of states, counties, and municipalities passed legislation designed to prevent employment discrimination based on sexual orientation.

## THE STANDOFF: OLD ANTAGONISMS, NEW ALLEGATIONS

As the November 1992 annual meeting approached, Cracker Barrel requested that the Securities and Exchange Commission make a ruling on the resolution offered by the New York pension fund administrators. The resolution, according to Cracker Barrel, amounted to shareholder intrusion into the company's ordinary business operations. As such, it should be excluded from consideration at the annual meeting and excluded from proxy ballots sent out before the meeting. The SEC agreed, despite previous rulings in which it had allowed stockholder resolutions regarding race- or gender-based employment bias.

Acknowledging that frivolous stockholder inquiries had to be curtailed, the dissenting SEC commissioner nonetheless expressed great dismay: "To claim that the shareholders, as owners of the corporation, do not have a legitimate interest in management-sanctioned discrimination against employees defies logic." A noted legal scholar warned of the dangerous precedent that had been set: "Ruling an entire area of corporate activity (here, employee relations) off limits to moral debate effectively disenfranchises shareholders."

Thus, the standoff continued. Queer Nation and its supporters persisted in the boycott. The Cracker Barrel board of directors and, with one exception, upper management remained all-white, all-male bastions. Lynn Cothren, Cheryl Summerville, and the other protesters arrested in Lithonia, Georgia, were acquitted on charges of criminal trespass. Jurors ruled that the protesters' legitimate reasons for peaceably demonstrating superseded the company's rights to deny access or refuse service. Charges stemming from the Union City, Georgia, demonstrations were subsequently dropped. Meanwhile, within weeks of the original policy against lesbian and gay employees, Cracker Barrel vice president for human resources, William Bridges, had left the company. Cracker Barrel declined comment on the reasons for his departure.

Lesbian and gay activists' charge of racism at Cracker Barrel seemed to be borne out over time. In the year 2000, a local human rights commission awarded $5,000 in damages to a black employee in Kentucky after she suffered racial and religious bias in the scheduling of shifts. Months later, the NAACP joined a group of employees and former employees in a class-action lawsuit against Cracker Barrel, alleging that the company repeatedly discriminated against African Americans in hiring, promotions, and firing practices. African-American workers further were said to have received less pay, to have been given inferior terms and conditions of employment, and to have been subjected to racial epithets and racist jokes, including one told by Dan Evins. In a second suit filed by the NAACP, along with 42 customers, and supported by over 400 witnesses,

Cracker Barrel was accused of repeatedly offering better, faster, segregated seating to whites and inferior service to blacks. A similar case was filed by 23 African Americans in Little Rock a year later.

## THE OUTCOME: POLICY REVERSALS

As of 2002, Cracker Barrel annual net sales surpassed two billion dollars. The company still had not issued a complete retraction of its employment policy with regard to sexual orientation, and those employees fired back in 1991 had never been offered their old jobs back. In contrast, for a year's work, Chairman Dan Evins regularly pulled in over a million dollars in salary, bonus, awards, and stock options.

A total of 14 states and the District of Columbia offered protections for lesbians and gays on the job, both in the public and private sectors. With over 400 restaurants in 41 states, Cracker Barrel now operated in 11 of those jurisdictions with protections: California, Connecticut, Maryland, Massachusetts, Minnesota, New Hampshire, New Jersey, New Mexico, New York, Rhode Island, and Wisconsin. (The other states with antidiscrimination statutes were Hawaii, Nevada, and Vermont.) Expansion had taken the company into areas even less receptive to employment discrimination. As one business editor had correctly predicted, "Cracker Barrel [wa]sn't going to be in the South and Midwest forever. Eventually they w[ould] have to face the issue—like it or not."

In 1998, the SEC reversed itself, allowing the New York City Employees' Retirement System to again offer a shareholder resolution, which was defeated yet again and again. By 2002, however, the tide was turning. In its proxy statement sent out in advance of the annual meeting, the Cracker Barrel board of directors still recommended that stockholders vote against the proposal. "[A]ny attempt to name all possible examples of prohibited discrimination other than those . . . specifically prohibited by federal law," it said, "would result in a long list" that was neither "appropriate" nor "necessary."

But shareholders were ready to defy the board. After 58 percent voted in support of the proposal in an informal vote, the board members unanimously agreed to add the category of sexual orientation to its equal employment opportunities policy.

## THE PROPOSAL: FEDERAL LEGISLATION

In 36 states it is perfectly legal to fire workers because they are gay—or straight. For example, a Florida bar owner decided to newly target a lesbian and gay clientele and so fired the entire heterosexual staff. Queer activists boycotted, and the bar eventually was forced out of business. Still, in most American jurisdictions, employment discrimination based on sexual orientation remains a constant threat.

The vast majority of Americans, 80 percent, tell pollsters that lesbians and gays should have equal rights in terms of job opportunities. In every region including the South, among both Democrats and Republicans, solid majorities support federal legislation to remedy the situation. Nonetheless, despite several close votes in

Congress, the Employment Non-Discrimination Act, or ENDA, has yet to be passed into law.

Although there are no federal laws to prevent discrimination based on sexual orientation, protections do exist for workers on the basis of religion, gender, national origin, age, disability, and race. Still, as the NAACP and other lawsuits against Cracker Barrel demonstrate, federal legislation does not ensure corporate compliance. Aggrieved parties and their supporters often must invest years of their lives in protest and litigation simply to achieve the equal treatment ostensibly guaranteed in the American marketplace. Even after the terms *race* and *sexual orientation* have been added to policy statements, broader cultural transformations will be required before these added burdens are removed from the shoulders of workers already greatly disadvantaged in our society.

## DISCUSSION QUESTIONS

1. Discuss the factors that make it more difficult to establish workplace discrimination based on sexual orientation than discrimination based on race.

2. Do franchise operations, which prize uniformity—and thus reliability—in store design, products, and operating procedures, require uniformity of personnel policies? Were the regional variations that Dan Evins proposed on February 27, 1991, a viable corporate strategy? Why or why not?

3. How does the Cracker Barrel case support or challenge the notion that federal legislation is warranted to stop employment discrimination based on sexual orientation?

4. Why are particular retail products—inanimate objects such as mammy dolls— perceived to be racist?

5. Which areas of corporate activity should be open to broader scrutiny through shareholder resolutions? How much stake in the company should a shareholder have in order to present a resolution?

6. If a controversial corporate policy is reversed only after a decade of defiance, how should the company's public relations officers present the change to the media?

## BIBLIOGRAPHY

*Atlanta Journal-Constitution*, 6, 11 July 1993; 2, 3 April 1992; 29 March 1992; 4, 18, 20 January 1992; 9 June 1991; 3, 4, 5 March 1991.

Carlino, B. (1991, December 16). Cracker Barrel profits surge despite recession. *Nation's Restaurant News*, 14.

———. (1991, April 1). Cracker Barrel stocks, sales weather gay-rights dispute. *Nation's Restaurant News*, 14.

CBRL Group, Inc. Annual Reports, 2002, 2001.

———. Notice of Annual Meeting of Shareholders to be held on Tuesday, November 26, 2002. 30 October 2002.

Cheney, K. (1992, July 22). Old-fashioned ideas fuel Cracker Barrel's out-of-sight sales growth and profit increases. *Restaurants & Institutions*, 108.

*Chicago Tribune*, 5 April 1991.

Cracker Barrel's emphasis on quality a hit with travelers. (1991, April 3). *Restaurants & Institutions*, 24.

Cracker Barrel Hit by Anti-Bias Protests. (1992, April 13). *Nation's Restaurant News*, 2.

Cracker Barrel Old Country Store, Inc. Annual Reports, 1999, 1996, 1992, 1991, 1990.

———. Notice of Annual Meeting of Shareholders to be held on Tuesday, November 26, 1996. 25 October 1996.

———. Third Quarter Report, 30 April 1993.

———. Second Quarter Report, 29 January 1993.

———. First Quarter Report, 30 October 1992.

———. Securities and Exchange Commission Form 10-K, 1992.

———. Securities and Exchange Commission Form 10-K, 1991.

Cracker Barrel sued for rampant racial discrimination in employment. (1999, October 5). NAACP press release.

Dahir, M. S. (1992, June). Coming out at the Barrel. *The Progressive*, 14.

Documented cases of job discrimination based on sexual orientation. (1995). Washington, DC: Human Rights Campaign.

Farkas, D. Kings of the road. (1991, August). *Restaurant Hospitality*, 118–22.

Galst, L. (1992, May 19). Southern activists rise up. *The Advocate*, 54–57.

Greenberg, D. (1988). *The construction of homosexuality*. Chicago: University of Chicago Press.

Gutner, T. (1993, April 27). Nostalgia sells. *Forbes*, 102–103.

Harding, R. (1991, July 16). Nashville NAACP head stung by backlash from boycott support. *The Advocate*, 27.

———. (1991, April 9). Activists still press Tennessee eatery firm on anti-gay job bias. *The Advocate*, 17.

Hayes, J. (1991, August 26). Cracker Barrel protesters don't shake loyal patrons. *Nation's Restaurant News*, 3, 57.

———. (1991, March 4). Cracker Barrel comes under fire for ousting gays. *Nation's Restaurant News*, 1, 79.

Investors protest Cracker Barrel proxy plan. (1992, November). *Nation's Restaurant News*, 2, 14.

*Larry King Live*. CNN television, aired 2 December 1991.

Lexington-Fayette Urban County Human Rights Commission. (2000, August 2). Press Release: Lexington woman awarded $5,000 in discrimination case against Cracker Barrel. Retrieved from http://www.lfuchrc.org/News/2000/Press%20Release%20080200.htm

*Los Angeles Times*, 28 February 1991.

*New York Times*, 25 June 1999; 11 November 1992; 22 October 1992; 9 April 1992; 20 March 1991; 28 February 1991.

*Oprah Winfrey Show*. Syndicated television, aired January 1992.

Queer Nation. (n.d.) Documents on the Cracker Barrel Boycott. N.p.

*San Diego Union-Tribune,* 30 July 2003.

SEC upholds proxy ruling. (1993, February 8), *Pensions & Investments*, 28.

Star, M. G. (1992, October 26). SEC policy reversal riles activist groups. *Pensions & Investments*, 33.

*The* (Nashville) *Tennessean*, 27 February 1991.

*20/20*. ABC television, aired 29 November 1991.

Wildmoon, K. C. (1992, December 10). QN members allowed to attend Cracker Barrel stockholder's meeting. *Southern Voice*, 3.

———. (1992, October 22). Securities and Exchange Commission side with Cracker Barrel on employment discrimination. *Southern Voice*, 1.

———. (1992, July 9). DeKalb drops most charges against Queer Nation. *Southern Voice*, 3.

Walkup, C. (1991, August 5). Family chains beat recession blues with value, service. *Nation's Restaurant News*, 100, 104.

*Wall Street Journal*, 9 March 1993; 2 February 1993; 26 January 1993; 28 February 1991.

Washington Lawyers' Committee for Civil Rights and Urban Affairs. (2003, July 30). Press Release: 23 African American patrons file lawsuit against Cracker Barrel Restaurants for civil rights violations. Retrieved from http:// www.washlaw.org/news/releases/073003.htm

┌─ **Diversity on the Web** ─────────────────────────────────────────

Be sure to do this assignment in the order in which it is presented.

1. Go the following Web site and read the press release, "Cracker Barrel Old Country Store, Inc, Reaches Agreement with U.S. Department of Justice on Procedures to Address Claims of Discrimination." If you have difficulty finding this press release, search for "diversity" on the Cracker Barrel Web site.

   www.crackerbarrel.com/about-newsandhappenings.cfm?doc_id5911

2. Next, read the article, "Cracker Barrel Customer Says Bias Was 'Flagrant,'" from *USA Today*, currently available at

   www.usatoday.com/money/companies/2004-05-07-cracker-barrel_x.htm.

3. After reading these two articles, how would you evaluate the current managing diversity efforts at Cracker Barrel? What are the strategic business implications of these two readings?

# Appearance and Weight Inclusion Issues in the Workplace

M. June Allard

*Assumption College*
*Worcester State College Professor Emerita*

**P**resident Lincoln used his homeliness as humor. When accused of being two-faced, he replied, "Do you think I would wear this face if I had another one?" Appearance counts. "The effects of attractiveness and physical appearance on the formation of positive impressions is well documented…" (Matsumoto, 1996). Good-looking people are judged to be happy, successful, kind, smart, honest, sociable, popular, and to have high self-esteem. Beauty carries a sort of "halo effect" that psychologists refer to as a "physical attractiveness stereotype," implying that good-looking people also possess many other positive characteristics.

Every culture has standards of physical beauty and these standards are "relatively constant across time and to some extent across culture, race and ethnicity" (Bell and McLaughlin, 2006, p. 456). In collectivist cultures, beauty equates with cultural good (Wheeler & Kim, 1997). The halo effect surrounding good-looking people works to disadvantage women and those with visible physical disabilities, who may experience prejudice and discrimination in the social and business arenas.

## Workplace

Physical attractiveness and pleasing body image have long been known to have marketplace advantages. In the workplace, good looks are generally an asset in hiring, performance ratings, securing plum assignments, promotion, and long-term salary growth (Bell & McLaughlin, 2006, p. 457). "…[F]avoritism toward good looks and prejudice against homeliness is pervasive in most jobs" and within most occupations (Carr-Ruffino, p. 483).

Attractive people earn about 5 percent more than those with average looks (Harvard Law Review 2035, 1987). Homely workers make about 7 percent less than those with average looks. The most aesthetically challenged members of our society face severe discrimination. In the words of Hamermesh and Biddle, there is a "salary premium for physical attractiveness and a salary penalty for 'plainness'" (Bell & McLaughlin, 2006, P. 457).

Height bias for example, can affect salaries. Research suggests that tall people (6 feet and over) earn, on the average, nearly $166,000 more over 30 years than men who are 5 feet 5, even when gender, age, and weight are considered (Dittman, 2004, p. 14). These findings are especially strong in sales and management positions, but occur in other positions as well.

There are gender differences for example, in the impact of good looks on the job. "Attractive women are advantaged in lower level jobs and in jobs held predominately by women but not at higher levels, in professional jobs or those perceived as men's jobs" (Bell & McLaughlin, 2006). How much impact good looks has in the workplace depends in part on many other factors such as gender, credentials, level of position, ethnicity, etc.

## APPEARANCE STANDARDS

> At the beginning of its 2005-2006 season, the National Basketball Association (NBA) made headline news when it announced that it had decided to impose an off-the-court dress code on its players.
>
> (King, Winchester & Sherwyn, 2006)

Businesses are increasingly rejecting casual dress (Armour, 2005). In late July 2007, even the U.S. White House imposed dress standards for tourists. Organizations set appearance standards for their employees not only to project a particular corporate image, but also to create a favorable working environment and/or to "limit distractions caused by outrageous, provocative, or inappropriate dress." Such standards generally take the form of requirements (e.g., uniforms) or restrictions on dress, grooming, personal hygiene, hair styles, beards, mustaches, tattoos, make-up, face piercing, tongue metals, jewelry, "overwhelmingly bare midriffs," and weight. Penalties for violation of these standards are often serious and can even result in termination (Personnel Policy Services, [n.d.]). Noncompliant or penalized employees in return are increasingly filing lawsuits. Consider these examples of standards and their consequences:

- *Harrah's Operating Company, Inc.* — fired a long-term employee who refused to comply with a new policy requiring female employees to wear facial makeup.

- *L'Oreal* — terminated an employee who refused to fire a sales associate who was "not sufficiently attractive."

- *Harvard* — was charged by a librarian with refusing to promote her because she didn't fit the librarian image — she felt that she was seen as "just a pretty girl" who wore "sexy outfits."

- *Costco Wholesale Corporation* — was sued by an employee, a member of the Church of Body Modification, who defied company policy prohibiting facial jewelry (except earrings) by refusing to remove eyebrow rings. The employee sued on the grounds of religious discrimination.

(Corbett, n.d., pp. 7, 8)

# APPEARANCE LAW

How legal are appearance standards? In general, "requirements for professional appearance may be legitimate and job related or illegitimate and discriminatory" (Bell & McLaughlin, 2006, p. 458). Generally, under federal law, it *is legal* for employers to discriminate on the basis of appearance, except for those characteristics such as sex and age that are protected under the antidiscrimination laws or when appearance standards conflict with religious beliefs or negatively affect women or racial/ethnic minorities. The exception is a BFOQ (bona fide occupational qualification).

Courts have occasionally recognized that sex and age and other protected characteristics *can* be relevant to some jobs. Under BFOQ, employers sometimes *can sometimes* legally discriminate in terms of certain protected characteristics *if* the characteristics are "reasonably necessary to the normal operation of that particular business." Southwest Airlines for example, was allowed to limit its hiring to females for ticket agent and flight attendant positions in order to project its "love in the air" image and Hooters was permitted to continue hiring only females as "Hooter girls" (Corbett, n.d., p. 10, 11, 16). Businesses such as airlines, fashion stores, restaurants, beauty salons, and real estate agencies often want to hire pretty people in the belief that attractive sales people engage customers and increase sales.

Although federal law may not prohibit appearance policies, employers are cautioned that a) creative attorneys often tie appearance codes to religious discrimination or race or sex stereotyping or discrimination, b) states and localities may have laws barring appearance-based hiring and c) union contracts may prohibit or regulate dress codes.

There is no single model for dress code or appearance policy. Employers creating or reviewing existing policies might do well to consider the checklist provided by King, Winchester, and Sherwyn (2006) and consult an attorney.

| 🏛 | **Points of Law** |
|---|---|
| **Sex** | Does this policy create a burden for one gender, but not the other? |
| **Age** | Is complying with this policy differentially difficult for workers older than forty? |
| **Race & National Origin** | Does this policy infringe on a cultural aspect of specific race or national origin? |
| **Americans with Disabilities Act** | Does any covered disability prevent an employee from complying with this policy? |

# WEIGHT

Weight counts. The visibility of excess weight, like other aspects of physical appearance, lends itself to stereotyping. Even though Americans are becoming increasingly heavy, there are severe social sanctions against obesity. Research by Hebl and Mannix

(2003) suggests that biases even exist against people who associate with overweight people.

Overweight people live with negative stereotypes that include being lazy, undesirable, stupid, and slow; lacking in self-control; being out of shape, depressed, and uneducated; being a slob, greedy, and glutinous; and having low energy levels. They are stigmatized and find themselves ridiculed, the butt of jokes, and the recipients of hostility and tasteless and cruel comments. Discrimination occurs in education, health care, daily life, housing, public accommodations, employment, and other areas.

"Discrimination may also exist for obese tenants seeking apartment rentals and in places such as fitness clubs and clothing stores" (Rudd, *b,* n.d.). Appropriate workplace clothing can be difficult to find and usually costs more than clothing for average size people. The Rudd Center (*b*, n.d.) further reports that " … obese people can experience problems in public settings such as restaurants, theaters, airplanes, buses, and trains because of inadequate seat or seatbelt sizes." Being excessively overweight is likely to lead to higher medical expenses, difficulty in obtaining health insurance, and life insurance premiums that are two to four times higher than those of their average-size peers (Darlin, 2006).

"In the workplace, the magnitude of bias against fat people far exceeds that for age or race or any other measure" (Smith, 2001).

> A stellar career path, a solid resume, and a call from a headhunter may be the ticket to a better job. But if you're overweight, there's a good chance you won't be selected as a finalist for an executive position.                                    Voros, 2007, March 11

Obesity bias weighs against job seekers. They are not hired as often as those of average size, are not promoted as often, have a harder time securing plum assignments, are assigned to non-visible jobs, receive more disciplinary actions, are paid less than their thinner counterparts, may be charged more for employee insurance coverage, and are sometimes fired because of their weight" (Fact Sheet, n.d.; Goldberg, 2003; Darlin, 2006). In the words of one worker, "Our culture thinks heavier people are not qualified to be picked for the job."

One large study "found that among those 50% or more above their ideal weight, 26% indicated that they were denied benefits such as health insurance because of their weight, and 17% reported being fired or pressured to resign because of their weight" (Puhl & Brownell, 2001, p 6).

## WEIGHT STANDARDS

Employer weight standards are especially resented and extremely contentious as they are often based on stereotypes about the control of weight and presumed characteristics of the overweight individual. Here are some of the standards and their effect on workplace experience:

- *Weight Loss Centers, Inc.,*—a company specializing in weight loss plans, refused to hire a 350-pound man as a sales associate (Corbett, n.d., p. 8).

- *Jazzercise*—(a company with 5,300 franchises in 38 countries) turned down a 240-pound job applicant because "Applicants must have a higher muscle-to-fat ratio and look leaner than the public" (Corbett, n.d., p. 8).

- ***Korn/Ferry*** — an international executive search firm, reports the case of a very qualified 300-pound manager who was refused a job interview at a telecommunications company because "he wouldn't fit in" (Voros, n.d.).

- ***Xerox Corporation*** — refused to hire an overweight applicant for a computer programming position because her obesity made her "medically unsuitable for the job" (Puhl & Brownell, 2001).

- ***Rivier College*** — removed a morbidly obese woman from her teaching position because of her weight (Puhl & Brownell, 2001).

- ***Agency Rent-a-Car Systems*** — fired an office manager because of his obesity in spite of his excellent employment record and excellent commendations (Puhl & Brownell, 2001).

- ***Southwest Airlines*** — terminated a flight attendant and denied his reinstatement because his weight exceeded airline requirements (Puhl & Brownell, 2001).

- ***Commonwealth of Virginia State Police*** — demoted a nine-year state trooper to dispatcher for failing a weight-loss program (Puhl & Brownell, 2001, pp. 6,7,23).

## IS FAT ALBERT OVERWEIGHT OR OBESE?

Obesity is increasing worldwide. "Of the 6.5 billion people in the world, more than 1 billion are overweight and at least 300 million are obese" (Bell, 2006, p. 424). In the United States, the National Center for Health Statistics reports that American population weight has been increasing since the 1980s" (NCHS, n.d.). On average, Americans gained 10 pounds during the 1990s (Warren, 2004). Approximately 65 percent of U.S. adults are overweight or obese, and almost 10 million (approximately 3 percent) are morbidly obese (Bell, 2006, p. 464; Darlin, 2006, p. 2; Smith, 2006, Dec. 8).

### Weight Categories

How heavy is "overweight"? "Obese"? "Morbidly obese"? Weight is defined both by culture and by the field of medicine.

*Cultural Standards:* "… media and advertising play roles in the perceptions of obesity, from the choices consumers make, to body images they strive for" (Rudd Center, n.d., p. 1). The message is: fat is bad; thin is in. American culture creates the ideal of slim beauty and condemns excess weight on one hand and on the other, encourages junk food diets and supersized food portions. Medicine has created its own standards for weight judgments.

*Medical Standards:* The Body Mass Index (BMI) used by the medical profession is the accepted standard for distinguishing excess weight from obesity in adult men and women. Calculation of the BMI is shown here.

| | |
|---|---|
| **BMI Formula** | **Divide your weight in pounds by the square of your height in inches. Multiply the answer by 703.** |
| **Alternative** | **Use a Web calculator:** <br> **www.nhlbisupport.com/bmi/ or** <br> **www.halls.md/ideal-weight/body.htm** |
| **BMI Diagnosis** | **Underweight:**    **18.4 or less** <br> **Normal:**        **18.5–24.9** <br> **Overweight:**     **25–29.9** <br> **Obese:**          **30–39.9** <br> **[1]Morbidly Obese: 40 and over** |

[1]Facing serious health problems

The BMI Index is considered to be a reliable measure of body fat, but the National Institutes of Health warns that it does have limitations:

- "It may overestimate body fat in athletes and others who have a muscular build."
- "It may underestimate body fat in older persons and others who have lost muscle mass."

   *http://www.nhlbisupport.com/bmi/*

The correlation between the BMI and fat varies by sex, race, and age. For children and teens, calculation of the BMI is the same as for adults, but interpretation of the resulting index number differs.

## WEIGHT LAW

As with other appearance characteristics, there are no federal laws prohibiting discrimination against obese individuals (Rudd *a*, n.d.). Only Michigan; the District of Columbia; Madison, Wisconsin; and San Francisco and Santa Cruz, California, provide legal protection (Puhl & Brownell, n.d.; Fryer & Kirby, 2005; Bell & McLaughlin, 2007).

"Overweight plaintiffs usually must prove that acts of bias against them are covered by federal laws prohibiting discrimination against disabled people" (ABCNEWS, 2004). Except for New Jersey, courts generally consider weight as under the control of the individual and therefore, not a disability (Puhl & Brownell, 2001). In New Jersey, obesity is a disability and is therefore protected from workplace discrimination.

Being *moderately fat* is *not* a disability unless it is accompanied by another impairment. Under EEOC guidelines *obesity* is *not* a disability unless the weight is related to a physiological disorder or if the weight is extreme as in cases of morbid obesity. *Morbid obesity* can meet disability requirements (Puhl & Brownell, 2001).

The Social Security Administration does not consider obesity an impairment for purposes of determining eligibility for disability payments. This policy doubles the impact on obese people, because they are then also denied opportunities for medical coverage afforded most people receiving social security disability benefits for two years or more (Puhl & Brownell, 2001).

*When obesity is not a disability*, there is no federal legal protection against discrimination. *When obesity is an impairment,* there is legal protection. When Xerox denied an obese computer programming applicant a job due to obesity that made her "medically unsuitable for the job" according to the company physician, she was protected (Puhl & Brownell, 2001, p. 23). The disability claim of the office manager fired by Agency Rent-a-Car System was upheld in court because he had sought medical treatment for his condition" (Puhl & Brownell, 2001).

"Being overweight isn't just a health issue, however. It's also a political issue, one tied up with body image, sexism, discrimination, and self esteem" (Schwartzapfel, n.d.).

## WEIGHT TIES TO WAGES, GENDER, RACE, AND AGE

An interrelated set of factors both blurs and compounds the effects of weight on wages. Weight and wages are related to each other and both are tied to gender, race, age, and social class. Since fat is more prevalent in certain racial and ethnic populations, more common in women than in men, and more common in older people than young…" (Goldberg, 2003, p. 97), weight discrimination is closely allied with discrimination of these protected characteristics. Among the relationships:

*Weight and Age*
- Weight gain often comes with age (Goldberg, 2003).

*Weight and Gender*
- "Fat women experience more negative outcomes than fat men" (Bell, 2007, p. 406).
- "Only 9% of top male executives are overweight" (Voros, n.d.).
- "Overweight women earn less than slim women" (Pagan & Davila, 1997).
- "…overweight men pay a salary penalty of $1,000 per year per pound they're overweight" (Voros, n.d.)

*Weight and Social Class*
- "…poor women [in the U.S] tend to be heavier than more affluent women making class issues yet another factor to be considered" (Bell & McLaughlin, 2006, p. 468).

*Weight, Wages, and Gender*
- Overweight women get paid less for the same work than thinner women (Puhl & Brownell, 2001, p.25).
- "…a weight increase of 64 pounds above the average for white women was associated with 9 percent lower wages" (Darlin, 2006, p. 5).
- "Men do not experience wage penalties until their weight exceeds standard weight by over 100 pounds" (Maranto & Stenoien, 2004, p. 2).

*(Continued)*

### Weight, Gender, and Race

- "Women of color tend to be heavier than white women" (Bell & McLaughlin, 2006, p. 412).

### Weight, Wages, Gender, and Race

- White women who are mildly obese (20% over standard weight) "experience greater wage penalties than do black men who are 100% over standard weight" (Maranto & Stenoien, 2004, p. 2).
- "Overweight men sort themselves into lower-level jobs."

### Weight, Wages, Gender, and Social Class

- "Overweight and obese women have lower incomes ($6,700 a year less) and higher rates of poverty (10% higher) than their non-obese peers" (NOW Foundation, n.d.).

Weight clearly is intertwined with other diversity characteristics. It is one of a person's multiple group memberships and the impact of excess weight has to be considered in conjunction with these other characteristics. If someone is old and obese and female—is this three strikes against the person, or do one or two factors outweigh all others in the behavior of the individual and in the way the individual is treated in the workplace?

## *Writing Assignment*

Hiring obese employees does cost employers. Write a report that details these costs to employers.

*Starting Sources*

Bell, M., & McLaughlin, M. (2006). Outcomes of appearance and obesity in organizations. In Konrad, A., Prasad, P. & Pringle, J. (Eds) of *Handbook of workplace diversity*. pp 461–462. Mason, Ohio: Thomson South-Western.

Minerd, J. (2007, April 24). Obese employees weigh heavily on bottom line. *Medpage Today*. Retrieved July 22, 2007, from http://www.medpagetoday.com/Pediataics/Obesity/tb/5490

Leopold, R. (2004, August 2). Reining in the rising cost of obesity. *Managed Healthcare Executive*. Retrieved July 29, 2007, from http://www.managedhealthcareesecutivecom/mhe/articleDetail.jsp?id=134273

## DISCUSSION QUESTIONS

1. What are the pros and cons of an airline implementing a policy that larger customers need to buy a second seat?

2. What can employers do to counteract the high costs of employees who are obese?

3. Should television networks and stations set appearance and weight standards for news reporters, newscasters, weather forecasters, etc.? Why or why not? Should these standards be different for male and females?

## BIBLIOGRAPHY

ABCNEWS. *Fat activists see diet industry draining, Tyranny of the slender?* (2004, August 2). Retrieved July 15, 2007, from http://www.spinwatch.org/content/view/402/9/

Armour, S. (2006, October 25). Dress codes gussy up. *USA Today.* Retrieved July 24, 2007, from http://www.usatoday.com/money/workplace/2005-10-25-dress-code-usat_x.htm

Bell, M., & McLaughlin M. (2006). Outcomes of appearance and obesity in organizations. In (Eds) Konrad, A., Prasad, P., & Pringle J. *Handbook of workplace diversity.* (pp. 455–474). Thousand Oaks, CA: Sage.

Bell, M. (2007). *Diversity in organizations.* Mason, OH: Thomson South-Western.

Bellizi, J. (2000). Does successful work experience mitigate weight and gender-based employment discrimination in face-to-face industrial selling? *Journal of Industrial Marketing, 15 (6).*

Bodypositive Forum. (n.d.). Retrieved September 5, 2007, from www.bodypositive.com/forum1.htm

Carr-Ruffino, N. (2003 ?). *Managing diversity: People skills for a multicultural workplace, 6th ed.* Boston: Pearson Custom Publishing.

Corbett, W. (n.d.). The ugly truth about appearance discrimination and the beauty of our employment discrimination law. *Duke Journal of Gender, Law and Policy.* Retrieved July 15, 2007, from http://www.law.duke.edu/journals/djglp/articles/gen14p153.htm

Darlin, D. (2006, Dec 2). *Extra weight, higher costs.* Retrieved July 10, 2007, from http://www.nytimes.com [*click:* December 2, 2006, *then* Business, *then* Darlin, Damon]

Fyer, B., & Kirby, J. (2005, May). Fat chance. *Harvard Business Review.* Reprint RO505A.

Goldberg, C. (2003). Citing intolerance, obese people take steps to press course. In Plous, S. (2007). *Understanding prejudice and discrimination.* (McGraw-Hill) Retrieved July 27, 2007, from www.understandingprejudice.org/anth.htm

Hebl, M., & Mannix, L. (2003). The weight of obesity in evaluative others: A mere proximity effect. *Personality and Social Psychology Blletin, 29,* 28–38.

King, G.R., Winchester, J., & Sherwyn, D. (2006). You (don't) look marvelous. Considerations for employers regulating employee appearance. *Cornell Hotel & Restaurant Administration Quarterly 47, 4.* pp. 359–368.

Leopold, R. (2004, August 2). Reining in the rising cost of obesity. *Managed Healthcare Executive.* Retrieved July 28, 2007, from http://www.managedhealthcareexecutive.com/MHE/articleDetail.jsp?id=134273

Maranto, C., & Stenoien, A. (2004, October 31). Weight discrimination: a multidisciplinary analysis. *Employee responsibilities and rights journal.* Retrieved July15, 2007, from http://www.springerlink.com/content/q7nhu072466g0136

McAdams, T., Moussavi, F., & Klassen, M. (2005, April 6). Employee appearance and the Americans with disabilities act: An emerging issue? Employee responsibilities and rights journal. Netherlands: Springer

NIH National Heart, Lung and Blood Institute. (n.d). What are the health risks of overweight and obesity? Retrieved July 29, 2007, from http://www.nim.nih.gov/medlineplus/ health-statistics.html

NOW Foundation. (n.d.). Fact sheet: Size discrimination. *National Organization for*

*Women*. Retrieved July 15, 2005, from http://loveyourbodynowfoundation.org/factsheet4.html

Pagan, J., & Davila, A. (1997). Obesity, occupational attainment, and earnings. *Social Science Quarterly, 78,* 756–770.

Panaro, G. (n.d.). Is hiring on the basis of appearance illegal? *H.R. Corner.* Retrieved July 29, 2007, from http://wwwbankersonline.com/operations/gp_appearance.html

Personal appearance of employees – dress code (n.d). Retrieved July 15, 2007, from http://www.hrpolicyanswers.com/preview/dresscode.pdf

Puhl, R., & Brownell, K. (n.d.). *Bias, discrimination, and obesity.* Retrieved July 15, 2007, from http://www.obesityresearch.org/cgi/content/full/9/12/788

Rudd Center (*a*). (n.d.) *Advertizing and the media.* Retrieved July 17 from http://www.yaleruddcenter.org/default.aspx?id=21

Rudd Center (*b*). (n.d.) *Other domains of weight bias.* Retrieved July 17 from http://www.yaleruddcenter.org/default.aspx?id=82

Rouen, E. (2004, February 16). *A heavy burden: fighting for fat acceptance.* Retrieved July 15, 2007, from http://www.jrn.columbia.edu/studentwork/cns/2004-02-16/358.asp

Schwartzapfel, B. (n.d.). The fat of the land. Retrieved July 21, 2007, from http://www.providencephoenix.com/features/other_stories/multi_1/documents/05207016.asp

Schweitzer, T. (2007, May 22). Obese employees cost companies more. *Inc.com.* Retrieved July 10, 2007, from http://www.inc.com/news/articles/200705/obesity.html

Smith, E. (2001, May 21). Obesity bias weighs against job seekers. Retrieved July 15, 2007, from www.magellanassist.com/mem/library/default.asp?TopicId=122&CategoryId=08&ArticleId=51 http://www.associatedcontent.com/article/95247/should_overweight_consumers_pay_extra.htm

Voros, S. (n.d.) *Weight discrimination runs rampant in hiring.* Retrieved July 15, 2007, from http://www.careerjournal.com/myc/climbing/20000905-voros.html

Warren, M. (2004, November 6). Cost of fat air passengers takes off. *The daily telegraph, London. News,* p.1.

Wheeler, L., & Kim, Y. (1997). What is beautiful is culturally good: The physical attractiveness stereotype has different content in collectivist cultures. *Personality and Social Psychology Bulletin, 23,* 795–800.

---

### Diversity on the Web

When business discriminates against "customers of size," there are costs to good will for the business as well as costs to the customers themselves.

1. Research the crash of U.S. Airways Express 5481 on Jan 8, 2003, shortly after takeoff from the Charlotte-Douglas International Airport, in North Carolina. Note: notice the youth of the pilot (age = 25) as well as the weight issue.

   Wald, M. (May 13, 2003, Section A, column 1). Weight estimates on air passengers will be increased. http://www.nytimes.com

   New flight risk: Obesity? (January 30, 2003, News, p. 12A) http://www.usatoday.com

2. Research the implications of a policy that people have to declare their weight before boarding a plane.

   Warren, M. (2004, November 6, News, p.1). Cost of fat air passengers takes off. *The Daily Telegraph, London.* Retrieved September 5, 2007, from www.telegraph.co.uk/news/index.jhtml

Southwest Airlines forces larger passengers to buy two tickets http://www.cswd.org/docs/airlineseating.html

Southwest Airlines' policy concerning overweight travelers http://www.everything2.com/index.pl?node_id=1343085

Smith, A. (2006, December 8). Should overweight consumers pay extra for services from Southwest Airlines & other businesses? http://www.associated-content.com/article/95247/should_overweight_consumers_pay_extra.htm

 # Points of Law

When obesity is not a disability, there is no federal legal protection against discrimination.

When obesity is an impairment, there is legal protection under ADA law.

# Choosing the Board

## M. June Allard

*Assumption College*
*Worcester State College Professor Emerita*

This exercise is based on the author's experiences serving on governing boards and board development committees. It represents common situations faced by boards of profit and nonprofit organizations.

Heritage Medical Center is a moderately sized suburban hospital currently plagued with financial and management problems so severe they are reaching the crisis stage. The hospital is governed by a board of directors composed of 12 members. At the moment there are four empty seats on the board.

The eight remaining board members are fiscally conservative, well-to-do industrialists who have known each other for years and who frequently see each other socially and at community affairs. Many of these men belong to an exclusive country club; a few to a very exclusive yacht club. Board members are expected to—and do—donate generously to the hospital fundraising campaigns.

There is friction among these Board members. They are very concerned about the future of the hospital, but they cannot agree on what course of action to take in the face of its mounting problems.

You serve on the Board Development Committee, which must now fill the four empty seats. Eight people have been nominated for the four seats. Brief biographies of the nominees are provided here. Read the biographies carefully to help you select the best candidates.

## NOMINEES

**Drake Covington II** is a very bright 23-year-old computer systems analyst. He marches to a different drummer and is considered "far out." He is the nephew of an influential board member and owes his nomination to his uncle.

**Layla Amini** is a successful 27-year-old financial analyst. She is very quiet and very conservative; a traditionalist with a solid reputation. She was nominated by her cousin, a state senator.

**Carmen Diaz** is a 33-year-old, highly respected medical doctor. She is very innovative and a self starter who has already set up a clinic. She has never met anyone on the board, but does know the hospital CEO. She was nominated by a group of doctors practicing at the hospital.

**Charles Wong** is a 35-year-old management systems analyst. He lives near the hospital and works out of his home. He is reputed to be a team player and a supportive person. He was nominated by the union representing the hospital staff.

**Peter Skylar** is a 46-year-old CEO of a Health Maintenance Organization (HMO), who, by the nature of his position, is very familiar with hospital operations. He is brilliant, a loner, and connected to the state regulatory agency. He is considered to be in the "out-group" by those members of the board that he knows.

**Sue Novenski** is a 42-year-old social worker who works in a battered women's shelter. She works well with groups and is low key and extremely collaborative. She knows no one on the board; she was nominated by the hospital's Patients Advisory Committee.

**Katherine Dobbs Courtney** is the 55-year-old widow of a very wealthy industrialist who served on the board. She has served on community boards previously. She is an idea person and an individualist, and is outspoken. She plays golf with the mayor, who nominated her.

**Lamar Leroy Woods** is a 56-year-old retired owner of a profitable manufacturing company. He is very wealthy and has donated large sums of money to the hospital. He is conservative, easygoing, intelligent, and comfortable to be with. He was nominated by the hospital CEO.

1. Which four of the nominees would be your choices? Please list them in order of preference.
   A. _____
      *Why?*
   B. _____
      *Why?*
   C. _____
      *Why?*
   D. _____
      *Why?*

2. Replacing one-third of the board members all at once will mean a radical change for this board. This is a source of concern for the board members and a serious concern of the hospital CEO, who deals frequently with the board. What will you do to ease the transition for the board members and for the CEO?

# Media Messages

## M. June Allard

*Assumption College*
*Worcester State College Professor Emerita*

*. . . cultures have enriched each other in all the great civilizations of the world . . . No culture has grown great in isolation (Sowell, p.43).*

**S**owell makes a compelling case for the importance of contact among cultures and one that modern cultures have been quick to appreciate. The last decades have witnessed the exponential expansion of communication among cultures with modern technological and electronic advances that transcend geographic barriers to provide limitless opportunities for cultural interaction and advancement. Cultures enrich each other through communication—communication through travel, trade, and migration, and communication through print and electronic media.

Cultural transfer through travel and migration are examined in *Cultural Transmission Today: Sowell Revisited* found in this text, while the discussion and exercises in the present article examine transmission occurring through print and electronic media.

## Electronic Media

Print and electronic media play an important role in transmitting culture in low context cultures, such as the United States, where meaning and messages are derived mostly from the words themselves and much less from the situation in which they occur.

In developed countries, TV, like radio, is universal. By 1995, more than 99 percent of all U.S. households owned at least one television set, with children between 2 and 11 watching primetime TV more than five hours per week and their teenage siblings watching almost six hours (NAA, 2004). Today the Internet, e-mail, and text messaging provide additional electronic means of cultural contact. Although these electronic advances are widespread in developed countries, they are the media of the more privileged. Even within the U.S., the "digital divide" often denies the less affluent these newest avenues of cultural exchange.

### "Print" and Entertainment Media

Newspapers and magazines, although not as widely read as before the advent of television and electronic media, are still very influential. Millions of U.S. adults read national circulation newspapers, with substantial percentages of all cultural groups reading magazines. Even the entertainment media—most particularly films and videos—are far-reaching conveyers of culture, as are other cultural products such as art, music, books, video games, toys, and the knowledge and products of science and technology.

## THE SHAPING OF CULTURE

What role does the communication media play in the shaping of culture today? How do newspapers, magazines, books, TV, radio, Internet, e-mail, text messaging, etc., function to influence and enrich cultures? The answer is complex, for the media serve as agents of transmission and cultural maintenance by passing down the culture to new generations and conveying it to newcomers. Media also become shapers of culture by serving to unite cultures and subcultures and, at the same time, to divide cultural groups from each other.

The complexity of the role is easily seen in the case of immigrants in the United States, where mass media (newspapers, radio, and television) serve to unite by teaching immigrants about the larger culture and teaching the larger culture about them. While the larger culture dominates the national news, ethnic-cultural and religious festivals are presented in feature stories locally. At the same time, however, e-mail, telephone, and broadcast media allow newcomers to maintain their ethnic and social class identities by providing easy contact with their home culture and with fellow immigrants within the United States. In recent years, language programs on radio and TV stations, and newspaper and magazines targeted to specific cultural groups further serve to maintain these cultures, while at the same time infusing into them elements of the larger culture. In the process, ethnic media serve to separate the ethnic cultures from the mainstream culture.

## THE MEDIA AND WHO IT REACHES

One size does not fit all groups. The interaction of the media with various segments of society is not uniform. Just as international travel and electronic media are readily available to only part of the society, other media forms are accessed in differing degrees by different segments of the society. Not all groups "tune in" to TV to the same extent, nor do they all read newspapers and magazines, much less the same papers and magazines.

### TV and Radio

In 2005 there were approximately 124.5 million TV households and 262 million TV viewers in the United States (U.S. Census, 2000). In 2003–2004, on average, Americans spent more than 6.4 hours per day watching TV. According to the Nielsen ratings, Hispanic-American households across all age groups watch even more television every week than U.S. households in general. African-Americans, the largest minority segment of TV viewers, generally spend more time watching television (9.2 hours per day) than other population groups (Ethnic Media Audience Trends, 2006). Some 21 percent of African- and Asian-Americans also watch cable TV, compared with 14 percent of

Latinos and 8 percent of whites (Nielson, 2003). Estefa reports that "[U.S.] minority ethnic viewers originating from the Arab world are more densely equipped with satellite receivers than the majority population in the U.S." (2004).

Over 40 percent of Asian-American viewers watch English-language channels with equal numbers watching both English and native-language channels. Some 40 percent of U.S. Hispanics view native-language channels with approximately 33 percent watching English and Spanish channels. Nearly half of Asians listen to English radio stations with 20 percent listening to Asian only or both languages. With Hispanics, over half listened to Spanish-only stations with less than one fourth listening in two languages.

## Newspapers and Magazines

Americans also spend countless hours reading newspapers and magazines, listening to the radio, and going to the movies. In 2007, newspapers were read by more than 154,353,000 adults reaching 70 percent of the adult population (NAA, 2007). In the second quarter of 2006, more than 59 million people, well over one-third of all active Internet users, visited newspaper Web sites on the average, spending a total of 7.2 billion minutes for a total of 1.4 billion visits (Sigmund, 2007). In addition, a recent survey found that 59 percent of Asian-Americans, 45 percent of African-Americans, 43 percent of whites, and 30 percent of Latinos read a magazine the previous day (DiversityInc, Sept. 10, 2003).

Approximately 41 percent of Hispanic readers read mostly the Spanish-language newspapers, while other ethnicities are more likely to read both English and native language newspapers (Journalism, 2004).

## Ethnicity and Media

There are historical as well as cultural reasons for ethnic differences in media use. Over the last decades of the twentieth century, the growing diversity in the United States led some media to avoid dealing with people of color as they moved into cities and tried to build audiences based on specific marketing niches such as age, education, income, racial, or gender target markets. Minority concerns were frequently ignored. Thus mass media developed into a segmented media—selective in *who* it transmits to and in *what* it transmits. Advertisers, the driving force behind the audiences targeted by newspapers, want predominantly affluent Anglo readers. In practical terms this means selectivity in terms of which stories are printed or aired and which are not. In some places stories about African-, Latino-, and Asian-Americans have actually been ignored.

As a result of this selectivity, the media *maximized* racial and ethnic division. As diversity numbers in the United States have grown; however, this exclusion from national media has given rise to newspapers and TV channels specifically targeting the excluded minorities. With an estimated 10.9 million Hispanic American television households in the United States by 2004–2005, Spanish-language TV channels became common in urban areas (ASNE, 2004). In September of 2003, large mainstream English-language newspapers launched several Spanish-language daily newspapers (*Hoy, Diario La Estrella, Al Dia*) to complement the small Spanish-language weeklies.

In addition to Spanish-language TV channels, satellite dishes now bring in stations from Mexico and Colombia, CNN in Spanish, and Fox Sports in Spanish. Cable operators serve geographically defined markets with programming geared to those areas. Smaller ethnic and cultural groups that are more diffused geographically—such as the Arabic, Russian, and Korean language groups—are serviced by satellite television.

# WHAT THE MEDIA TRANSMITS

Ethnic-targeted media focus on culture-specific entertainment and news. Aimed at the young, Americanized Latinos, Spanish-language networks feature Spanish-language soap operas *(telenovelas)* that provide satire and moral dilemmas focusing on issues distinct to U.S. Latinos. The Spanish-language dailies are far more than translations of English-language papers. They cover local, national, and international news, concentrating on sports like soccer, classified ads, and news from Latino countries—topics of high interest to U.S. Latinos. Late in 2003 when Comcast, the nation's largest cable company, launched new packages of Spanish-language programming, the Associated Press quoted Mauro Panzera, senior director of multicultural marketing at Comcast, Philadelphia:

"We launched the package to give them the best possible way of keeping a lifeline not only to the Hispanic market here but also back home, to connect with their heritage and what's important in their lives" (Lopez).

## Stereotypes

All forms of media engage in the transmission of cultural stereotypes. Traditional type-casting of African Americans and native Americans by advertisers has decreased markedly in broadcast and print media. Unfortunately other forms of stereotyping are alive and well, often in the character roles portrayed in TV dramatizations. In the last few decades, many studies have examined the stereotypes fostered by media. A sample of the stereotypes emerging from Nielson research and other studies includes the following:

*Businessmen.* Compared with characters in other occupations, this group is portrayed twice as often in a negative way as in a positive way. They commit 40 percent of the murders and other crimes three times as often as characters in other occupations.

*Public Officials.* This group has the worst negative image of any occupational group (civil servants were a close second). They commit crimes twice as often as other characters, take bribes, or do the bidding of special interest groups. Most political and legal institutions are portrayed as corrupt. Noteworthy exceptions: law enforcement officials and public school teachers—who have positive images, but are rarely portrayed as government representatives.

*Arabs.* Positive images are hard to find. People of Arabic descent are presented as "billionaires or bombers" and rarely as victims or as ordinary people doing ordinary things.

*Italian Americans.* Far more male than female roles are found. Portrayals are more negative than those of other groups with one in six engaged in criminal activity (e.g., The Sopranos) or with most holding low status jobs and not speaking proper English.

*Latinos.* Latinos are portrayed as living in poverty and as criminals—"a dysfunctional underclass that exists on the fringes of mainstream U.S society." Some 66 percent of all network stories about Latinos last year involved "crime, terrorism and illegal immigration" (Mendéz-Méndez & Alveiro, 2002).

*Gender.* The overshadowing of women in network anchor positions in prime time news by male anchors (Wilson et al, 2003) sends the message that women lack credibility. Sunday comic strips feature more males than females with males more likely to be central characters, authority figures, and nonemotional in nature. Both genders engage in stereotypical occupations such as the comic strip's Dagwood in an office and Blondie in a catering business. Video game heroes are primarily white males (over 80 percent) with females often depicted as sexy and seductive and as secondary or irrelevant characters (Berkeley Daily Planet, 2001).

*Obesity.* Obesity is linked to gender. On prime time TV, 3 percent of the females are obese and 33 percent are underweight (compared with real U.S. population figures of 25 percent and 5 percent, respectively). TV males are one-third as likely to be obese as real life males and male TV characters are six times more likely to be underweight as real life males (White, 2001).

*Social Class.* Research on social class in television programming or in audience research is sparse. A few studies focused on drama programming often using occupation as an indicator of class of the television characters (Butsch, n.d.).

*The Poor.* Mantsios reports that very little coverage occurs of the poor and poverty. The messages sent suggest that they are faceless, are undeserving (e.g., welfare cheats, drug addicts, greedy panhandlers), are an eyesore (e.g., homeless shelters and panhandlers are problems for the community), do not exist (the 40 million poor get scant press coverage), are down on their luck (soup kitchens and charity by the rich get coverage), and have only themselves to blame for their condition. (Census figures reveal poverty to be greatest in rural areas among whites holding jobs at least part of the year, but the media imply that the poor are urban unemployed blacks and minorities entrapped by attitudes and culture.)

*The working class* is coded by gender with gender status reversed, i.e., working class males are lovable and bumbling (sometimes buffoons), while females are more intelligent than males often acting like mothers to their husbands (Butsch, n.d.).

The *middle class* is generally portrayed as the universal class and as a victim of the lower class (middle class pays their welfare costs and are the victims of their crimes). The middle class receives positive treatment—almost as the American ideal with "exaggerated displays of affluence and upward mobility" (Butsch, n.d).

The *wealthy* are seen as fascinating (celebrities, superstars, society stars, and corporate empire builders appear in stories and gossip columns) and benevolent with an occasional bad apple. Newspapers and TV cater to this group far in excess of their numbers.

*Youth.* Positive images are largely absent. Youth are stereotyped by exclusion from mass media suggesting their lack of importance. In local news they are often portrayed in the context of crime and other at-risk behaviors. A considerable gender imbalance in youth stories occurs with most stories about males. Racial imbalance occurs with 35 percent of the news about white youths involved in crime, compared with 52 percent for nonwhite youths.

*Gays.* Once nonexistent, gays are now a presence on TV, having emerged from the shadows in the last decade. Critics charge however, that gay portrayals are stereotypical: "Gays are often presented in extreme circumstances on television . . . They're either perpetually giddy and flamboyant . . . or traumatized by AIDS and social and emotional hardship" (Boone, 2003).

*Religion.* Positive and negative portrayals are evenly balanced (35 percent and 34 percent, respectively). In 2003–2004, religion came up 2,314 times, dropping to 1,425 in 2005–2006 (Learmonth, 2006). The bashing of Muslims by syndicated talk show hosts continues, with name calling such as "rag heads," "goat-humping weasels," etc. (Akbar, 2007).

*Nonwhites.* Nonwhites are underrepresented in TV dramatizations and when present, are often in roles that reinforce stereotypes.

*Class, Age, Gender, Appearance.* Nowhere is the effect of discrimination more apparent than in the disparate coverage of missing persons. "If a missing person is white, female, young, attractive, and has an upper-middle-class background, media coverage of her case will be far more thorough than coverage of missing men, minorities or the elderly" according to Roy Clark, vice president at the Poynter Institute (Santos, 2007).

## WHO TRANSMITS

The stereotypes and other cultural messages transmitted by media are a product in part of "who" within the media decides on the messages to be transmitted. Unfortunately, the mass media have long been charged with a lack of diversity within their ranks. Ron Smith of the *Milwaukee Journal Sentinel* writes,

"Diversity is a word journalists often hear. In fact you can't go to a conference without hearing about it. But you can walk into just about any newsroom in the country and never see it" (2003).

Ownership and control of the mass media (television, movies, music, radio, cable, publishing, and the Internet) have dwindled from the 50 of two decades ago, to "less than two dozen with power concentrated in 10 huge conglomerates" (Free Press, n.d.). Thus, diversity imbalance among the producers of mass media messages has serious consequences for what is aired for everyone.

NewsWatch reports that in 1999 there were only 24 percent female and 14 percent minority network reporters with on-air stories. In 2004 the picture improved with women in the TV news workforce numbering 39 percent and minorities, 21 percent. Some 21 percent of the TV news directors are women and 24.7 percent of the radio directors are women. For minorities, 12 percent were TV and 11 percent are radio directors (2005, July 20). The percentage of Hispanics in the newsroom is 9.6 percent; Asian Americans, 2.7 percent and Native Americans, .05 percent. For the first time ever, two Asian Americans cracked the list of the top 50 most visible reporters in 2003.

Interestingly, "...African Americans, Asians, Hispanics and Middle Easterners tend to trust English-language media outlets more than native-language ones" (Journalism, 2004).

"On both sitcoms and dramas, exclusion is pervasive. Black, Latino and Asian performers have a hard time landing recurring roles" (Seitz, 2002) and behind the scenes—writers, directors, producers, and crew members are mostly Caucasian.

## SUMMARY

Media coverage and employment of minorities within the field still reflect discrimination. Media messages foster stereotypes, as well as the ideals of a culture, as they reflect and reinforce cultural values. Media messages are often multiple in that they contain combinations of gender, age, social class, and/or ethnic values in the same message.

## EXERCISES

To examine media messages, select one of the following media to investigate. **Note**: Your instructor will provide the recording forms from the Instructor's Manual to aid you in recording your observations.

### 1. Electronic Media: Prime Time TV

Watch prime-time television selecting Option A or Option B from the following list. Record the information (role, gender, ethnicity, social group, and behaviors) about the principal and secondary characters on the Recording Form. You will need several copies of the Recording Form for each program. Be sure to use separate forms for each program.

a.  Watch two hours of prime-time TV drama (6–11 p.m.) or
b.  Watch three different prime time crime dramas (6–11 p.m.).

After you have made your observations, answer the following questions:

i.   What audience do you think each program targets? Why?
ii.  What stereotype and cultural messages do you think the programs send? Explain.
iii. What audience do you think the commercials target? Why?
iv.  What stereotype and cultural messages do you think the commercials send? Explain.

### 2. Print Media: Magazines

Visit a library or bookstore. Select three magazines, one from each of the following columns. Use the Recording Form for your observations of the ethnicity, gender, social class, and the tone of the commentary. You will need several copies of the Recording Form for each magazine.

| | | |
|---|---|---|
| *Cosmopolitan* | *Brides* | *Business Week* |
| *Good Housekeeping* | *Maxim* | *DiversityInc* |
| *Instyle* | *Money* | *Jet* |
| *Marie Clair* | *Seventeen* | *Real simple* |
| *Martha Stewart Living* | *Sports Illustrated* | *Time* |
| *Shape* | *Travel & Leisure* | *Vanity Fair* |

After you have recorded your observations, analyze the media messages and answer the following questions for each magazine:

a. What group(s) (gender, class, race/ethnicity, age, etc.) does each magazine seem to target? Explain. Give examples.

b. What messages (cultural value, stereotypes, etc.) does each magazine seem to convey? Explain. Give examples.

c. What group(s) (gender, class, race/ethnicity, age, etc.) do the advertisements in each magazine seem to target? Give examples.

d. What messages (cultural value, stereotypes, etc.) do the advertisements in each magazine seem to convey? Explain. Give examples.

### 3. Print Media: Mass Circulation Newspapers

Examine a single issue of a mass circulation daily or Sunday newspaper and record your observations of the ethnicity, gender, social class, and tone (i.e., positive, negative, neutral) of the commentary in either a) the stories or b) the features on the Recording Form. You will need several copies of the form.

a. Newspaper stories.

b. Features including wedding, engagement, anniversary and death notices, financial reporting, clothing, travel articles, etc.

After you have recorded your observations, answer the following questions:

  i. Are the groups treated in proportion to their numbers in the population? Explain.

  ii. Do you think the groups are treated equally in tone (i.e., positive, negative, neutral)? Explain.

  iii. What audience do you think they may target? Explain.

  iv. What stereotypes do you think they may foster? Explain.

### 4. Other Cultural Products

Transmission of cultural expectations for both genders begins at birth and continues throughout childhood. Verify this by making observations of one the following cultural products. Your instructor will supply Recording Forms to aid you in making your observations. You will need several copies of the Recording Form.

a. Baby Cards. Visit a store selling baby cards and record the gender differences in color, design, and message. Use separate Recording Forms for male and female cards. Do not use cards from the Internet.

b. Toys. Visit a large toy store and record gender and racial differences in color, design, and message. Use separate Recording Forms for male and female toys.

c. Comic Books. Examine three different comic books and record social identity information, such as gender and race, about the principal and secondary characters on the Recording Form. Use separate forms for each comic book.

d. Children's Books or Elementary School Textbooks. Visit a library or bookstore and examine the textbooks used in a single grade or examine subject textbooks (e.g., social science) for several grades recording information about the characters in the book on the Recording Form. Use separate forms for each book.

e. Video Games. Examine three different video games, noting information about the principal and secondary characters on the Recording Form. Use separate forms for each game.

After making the observations answer the questions:

i. What stereotypes and cultural messages do you think are being sent? Explain.

ii. How are ethnic and racial groups represented? As leading characters? As villains? Heroes? What are the gender roles? Explain.

### 5. Additional Assignments

*Anatomy of an English-Language Newspaper*

a. Select one newspaper. One person will examine each of the following parts of the paper for a single day (issue). Other individuals will examine the paper on different days. Use Recording Forms to make observations.

i. comic strips
ii. advertising
iii. letters to the editors
iv. features
v. news stories
vi. photographs

b. Assemble group members to combine their observations into a "profile" of the newspaper.

*Anatomy of Foreign-Language Newspapers*

If possible, dissect foreign-language newspapers in the same fashion as the English-language newspapers.

*Magazines*

Select an unusual magazine (such as a biking magazine or skiing magazine or Travel Over 50) and analyze it to determine what segment of society it targets in terms of race/ethnicity, age, social class, gender, etc.

*Television*

Select TV networks targeting special groups, such as the Home and Garden channel or ESPN, and compare their programming (messages) with those of mass TV.

## BIBLIOGRAPHY

Akbar, M.T. (2007). We are not done with racism – yet. Media Monitors Network. Retrieved September 4, 2007, from http://usa.mediamonitors.net

American Society of Newspaper Editors. (2001, April 3). *2001 ASNE census finds newsrooms less diverse: increased hiring of minorities blunted by departure rate.* Retrieved on November 11, 2003, from http://www.asne.org

Barnes, K., & DeBell, C. (1995). *The portrayal of men and women workers in Sunday Comics: no laughing matter.* Paper presented at the American Psychological Association Convention, New York, August 1995.

Bennett, W. (1994). *The index of leading cultural indicators.* NY: Touchstone, p. 102–106.

Berkeley Daily Planet. (2002, December 11). Videogames lack diversity. Retrieved

September 4, 2007, from http://www.berkeleydailyplanet.com

Boone, M. (2003). Television's gay characters aim to add diversity, but unintentionally reinforce negative stereotypes. The Daily Orange. Retrieved on September 7, 2007, from http://www.dailyorange.com

Brown, C.S. (2003, August 12). *Univision/Hispanic broadcasting merger: what's at stake for marketers, latinos?* Retrieved on November 26, 2003, from http://www.diversityinc.com

Butsch, R. (n.d.). Social class and television. The Museum of Broadcast Communications. Retrieved September 4, 2007, from http://www.museum.tv/archives/etv/S/htmlS/socialclass/socialclass.htm

Center for Media and Public Affairs. *Factoids. Demographics of network reporters 1989 –1999.* Retrieved on November 18, 2003, from http://www.cmpa.com/factoid/diverse.htm

Center for Media and Public Affairs. (2003, February 28). *Minorities, women make network news history.* Retrieved on November 17, 2003, from http://www.cmpa./preeerel/ MinRelease 2003.htm

Cole, Y. (2003, July 21) *U.S. 'telenovelas': bringing Latino generations together.* Retrieved on November 26, 2003, from http://www.diversityinc.com

DiversityInc. (2003, September 10) Diversity Factoids: September 10. Retrieved on November 26, 2003, from http://www.diversityinc.com

DiversityJobs. (2007). Broadcast news workforce lacks diversity. Retrieved September 4, 2007, from http://www.diversityjobs.com/node/3460563

Estefa, A. (2004). Satellite television viewing among Arabs in the U.S. Retrieved September 12, 2007, from http://www.allacademic.com/meta/p113211_index.html

Fitzgerald, M. (2003, January 8). *Newspaper outlook 2003.* Retrieved on November 27, 2003, from http://www.editorandpublisher.com.

Free Press. (n.d.). Media ownership. Retrieved September 4, 2007, from http://www.freepress.net/issues/ownership

*Government goes down the tube: images of government in TV entertainment. Executive summary.* Retrieved on November 18, 2003, from http://www.cmpa.com

Huang, T .T. (2003, November 17). Poynteronline. *The battle for inclusiveness.* Retrieved on November 18, 2003, from http://www.poynter.org

*Italian-American characters in television entertainment. Executive summary.* Retrieved on November 18, 2003, from http://www.cmpa.com

Journalism. (2007). The state of the news media 2007. Retrieved September 10, 2007, from http://www.journalism.org

Journalism. (2007). Ethnic media audience trends 2007. Retrieved September 11, 2007, from http://www.journalism.org/node/465

Learmonth, M. (2006). PTC unhappy with TV's religious stereotypes. Retrieved September 4, 2007, from http://www.variety.com/article/VR1117955772.html

Lichter, S. R., & Amundson, D. Distorted reality: Hispanic characters in TV entertainment *1955–1992. Executive Summary.* Retrieved on November 18, 2003, from http://www.cmpa.com

Lichter, S. R., Lichter, L., & Rothman, S. *Video villains: the TV businessman 1955–1986. Executive summary.* Retrieved on November 17, 2003, from http://www.cmpa.com

Lopez, E.M. (2003, September 4). *Can new Spanish-language dailies help save the newspaper industry?* Retrieved on November 26, 2003, from http://www.diversityinc.com

Mantsios, G. (1998). *Media magic. Making class invisible.* From Paula Rothenberg (ed.), Race, Class and Gender in the United States: An Integrated Study. 4th ed. NY: St. Martin's Press, 1998.

Media Monitor. (2002, September/October). *What's the matter with kids today? Images of teenagers on local and national TV news.* Retrieved on November 17, 2003, from http://www.cmpa.com

Méndez-Méndez, S., & Alveiro, D. (2003). Network Brownout 2003: The portrayal of Latinos in network television news, 2002. National Association of Hispanic Journals (Access: Google senior author).

Mitchell, B. (2003, November 17). *It's about hiring, too.* Retrieved on November 18, 2003, from http://www.poynter.org

NAA. (2007, July 24). *NAA launches next phase of industry trade campaign.* Newspaper

Association of America. Retrieved on September 11, 2007, from http://www.naa.org

NAA. (2007). *Trends and numbers.* Newspaper Association of America. Retrieved on September 11, 2007, from http://www.naa.org

Nakamura, L. (2000). "Where do you want to go today?" Cybernetic tourism, the Internet and transnationality. From Dines, G. and Humez, J., eds. *Gender, race and class in media text reader Second* ed. Thousand Oaks, CA: Sage 2002 p. 684–687.

Nielsen Media Research (2007). *Hispanic-American Television Audience.* Retrieved on September 4, 2007, from http://www.nielsenmedia.com/ethnicmeasure

Nielsen Media Research (2003). *The African-American Television Audience.* Retrieved on November 18, 2003, from http://www.nielsen-media.com/ethnicmeasure

Online NewsHour. (1999, August 23). *Diversity in the newsroom.* Retrieved on November 27, 2003, from http://www.pbs.org/newshour

Readership Institute. (1999). *Newspaper staffing, diversity and turnover.* Retrieved on November 27, 2003, from http://www.readership.org

Santos, M. (2007). Part 1: Missing people face disparity in media coverage. MSN Lifestyle. Retrieved September 4, 200 from http://www.lifestyle.msn.com

Seitz, M. Z. (2002, July 16). Despite some progress, minorities remain an unseen presence. *Star Ledger,* p. 28.

Shaheen, J.G. (1989) TV Arabs. From New Worlds of Literature, Jerome Beatty and J. Paul Hunter, eds. In Rothenberg, *Race, Class and Gender in the United States. An Integrated Study. Sixth ed.* NY.: Worth 2004 p. 356–357.

Sigmund, J. (2007). NAA launches next phase of industry trade campaign. Newspaper Association of America. Retrieved September 3, 2007, from http://www.naa.org/sitecore/content/Global/PressCenter/2007

Smith, R. (2003, October 24). *Copy editing for diversity.* Poynteronline. Retrieved on November 18, 2003, from http://www.poynter.org

Sowell, T. (1991). A world view of cultural diversity. *Society.* vol. 29, no. 1, pp. 37–44.

Television's impact on ethnic and racial images: a study of Howard Beach adolescents *Executive summary.* Retrieved on November 17, 2003, from http://www.cmpa.com

The Associated Press. (2003, October 7). *Cable TV seeks Spanish-speaking customers.* Retrieved on November 26, 2003, from http://www.diversityinc.com

UNITY: Journalists of Color, Inc. (2003, April 7). *Unity: newspapers face diversity crisis and need crisis reaction.* Retrieved on November 27, 2003, from http://unityjournalists.org/news3a.html

U. S. Census Bureau. *Population Estimates.* Retrieved September 8, 2007, from http://www.census.gov

Video games. (2002). Retrieved September 4, 2007, from http://www.units.muohio.edu

Wilson, C.C. II, Gutierrez, F., & Chao, L. (2003). Racism, sexism and the media. The rise of class communication in multicultural America. 3rd ed. Thousand Oaks: Sage 2003, pp 25–34.

White, R. (2001). TV portrayals of obese people perpetuate stereotypes. Retrieved September 4, 2007, from http://cas.msu.edu

Zafar, S. (2003, January). Going beyond words. *Managing Diversity,* vol 12, no. 4, p.1.

# Being an Only: A Field Assignment

## Carol P. Harvey
### *Assumption College*

**G**iven the demographic changes in today's workforce, it is important to understand what it feels like to be a visible minority. Sometimes, differential treatment is due to the context of the workplace situation, rather than to discrimination. When an organization or a department has one or a few people who are different in terms of some visible social identity group membership, the majority may—often unconsciously—treat them differently. In turn, the minority employees may find that they react differently to their contextual situation than they would if there were more balanced numbers in the work situation. If one is a part of the majority, it may be difficult to recognize the impact of this phenomenon. One of the most effective ways to recreate this learning experience is to watch the award-wining video, "A Tale of O" (Goodmeasure) and to complete the following field assignment.

## INSTRUCTIONS

1. Watch the film, "A Tale of O," and take meaningful notes about the experiences of the O's (minority) and X's (majority).

2. Think creatively about how you could place yourself in a safe, alcohol-free field situation where you would be a visible minority, i.e., be an "O." (Some examples include a female student going truck shopping at a local automotive dealer, a male student attending a Tupperware party, a young student going to a water aerobics class with senior citizens, an able-bodied student shopping in a mall in a wheel-chair, and others attending religious services of faiths very different from their own, etc.) Submit your idea to your professor for approval. (Note: Some experiences are inappropriate for this assignment. For example, attending an Alcoholics Anonymous meeting, going to a gay bar, or trying to recycle your study abroad semester, or any additional situations that your instructor considers inappropriate will not fulfill the requirements of the assignment. Also, sometimes, you may need

to obtain permission from the person in charge of the organization, such as the minister, rabbi, etc.) to attend the activities of an organization.

3. Once your idea is approved, complete the field experience, keeping in mind the material from the video. Do not have a friend accompany you on the field experience.

4. Write a 3- to 4-page typed report that analyzes your field experience from the perspective of the consequences of being an "O." How does it feel? How did you act differently in this situation? How did people treat you differently? What did you learn about yourself and others? Try to relate your experiences closely to the information presented in the video.

# Diversity Challenges in Tomorrow's Organizations: The Symposium

Pamela D. Sherer

*Providence College*

Organizations deal with a multitude of diversity-related issues on a daily basis (e.g., age, social class, ethnicity, gender, health/disability, race, religion, sexual orientation, etc.). This course affords the opportunity to increase awareness of diversity-related issues, to understand how diversity affects individuals and organizations, and how to take an active role in an organization's diversity initiatives. This integrative assignment requires you to identify and explore *future* organizational challenges with respect to a particular diversity-related topic. The effort required for the assignment will be undertaken both individually and in assigned groups.

## INSTRUCTIONS

You will be assigned to small groups based on your interest in one of the course diversity topics (e.g., age, social class, ethnicity, gender, health/disability, race, religion, sexual orientation).

### Group Instructions

- Subdivide your topic among your group members (see examples A and B).

- Interact, both inside and outside of class, to share information and relevant resources on your topic.

- Plan and conduct a symposium where each group member will present key findings and the group will conduct a question-and-answer session.

---

## EXAMPLE A

Assume that your group topic is **gender diversity** and individual group members decide to each select a different *organization/industry* for his/her research. As a result, each group member's research has a different lens to look at future organization challenges with regard to gender. For example, students might focus on gender issues in, for example, the entertainment, financial services, and/or hospitality industries; law firms; local government; hospitals; military; police/fire (public service); religious organizations; schools and universities; social work; and/or sports organizations.

Once your individual research is complete, your group will plan a 30-minute symposium, titled, for example, "Future Gender Diversity Challenges: The Military, Education, and Religious Organizations." Each group selects a chairperson who will introduce the symposium and the individual speakers. Each member will individually summarize his/her key research findings and, as a group, conduct a question-and-answer session.

---

## EXAMPLE B

Assume your group topic is **racial diversity** and your group selects one industry, the *sports industry*, for example. Individual group members each select a different organization lens to look at future organizational challenges with regard to race and a sport, such as race and golf, race and tennis, and race and ice hockey.

Once your individual research is complete, your group will plan a 30-minute symposium, titled, for example, "Future Racial Diversity Challenges in Professional Sports: Golf, Tennis, and Ice Hockey." Each group selects a chairperson who will introduce the symposium and the individual speakers. Each member will individually summarize his/her key research findings and, as a group, conduct a question-and-answer session.

---

### Individual Instructions

- Conduct secondary and primary research on your individual topic (see Research Suggestions).
- Summarize your research in a 6-to-8 page paper that includes the following:
  a. the major future trends and challenges for your topic/organization in terms of diversity,
  b. the major reasons for these challenges (e.g., internal and external factors such as demographics, laws, cultural changes, employee initiatives, technology, etc.),

c. suggestions for action steps organizations can take to address these future challenges, and

d. a list of references (requirements described in the next section).

## RESEARCH SUGGESTIONS

1. *Secondary Research.* In addition to class readings, you will need to locate journal articles, newspaper sources, etc., to guide you in your analysis. Your paper must include a minimum of five references from professional journals and/or books, five references from the *Wall Street Journal* or other major business/organization-related publications, and three Internet sites that provide resources about the future and your selected issue. The Internet sources should be annotated (see http://library.umcrookston.edu/annotate.htm for sample annotation).

2. *Primary research.* Another major source of information is from an interview with someone who works in the type of organization you have selected (e.g., military, law, schools) and who has experience in dealing with diversity issues. If you do not know someone to interview, a helpful source for identifying individuals can be your campus alumni/development office; or you may directly contact an organization or association that represents specific professional groups (e.g., American Bar Association, American Federation of Teachers, and American Nurses Association). Usually there are local chapters in your area that will be helpful in your research.

## EVALUATION

Presentations will be graded for *style* (preparation, organization, clarity, enthusiasm). The paper should be written clearly, free from typos, spelling errors, etc., and with correctly cited references. A second grade for *content* (the quality and quantity of information presented) will also be given.

# Decisions

## Carol P. Harvey
### *Assumption College*

Assume that you are an exempt, i.e., not paid by the hour, employee who has a decision to make. The management of your company has offered that one of their employees would do a special research project for a nonprofit organization in the community. Your boss thinks that you would be the best employee to write this report. This task would be in addition to your regular work, will involve a lot of time, and is due in a month. You would like the experience of doing this project, but you tell your boss that the company should give you "something" in return for the extra work. There is currently a wage freeze in your organization, so your boss can't reward you with extra salary or a bonus. However, she does offer you the choice of one of the following:

---

A. You can work at home two days a week for the next month.

B. You can add two vacation days to the two weeks that you receive this year.

C. Your company will pay the premium for a $50,000 life insurance policy for a year.

D. You can have a reserved parking space in the underground lot where the executives park for a month.

E. Your company will give you two box seat tickets on the 50-yard line for one of the local pro football team's games.

---

1. Which of these options (A–E) would you select as a reward for the extra work? Why?

2. Which of these options (A–E) is the least attractive to you as a reward? Why?

# SECTION

# A Framework for Understanding Organizational Diversity and Inclusion

## Introduction

**Goals of Section III**

- To understand why organizations are changing in terms of their approaches to diversity

- To understand the implications of the business case for diversity

- To explore some of the models for understanding organizational diversity

- To learn how to evaluate an organization's diversity programs and progress

In this section of the text, we consider how organizations need to adapt to the changing workforce and learn what they will need to do in the future to fully benefit from diversity.

From a business perspective, organizations implement diversity initiatives for a variety of reasons. Sometimes they implement these changes to avoid costly lawsuits and negative publicity; or to attract and retain a wider pool of employees, especially in a tight labor market; or to improve customer and supplier relationships; or to improve workplace performance (DeLong, 2006).

While some organizations—like Coca-Cola—need the power of the law as a catalyst for change, others—like Pitney Bowes—consider integrating diversity initiatives into the mission of the organization as a proactive way to adapt to changing times and as the right thing to do. Today, workplace diversity programs have evolved from "predominately legal compliance to a focus on inclusion and valuing diversity for the skills, competencies and experiences brought to the organization" (Lockwood & Victor, 2007, p. 1).

In the last ten years there has been a growing but controversial attempt to make what is called "the business case for diversity"—i.e., to prove that diversity pays off financially for an organization. Most of the research that has been done has produced mixed results (Kochan et al., 2002; Fegley, 2006). Since diversity initiatives require significant and long-term organizational changes within a business culture that tends to value short term returns on its investments, it should not be a surprise that its effects are somewhat intangible and difficult to measure. However, what can be measured are the costs of product innovation, decreased turnover and absenteeism, among diverse employees.

Thomas and Ely (1996) recognize that organizations can be in different stages in terms of managing diversity. Some are still operating in the *discrimination and fairness paradigm*—i.e., avoiding lawsuits through recruitment and retention of diverse employees who are expected to assimilate into the dominant group. Others are in an *access and legitimacy paradigm,* where diversity is considered a competitive advantage in terms of understanding changing customer markets. To make managing diversity really work, organizations need to be operating in a *learning and effectiveness paradigm,* where an organization internalizes diversity as part of its mission, connects the needs of diverse workers to the way that work is done, and makes workers feel valued and included.

Thomas and Ely suggest that the best way to build a business case is to link diversity to the specific needs of an organization, such as optimizing market opportunities, developing creative solutions to problems, or decreasing the turnover of talented diverse employees. Then make a plan to achieve these goals and track and measure the long-term results, both quantitatively and qualitatively, adjusting as necessary.

An example of the implementation of the learning and effectiveness paradigm is the diversity program at the National Institutes of Health (NIH), the United States' medical research agency. NIH has developed a Diversity Life Cycle Model (see Figure 1) that recognizes diversity as an ongoing, long-term organizational change process. The NIH diversity initiatives were developed at a 1995 Diversity Congress, where 115 delegates, representing the Institutes and Centers (IC) met to develop a diversity program.

> It is the policy of the NIH to manage the diversity of its approximately 18,000 employees by building an inclusive workforce, fostering an environment that respects the individual, and offering opportunities for all persons to develop to their full potential in support of science (National Institutes of Health, 2007).

With continual support from the directors, this model has worked because it includes several important elements necessary for effective diversity change initiatives. Taking into account the unique culture and mission of this organization, it goes beyond making employees "aware" of others' differences to include managing diversity (i.e., actions) and assessment (i.e., evaluations) to determine which diversity programs are effective at NIH. This process creates a feedback loop that leads to ongoing diversity change efforts.

In terms of creating a climate of inclusion, NIH has employees representing all levels, from blue-collar to highly educated scientists, who serve as Diversity Catalysts in each IC and on a organization-wide Diversity Council that advises "the NIH Director and management officials on policies, programs, and areas to be addressed through the WDI (Workplace Diversity Initiatives) Strategic Plan" (NIH, 2007).

## Components of the Diversity Life Cycle

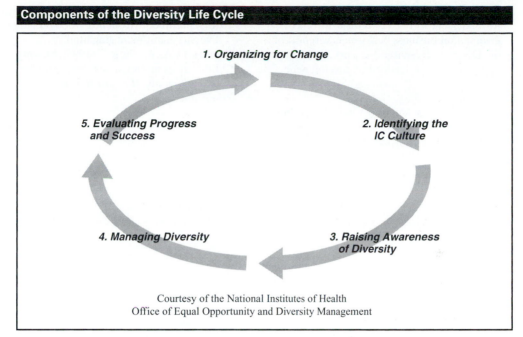

1. Organizing for Change

2. Identifying the
IC Culture

3. Raising Awareness
of Diversity

4. Managing Diversity

5. Evaluating Progress
and Success

Courtesy of the National Institutes of Health
Office of Equal Opportunity and Diversity Management

Available at *http://oeo.od.nih.gov/diversitymgmt/cycle.html* and used with permission of the National Institutes of Health.

Yet, there is still much progress to be made and much to learn about understanding how diversity has changed the ways that we manage in the workplace. DeLong writes,

> The gains associated with diversity rarely materialize until a company reaches a sufficient threshold. Research shows, for instance, that teams work best when they are either extremely diverse or completely homogenous: they function least well when they are stuck in the middle (2006, p. 9).

Section III opens with an explanation of why it is important for organizations to achieve inclusion and a description of the changes that organizations need to implement to truly "unleash the power of diversity." Next, the article on human capital as a strategic issue, and the Pitney Bowes case, offer examples of how well-designed organizational change efforts can help to make diversity a strategic advantage. The next three cases illustrate what happens when organizations ignore their human capital issues (Coca-Cola), try to deal with diversity through assimilation (the Air Force Academy), and subtly let stereotypes and prejudices stand in the way of hiring the most qualified but diverse candidate (Fairfax Memorial). This section concludes with a capstone assignment (the Diversity Audit) that will allow you to integrate the semester's material into the evaluation of a real organization.

## BIBLIOGRAPHY

DeLong, T. (2006). A framework for pursuing diversity in the workplace. *Harvard Business School reprint*, #9-407-029, August 22. Boston MA: Harvard Business School Press.

Fegley, S. (2006). SHRM 2006 workplace diversity and changes to the EEO-1 process Survey report. Alexandria, VA: SHRM.

Kochan, T., Bezrukova, K., Ely, R., Jackson, S., Joshi, A., Jen, J. et al. (2002). The effects of diversity on business performance: report of the Diversity Research Network, building opportunities for leadership development initiative. Alfred P. Sloan and SHRM, October.

Lockwood, N.R., & Victor, J. (2007). Recruiting for workplace diversity: a business strategy. *SHRM Staffing Research*, Spring, p.1.

National Institutes of Health. (2007). Retrieved on September 5, from http://oeo.od.nih.gov/diversitymgmt/managing.html.

Thomas, D. A., & Ely, R. J. (1996). Making differences matter: a new paradigm for managing diversity. *Harvard Business Review*, Sept-Oct.

# The Inclusion Breakthrough: Unleashing the Real Power of Diversity

*A Summary Prepared by*

## Kristina A. Bourne

*from*
*The Inclusion Breakthrough: Unleashing the Real Power of Diversity*
*by Frederick A. Miller & Judith H. Katz*

An *inclusion breakthrough* is a powerful transformation of an organization's culture to one in which *every* individual is valued as a vital component of the organization's success and competitive advantage. In the past, diversity has been seen as something that must be managed, tolerated, or molded to fit the dominant culture. Even those organizations that embrace diversity usually see it as an end in itself, rather than connected to the main mission of the organization. Such views create a *diversity in a box* strategy for most organizations, limiting the potential and power of diversity. With an inclusion breakthrough, differences are understood as mission-critical, not something extra linked only to human resource policies and practices.

Underpinning an inclusion breakthrough is the assumption that *diversity can be found in all individuals.* Everyone has his or her own unique backgrounds, experiences, and perspectives. Hiring people from different backgrounds, however, is not enough if the organization values sameness in ways of thinking, style, and behavior. Organizations can break out of the diversity in a box model by transforming their culture to one that values and supports the various dimensions of diversity, and unleashing its power.

Barriers to inclusion, ranging from blatant disregard for differences (such as the lack of accommodations for people with disabilities) to more subtle forms (such as exclusion from the afternoon golf game) are still widespread. Change efforts, however, should not stop at leveling the playing field by breaking down these barriers. Creating an environment where all people can be more productive means raising the playing field by continually examining processes to ensure that everyone feels valued for their contribution to the organization's success. *Leveraging diversity requires a culture of inclusion to support it.*

## THE FUNDAMENTALS OF AN INCLUSION BREAKTHROUGH

An inclusion breakthrough is a cycle—each element builds on the previous to raise the entire bar of expectations for organizations. This cycle positively impacts organizations by continuously increasing job satisfaction, attracting and retaining talented individuals, developing thriving communities, and tapping into market potential. Creating a culture of inclusion requires organizations to examine the following five key processes:

- Defining a new set of competencies
- Aligning policies and practices
- Leveraging a diverse labor force
- Connecting with local community
- Increasing value to marketplace

### Defining a New Set of Competencies

Organizations today are plagued with incompetence such as inadequate communication skills, underutilized assets, internal rivalry, turnover of talented workers, and lack of cooperation across units. To unleash creativity and enable people to perform at their highest level, organizations must require new competencies and develop infrastructures that support them.

Working collaboratively and partnering across a diverse pool of people requires an environment in which individuals feel their unique perspective contributes to the overall success of the organization. People's experience of an organization is often based on the behavior of their immediate supervisor and members of their work group. A culture of inclusion, therefore, requires *all* people, no matter what position or level in the organization, to demonstrate the following new *inclusive competencies:*

- Greet others genuinely
- Understand difference as a force for new ideas and resolve disagreements
- Listen to each team member's ideas and perspectives
- Share information clearly and honestly
- Ensure that everyone understands the overall vision and how each task relates to it
- Realize that every member has a contribution to make
- Understand that others' experiences and perspectives can add innovative ideas
- Encourage quiet members to share their thoughts
- Respect other team members' time and personal/family responsibilities
- See mistakes as learning opportunities for improvement

These key competencies create a workplace that encourages communicating across differences, resolving conflict, and valuing every individual as a contributor to the overall mission. These new competencies, however, are not static and must be continuously re-evaluated in light of changes in the external and internal environment.

## Aligning Policies and Practices

Developing a new set of inclusive competencies will only be effective if they are integrated into the formal rules and policies of the organization, requiring both the written and unwritten practices to change. Even the so-called "soft policies," those that help people feel connected to and supported by the organization, must be reevaluated to enable individuals to feel respected for their unique contribution while working in diverse situations. Old assumptions must be abandoned. For example, no longer is the office Christmas party "everyone's holiday."

In order to achieve an inclusion breakthrough, organizations must go beyond what they are already doing, raising the bar of the old baseline of actions to new levels. Table 1 lists current and updated policies and practice that allow people from a variety of social identity groups to perform at their highest level. The goal is not to treat everyone the same. *Fairness gets redefined as treating everyone according to their needs so that they can do their best work.*

### The Old and the New Baseline for Inclusive Policies and Practices

| *Addressing Issues Relating to . . .* | *The Old Baseline* | *The New Baseline* |
| --- | --- | --- |
| Age | • Recruits young people | • Recognizes that young people are investments in the future |
| | | • Develops young people quickly |
| | • Values the experience of people who are 50 and older | • Extends the retirement age |
| | | • Includes 50+ people in high-potential groups |
| Lesbians, Gays and Bisexuals | • Creates an environment that is safe for people to come out | • Invites people's partners to company events |
| | • Offers domestic partner benefits | • Encourages people to talk about personal lives |
| | | • Offers benefits that take into account the unique needs of lesbians and gays |
| | | • Recognizes that not all customers are heterosexual |
| Nationality | • Offers additional pay for language skills | • Recognizes a variety of holidays and customs |
| | • Recruits people from different countries | • Includes representatives from all the organization's geographic locations on board of directors and senior management team |
| | | • Develops local talent |
| Organizational Hierarchy | • Values and respects people at the lower levels | • Recognizes that all people contribute to the organization |

*(Continued)*

**Continued**

| Addressing Issues Relating to . . . | The Old Baseline | The New Baseline |
|---|---|---|
| | • Provides career development opportunities for all people | • Listesns to all voices at all levels |
| | | • Creates participatory decision-making processes |
| People of Color | • Actively recruits and retains people of color | • Demonstrates a critical mass throughout organization |
| | • Has minimal representation at all levels | • Acknowledges multiracial identity |
| | • Acknowledges differentiation between groups (e.g., African American, Latinos) | • Develops two-way mentoring across racial lines (versus one-way mentoring to fit into old culture) |
| People with Disabilities | • Complies with the Americans with Disabilities Act | • Creates an environment where people feel safe to express their unique needs |
| | • Provides medical benefits that address disabled people's particular needs | • Proactively recruits and retains people with disabilities |
| | • Recognizes the contributions of people with disabilities | • Represents people with disabilities in marketing campaigns |
| | | • Provides more funding for accommodations |
| White Men | • Ensures that the white men are included in inclusion efforts | • Develops two-way mentoring so white men can learn about their own diversity and expand their perspective |
| | • Recognizes that there is more than one type of white man | • Acknowledges work/family issues |
| Women | • Shows representation at all levels | • Eliminates subtle forms of harassment |
| | • Addresses sexual harassment | • Addresses the sticky floor (i.e., barriers that keep women of color at the bottom) |
| | • Acknowledges the structural barriers to women's advancement | • Develops two-way mentoring across women and men |
| | • Values the work women do at all levels | • Applies flexible scheduling to all levels of the organization |
| | | • Includes men in parental policies |

## Leveraging a Diverse Labor Force

*Just having people who represent diverse social identity groups in the organization is not enough; an environment must be created that unleashes that diversity.* Diversity in a box creates a situation where everyone is expected to fit within its walls. Dismantling these limits creates an environment where people feel safe to bring forward new ideas and perspectives when their difference is valued and respected as integral to the organization's strategic mission.

**The Biases Among Us**  Unleashing the potential of a diverse workforce requires organizations to address the barriers preventing everyone from succeeding. Organizational practices reflect societal and individual belief systems. Racism, sexism, heterosexism, ageism, and other prevalent "isms" are like a boulder of oppression that builds momentum as it rolls down the hill. Condescending and patronizing comments maintain the dominance of the one-up group. Sexism is prevalent when men are admired for leaving early to go to their child's school activity, while women are judged negatively for leaving early to pick their child up from daycare. Systematic racism exists when white women express concern about their organization's glass ceiling, while ignoring the fact that more women of color are concentrated at the lower levels. Doing nothing allows the boulder of bias to roll on. The only way to have a true inclusion breakthrough is to stop this boulder of oppressive beliefs with sustained, positive action.

## Attracting and Retaining a Talented Workforce

Hanging on to new talent is difficult in today's high-turnover environment. Most people change jobs and/or organizations every few years, making recruitment and retention of talented individuals a strategic priority. When people walk out the door in a year or two, they take with them their talent and training, often heading to the competitor's door. The traditional strategy of "bringing them along slowly" doesn't work when employee turnover is high. Further, "outsider status" must be eliminated. People of color, people with an accent, and people from other social identity groups must not be ignored or made to prove that they can fit in. All members must be nurtured and developed, because all members create value for the organization.

**An Employer of Choice**  Becoming an employer of choice means asking why, given complete freedom, people would work for your organization. The following are key characteristics that talented individuals from diverse backgrounds report as significant in selecting an employer.

- The leaders are highly knowledgeable and inspirational.
- The organization is positioned for growth.
- Policies support work, life, and family integration.
- Ample growth and development opportunities exist (e.g., educational support).
- People feel respected by their colleagues.
- The environment is physically and emotionally safe.
- People are recognized as business partners (e.g., profit-sharing programs).
- People have access to all job-relevant information.
- Roles, responsibilities, performance expectations, and reward systems are openly stated.

If organizations want their employees to invest their time and energy into the organization, then organizations need to invest their time and energy into those people; this is the new two-way employment agreement.

### Connecting with the Local Community

To be competitive, an inclusion strategy should not only focus on the inside of the organization, but the outside. Attracting talented people requires attractive communities in which they will live. The quality of the water supply, school systems, transportation, and other community resources must be high. Organizations should go beyond a one-way relationship with local communities based on tax breaks and other incentives to investing in educational, recreational, and health facilities. Organizations are, after all, dependent on local communities for people, suppliers, distributors, customers, and investors.

### Increasing Value to the Marketplace

Diversity in a box places customers outside of its walls. An inclusion breakthrough sees customers as central players in the organization's success. Traditionally, diverse customers are segmented into niches, which treats social identity groups as monolithic categories. Leveraging diversity in the marketplace requires organizations to expand their view of customers and link them to their core business strategy. The range of tastes and preferences within each social identity category must be recognized. Tapping into this market potential requires more than the token representative of each social group. *All* people in the organization must have the competencies to understand the unique features of each social group.

## BUILDING AN INCLUSION BREAKTHROUGH

Creating an environment in which all members of the organization feel supported to perform at their highest level requires a methodology for an inclusion breakthrough. Most organizations will go through four phases: laying the foundation for change, mobilizing change efforts, making change an everyday activity, and sustaining and challenging the new change.

### Phase I: Laying The Foundation for Change

The most important piece of the foundation is the support from the top. Senior executives must lead and model the new competencies and provide resources to help people change to new, and initially uncomfortable, ways of behaving and interacting. Senior leaders need to link the change to the core business mission by creating an organizational imperative that clearly describes how a culture change will positively impact the organization as a whole, thereby creating value for each individual.

Laying the platform for change also requires a comprehensive organizational assessment that examines and documents a baseline of the current culture, resources, practices, and opportunities. Assessment is itself a tool for change; asking people about their experiences and concerns opens a space for change to occur. Data can be collected from surveys or by focus groups that assemble people by different social identities—part-time workers, individuals over 55, Asian-American managers—providing a forum for a diversity of views. Senior leaders must be receptive to honest and frank feedback about the organization's culture.

Senior leaders cannot create the change alone; learning partners should be selected to share their experiences and perspectives with senior leaders on a continuous basis. These individuals should not be seen as token representatives for differences, but as vital partners in the change effort, who offer insights to voices in the organization that otherwise go unheard. Further, a change leadership team, including individuals from various social identity groups and the dominant group, should be created to broaden the scope of the efforts.

## Phase II: Mobilizing Change Efforts

This phase begins with developing an initial 12- to 18-month plan to implement the widespread culture change. At this stage, senior leaders should provide frequent and clear communication so that everyone in the organization is aware of the forthcoming changes. For example, the CEO can send a personal letter to each employee that describes the inclusion breakthrough as mission-critical. A core group should be selected to model the changes by integrating the new competencies into their everyday work lives. Intense education sessions will also allow groups of people in the organization to learn the new competencies. For example, human resource staff will need to learn how to integrate the new inclusive policies. Further, managers at all levels will need to integrate the new skills for leveraging diversity into their behaviors. Managers can often resist the culture change because in order for them to have climbed to their current position, they had to follow the rules of the old culture, to which they became comfortable.

Breaking down both overt and subtle forms of discrimination is also an integral component of this phase. For example, organizations need to take a close look at the gender wage gap, lagging advancement opportunities for people of color, and disregard for the family needs of lesbian and gay members. Processes must be created to address these forms of discrimination.

Finally, networking groups and buddy systems should be formalized. In one organization, a networking system was established in which each group linked its existence with the overall mission, was supported by a senior executive (usually not from the group's primary identity group), and belonged to an overall group of networks, which regularly meet to align each group's activities with business objectives. After two years, the benefits of such a networking system included new talented recruits, new relationships with business partners from various social identity groups, and new products that met the needs of different customers. In buddy systems, the success of new hires is both the responsibility of the new employee and the established team member, who are matched in the recruiting process.

## Phase III: Making Change an Everyday Activity

For the culture change to become a core part of the organizational mission, a longer term strategic plan must be developed to integrate the new diversity concepts into every aspect of the organization, especially training and education. Managers, with their vital role in training and mentoring, must practice the new behaviors and hold their direct reports accountable for them. As new competencies get cultivated, effective performance-measuring systems must be established and formalized in order to verify that people's, including managers', behaviors align with the new inclusion policies and practices.

In one organization, a comprehensive plan to make the inclusion breakthrough an everyday reality included mandatory education sessions on the organizational imperative for every employee, a multi-day training on leveraging diversity for managers, a reorganization of managers according to the new competencies, and the identification of change agents to model the new skills in their teams. Just two years after the changes were made, people felt more than twice as favorable toward their managers and were more committed to the organization.

### Phase IV: Sustaining and Challenging the New Change

An inclusion breakthrough is not static; rather, it is a dynamic process that must be continually recreated. Periodic reviews allow organizations to assess the change progress. Revisiting the organizational imperative will show where advancements have been made and where gaps are still present.

Leadership groups will evolve, bringing in new ideas and perspectives. Communication of the new culture should remain open both internally and externally. *To be successful, an inclusion breakthrough must be ever changing, and continuously improving as people, strategies, customers, and environments change.*

## BREAKING DIVERSITY OUT OF THE BOX

Diversity in a box may feel more comfortable in the short run, but breaking out of the box will set free the organization's underutilized human potential. Stepping out of the box opens a space for individuals to feel respected, valued, and supported so they can perform to their highest level. Changing one organization at a time just might change the world by unleashing the real power of diversity.

## DISCUSSION QUESTIONS

1. The author writes that, "Diversity can be found in all individuals." Since much of the attention of diversity initiatives has focused on racial and gender diversity in organizations, what can managers do to be more inclusive of other types of diversity?

2. In phases #3 and #4, the author stresses the importance of measuring, reevaluating and assessing progress in terms of diversity initiatives. Why are these steps so important to creating an inclusive organizational culture?

3. Are the four phases of an inclusion breakthrough only applicable to diversity initiatives or might these just be good management practices? Why or why not?

# Responses to the Changing Workforce:

## Human Capital and Strategic Issues

Carol P. Harvey

*Assumption College*

Since the American workforce is becoming increasingly diverse, proactive organizations have become more creative with their policies, practices, and programs. Women currently represent 46 percent of the total U.S. workforce. The United States Department of Labor estimates that "women will account for 55 percent of the increase in total labor force growth between 2002 and 2012." In the 2000 census, 69 percent of the U.S. population was reported as non-Hispanic Caucasian. By 2030 this percentage is expected to decline to 59 percent and by 2050 to 52 percent with the largest growth occurring in the Hispanic populations (U.S. Department of Labor, 2005). To recruit, retain, and motivate this new workforce, many organizations have taken a proactive approach by instituting diversity training programs, employee resource groups, and more flexible work arrangements.

## DIVERSITY TRAINING PROGRAMS

One of the most common organizational responses to the dynamics of the new workforce is to educate the workforce by implementing diversity-training programs. These range in content from just providing demographic information about the changing workforce to personal explorations of stereotypes and prejudices to building skills for managing diverse employees. In terms of methodology, some programs are entirely online, while others involve more interactive training methods.

In a survey of more than 2,000 employers conducted by the Novations Group, 22 percent of the organizations surveyed said that they will spend more on diversity and inclusion training in 2007 than they did in 2006 and 51 percent will spend as much as they did the previous year (Chief Learning Officer, 2007). The history of discrimination and the recent changes in the workforce, clearly necessitate effective diversity education that imparts the essential skills for twenty-first century managers; however, diversity-training programs have produced mixed results (Dobbin, Kalev, & Kelly, 2006). The motivation for organizations to invest time and money in training programs ranges from legal compliance and avoidance of lawsuits to making such programs an integral part of their business case for diversity efforts.

Research shows that diversity-training programs which produce the most positive outcomes share some common elements: support from management, customization based on organizational needs, on-going implementation, accountability and evaluation requirements, competent instructors, and a clearly defined connection between diversity and the mission and goals of the organization (McLaughlin, and Clemons, 2005). Less successful programs tend to be those that were developed without a needs assessment or diversity audit; those required only for lower level employees—especially to avoid potential lawsuits; those that are off-the–shelf, rather than customized to match organizational needs; those that lack follow-up, and those that do not have a clear connection to the uniqueness of the organization's mission (Velasquez, 2004). Mulvaney (2003) identified three major problems with current diversity-training programs: a tendency to foster stereotypes, administration by HR personnel rather than managers with bottom-line responsibilities, and not allowing participants to hold divergent opinions.

Some of the more superficial programs are referred to as diversity with a "carwash approach," i.e., running many employees through a short, one-shot training session with the expectation that they will emerge changed—i.e., "squeaky clean"—on the other side. However, just like the carwash experience, this type of training does not produce lasting results.

## AFFINITY GROUPS/EMPLOYEE RESOURCE GROUPS

While differences can be seen as assets in organizations in terms of multicultural marketing, creativity, and innovative decision making, in many cases being a member of a nondominant race, ethnicity, gender, etc., may lead to issues of isolation. An organizational response to employees' need for role models, mentoring, and inclusion is the formation of employee groups that are based on a common social identity, affinity, or interest. Currently, JP Morgan supports over seventy of these networks for employees who share a common cultural heritage, gender, age, or interest such as *ujima,* which is Swahili for collective work, for employees of African descent and Access Ability for employees with disabilities (J.P. Morgan, 2007).

The origin of these groups goes back to the 1960s, when corporations such as Digital Equipment and Xerox pioneered efforts to diversify their workforces and learned that it was not such an easy transition. These new recruits, then primarily women and people of color, often felt isolated, unwelcome, and misunderstood in organizations long dominated by white males. Additionally, many of these employees faced backlash and were branded as "tokens," i.e., unqualified people hired to comply with EEO/AA laws, even if they were fully qualified for their positions. In the 1960s, the black employees at the Xerox Corporation formed regional caucus groups. Although the main purpose of these groups was to secure fair treatment for black employees, they also served as a mentoring resource for newer minority employees and as a source for the recruitment of additional minorities.[1]

---

[1]For a complete history of these pioneering groups, see Mary Gentile. (1960). The Black Caucus Groups at Xerox Corporation (A) Case. *Managing Excellence Through Diversity,* Waveland Press.

From their informal beginnings, these groups have evolved into more structured "employee resource groups." The primary difference is that the affinity groups functioned more as support groups for nondominant workers. Although the "employee resource groups/networks" still provide mentoring support to diverse employees, today they are tied more closely to the mission of the organization. In employee resource groups, as the name implies, diverse employees become a business resource. Often, these efforts take the form of offering marketing advice for products targeted to diverse populations and assistance in linking the company with diverse communities for employee recruitment.

The most successful employee resource groups capitalize on the idea that diverse employees can be a competitive advantage and are tied to the business case for diversity. For example, Verizon Communication consulted its black employee resource group in the development of its "Realize" advertising campaign, which was produced by Burrell Communications, a black advertising agency. This promotion, which targeted African Americans because they spend more monthly on communication services than any of Verizon's other market segments and represent 28 percent of Verizon's customer base, achieved over 200 percent of its sales goal (Lowrey, 2006). At the Ford Motor Company, the African-American employee resource group members have made referrals through the "Friends and Neighbors Program." These referrals have resulted in $260 million in vehicle sales since 2003 (Ortiz, 2006). In 2005, PepsiCo's CEO, Steve Reinemund, attributed much of the corporation's sales growth to product development ideas such as Frito-Lay Guacamole, Lay's Chili Limon, and Mountain Dew Code Red, which all came from company employee resource groups (Sherwood, 2005).

## WORK-LIFE BALANCE: FLEXIBLE WORK ARRANGEMENTS

Offering flexible work arrangements like job-sharing, compressed workweeks, telecommuting, leaves, flexible schedules, on and off ramps, and part-time employment may attract a larger pool of potential applicants, decrease absenteeism and turnover, and increase employee satisfaction and motivation. A recent survey by Work-Life Benefits Consultants found that more than 25 percent of all employee absences were caused by family issues, which was up from 11.5 percent six years ago (2007). In 1998 Work/Family Directions conducted a study that revealed that "for every $1 an employer spends in helping employees balance their home and work lives, the company will get a return investment of $3 to $4 in work hours saved, insurance costs, sick leave, decreased absenteeism and fewer on-the-job injuries" (Ortiz, 2005).

In spite of these advantages, a 2002 U.S. Chamber of Commerce report revealed that only 19 percent of the organizations surveyed offered any type of flexible work options and these tend to be in the service, federal, and nonprofit sectors. Objections to flexible work arrangements include resentment from employees who may not be eligible for such schedules, supervision concerns, difficulties in scheduling meetings, and staffing-level issues during peak times (Carlson, 2004). In addition, many of the organizations that do have flexible work policies indirectly discourage their use and/or fail to promote those who take advantage of such options (Frankel, 2007).

The demanding schedules in the legal and accounting professions have led to serious retention and turnover issues, particularly for women who often tend to carry more of the child-rearing responsibilities and for both genders in terms of elder care. Within these industries there are interesting examples of innovative responses that have led to change. For the past twenty years, women represented over 40 percent of the law school graduates. However, today, they still comprise only 17 percent of the partners at major law firms. Only 4.7 percent of lawyers work part-time and 4 percent of these are women. In comparison, 14 percent of the U.S. professional workforce was employed part-time in 2005. Although many law firms have part-time work options in place, these often lead to deadend careers. Lawyers at top firms are expected to bill 1,800 hours a year but work 2,100 hours or more (National Association for Legal Professionals, 2007).

An example of a law firm that has made progressive changes to accommodate work-life responsibilities is Kirpatrick & Lockhart, Preston, Gates, & Ellis (K & L). As the thirty-sixth largest law firm in the United States, with 1400 lawyers, offices in twenty-two cities and three countries, K & L supports diversity initiatives in many ways. The seven-member Executive Committee includes two women and two men of color. The firm considers diversity a "core value," has a chief diversity officer who reports directly to the chairman and a global managing partner, and publishes a diversity newsletter.

This support from the top has resulted in policies and practices that support better parental work-life balance. Years ago, attorney Kari Glover, a managing partner at K & L, took a year off to be with her children, but she points out that this was not a common practice at that time. Today, her firm takes a long-term approach to retaining talented attorneys. Both mothers *and* fathers are allowed 12 weeks of paid parental leave and there is a room set aside in the office for nursing mothers. In an effort to retain talented employees, her firm recently elected two mothers who work part-time to partnership positions (Vault, 2006).

A 2004 study conducted by AICPA's Work/Life and Women's Initiatives Executive Committee revealed that excessive time requirements of the accounting profession and work-life issues were the two major reasons that CPAs leave their firms (Lewison, 2006). Unfortunately, many legal and accounting firms are not as progressive about flexible work arrangements. However, to reduce turnover costs and to increase retention rates, particularly for young female employees, these professions will need to develop and implement more flexible work programs that employees can use without career penalties.

While this article presented many examples of organizations that adopted progressive policies and practices that better meet the needs of the twenty-first century workforce, it is important to remember that these are the models and not necessarily the norm for most organizations. In addition, corporate cultural values must support effective training programs, the utilization of employee resource groups, and work-life balance options. For example, a 2004 Catalyst study revealed that 91 percent of women and 94 percent of men surveyed said that flexible work options were available to them for family emergencies or personal matters. However, only 15 percent of the women and 20 percent of the men felt that they could use these options without jeopardizing their careers. To achieve the benefits that diversity can bring, organizations need to remember that the practices and policies that motivated workers, retained employees, and produced productivity in the past may not be as appropriate for today's workforce.

# INNOVATIVE IDEAS: 10 TIL 2—PART-TIME OPTIONS FOR PARENTS

Although 54 percent of the mothers with children under three years old are in the labor force, either full or part time (Current Population Statistics, 2006), some parents may find the demands of full-time work a difficult balance. For those who choose to leave the workforce during their children's younger years, reentry is often an issue.

A Denver, Colorado, placement firm, 10 til 2, bases its business model on matching college-educated parents needing flexible work schedules with organizations that will hire on a part-time, long-term basis. Started by four stay-at-home mothers, 10 til 2 considers its business model "win, win, win, win." Parents get the flexibility that they want and organizations get access to an experienced, college-educated talent pool (Tillman, 2005). Job listings on the Web site include a range of positions, such as a part-time attorney with the possibility of telecommuting and a Web information coordinator. Recently, 10 til 2 expanded by offering part-time positions to retirees and selling franchises on a national basis.

## BIBLIOGRAPHY

Carlson, L. (2004). Flextime elevated to national issue. *Employee Benefit News,* September, 8, (12), 1–2.

Catalyst. (2004). Women and men in U.S. corporate leadership: same workplace, different realities? Retrieved May 17, 2007, from http://www.catalyst.org/files/fact/2005%20COTE%20-20Fact%20sheet.pdf.

Chief Learning Officer. Survey: employers plan to raise diversity training spending this year. Retrieved on May 16, 2007, at http://www.clo-media.com/content/templates/clo_section.asp?articleid+1663zoneid=142

Current Population Statistics, table 6, Employment status of mothers with own children under three years old by age of youngest child and marital status, 2004–05 annual averages. Retrieved May 17, 2007, from http://www.catalyst.org/files/quicktakes/Quick%20Takes%20-%20Maternity%20Leave.pdf

Frankel, B. (2007). Who really benefits from work/life? *DiversityInc.* March 6, (2), 22.

Gentile, M. (1996). The Black caucus groups at Xerox Corporation (A) case, found in

*Managing Excellence Through Diversity.* Long Grove, IL: Waveland Press.

J. P. Morgan. Employee networks. Retrieved April 11, 2007, from http://www.jpmorgan-chase.com.

Kalev, A., Dobbin, F., and Kelly, E. (2006) Best practices or best guesses? Assessing the efficacy of corporate Affirmative Action and diversity policies, *American Sociological Review, 70,* 589–917.

Lewison, J. (2006). The work/life balance sheet so far. *Journal of Accountancy,* 202, (2), 45–49.

Lowrey, M. (2007). Three of the best multicultural advertising campaigns ever. *DiversityInc.* Special issue 2007, vol. 6, (2), 34–38.

McLaughlin, J., & Clemons, L. (2005). Diversity training: the often-forgotten but necessary ingredient of any employment training program. *Managing Diversity,* 14, (1), 1 & 6–7.

Mulvaney, T. (2003). Diversity in practice: three things missing. *Managing Diversity,* 12 (11), 1 & 4.

National Association for Legal Professionals (2006). Few lawyers work part-time, most who do are women. Retrieved April 14, 2007, from http://www.nalp.org/press/details. php?id=65.

Ortiz, P. (2006) Employee resource groups: the hidden assets. *DiversityInc,* special issue, fall, 75–78.

Pine, J. (2001, December 12). Avoid the diversity car wash: diversity training that sticks. *DiversityInc.* Retrieved December 12, 2006, from http://www.diversityinc.com/members/1941print.cfm

Sherwood, S. (2005). Lessons learned from the top 50 CEO commitment: PepsiCo's Reinemund takes his faith in diversity to a new level. *DiversityInc,* 4, (8), 35–38.

Tillman, A. (2005). Attitude at altitude. *Colorado Business Magazine.* August, 32,

available at http://www.tentiltwo.com/news-ColoBiz.cfm.

U.S. Census Bureau (2005) available at http://www.census.gov/.

Vault. (2006). View from the top highlights: questions and answers with legal women leaders. *Vault Inc. Newsletter.* Retrieved April 16, 2007. Available at www.klgates.com/.../PublicationAttachment/05a841dc-e057-42fa-8a3d-4e1f59173aec/Preston_VFTT_2007.pdf-2006-12-04.

Velasquez, M. (2004). Successful vs. failed diversity programs. Retrieved May 13, 2007, from http://www.diversitydtg.com/articles/topten.html.

Work-Life Benefits. Retrieved May 13, 2007, from http://www.wlb.com

## DISCUSSION QUESTIONS

1. Many organizations use e-learning as their delivery model for diversity training. What are the pros and cons of Web-based diversity training?

2. What are the advantages and disadvantages of having diversity training conducted by internal employees vs. using an outside consultant?

3. While family-friendly policies may be beneficial to working parents, these may cause resentment and allegations of "unfair" treatment from employees who are not parents. How should managers handle the backlash that may occur as a result of these programs?

4. If an organization has "employee resource groups" for gender, race, ethnicity, sexual orientation, etc., how can a manager prevent white, straight males from feeling left out?

---

**Diversity on the Web**

In the state of California, a new law, AB 1825, was recently passed that mandates all employers with 50 or more employees *doing business* in the state (but not necessarily located in CA), to provide two hours of interactive sexual harassment training to all supervisory employees once prior to January 2006 and then every two years thereafter. To comply with this legislation, many organizations are turning to Web-based training.

Visit *www.californiaharassmentlaw.com* and click on the course demo for AB 1825 Sexual Harassment Prevention for Managers.

Do the training program and evaluate the training in terms of its strengths and weaknesses. Based on this sample, if you were a manager in California, would you adopt this program for your employees? Why or why not?

## Points of Law

The Family Medical Leave Act requires employers of 50 or more employees to provide up to 12 weeks of unpaid, job-protected leave to employees for the birth or adoption of a child or for the serious illness of the employee or a spouse, child, or parent.

http://www.dol.gov/opa/aboutdol/lawsprog.htm#fmla

# The Ethics of Workplace Diversity

## Jeanne McNett
### *Assumption College*

**S**pike Lee's suggestion in his 1989 classic film *Do the Right Thing* that we "do the right thing" on the issue of diversity seems a reasonable one to most people, on the face of it. But when we ask, "Why?" in a business environment, we are likely to hear that we should do the right thing because such actions are good for business results. That may be fine, but is it enough? Is there more than a pragmatic justification for diversity in the workplace? Is there an ethical justification for valuing diversity (the right thing) in the workplace?

In our exploration of this question, we begin with a brief review of the pragmatic business arguments that are used to suggest that diversity is desirable in business. These arguments are not, though, based on an ethical analysis, but rather on an economic one. We then explore what ethical theories might tell us about valuing diversity in the workplace. Our conclusion then moves to an attempt to bridge the practical (business) and the good (ethics).

Let's begin with definitions. By valuing *diversity*, we mean valuing, respecting, and appreciating the differences (such as age, culture, education, ethnicity, experience, gender, race, religion, sexual orientation, among others) that make people unique. Note that our definition has to do with *valuing* differences, so it is a frame of mind, a way of thinking, rather than a result. This is an important distinction, because if we were to think of diversity as only a result and not a way of thinking, such an approach might lead to false conclusions. For example, we might observe that a workforce is diverse and then be tempted to infer that valuing diversity has led to the workforce composition. Yet we all recognize that a diverse workforce could be explained by many other factors, such as differential wages, poor work conditions, and business location. This workforce could have been arrived at by values that are not connected to diversity except by coincidence.

## ECONOMIC ARGUMENTS FOR DIVERSITY

Most of the economic arguments for the desirability of a diverse workforce are based on a connection made between diversity and desired business outcomes. Most compelling is the connection made between a workforce that brings valuable and different perspectives and abilities to connect with a wide spectrum of customers. This market-driven argument for diversity becomes increasingly important because globalization has strengthened the role that relationships play in business transactions. Globalization has led managers to realize that business is all about relationships. The more diverse the workforce, the wider and deeper is the ability to communicate across cultures, and the greater the potential for deep, long-lasting relationships. An additional economic argument for diversity is that when the firm is recruiting from a larger, more diverse labor pool, the likelihood of hiring capable managers increases (Schraeder, 1997).

There is also the argument that a diverse workforce is nontraditional, and therefore likely to be more creative and more capable of instituting and accepting change, because diverse workgroups tend to be more accepting of ambiguity (Rosener, 1995). Research suggests that the Western assumption that innovation comes from the center of the firm (which traditionally is the less diverse part) may be seen as a dying vestige of essentially an imperialist way of thinking. Prahalad and Lieberthal conclude that "over time . . . as multinationals develop products better suited to the emerging markets, they are finding that those markets are becoming an important source of innovation." That is a good explanation of how diversity may increase the potential for creativity (Prahalan & Lieberthal, 1998).

These arguments for diversity rest on a way of thinking about business known as the resource-based theory of the firm (Barney, 1991). According to this theory, the firm is conceptualized as a bundle of resources that are poised, ready to take advantage of opportunities in the external environment. The more distinctive these resources are, the more difficult would be their imitation by a competitor. A diverse workforce with established customer relationships is an example of such a difficult-to-imitate resource. Lord Browne, former group chief executive (CEO) of British Petroleum, offers an example of this economic rationale for diversity and its primacy over an ethical justification in his comments to the Women in Leadership Conference (2002, Berlin, Germany).

> For BP the issue is no longer about whether diversity is a good thing . . . . the issue is how to deliver strategy. How to take immediate, real actions . . . We're competing for resources. . . . And we're competing for markets. . . . And therefore we're competing for talent. If we can get a disproportionate share of the most talented people in the world, we have a chance of holding a competitive edge. That is the simple strategic logic behind our commitment to diversity and to the inclusion of individuals—men and women regardless of background, religion, ethnic origin, nationality or sexual orientation. We want to employ the best people, everywhere, on the single criterion of merit. And the importance of that goal as a part of our overall business strategy has grown as competition has intensified.

BP is an energy company that needs to establish relationships that will allow it to extract oil and gas in Mexico, Indonesia, West Africa, and Russia, while it competes for markets in America, China, South Africa, and Europe. BP's approach to diversity, based on market economic arguments, makes a lot of sense. The rationale is not ethics, but rather, the strategic outcomes BP seeks. Such motivations, regardless of their impact on diversity, go to an assertion that the purpose of business is to increase profits, not to do good. The fundamental argument of this understanding is best articulated by the economist Milton Friedman in his oft cited essay, "The Social Responsibility of Business is to Increase Its Profits."

> There is one and only one social responsibility of business—to use its resources and engage in activities designed to increase its profits so long as it stays within the rules of the game, which is to say, engages in open and free competition without deception or fraud.

> (http://ca.geocities.com/busa2100/miltonfriedman.htm/)

In contrast, an ethical approach would be an approach that considers judgments about right and wrong, good and bad, and what ought to be in our world (Hartman, 2002).

Another difference between a pragmatic/economic justification for diversity and an ethical one has to do with the judgment criteria. In economic business arguments, the business results are essential. Making a decision about diversity is, at a superficial level, pretty easy: we look at the economic business results of a decision. In contrast, ethically based decisions are judged sometimes by the reasoning that leads to the decision, not necessarily the decision's outcomes. The ethical dimension of a decision may not always be obvious from a surface consideration of that decision or an examination of the decision's outcomes.

## CATEGORIES OF ETHICAL THEORIES

So what might an ethical justification for valuing diversity be? In order to move toward that answer, let's first look at the three categories that are often used to describe Western ethical theory. First is the set of theories that looks at the process or the means of a decision; that is, how do we arrive at the decision? Second are the theories that address what is good and bad by looking at likely outcomes or consequences of a decision. Third is a set of theories that looks at the caring aspects of decisions. These three categories remind us that the assumptions upon which ethical claims can be made may vary widely.

F. Neil Brady developed a matrix for these distinctive categories of ethical theories that offers a helpful summary (Brady, 1996). Exhibit I is a modification of Brady's chart. His correlation of these approaches with the three virtues of faith, hope, and charity is an added benefit as we think about the possible ethical bases for workplace diversity. The columns on the right describe the three main theoretical bases for ethical judgment, with Brady's suggested equivalents in parentheses. We discuss each of them and their likely application to a diversity claim: that a valuing of differences—our definition of diversity—is good or produces the quality of goodness either by process (deontological) or outcomes (teleological), or through caring for others. We also consider whether the theory is universal in nature, for all times and all places, or particular, depending on the context.

The reason to consider universal or particular applications of an ethical theory has to do with culture. The cultural context in which a diversity decision is made may well affect the shared understanding of what *ethical* actually means. A short example of the results of different assumptions about what is ethical may be found in the consideration of the quality of difference in Japan. The Japanese culture is homogeneous, and the introduction of difference is generally not seen as good. In fact, families and

## EXHIBIT 1   Three Categories of Ethical Theories

|  | Deontology (Faith) | Teleology (Hope) | Caring (Charity) |
|---|---|---|---|
| **Universal application** (all times, all places) | Universal duty: universal principles, The Way | Universal ends: Character ethic, utilitarianism, other -isms | Universal care: love for humanity |
| **Particular Application** (depends on context) | Particular duties: situation ethic, case by case approach | Particular ends: self-actualization | Particular care: personal relationships |

*(adapted from F. Neil Brady)*

the individual's company will conduct a background investigation of an engaged employee's potential spouse to make certain he or she is pure Japanese and not from an outcast group such as the *borakumin*. Such activity is seen as fulfilling an ethical responsibility. In North America, especially on the part of the employer, such an investigation would likely be regarded not as a moral duty but as an immoral action, on the grounds of both privacy and what we in North America would consider racial prejudice.

Brady's categorization describes various ethical theories based on the claims that their application makes: is the theory universally applicable (*the* rule, built on understood similarities) or does it claim a situational focus (it all depends, built on differences)? This distinction is helpful as we consider the ethical bases for diversity because it incorporates the idea of the decision's context. The distinction also corresponds in interesting ways to the universalism–particularism dimension used to describe culture differences by Fons Trompenaars (Hampden-Turner and Trompenaars, 2000). In cultures that measure high on the universalism dimension, such as the United States, Switzerland, Australia, and Canada, rules are seen to apply to all equally. In particularist cultures such as China, Japan, Venezuela, Greece, and India, rules are seen as more variable, depending on the context and the actors.

The implications of these assumptions in the area of diversity are significant, especially if we consider the effects of a diverse workgroup on an organization's ethics. For example, Chinese assumptions about ethical decisions tend to be particularist and relationship-based. Awareness that American business ethics decisions, in contrast, tend to be universalist and rule-based would help an international partner from a particularist culture such as China understand the assumptions that underpin Title VII of the Civil Rights Act of 1964. This act as amended prohibits "discrimination in hiring, promotion, discharge, pay, fringe benefits, job training, classification, referral, and other aspects of employment on the basis of race, color, religion, sex, or national origin."

We now look at how each of these ethical theories might be applied to diversity in the workplace. The ethical argument would be that these differences are good or produce the quality of goodness either by process (deontological, faith) or outcomes (teleological, hope), or by caring for others (care, love, charity).

## DEONTOLOGICAL CATEGORY OF ETHICAL THEORIES

The first category of ethical theories in our framework is deontological, and it stems from duties and moral obligations (the Greek *deont* means duty). Probably the most well-known deontological theory is Emmanuel Kant's categorical imperative, which dictates that one has a duty to "act only on that maxim by which you can at the same time will that it should become a universal law" (Kant, 1785). We all know the popular paraphrase of Kant's categorical imperative, "Do unto others as you would have them do unto you." Deontological theories are based on duties, rules, and obligations that lie outside the person. Religious practice tends to rest on a deontological approach to ethics. For example, we can think of the Ten Commandments as a series of duties. Brady uses the term *faith* to capture this characteristic.

## DEONTOLOGICAL ETHICAL SYSTEMS AND DIVERSITY

Can a claim that workplace diversity rests on duty be made in a convincing way? Such a claim would establish that we have a duty to at least tolerate differences. This tolerance would be not because of the *results* of these differences, but simply because, for some reason, having differences is a duty that is a good in itself.

To explore our sense of duty in this regard, let us go to an example of which we all are a part, the U.S. housing market. We all live somewhere. Consideration of the nature of the U.S. housing market, segregated as it is by race and economic class, might suggest that there is no widely accepted duty to incorporate or tolerate difference, at least in this narrow but universally inhabited sector, despite federal law prohibiting discrimination. At the particularist level though, we can recognize that we might have specific duties we hold to one another with regard to diversity, depending on the context. For example, when we find ourselves part of a public group, say, a search committee, we may well accept that there is a duty to diversify the committee membership, simply for the sake of diversity and not for a pragmatic reason. Of course, we may well want to diversify for reasons other than duty, for example, to meet legal obligations, ensure compliance with the choice by including various constituencies or stakeholders and their varied points of view in the search process, and so on. Yet we can see that in some situations, diversity may be understood to be a duty, a good in and of itself. On balance though, deontological approaches to diversity are probably few in the work situation.

This observation is in accord with sociologist William Julius Wilson's application of Blalock's theory of social power, which suggests that when majority or minority members change their beliefs about minority or majority members, these changes are initially a result of power shifts (in this case, Civil Rights legislation), and only secondarily, value shifts. Diversity in our workplaces developed initially as a response to a power shift, federal legislation (for example, Title VII of the Civil Rights Act of 1964, the Americans with Disabilities Act of 1990, the Equal Pay Act of 1963, the Age Discrimination in Employment Act of 1967) rather than as a response to a changed belief system about what is right.

In our discussion of deontological approaches, we have considered individuals as the location of ethical decisions. This approach is justified because decisions are made in the minds of individual managers. Yet we may think of organizations themselves as having a limited kind of personhood, at least in a legal sense. Considered from the perspective of an organization capable of ethical decision making, we find another example of deontological ethics in the workplace when we consider the ethics codes of these organizations. Ethics codes are rule-based and suggest that the corporate citizen is bound by duty to follow the rules, some of which may address respect for diversity.

## TELEOLOGICAL CATEGORY OF ETHICAL THEORIES

The second category of ethical approaches is teleological, addressing the good that comes from a focus on the ends achieved by a contemplated action (the Greek *telos* means end). The teleological approach holds that decisions are right or good if they produce a desired goodness and bad if they produce some undesirable state (badness or pain). So teleological approaches are action-based, connected with implementation — while deontological approaches concern the process (Hopkins, 1997). Utilitarianism, the greatest good for the greatest number, illustrates such an action-based, results-oriented approach. A business example is found in cost–benefit analysis, through which the benefit is weighed against its cost. The decision is then made to follow the path that provides the greatest overall gain for the least cost. In fact, research suggests that many American managers hold to utilitarian principles in their decision making (Fritzsche & Becker, 1984). For example, a manager might structure a layoff list with the least trained and newest members of the organization as the first to face cuts, on the basis that keeping people with seniority will lead to the retention of higher levels of knowledge, which, in turn, may lead to better results for a larger number of people.

Distributive justice, concerned with fair and equitable outcomes, is another ethical theory within the teleological category. Distributive justice suggests that ethical decisions are those that lead to a fair distribution of goods. John Rawls (1971) has developed a test for distributive justice: is the decision the one that we would make if we were cloaked in a *veil of ignorance*? This veil of ignorance would not allow us to know our status and position, so it protects us from our own self-interests playing a role in decisions on distribution of goods. Laura Hartman describes how Rawls sees the veil of ignorance working and the ends it would achieve (2002). First of all, we would make decisions unaware of their immediate consequences to ourselves. We would develop a cooperative system in which the benefits would be distributed unequally only when doing so would benefit all, especially those who were least advantaged. Ethical justice would be measured by the capacity of the decision to enhance cooperation among all — by its fairness. Because these theories rely on outcomes that depend on actions, but we don't know the outcomes of an action often until well after it is completed, Brady connects these approaches to *hope*.

## TELEOLOGICAL ETHICAL SYSTEMS AND DIVERSITY

Utilitarianism, in its assertion that a good or ethical decision is one that produces the greatest good for the greatest number, seems on first examination to be business-friendly. As a justification for diversity, a utilitarian approach might argue that valuing differences would lead to behaviors that would be likely to lead to better results for the company's stakeholders, through a diverse workforce that is, perhaps, better at decision making and that possesses increased creativity, better knowledge of markets, and increased communication abilities. Such a work team would be likely to produce better results for a broader array of people, the various stakeholders. We would expect utilitarian approaches to the valuing of diversity in the workplace to be frequent, since both the management environment and utilitarianism share a focus on results. Note, though, that for an ethical decision, results have to show greater good, not simply bottom line good.

An example of the distributive justice theory applied to diversity is found in human resource processes that rest on principles of fairness and justice: all employees—regardless of level and type of contract (part time/temporary)—would receive medical and other benefits, profit sharing, retirement contributions, and bonuses. Selection, compensation, and promotion systems might also offer examples of distributive justice in the area of diversity. The ethical rationale would be that we make this decision because it is the right thing to do in order to produce equity, not that we make this decision because it will be good for business. These are all examples of universal application.

Teleological theories in a particularist context would be theories that apply to differences among people and also consider the ends or outcomes in order to judge the ethical nature of a decision. Self-actualization might be considered to be an example here, that we have a moral duty to fully develop our skills and talents, and that organizational decisions that lead in that direction (support for education, training programs, mentoring systems) are ethical ones. This approach, on a case-by-case basis, would have powerful application to diversity, since it would support individual learning and development within the company. Note that the increased learning could be thought to lead to improved results for the company, too, and this would be a utilitarian justification. Another application of distributive justice theories in a particularist context can be found in the justification (or failure of justification) of Affirmative Action legislation. The desired outcome (an increase in social equity universally) was thought to outweigh what some understood to be unfair processes (individual, particular decisions).

## CARING ETHICAL THEORIES

The final category of our ethical framework addresses caring, which is—unlike deontology and teleology—a nonrational, emotional claim. These are the theories that come, not from a reasoned sense of duty nor from desired outcomes, but, because they are psychological and emotional in nature, "from an interpersonal connectedness"—an ethic of *charity*, as Brady suggests. On the universal side of this theory, examples drawn from religious situations and philanthropy come to mind readily: belief systems that value a love for humanity, for example, and a love for individuals, because they are a part of that humanity. On the particular side, someone who joins the Peace Corps to do volunteer work in a specific setting or who does community volunteer work in a specific effort might offer us examples of particularized caring ethics. The layoff situation we discussed as an example of teleological ethics (the greatest good is achieved by keeping those who have the most seniority and knowledge) may also rest on an ethic of caring (the manager keeps the people about whom he/she cares most, those with the most seniority).

## CARING THEORIES AND DIVERSITY

We can find a caring ethic basis for diversity in the workplace in Pope John Paul's belief that "the evil of our times consists in the first place in a kind of degradation, indeed in a pulverization, of the fundamental uniqueness of each person." He argues that the "fundamental error of socialism is anthropological." It tries to reduce humans to something less than they are, as did the Nazis (racial makeup) and the Marxists (class status) (Brooks, 2003). Pope John Paul's argument is caring-based. David Brooks points out that when Pope John Paul told his audiences in Poland and Cuba, "You are not what they say you are," the result was a revolution. The Pope's claim is that our human diversity is good and we are fundamentally unique in our personhoods. This uniqueness should be recognized. Such ethical arguments for diversity would be strong in the workplace because they would offer the individual liberation from the crushing anonymity of a cubicle existence, for example. The ethics of caring leads to powerful emotional connections among people. Although we may not find it often at an official, articulated level (How does a CEO convincingly claim to care about 25,000 employees personally?), it may be more common, unarticulated, yet in the minds of organization members, than we realize. The college at which I teach is infused with the ethics of caring—caring about each other and about our students. Yet, as is frequently the case with ethics of caring, we don't know how to talk about it. When students come on campus, they feel this emotional connection and are often drawn to the school for this reason.

The diversity claim offered by the ethics of caring might be stated as follows: we value diversity in our organization because we value every individual and his/her dignity and right to contribute and be a part of our organization. This particularist approach in a business setting seems more likely than does its universal aspect: we value individual, diverse members of our organizational community because we have come to respect, care for, and, perhaps, love them.

## BUSINESS PRAGMATISM AND AN ETHICAL APPROACH

The economic business arguments for diversity with whose review we began our exploration are each premised on the resource-based view of the firm and are all *pragmatic* in that they are concerned with *what works best* to meet business objectives. The American William James (1842–1910), whose work bridges psychology and philosophy, captured pragmatism's essence in slightly different words:

> Pragmatism asks its usual question. Grant an idea or belief to be true, it says, 'what concrete difference will its being true make in anyone's actual life? How will the truth be realized? What experiences will be different from those which would obtain if the belief were false? What, in short, is the truth's cash-value in experiential terms?' (James, 1907)

We examine pragmatism here because it may offer us a way to better understand and pin down the ethical claims for workplace diversity. Such an approach to decision making, including that about diversity, is the cornerstone of business practice: *if it works, do it*, or as James suggested, if it works, it is true. The question that now faces us is, how do these pragmatic approaches square with the ethical options we have just reviewed? In order to summarize this issue, we use a four-cell grid with the horizontal axis representing ethics (highly ethical to unethical), and the vertical axis representing the level of pragmatism, (fully pragmatic to nonpragmatic). We now have a way to categorize our theoretical justifications of workplace diversity that makes sense and is useful because it considers the practical aspect, "the cash value." We will see if any of our ethical theories can offer what is good and good for business at the same time.

This matrix is a useful way to think about the possible relationships between pragmatism and ethical choices (Henderson, 1982; Lane, 2000). Quadrant I is where most business people would like to be, pragmatic (good numbers) and ethical (good results). Quadrant I is also where the teleological ethical theories we have reviewed would be—utilitarianism and distributive justice. They are judged by outcomes and the good that constitutes those outcomes. What we see by considering Quadrant I is that an argument for diversity in the workplace can be pragmatic (good for business) and also ethical. Such an argument might be, for example, that diversity is good—the right way to select personnel—because when we have a diverse team, we communicate better with diverse markets and are more innovative within the organization because we are always trying to question our unarticulated assumptions. Such an environment is good for its participants and for business results.

The argument for a diverse workplace because it is simply beneficial for business (the bottom line) is an example of a pragmatic and nonethical argument, which is where the economic arguments for diversity that we reviewed earlier are located: Quadrant IV. Often, when posed, such an argument is nonethical, because it does not consider the

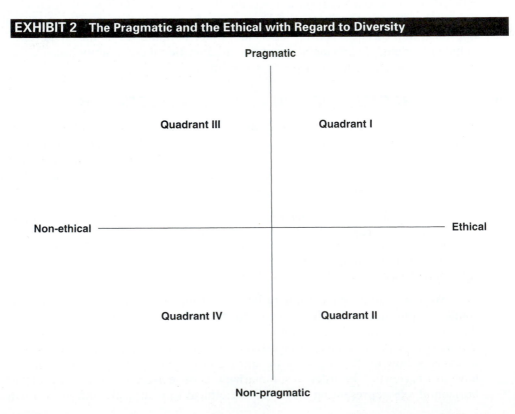

**EXHIBIT 2** **The Pragmatic and the Ethical with Regard to Diversity**

Pragmatic

Quadrant III | Quadrant I

Non-ethical ——————————————— Ethical

Quadrant IV | Quadrant II

Non-pragmatic

treatment of humans in ethical terms; humans are inputs, parallel to semiconductors and motherboards. This brings to mind that horrible phrase, *human resources*.

Note that the arguments in Quadrant I (teleological) and IV (pragmatic without an ethical base) are close, and yet a world apart. The danger of the pragmatic, nonethical approach is that it might do harm to people. One can imagine a woman engineer being assigned to a project in the mainly male profession of construction engineering because the company wants to qualify to compete on projects that require a diverse workforce. In such a case, the woman engineer is there on the project for the business ends, almost as a token, but the company does nothing to support her integration into the work team. The hostile work environment that might result from the company's unconsidered approach to building a diverse workforce would be a harm.

In passing, we note that Quadrant III is where we would locate nonpragmatic, nonethical efforts, a combination difficult about which to think. Perhaps some business decisions with regard to diversity are the result of personal prejudice or blindness that considers neither the practical aspects of the market nor the decision's ethical content. Consider a family consumer business in a geographic area that attracts many gays and a decision maker who has unexamined homophobic values in the personnel selection process. Such an example would be nonpragmatic and nonethical.

Quadrant II represents ethical, nonpragmatic approaches. Because for-profit business has to take care of the bottom line, has to show that outputs have added value over inputs, such approaches to ethics would be unusual, but they exist. Ben and Jerry's Ice Cream sources ingredients for their product from worker collaboratives in impoverished areas in the United States, Africa, and Latin America. This commitment to the support of businesses owned by minority groups may increase the production costs, but it appears to be a cost the consumer is willing to pay. The consumer subsidizes the ethical, nonpragmatic approach Ben and Jerry's takes. One could argue that Ben and Jerry's has changed the nature of the product; it is not premium ice cream that the consumer purchases, but premium ice cream *and* a contribution to greater good in the world. In contrast to the for-profit sector, the nonprofit sector has an abundance of ethical, nonpragmatic approaches. Think of the local art museum, symphony, opera, and other community efforts that by their very natures are nonpragmatic.

Our analysis illustrates that Quadrant I is where most of the ethical arguments for diversity in the workplace are likely to be located. These teleological ethical arguments, because they focus on outcomes, are similar on the surface to the pragmatic economic justifications for diversity. They add an important dimension, though—an ethical consideration that is missing in the economic approach. It does seem that with some ethical analysis in the decision-making stage, business can do well and do good.

## DOING WELL AND DOING GOOD

As a final step moving toward our conclusion, we need to consider how the process of workplace decision making about diversity might maintain a practical focus and at the same time be encouraged to incorporate an ethical one. One key point we can draw from our earlier discussion is that if there is an ethical consideration present in a diversity-related decision, it is usually tacit—unarticulated—in the decision maker's private thoughts. Laura Nash calls for discussion-based ethical analysis to become part of any organizational decision (Nash, 1981) and she offers a process to encourage

discussion around these usually tacit elements. This review would be especially revealing of hidden assumptions in diversity-related decisions. The twelve questions to open
such a discussion are as follows:

1. **Have you defined the problem accurately?**
   A moral decision cannot be built on blind or convenient ignorance. Convenient
   ignorance is frequently a part of diversity-related issues.

2. **How would you define the problem if you were to stand on the other side of the
   fence?**
   There is power in self-examination that may lead both to an awareness of the role
   of self-interest in a decision and to a tendency to dampen the expedient over the
   responsible action.

3. **How did this situation occur in the first place?**
   This course of questioning helps to distinguish the symptoms from the disease and
   helps to work against the tendency to ignore problems until they become crises.

4. **To whom and what do you give your loyalties as a person and as a member of the
   corporation**?
   The area of divided loyalties is a difficult one in the diversity area. The first steps
   to addressing such issues are to articulate them and then examine them.

5. **What is your intention in making this decision?**

6. **How does this intention compare with the likely results?**
   Intentions do matter. They can have effects on attitudes inside and outside the
   organization. Thus, their communication is important.

7. **Whom could your decision or action injure?**
   This question helps to discover whether any resulting injury would be intentional.

8. **Can you engage the affected parties in a discussion of the problem before you
   make your decision?**
   Participation of all or many stakeholders insures that affected parties can discuss
   what among the action alternatives may be in their best interests. At the same
   time, they learn of possible decisions that may cause them difficulties and thus
   have the opportunity to see these issues in a larger context.

9. **Are you confident that your position will be as valid over a long period of time as
   it seems now?**
   Articulation of values should anticipate good and bad times. A difference in time
   frame can make a huge impact on the problem's meaning.

10. **Could you disclose without a qualm your decision or action to your boss, your
    CEO, the board of directors, your family, or society as a whole?**
    This test, referred to by some as the billboard test, helps to uncover conscience
    and loyalties.

11. **What is the symbolic intention of your action if understood? If misunderstood?**
    How the symbol is perceived or misperceived is what matters. Getting intent out
    there early (see 5 and 6) helps to frame how the symbolic aspect of an action is
    understood.

12. **Under what conditions would you allow exceptions to your stand?**
   It is important to discuss under what conditions the rules of the game may be changed.

   Now we can begin to do the right thing as we implement diversity in the workplace, to make good and pragmatic business decisions.

# DISCUSSION QUESTIONS

1. Describe an approach to a business diversity program that would be pragmatic and ethical.

2. What are some possible explanations for the hesitancy to discuss ethics in the workplace?

3. This discussion's definition of diversity rests on a valuing of differences across many groups of people. Explain why valuing (the process) is what should serve as the foundation for diversity and not the results.

4. Which of the final 12 discussion areas would be most difficult for you as a manager to discuss in the organization with your colleagues? Why?

## BIBLIOGRAPHY

Barney, J. (1991). Firm Resources and Sustained Competitive Advantage. *J. of Management,* 17(1) 99–120.

Brady, F. N. (1996). Introduction: a Typology of Ethical Theories. *Ethical Universals in International Business,* p. 6. Berlin: Springer.

Brooks, D. (2003). Bigger Than Nobel. *The New York Times,* October 11. http://www.nytimes.com/2003/10/11/opinion/11BROO.html/

Fritzsche, D., & Becker, H. (1984). Linking Management Behavior to Ethical Philosophy: An Empirical Investigation. *Academy of Management Journal,* 27(1) 166–176.

Goleman, D., Kaufman, P., & Rae, M. (1992). *The Creative Spirit.* New York: Dutton.

Hampden-Turner, C., & Trompenaars, F. (2000). *Building Cross-cultural Competence.* New Haven: Yale University Press.

Hartman, L. P. (2002). *Perspectives in business ethics, 2nd ed.* Burr Ridge, IL: McGraw-Hill Irwin.

Henderson, V. (1982). The Ethical Side of Enterprise. *Sloan Management Review,* 23:1982, 37–47. Henderson's matrix categorizes ethical and legal behaviors.

Hopkins, W. (1997). *Ethical Dimensions of Diversity.* Thousand Oaks, CA: Sage.

Kant, I. (1785). *The Foundations of the Metaphysics of Morals,* section one.

Lane, H., DiStephano, J., & Maznevski, M. (2000). *International Management Behavior,* 4th edit. Malden, MA: Blackwell Publishers. This matrix is an adaptation of Henderson's.

Nash, L. (1981). Ethics without the sermon. *Harvard Business Review,* 56(6) 79–90. The questions and the slight commentary are summarized from the author's more extensive and richer discussion, with applications to diversity added.

Prahalad, C., & Lieberthal, K. (1998). The End of Corporate Imperialism. *Harvard Business Review,* 76(4) 68–79.

Rawls, J. (1971). *A Theory of Justice.* Cambridge, MA: Harvard University Press.

Rosener, J. (1995). *America's Competitive Secret: Utilizing Women as a Management Strategy*. New York, NY: Oxford University Press. Quoted in Schraeder (1997).

Schraeder, C., Blackburn, V., & Iles, P. (1997). Women in management and firm financial performance: An exploratory study. *Journal of Management Issues,* 9(3), 355–372.

---

### Diversity on the Web

1. Investigate the inclusion (or lack of inclusion) of diversity/discrimination in the ethical codes of businesses. You can begin by searching for the words "diversity" or "discrimination" in the codes, but note that diversity concerns may be covered by words other than these, e.g., "respecting the rights and privileges of all workers, regardless of race, gender ..."

2. Compare the codes of ethics for businesses with those of another profession in terms of inclusion of diversity or nondiscrimination policies.

3. Compare and contrast the codes of two competing companies within the same industry, e.g., the Marriott and the Hilton hotels in the hospitality industry.

### SAMPLE CODES OF BUSINESS ETHICS

The following Web site, compiled by the Center for the Study of Ethics in the Professions at the Illinois Institute of Technology, contains hundreds of codes of ethics from corporations, professional societies, academic institutions, and government agencies. The codes are organized into 25 professional categories, such as arts, business, communications, etc. The codes can be searched for key words.

http://ethics.iit.edu/codes/coe.html

The Your Code of Ethics site, created by Irwin Berent, is a clearinghouse for "codes of ethics, oaths, pledges, and other forms of verbal commitment, statements of purpose, or declared standards of conduct." This site is organized into categories including three categories of business association codes: General, Management, and Sales or Selling, as well as "Companies' (US) codes."

http://www.yourcodeofethics.com

The Business Ethics site by Sharon Stoerger lists business codes of ethics alphabetically by company name.

http://www.web-miner.com/busethics.htm

# Ethics and Diversity: Applications in the Workplace

M. June Allard

*Assumption College*
*Worcester State College Professor Emerita*

## CASES AND SITUATIONS

The managers of today have gone far beyond consideration of workers in terms of single diversity dimensions. Managers deal daily with composites: a worker who is not just old, but who is old and female and black, or a male who is Latino and has a visual disability. The judicial system, however, still deals in single dimensions. Discrimination charges and lawsuits are not filed in terms of composites; they are filed in terms of age or gender or race or religion or disability or any other **single** dimension of diversity.

Each of the following cases and situations involves ethical issues in diversity:

1. For each case or situation, consider the ethical implications from your perspective. What do you personally think should be the outcome or resolution?
2. How would McNett characterize each situation in terms of the ethics involved? (Use the three categories of ethical theories found in Exhibit 1 of *The Ethics of Workplace Diversity* article in this text).
3. Investigate the resolution or current status of each case or situation. What was the rationale? Why was this outcome reached?

*Legal Commentary*

> *A key to the analysis of almost any discrimination case is whether an employer's given reason for taking action against an employee is the real reason, or a lie that covers up intentional discrimination in the decision. This is known as a pretext analysis . . .*

Michels, L. (2006, July 6). The Truth and Nothing But. *Suits in the Workplace*. Retrieved May *19*, 2007, from http://suitsintheworkplace.com/blogs

# Cases and Situations

## 1. Mammone vs. President & Fellows of Harvard College

### *Diversity Issue: Mental Illness*

Michael Mammone was a museum receptionist at Harvard with bipolar disorder. He worked for seven years with no problem, but then his behavior changed in August of 2002. He began singing and dancing in the reception area, had loud conversations and phone calls and established a Web site denouncing the low pay at Harvard. Later he began wearing East Indian dress with necklaces, rings, and bracelets and refused to stop using his personal laptop. He refused to meet with his supervisor, to whom he used 'abusive, threatening, and sexually derogatory language' and refused police instructions to leave the premises. After receiving disability benefits from Harvard for six months, he was terminated. Mammone charged Harvard with disability discrimination.

> Weintraub, B. (2006, May 15). University Wins AntiDiscrimination Suit. *The Harvard Crimson.* Retrieved May 19, 2007, from http://www.thecrimson.com/article.aspx?ref=513483

### *Legal Commentary*

> *Employers should be especially vigilant in defining and articulating essential job functions, and documenting the risks associated with an employee's failure to perform such functions.*

> Satterwhite, R. (2007, March 9). Thin Line Between Misconduct and Disability. *Suits in the Workplace.* Retrieved Mary 19, 2007, from http://suitsintheworkplace.com/blogs/

## 2. Minnesota and Muslim Cabbies

### *Diversity Issue: Religion*

In 2000, over 600 Minneapolis–St. Paul Airport Somali Muslim cabbies (approximately ¾ of the fleet) began refusing to pick up passengers carrying duty-free liquor, stating that Islamic law forbade them from doing so. By 2007, over 5,000 passengers had been refused. The Muslim American Society tried using a different top light on cabs refusing to transport liquor, but public reaction was overwhelmingly negative.

> Van Biema, D. (2007, January 19). Minnesota's Teetotal Taxis. *Time.* Retrieved May 19, 2007, from http://www.time.com/time/printout/0,8816,1580390,00.html

## 3. Brown vs. City of Salem

### Diversity Issue: Sleep Apnea Disability

Brown, a 911 emergency dispatcher for almost 25 years, was diagnosed with sleep apnea (involuntary short sleeps) 10 years ago. The city excused him from night duty and gave him a fan in accordance with his doctor's recommendation. In 2003 he was terminated at least in part because he still fell asleep while on duty. Brown sued.

> Satterwhite, R. (2007, March 9). Thin Line Between Misconduct and Disability. *Suits in the Workplace.* Retrieved May 18, 2007, from http://suitsintheworkplace.com/blogs/

## 4. Walgreens Drug Stores vs. State of Illinois

### Diversity Issue: Religion

Walgreens policy allowed pharmacists to decline to dispense birth control prescriptions as long as there was another pharmacist in the store or nearby to do so.

In April 2005, Illinois passed a law requiring all pharmacists to fill all prescriptions. A follow-up letter from the governor indicated that pharmacists refusing to comply would subject their employers to heavy penalties. In September 2005, disciplinary actions against the pharmacies, including Walgreens, began. Walgreens suspended non-complying pharmacists, offering to help those in southern Illinois to get licensed in Missouri. The pharmacists declined to relocate to Missouri. Suspended Illinois pharmacists and Walgreens both sued the state.

> Michels, L. (2006, Sept. 25). Conflict Over Contraception. *Suits in the Workplace.* Retrieved May 18, 2007, from http://suitsintheworkplace.com/blogs/archive/2006/09.aspx

## 5. Domino's

### Diversity Issue: Worker Safety or Social Class/Ethnic Discrimination?

Domino's refused to deliver pizza to a home in a high crime area in San Francisco. Like other pizza chains, they practiced redlining. They coded neighborhoods as red (high crime areas where they would not deliver pizza), yellow (customers must come out to street to get pizza from delivery car) or green (delivery to home) areas. Red areas were almost always high-minority areas. A customer in a red area claimed delivery people had been discriminating; Domino's claimed that their delivery policy was for worker protection—several pizza delivery people had been robbed and assaulted.

> The New York Times (1996, July 14). San Francisco Tells Pizza Shops to Hold the Excuses. *New York Times.* Retrieved May 19, 2007, from http://query.nytimes.com

## 6. Football Referee

### Diversity Issue: Visual Disability

When a Big Ten football official lost an eye, he informed the head of the Big Ten officiating and was told to continue working. He officiated games for six years, including two

Orange Bowl games, until the commissioner of the Big Ten learned about his vision; he was then terminated. He sued for violation of the Americans with Disabilities Act.

> Michels, L. (2006, July 20). Let's Hope the Judge Isn't a Michigan
> Fan. *Suits in the Workplace.* Retrieved May 18, 2007, from
> http://suitsintheworkplace.com/blogs/archive/2006/09.aspxu

---

**Outsourcing**

**Case 7** examines the practice of removing expensive labor costs from the payroll by forced retirement. **Cases 8 and 9** examine two different practices intended to accomplish the same end: a) forcing payroll labor into contract labor and b) transferring American jobs to countries where labor is cheaper. There are both positive and negative effects of these practices.

*"Full-time jobs become contract work without benefits, and then vanish overseas."*

> Reingold, J. (2004, April). Into Thin Air. *Fast Company.* Retrieved May 18, 2007, from
> http://www.fastcompany.com/magazine/81/offshore.html

*"In the absence of a public policy that tells me what to do ... I have no choice as corporate manager, nor do my colleagues ... [but to make decisions] that very often involve moves of jobs into other countries."*

> Andrew Grove (former Intel CEO) quoted in Reingold, J. (2004, April) Into Thin Air. *Fast
> Company.* Retrieved May 19, 2007, from http://www.fastcompany.com/magazine/81/offshore.html

---

## 7. Sidley Austin Brown & Wood vs. EEOC

### *Diversity Issue: Age*

Sidley, a giant, Chicago-based international law firm with 1,500 lawyers practicing on three continents, has used a mandatory retirement policy to involuntarily retire partners since 1978. Further, in 1999, it demoted 31 partners thereby forcing them out also. The EEOC filed a class action suit charging that Sidley selected partners for expulsion from the firm on the basis of their age. "The New York Bar Association recently criticized mandatory retirement programs for older attorneys saying that the requirements effectively cheat the public out of competent counselors with a wide body of experience."

> Michels, L. (2007, January 27) . Sidley Update. *Suits in the
> Workplace.* Retrieved May 19, 2007, from
> http://suitsintheworkplace.com/blog

## 8. Allstate Insurance

### *Diversity Issue: Age—demotion to contract work*

In 1999 Allstate fired 6,400 home and auto insurance agents, of which 90% were over age 40. Allstate offered to rehire them as independent contractors with slightly higher pay, but without their expensive health and pension benefits—provided that they waived their rights to sue Allstate for age or any other discrimination. Allstate also imposed a one-year freeze on rehiring former sales agents in other positions. This situation has now been repeated with 650 life insurance agents, 80% of whom are over 40. A class-action suit was filed by employees, who were joined by EEOC. Allstate countersued for fraud.

Sachs, S. (2002, May 22). Not in Good Hands. *The Harvard Crimson.* Retrieved May 18, 2007, from http://www.thecrimson.com/article.aspx?ref=214776.

Appelson, G. (2007, May 14). Baby Boomers Battle Bias. *Houston Chronicle.* Retrieved May 20, 2007, from http://www.chron.com/disp/story.mpl/business/4798277.html

## 9. WatchMark Corp. (Now WatchMark-Comnitel)

### Diversity Issue: Off-Shoring (Outsourcing Jobs Overseas)

WatchMark (a software company) terminated 60 people and sent their jobs to India. Some of the terminated workers were asked to stay and train their Indian replacements with the clear understanding that their severance pay and unemployment benefits were contingent upon them doing so.

Ethical dilemma: Cost savings and benefits to economy (increased productivity, lower prices and greater demand for American products) vs. downward mobility and suffering of the displaced workers.

Reingold, J. (2004, April). Into Thin Air. *Fast Company.* Retrieved May 18, 2007, from http://www.fastcompany.com/magazine/81/offshore.html

## 10. Supplier Diversity Programs

### Diversity Issue: Preferential Treatment of Women and Minorities

Many large corporations, such as Sprint and Bank of America, target a percentage of their purchasing budgets for goods and services toward businesses owned by women and minorities (WBEs and MBEs). Some, like Xerox and Eastman Kodak, even include businesses owned by other social identity groups, such as gays and lesbians and people with disabilities. The intention is to foster the growth and success of businesses owned by nondominant group members.

Tier I suppliers are considered to be the direct contractors. However, many corporations that have supplier diversity programs also require that their Tier I suppliers in turn contract some of their purchasing out to businesses that are also owned by nondominant groups (Tier II suppliers) and report back the dollar amounts that they spend. In addition, some corporations with supplier diversity programs may provide loans, advice, and specialized training to the Tier I suppliers.

Because of unethical past practices, such as male owners falsely reporting that over 51% of their business was owned and managed by their wives, certification programs such as those offered by the National Minority Development Council and the Women's Business Enterprise National Council are usually required as proof of ownership and management.

## LEGAL BACKLASH

### Academia and Reverse Discrimination

The changing landscape of state laws first required colleges to increase diversity among students and staff but now requires them to undo the very procedures they put in place to comply with the original diversity mandate.

### Diversity Issue: Race

**Admissions Policies**. University admissions policies *favoring* minorities are increasingly under attack. Attempting to provide greater minority access to primarily white campuses, universities employed practices such as the awarding of extra points for minority status and separate applicant pools with separate standards for whites and minorities. Legal challenges to policies such as these have been mounted at major institutions, including the universities of Michigan, Texas, Washington, Georgia, California, Maryland, Oklahoma State Regents (University of Tulsa), and the Commonwealth of Virginia Universities.

Reverse discrimination lawsuits have also been filed by white students denied access to federally funded academic programs, such as the National Science Foundation Minority Graduate Research Fellowships, and summer science programs conducted on university campuses.

### 11. Faculty Hiring

An example of reverse discrimination is that of the white female applicant who was a finalist for a position in the sociology department at the University of Nevada at Reno. The university hired an African-American male instead, paying him more than the posted salary range. One year later, the white female applicant was offered a position at $7,000 less than the black male at his hiring the year before. The female sued, arguing violations of the Equal Pay Act and the Civil Rights Act. The university argued that since only one (1) percent of its faculty members were black, it followed a "minority bonus program," whereby a department could hire an additional faculty member if it first hired a minority faculty member.

AAUP. (2005). University and Affirmative Action Update. *AAUP*. Retrieved May 20, 2007, from http://www.aaup.org/AAUP/ protectrights/legal/topics/aff-ac-update.htm

# The Pitney Bowes Case: A Legacy of Diversity Management

### Carol P. Harvey
*Assumption College*

*On July 2, 2004, Pitney Bowes' CEO Michael Critelli said,*

> Diversity is a part of our DNA at Pitney Bowes. We view diversity as a competitive imperative that helps drive innovation, deliver customer value, reach new markets and serve businesses of all sizes in over 130 countries worldwide. We also recognize that our future success is closely tied with our ability to attract, develop, and retain top talent and our inclusive culture will help us regardless of race, gender or ethnicity (Critelli, 2004).

*In April 1942, Pitney Bowes' CEO Walter Wheeler, said,*

> There has never been any management policy in Pitney Bowes which would preclude any individual qualified to do a job from obtaining it. Human nature being what it is, however, I have no doubt but what prejudices on the part of individuals already employed may have prevented some applicant from obtaining employment with us. It is the responsibility of the Personnel Department to see that these personal prejudices do not prevent the employment of qualified people regardless of race, color, or religion (Cahn, 1961, p. 204).

As the opening quotations illustrate, Pitney Bowes, the world's leading provider of integrated mail and document systems and services solutions is an example of a corporation with a long tradition of diversity management. Pitney Bowes' business success is built on a culture that values innovation, change, and growth—and diversity is an integral part of that culture. Managers are held accountable for diversity, recruiters form partnerships with community organizations that help bring the most talented minority interns and workers into the organization, the company has an award-winning diversity supplier program and diversity is incorporated into the strategic planning process.

## EARLY COMPANY HISTORY

To improve the efficiency of the U.S. Post Office, prevent stamp thefts, and simplify the business mailing process, Arthur H. Pitney patented the first practical postage meter in the United States in 1901. Although somewhat successful with his invention, the growth of his business, the American Postage Meter Company, was complicated because the post office would not approve its use for first class mail. In the meantime, the Universal Stamping Machine Company, under the leadership of its founder, Walter H. Bowes, was renting stamp-canceling machines to U.S. Post Offices. Rather than continue to compete with each other, the two men recognized their complementary talents of marketing (Bowes) and technology (Pitney) and merged into the Pitney Bowes Postage Meter Company in 1920. In the same year, Congress and the U.S. Post Office approved the postage meter for first class mail (Critelli, 2000).

In the 1920s and 1930s, Pitney Bowes, located in Stamford, Connecticut, benefited from decreased government regulations on metered mail and achieved much of its growth through technological inventions that solved specific customer mailing problems. Even in these early years, Pitney Bowes was progressive in its treatment of employees. Rather than lay off employees during the depression, the corporation cut wages by 10 percent and eliminated stockholder dividends. Efforts to unionize the employees were unsuccessful due to the company's generous benefits programs (Pedersen, 2002).

## A TRADITION OF DIVERSITY LEADERSHIP: THREE CEOs

Understanding diversity at Pitney Bowes today requires an historical examination of leadership and organizational culture. In 1937 Walter H. Wheeler, Jr., who is credited with the origins of Pitney Bowes diversity initiatives, became company president. Wheeler, the stepson of Bowes, was educated at Worcester Academy "where the headmaster, Daniel Webster Abercrombie, had his own form of democracy where all the boys were treated equally at least in class, in the dining hall, assemblies, student government, etc." (Frank Callahan, 2006). This school was "one of the earliest schools to accept students regardless of race or nationality . . . It was here that Walter was first introduced to certain principles of democracy that were to have dramatic applications years later" (Cahn, p. 76).

To understand how innovative Wheeler's diversity values and policies were at this time, it is necessary to understand the historical context. In the 1940s there was no national Civil Rights legislation in the United States. It was perfectly legal to refuse to hire, promote, or fire someone because of his/her race, ethnicity, gender, religion, etc. In some parts of the country, blacks still drank from separate water fountains, rode in the back of the bus, and attended separate public schools. Women were relegated to applying only for jobs that were advertised in newspapers as "help wanted, female." These positions consisted mainly of low-paying clerical and retail jobs, and jobs for highly educated women were limited mostly to helping professions, like teaching, social work, and nursing. AntiSemitism was rampant. In fact, Wheeler once resigned from a local yacht club because of their policy to deny membership to Jews.

There are many examples of Wheeler's infusion of his personal values into the corporate culture and management policies of Pitney Bowes. Predating the Civil

Rights Act by twenty years, he directed his managers to hire the same percentage of "colored workers" and "Hebrews" as were living in the Stamford area (Cahn, 2000, p. 204). He walked out of a New Orleans hotel when management refused to register a black Pitney Bowes employee. During World War II, like many U.S. manufacturing plants, Pitney Bowes suspended production of its own products to manufacture replacement parts for planes, guns, etc. At Wheeler's direction—unlike the situation in many U.S. corporations—after the war, Pitney Bowes retained the women and racial minorities who had been hired to replace the white male workers deployed overseas.

Wheeler also recognized that just hiring diverse workers was not enough. The corporation also had to make an effort to integrate them into the organization. Open communication and honesty have long been a crucial element of the diversity initiatives at Pitney Bowes. In 1946 Pitney Bowes hired its first African American office employee, Gladys Robinson. Although she was selected on the basis of her interviews and aptitude test (i.e., fully qualified), she was also prepared by management for any negative comments that she might receive from coworkers. Management discussed her hiring with the employees in her department before her arrival. This preparation of both employee and coworkers resulted in a friendly welcome from her new coworkers and became a standard procedure for new workers for some time. Mrs. Robinson said that she

> Detected an attempt on the part of my fellow employees to reassure me that I was wanted. After about six months I noticed the self-consciousness on the part of my fellow employees was beginning to wane. I was merely accepted as another worker and this suited me just fine ... By now, however, most people have become accustomed to the fact that Negroes are employed in most every department in the company. (Cahn, 1961, p. 207)

When antitrust legislation threatened Pitney Bowes in the late 1950s, the corporation embarked on a strategy of diversification into copiers, leasing equipment, retail supply chain products, etc. However, Chairman Wheeler stated that his company's dominance in the postage meter industry was due, not to anticompetitive business practices, but to positive employee relations that resulted in productive workers, lower costs, and innovative products (Pederson, 2002, pp. 296–7).

In the late 1980s George Harvey became the CEO at Pitney Bowes and took Wheeler's value of inclusiveness to the level of a business imperative. He recognized that "those who have previously been denied opportunity are often better performers who are more committed to excellence when they are given a chance" (Critelli, 2001, p. 19). His diversity focus was to see that all employees had the opportunity to advance their careers and become part of the leadership team—not just because it was the right thing to do, but also because it would enable the company to remain competitive by recruiting and promoting the most talented workers.

According to Sheryl Battles, long-time employee and now vice president of Corporate Communication, Harvey once looked out at a room full of managers and said that too many of them looked just like him and that was going to change. When women were hired away from traditional low-paying jobs into the sales force, where they could earn commissions and bonuses, they started to outperform the men. Harvey was quoted as saying "if this is what diversity does for business results, I want more diversity" (Battles, interview 6/16/06).

Along with the twenty-first century challenges of continued growth in a slow economy, increased competition, and the threat of terrorism through the mail, the current CEO and chairman, Michael J. Critelli, continues the legacy of diversity leadership. Currently serving his second term as chairman of the board of the National Urban League, the country's largest and oldest African-American organization, Critelli sees three dimensions to diversity management today at Pitney Bowes: becoming the employer of choice for a diversified workforce; understanding the challenges of global diversity; and implementing supplier diversity programs that create jobs for women and minority entrepreneurs (Bean, 2003, p. 54). Currently, women comprise 25 percent of the CEO's direct reports and 40 percent of the sales force. Twenty percent of the companies' officers and managers are people of color. Worldwide, 40 percent of the corporation's 33,000 employees are people of color. In 2000 Pitney Bowes purchased 47.5 million dollars' worth of goods and services from women and minority-owned businesses (Business Wire, 2001).

## PITNEY BOWES TODAY

Although this corporation was built on the success of manufacturing, leasing, and repairing postage meter equipment, Pitney Bowes, like all other U.S. manufacturers, is facing new challenges. In response to globalization, Pitney Bowes is now doing business in 130 countries and has over 34,000 employees worldwide. International operations account for 17 percent of their total revenues. With the shift from a manufacturing to a service economy, Pitney Bowes has retrained its workers to move from a manufacturing to an assembly model of production. In addition, the corporation has broadened its mission to focus on "integrated mail and document management" or "mailstream" services, such as package tracking and logistical transportation software.

Rather than be threatened by the impact of technology, such as the Internet and mobile phones, on decreasing volumes of traditional mail, Pitney Bowes considers these as business opportunities. Pitney Bowes provides customized U.S. postage stamps available on Zazzle.com and has formed a partnership with eBay to provide Web-based postage applications. Based on a system of longitude and latitude, T-Mobile uses Pitney Bowes' GeoTAX software to apply the correct federal, state, and municipal taxes to 20 million customer bills each month. In 2005 the company continued to grow through innovative services and acquisitions with nearly 25 percent of Pitney Bowes $5.4 billion revenues coming from companies that they acquired since 2001 (Pitney Bowes, 2005). Standard & Poor's recently rated Pitney Bowes stock, as a "buy" with an expectation that gross margins will soon hit 55 percent (Marcial, 2006).

## DIVERSITY INITIATIVES: USING A HUMAN CAPITAL APPROACH

Considering employees as human capital means that an organization realizes the economic value of its employees and their role in achieving profits, innovation, productivity, and long-term growth. Because being inclusive offers an organization a wider selection of talented people, it is a key element in the implementation of a business strategy based on the human capital approach. However, having diverse employees— i.e., the "numbers"—is not enough. Diverse employees can only become a competitive advantage if an organization capitalizes on the variety of perspectives and viewpoints of its employees in a supportive and cooperative organizational culture (Kochan, et al., 2003).

## RECRUITMENT

At Pitney Bowes, the key human resource functions of selection/recruiting, evaluating performance, training, benefits, etc., reflect the systemic nature of diversity as an organizational value. In order to have access to the best and the brightest diverse employee pool, the corporation uses a multilevel approach that includes advertising in publications targeted to the diverse community, forming external partnerships and alliances with organizations that represent a diverse talent pool, and sponsoring diversity-related events and causes. Some of these partnerships include Inroads (for interns), the National Urban League, the U.S. Hispanic Chamber of Commerce, Women's Business Enterprise National Council, National Society of Hispanic MBAs, National Black MBA Association, the Association of Latino Professionals in Finance and Accounting, the Connecticut Asian Pacific American Bar Association, Society of Women Engineers, National Society of Black Engineers, etc. Recently, Pitney Bowes' Literacy and Education Fund donated $50,000 to the National Action Council for Minorities in Engineering, Inc., (NACME) to develop a community college recruitment program that would help prepare African Americans, Native Americans, and Latinos for careers in math, engineering, and science (Pitney Bowes, 2006).

These relationships give Pitney Bowes a positive image in diverse communities and result in a more diverse but qualified pool of directors and job applicants. Currently, 25 percent of the board of directors are female or racial minorities. As of April 19, 2004, Pitney Bowes had a workforce composed of 26 percent African Americans, 10 percent Latino, and 5 percent Asian Americans (Torsone, 2006).

## EVALUATION OF DIVERSITY MANAGEMENT

Diversity management plays a key role in the evaluation process and is included as one of the criteria for each business unit president and his/her managers' performance appraisals. In 1992 the Diversity Task Force (DTF) was established to develop a mission statement and implementation plan for accountability for diversity within the organization. A year later the DTF proposed a diversity strategic planning process that is still in place today. Each business unit develops a strategic plan based on corporate goals. These plans address communications and training, employee development and work/life balance, business diversity, and community relations.

Within each unit there is a Diversity Leadership Council made up of employees who meet frequently to ensure that these goals are met. Achievement of these goals is taken into consideration when determining executive compensation (Pitney Bowes, 2006). Susan Johnson, vice president of Strategic Talent Management and Diversity Leadership, said that this process turns something "soft and mushy into something measurable" and "the planning process becomes part of the fabric of diversity" (Johnson, 2006).

## WORKPLACE BENEFITS

Even the benefit program at Pitney Bowes reflects the intersection of sound business practice with a focus on the preventing illness and recognizing that employees are individuals with different needs. Great Expectations is a program available to employees and spouses that provides prenatal care, risk assessment, and monitoring to prevent high-risk pregnancies. Employees with chronic conditions like diabetes or high blood pressure are offered on-site medical care and free prescriptions to encourage them to manage their illnesses. Employees who attend health care seminars can reduce their out of pocket health care costs and premiums. The Choice Time Program allows nonexempt employees to bank time off (vacations, flex days, etc.) to use for unplanned absences (Torsone, 2006).

## RECOGNITION FOR DIVERSITY

Although Pitney Bowes has received numerous awards from external organizations and publications for its diversity efforts (Figure 1), the corporation also rewards employees who demonstrate excellence in diversity through the annual PRISM award. Any individual employee or team can be nominated for the crystal trophy, cash award, and lunch with the CEO and senior management. Recently, this award was given for a program that employs people with disabilities in the outsourced mailrooms that Pitney Bowes manages in other companies (Torsone, 2006). In the fall, the Sheldon, Connecticut, campus hosts a family day, called a Diversity Festival, that is open to all local employees. The event features entertainment, exhibits, and food from a variety of cultures.

## ORGANIZATIONAL COMMUNICATION

At Pitney Bowes, the management/employee communication process also is rooted in a tradition of systemic inclusiveness. In the 1940s Wheeler felt that he should be as accountable to his employees as he was to his shareholders. So he began a series of *Job Holders* meetings based on his philosophy that everyone has something valuable to contribute to Pitney Bowes. At these meetings managers explained the state of the business and then answered employees' questions in a two-way dialogue. Today, since the corporation has expanded and become less centralized to Stamford, Connecticut, these meetings take the form of *Town Hall* forums. Each of the direct reports to the

---

**FIGURE 1   Recent Diversity Awards Received by Pitney Bowes**

Business Ethics magazine's **100 Best Corporate Citizen's List**

National Society of Hispanic MBA's **Corporate Partner of the Year**

*DiversityInc.* Ranked **#1 on Top 10 Companies for Diversity List**

Fortune magazine's **Best Companies for Minorities List**

Working Woman's magazine's **Top 25 Public Companies for Executive Women**

Hispanic magazine's **Top 25 Vendor Programs for Latinos**

CEO travels around the country to present an overview of the business and then responds to employee comments and questions in an open forum format.

When 9/11 and the anthrax mail crises occurred, Pitney Bowes stayed in constant contact with its employees through its voice mail system. The effectiveness of this communication evolved into *Power Talk*, a weekly short voice mail from the chairman or one of his direct reports that is broadcast over the entire voice mail system. These brief messages cover topics that affect employees—such as postal reform, announcement of company awards, company strategies, etc. This practice ensures that employees hear company news firsthand, rather than depending on the media or informal networks (Battles, 2006).

It is clear that diversity is integrated into the systems and management practices at Pitney Bowes. Because diversity has a long history at the corporation and because there has been continual support at the corporate and board levels, currently, Pitney Bowes provides an example of a corporation that has used diversity to its competitive advantage. However, as the company continues to grow, particularly by acquisition and global expansion, maintaining diversity as a corporate value will be the challenge of the future.

## DISCUSSION QUESTIONS

1. Given Pitney Bowes' growth and globalization strategies, analyze the forces for and against maintaining an organizational culture that supports diversity as a business imperative.

2. Provide specific examples of ways that Pitney Bowes has aligned diversity goals with a market-driven approach to meeting customer needs.

3. At Pitney Bowes, diversity in addition to being an ethical imperative, is a business imperative. How does diversity create competitive advantages for this corporation?

4. Into which of Thomas and Ely's three paradigms (see Introduction to Section III) does Pitney Bowes fit? Why?

## BIBLIOGRAPHY

Battles, S. (2006). Interview, June 16.
Battles, S. (1999). Pitney Bowes creates guide for Latina business women. *Business Wire,* November 23.
Bean, L. (2003). Pitney Bowes' CEO Michael Critelli: this change agent understands the value of diversity. *DiversityInc.* October–November, 50–54.
Business Wire Inc. (2001). Pitney Bowes creates Web link to expand opportunities for minority and women suppliers: diversity 2000 partners to launch Pitney Bowes Information. February 15.

Cahn, W. (1961). *The story of Pitney-Bowes.* New York: Harper and Brothers.
Callahan, F. Worcester Academy. e-mail received July 1, 2007.
Critelli, M.J. (2001). *Pitney Bowes, Inc. from mail to messaging: the leading provider of informed mail and messaging management.* Address to the Newcomen Society.
Johnson, S. (2006) interview, June 14.
Kochan, T., Ely, R., Jackson, S., Joshi, A., Jehn, J., Leonard, J., Levine, D., and Thomas, D. (2003). The effects of diversity on business

performance: Report of the diversity research network *Human Resource Management,* 42, #1, 3–22.

Marcial, G. (2006). For Pitney Bowes, a stamp of approval. *Business Week,* 3988, June 12.

Pedersen, J.P. (ed). (2002). Pitney Bowes. *International Directory of Company Histories.* Farmington Hills, MI: St. James Press. 47, 295–299.

Pitney Bowes. (2006). Retrieved from Web site pb.com on June 6, 2006.

Pitney Bowes, (2005). Annual report. Stamford, CT.

Tessler, C. (2004). Fortune magazine ranks Pitney Bowes one of America's 50 best companies for minorities. *Fortune Magazine.* July 2, 2004. (11A)

# What Happened at Coca-Cola?

## Carol P. Harvey
### *Assumption College*

**Coca-Cola . . .**

- is considered the world's most recognized brand name.
- controls 53 percent of the world's soft-drink market.
- was an international brand by 1900.
- was instrumental in the racial integration movement in Atlanta in the 1960s.
- was rated thirty-second on *FORTUNE's* 2002 list of the 50 best companies for minorities.
- agreed to spend $200 million to settle recent racial and gender bias lawsuits.

How did a company with a history of international business, that long targeted many of its products to minority groups and that is headquartered in a state where 28 percent of the population is black, lose the largest racial discrimination lawsuit (*Ingram et al. v. The Coca-Cola Company*) in U.S. history? The case illustrates the contrast between a corporation's public image and the acceptance of racism within its organizational culture. Although Coca-Cola contributed to civil rights groups such as the Southern Christian Leadership Conference and the Rainbow Push Coalition, according to Foust (2000b).

> When it came to its own workforce, the story was quite different. . . . According to allegations filed in the discrimination lawsuit, former CEO Ivestor told a transferee stunned by the latent racist culture at its headquarters that it would take "15 to 20 years before blacks would be fairly represented in the company" (p. 58).

However, this was not the first time that racism at Coca-Cola had been an issue.

> The company's Southern bottlers taunted and terrorized Coke's first black salesman. Privately, legendary chief executive, Robert S. Woodruff questioned civil rights legislation in the 1960s. And if the worst excesses of the past are gone, according to internal Coke documents released as part of a current lawsuit, even today the median salary for black employees is 44 percent less than that for whites" (Foust, 2000b, p. 58).

## INDUSTRY BACKGROUND

The soft-drink industry has its roots the United States when physicians in the 1800s began prescribing the bubbling waters discovered in New York as a cure for ailments ranging from arthritis to headaches and including everything in between. Later, the development of artificially carbonated water by laboratory scientists, the addition of flavors like lemon and root beer by pharmacists, and the growing popularity of the local pharmacy soda fountains as social gathering spots, led to increased demand for these products.

From its humble beginnings, the soft-drink industry enjoyed a phenomenal growth rate. One in every four beverages consumed in the United States is a soft drink, which amounts to an annual consumption of 53 gallons for every man, woman, and child in the country (www.nsda.org, 2003). However, due to the consumer shift to bottled waters, teas, fruit juices, and product variations in coffee, the consumption rate for soft drinks has become stagnant in the United States. To increase sales, soft-drink producers diversified into other bottled beverage products and aggressively compete in a market that is highly saturated, except in developing countries.

## EARLY COMPANY HISTORY

The history of the Coca-Cola Corporation, the producer of two of the world's three most popular carbonated drinks, parallels the industry trends in terms of growth and product lines. Pioneering a sophisticated distribution system of local bottlers who purchase the coke syrup from the corporation and implementing aggressive growth strategies of seven percent to eight percent a year, Coke now controls 51 percent of the carbonated beverage sales in the world and 18 percent of the noncarbonated beverage market. In 2002 the corporation had $19 billion in operating revenues and netted $3.9 billion from its 300 brands sold in over 200 countries (www.coca-cola.org, 2003).

However, the organization had humble beginnings when John S. Pemberton began a patent medicine business in Atlanta, Georgia, in 1886, where he invented such products as liver pills, hair dye, and the beverage known today as Coca-Cola. With caffeine and cocaine in his sugary syrup concentrate, the product was marketed as a cure-all remedy. Pemberton and his partners grossed a mere $50 in sales during the first year. In 1891 they sold the business and its secret formula for coke syrup for $2300 to Asa Candler. The new owner, a druggist, improved the original formula, removed the cocaine, and hired a sales force that blanketed the United States and beyond, selling syrup concentrate to local bottlers. He promoted the business using such progressive marketing techniques as free samples and product logo premiums, and by 1904 the company had sold a million gallons of syrup and, by 1969, six billion gallons (Derdak, 1988).

During WWII, General Eisenhower requested that Coke be made available to American soldiers serving in North Africa and Europe. So the company set up multiple foreign bottling plants that paved the way for a global business presence after the war. During the 1950s the company expanded rapidly internationally and opened 15 to 20 plants per year. As early as the 1950s, Coke recognized the potential of minority markets and included racial minorities in their advertisements (Pendergast, 2000).

Although Coca-Cola was a one-product company until the 1960s, it quickly became synonymous with the American way of life with its growing success and in its promotional messages. The company's "advertising never reflected the problems of the world, only a good and happy life" (Derdak, 1988, p. 233).

For Coke, the 1960s were a time of diversification, product development, and increased competition. Because Pepsi began to aggressively challenge Coke for market share, Coke bought Minute Maid and Belmont Springs Water and launched Tab, Sprite, and Fresca, making significant inroads into the diet soda market. During the 1970s Coca-Cola focused on foreign expansion, particularly into China and Russia. As a result, by 1984, Pepsi outsold Coke with a 22.8 percent market share, compared with Coke's 21.6 percent (Derdak, 1988, p. 234). Although the introduction of Diet Coke, now the world's #1 diet beverage, pumped up sales, the introduction of a reformulated "New Coke" was a marketing and public relations disaster. "Coke's great (financial) returns in the 1990s were based on the notion that it could keep increasing earnings at 20 percent or more per year. It can't" (Sivy, 2000, p. 42).

## CORPORATE CULTURE AND LEADERSHIP

Fueled by phenomenal marketing and financial successes, Coca-Cola was "run by bureaucrats and accountants focused more on getting the most out of what they had . . . than of thinking of new ideas" (New Doug, 1999, p. 55). Described as "insular" and "predominated by the good ol' boys from the University of Georgia" (Foust, 2000a, p. 56), the organization was "a marketing machine that created desire for the Coke brand (at whatever price), rather than a sales company that gave consumers what they wanted" (Feldman, 2000, p. 33). In some parts of the world, Coca-Cola was seen as representing American imperialism. This attitude is exemplified by former CEO Roberto Goizueta's wish that one day Coke should replace tap water. In 1997 when Goizueta suddenly died, the board replaced him with his protégé, M. Douglas Ivestor. Refusing to appoint a chief operating officer, "Ivestor did what accountants do best, he put his head down and carried on with the old way of doing things" (New Doug, 1999, p. 55). Over the next two years, Ivestor, described as "arrogant and insecure" (Morris & Sellers, 2000, p. 15), inherited many problems, including a tainted Coke scare in Europe that resulted in the largest product recall in company history (Europe Shuns, 1999), a decline in earnings for two straight years, and the need to steeply increase the price of Coke syrup sales to bottlers in an attempt to bolster profits.

## THE LAWSUIT

In 1999, just when things seemed like they couldn't get worse for Ivestor, Coca-Cola was served with a lawsuit that accused the company of systemically discriminating against black employees in promotions, evaluations, terminations, and pay. "Publicity surrounding the case troubled Coke, whose U.S. customer base is disproportionately made up of African Americans and Latinos" (Mokhiber, 2000, p. 30).

Could this lawsuit have been prevented? Earlier when black employees shared their complaints with the Rev. Joseph Wheeler, president of the local NAACP, he brought these concerns to Coca-Cola officials. He was told that the company was under no obligation to talk to him because he was not a lawyer. Greg Clark, one of the plaintiffs, said, "that he would never have sued had he felt that his concerns were taken seriously: 'They ignored me, ignored me, ignored me, to the point where I felt that I had no other recourse' " (Harrington, 2000, p. 188).

In response to the lawsuit, Ivestor appointed Carl H. Ware, the highest-ranking black executive in the company, as the co-chair of the Diversity Advisory Council along with senior vice president, Jack Stahl. Ware, a Harvard graduate, joined the company in 1974 to work in the area of urban and government affairs. As vice president of the Africa group, Ware focused on "cultivating African governments and bridging cultural hurdles so that the company can do business, often in partnerships, with local governments" (Holsendolph, 1999, p. 1). He is credited with influencing Coca-Cola's decision to divest its South African assets in support of the anti-apartheid cause. In 1994, Ware helped to organize Nelson Mandela's fund-raising tour in the United States, which is credited with smoothing the way for Coke sales in post-apartheid South Africa, where Coke sales now exceed 400 million cases a year (Foust, 2000b, p. 138). Having worked 26 years at the company, Ware was known for his ability to defuse problems before they became full-blown crises. In 1981, Jesse Jackson, critical of Coke's hiring record and its weak support for black-owned businesses, was set to kick off a "Don't choke on Coke" boycott. Jackson called it off after Ware helped craft a $50 million program to help support black vendors (Foust, 2000b, p. 138).

As the lawsuit wound its way through the court system, the number of plaintiffs increased, and both sides turned up the pressure. What began with four current and ex-employees (administrative assistant Motisola Abdallah, security officer Gregory Clark, consumer information specialist Linda Ingram, and a former director, Kimberly Orton) eventually became a major class-action suit with approximately 2,000 plaintiffs. The claim was that Coca-Cola had "systematically discriminated against African Americans by paying them lower salaries than whites for the same work, passing over them for promotions, and subjecting them to harassment" (Mokhiber, 2000, p. 30), since at least 1995. Coincidentally, 1995 was the same year that Carl Ware presented Ivestor, then Coke's COO with a report documenting racial disparities in pay, performance evaluations, and promotions for black employees. The plaintiffs asked both for monetary damages and a court order that required the company to change some of its employment practices. The lead co-counsel in the case was Cyrus Mehri, a 37-year-old lawyer, who had successfully won the $176 million Texaco racial discrimination lawsuit.

Coca-Cola denied the charges of discrimination, claiming that the plaintiffs' claims had nothing in common but their race. Carl Ware said, "I think we've made great strides in developing a gold standard for diversity management" (Foust, 1999, p. 2) and "I myself am a good example, a proof that glass walls do not exist at the Coca-Cola Company" (Holsendolph, 1999, p. 1). However, "the company's dithering continued even after the suit was filed. For starters, rather than pursue the almost inevitable settlement, Coke first engaged in a vigorous pre-trial defense" (Harrington, 2000, p. 188) and attempted to stop the class-action status of the lawsuit. U.S. District Court Judge Richard Story instructed the company to add a disclaimer to company e-mails to employees about the case that read, "The foregoing represents Coca-Cola's opinion of the lawsuit. It is unlawful for Coca-Cola to retaliate against employees who choose to participate in this case" (Unger, 1999a). The company did not add the statement.

In October 1999, while the case was pending, Ivestor effectively demoted Ware, the company's highest-ranking black executive, by having him report to a fellow senior vice president. "In response, Ware announced that he would retire at the end of the year. The episode fueled questions about Coke's commitment to diversity" (Smith, 2000, p. 52).

Although Ivestor's tenure was fraught with financial problems, the demotion of Ware seemed to be one of the catalytic events and public relations problems that moved influential board members to strongly suggest to Ivestor that he was no longer the man to run Coke. On December 5, 1999, Ivestor submitted his resignation at an emergency board meeting called on a Sunday evening. Morris and Sellers wrote

> Ivestor's sudden fall from one of the world's premier corporate jobs is more than just a tale of bad luck or plans gone wrong. It is a management story full of leadership lessons. It features colossal arrogance and insecurity. Its main character was blind to his own weaknesses and unwilling to take advice. . . . But the ultimate measure of a CEO is how he handles crises, and again and again, in the view of certain directors and the powerful bottling executives, Ivestor was a day late and a dollar short. . . . He took pride in being a substance-over-style guy, but that translated into taking no heed of image and perception issues, which are merely all important to a company like Coke (2000, p. 78).

The board elected Douglas Daft—a 56-year-old Australian with 30 years experience at Coke, primarily in their Asian and Middle Eastern markets—as president and CEO. In contrast to his predecessor, Daft was a delegator, who spoke of repositioning the company from three perspectives: building brand, thinking and acting locally in global business relations, and being seen as a model citizen. In a speech delivered to the Chief Executive's Club in Boston, he said, "I want the Coca-Cola Company to be one of the most desired employers in the world. I have told our people that we are going to take our company to the head of the class when it comes to the diversity of our workforce and our business" (Daft, 2000, p. 606). He quickly mended fences with Carl Ware by naming him vice president for Global Public Affairs, reporting directly to him, and adopted two of the suggestions from Ware's 1995 report: clear support for diversity from the top executives and tying compensation increases to the achievement of diversity goals. As a result, Ware rescinded his retirement plan.

In November 2000, as a result of a court-ordered mediation, Coca-Cola settled the lawsuit with almost all of the 2,200 plaintiffs for $192.5 million. Approximately 1 percent of the plaintiffs decided to "opt-out" of the settlement agreement. On June 7, 2002, the U.S. District Court for the Northern District of Georgia approved the settlement agreement in what is formally known as *Ingram et. al. v. The Coca-Cola Company*. The agreement applied to all nonhourly U.S.-based employees of the company, but not to employees of its bottlers. The terms of the agreement called for back pay to current and former employees, future pay equity adjustments, linkage between senior managers' compensation and the company's EEO performance, and the creation of an outside seven-member Task Force to provide independent oversight of Coca-Cola's compliance. The Task Force was responsible for preparing four annual reports evaluating the implementation of these programs. Cyrus Mehri, head of the plaintiffs' legal team, summed up his opinion of the case.

> The biggest problems at Coke were their HR practices. They had almost as many job titles as they did jobs, there was no consistent form of job posting, and promotional practices were not consistently applied. This gave undue discretion to managers and

prevented employees from having a fair chance to compete for these positions. Coke had cultivated an image of being extraordinarily progressive and generous in the African-American community. Unfortunately, Coke—like so many companies—got very arrogant and believed their own PR. They valued minorities as consumers, but not as employees (Wiscombe, 2003, p. 34).

When asked to comment on the case, Coca-Cola corporate media relations spokesperson Karyn Dest wrote

> Clearly we learned a valuable lesson from the lawsuit. But, in addition to the learning around diversity, another great learning for us was that we had no documented proof when it came to the lawsuit of our efforts. We didn't measure the growth and development of minorities and women at the company (personal communication, November 5, 2003).

## AFTER THE LAWSUIT

Alexis Herman, a former U.S. secretary of labor, chaired the Task Force that issued its first report in September 2002. Since the settlement, Coca-Cola has implemented numerous systemic changes in its policies and procedures (Exhibit 1) with measurable results (Exhibit 2). Although the report was generally positive, the Task Force cited key areas that needed additional work: identification of employees for senior management positions and improvement in the perceptions of minority employees that their career opportunities are comparable to those of white employees. Currently, "about a third of Coke's employees are minorities, but most top employees are white. . . . All minorities, the report said, are overrepresented in lower-paying support jobs" (Wyatt, 2002, p. 1).

---

**EXHIBIT 1   Programs and Policies Implemented by Coca-Cola since the Settlement Agreement was Accepted**

- Established uniform processes for employee reviews
- Required that all job postings attract at least three candidates, one of whom must be a woman or minority
- Implemented mandatory diversity training for managers and employees
- Conducted human resources audits and adverse-impact analyses
- Tied performance appraisals and compensation for managers to their effectiveness in performance management
- Implemented a uniform compensation system based on job-related measures, including a market-based salary structure, a common review date, and additional compensation training for managers
- Established a mentoring program
- Initiated executive briefings for senior management concerning diversity strategy
- Implemented a "Solutions" program that included an ombudsman and a hotline to resolve employee disputes

Adapted from the *First Annual Report of the Task Force* (Herman et al., 2002)

| EXHIBIT 2 | Key Findings from the First Annual Report of the Task Force |
|---|---|

- Of the 6,864 nonhourly U.S. Coke employees, 30 percent are minorities, up 4 percent since 12/00. Two-thirds of the minorities are African Americans.
- In the first six months of 2002, white men were promoted at the rate of 4.7 percent, women at 5 percent, and minorities at 5.7 percent; of the 301 new hires 29 percent were minorities and 55 percent were women.
- Minorities make up only 20 percent of the workforce at the executive level and are overrepresented at 47 percent among the lowest paid support personnel.

The Task Force also chided the corporation for missing an opportunity to diversify the board of directors, which was then composed of nine white men, two white women, and one African-American man. In the spring of 2002, when the board membership was expanded from 12 to 14 members, two white men were selected. "The company's failure to consult with the task force with respect to the nominations undermined its diversity efforts and suggested a lack of sensitivity to diversity goals" (Bean, 2002b, p. 1).

Shortly after the report was published, CEO and chairman Daft wrote a memo to employees that said, "There is still work to do. Our commitment to diversity is a journey not an endpoint. Diversity is not an initiative; it is a fundamental element of our business success" (Day, 2002, p. 3). In 2002, Coca-Cola began a five-year, 800 million-dollar supplier diversity program. That year alone $181 million worth of goods and services were purchased from women- and minority-owned businesses. In 2003, Coca-Cola extended health care benefits to same-sex domestic partners and named the first Hispanic female, Maria Elena Lagomasino, chief executive of J. P. Morgan, a private bank, to its board of directors. Coca-Cola is currently ranked number 25 on *FORTUNE* magazine's list of best companies for minorities and at number 18 on DiversityInc.'s survey of the top 50 companies for diversity (Dest, personal communication, November 5, 2003).

However, Coca-Cola's public relations problems with diversity were far from over. A recent article on the DiversityInc Web site questioned Coca-Cola's commitment to diversity in terms of the company's minority supplier program in contrast to the amount spent by other *FORTUNE* 100 companies. In addition, it was mentioned that a recent article written by Johnnie Booker and published in *Corporate Corridors* magazine on Coke's supplier diversity program's progress neglected to state in the byline that Booker was Coca-Cola's director of supplier diversity (Cole, 2002).

At the 2002 annual shareholders meeting at Madison Square Garden, some African-American employees protested because they believed that blacks remain underrepresented in the top corporate ranks, get fired more often, and are still paid less than white employees. "Protesters handed out material claiming that 16 percent of the Coke workforce is black but that blacks have just 1.5 percent of the top jobs" (White, 2002, E03).

In May of the same year, some employees in Texas accused Coca-Cola of repackaging nearly out-of-date soda, marking it down, and then reselling it in minority neighborhoods since 1993. Coca-Cola management denied the allegation.

On May 24, 2002, the Coca-Cola Company, in a conciliation agreement with the U.S. Department of Labor, agreed to pay $8.1 million in back pay to over 2,000 female employees. The agreement followed an audit by the Office of Federal Contract Compliance (OFCCP), which enforces federal rules against discrimination at companies holding government contracts. The audit revealed wage disparities between male and female employees between 1998 and 2000 (Bean, 2002a).

## DISCUSSION QUESTIONS

1. Considering that minority groups are one of Coca-Cola's major target markets in the United States and that the company sells its products all over the world, how could a diverse workforce be considered as a strategic advantage to the organization (See introduction to Section III)?

2. With all of the positive changes that have been instituted at Coca-Cola since the settlement of the lawsuit in 2000, how is it possible that the survey administered by the Task Force revealed that minority employees still perceive that their career opportunities are not comparable to those of whites?

3. How does Parker's triangle, "The Emotional Connection of Distinguishing Differences and Conflict," help to explain (a) why so many minority employees joined the class action lawsuit and (b) how Coca-Cola failed to "manage diversity"?

---

### *Writing Assignments*

1. Research the details of other major discrimination cases, such as Texaco, CSX Transportation, Winn-Dixie, Denny's, Johnson & Johnson, Adams-Mark Hotels, or Bell South. How are these current or settled cases similar to or different from the Coca-Cola case? Apply Thomas & Ely's framework to each of these organizations. What can be learned about managing diversity by applying their model?

2. *At the time that the lawsuit was filed:*
   a. What were the internal and external pressures for and against diversity at the company? Were the priorities for managing diversity low, moderate, or high? Why?
   b. Repeat this analysis (step a) for Coca-Cola at the *conclusion* of the case.

---

## BIBLIOGRAPHY

Bean, L. (2002a, September 30). *Coca-Cola to pay $8 million to resolve salary discrimination.* Retrieved September, 30, 2003, from http://www.diversityinc.com/members/3034print.cfm

Bean, L. (2002b, September 30). *Coca-Cola rebuked for missed opportunity to diversify board.* Retrieved October 20, 2003, from

http://www.diversityinc.com/members/3597print.cfm.

Coca Cola Corporation. (2003). *The Coca-Cola Company 2002 annual report.* Atlanta: Author.

Cole, Y. (2002, September 12). *Baloney meter measures Coca-Cola's claims of supplier-diversity progress* (electronic version). Retrieved

September 30, 2003, from http://www. diversityinc.com/members/351printcfm

Daft, D. (2000). Speech delivered to the Chief Executives Club of Boston, May 3, 2000. *Vital Speeches of the Day, 66*(19), 606–609.

Day, S. (2002, September 26). Antibias task force gives Coca-Cola good marks but says challenges remain. *The New York Times*. p. C3.

Derdak, T. (Ed). (1988). *International directory of company histories* (pp. 232–235). Chicago: St. James Press.

Europe shuns tainted Coke. (1999). *MacLean's, 112,* 26, p. 78.

Feldman, A. (2000). The real thing. *Money,* 29, 33–36.

Foust, D. (2000a). Coke: Say goodbye to the good ol' boy culture. *Business Week, 3683*(55), 58.

Foust, D. (2000b). Will Coke go better with Carl Ware? *Business Week, 3665* (55), 138.

Foust, D. (1999). A different cola war. *Business Week,* 3632(54), 38–39.

Harrington, A. (2000) Prevention is the best defense. *Fortune, 142*(2), 188.

Herman, A., Burns, A., Casellas, G. F., Cooke, E. D., Jr., Knowles, M. F., Lee, B. L.

Holsendolph, E. (1999, June 1). Once again, Carl Ware takes on an assignment, a big one. *The Atlanta Journal and Constitution.*

Mokhiber, R. (2000). Coke settles race suit. *Multinational Monitor, 21*(12), 30.

Morris, B., and Sellers, P. (2000). What really happened at Coke. *Fortune, 141*(1), 14–17.

National Soft Drink Association (NSDA), (2003). Growing Up Together: The Soft Drink Industry and America Retrieved from nsda.org/softdrinks/History/growup.html

New Doug, old tricks. (1999, December 9). *Economist, 353*(8149), 55.

Pendergast, M. (2000). *For god, country and Coca-Cola the definitive history of the great American soft drink and the company that makes it.* New York: Basic Books.

Sivy, M. (2000). Why Coke still isn't it. *Money, 29*(2), 42.

Smith, V.E. (2000). Things are going better with Coke. *Newsweek, 135*(3), 52.

Unger, H. (1999a, May 12). Plaintiffs in suit against Coca-Cola to meet in court. *Knight Rider/Tribune Business News.*

White, B. (2002, April 12). Black Coca-Cola workers still angry: Despite 2000 legal settlement, protesters say little has changed. *The Washington Post*, p. E03.

Wiscombe, J. (2003). Corporate America's scariest opponent. *Workforce, 82*(4), 34–40.

Wyatt, K. (2002, September 25). Coke's diversity work gets approval. *Associated Press News Release.* Retrieved October 31, 2003, from http://www.ap.org

## Diversity on the Web

Now that you have read the Coca-Cola case, visit the following Web site, where you will find the five Task Force reports that were part of the legal settlement of the Coca-Cola discrimination case. Within each annual report, you will find an "executive summary" section. Read at least that section and develop a time line that tracks the yearly actions Coca-Cola took to remedy the situation as it existed at the close of this case.

According to these summaries, were these changes always easily implemented or were there some problems along the way?

In 2007 the Coca-Cola Corporation was named number 4 on *DiversityInc.*'s Top 50 Companies for Diversity List. Do you think that this would have happened if it were not for the work of the external Task Force? Why or why not?

http://www.thecoca-colacompany.com/ourcompany/taskforce_report.html

# The U.S. Air Force Academy: Organizational Culture and Diversity Issues

Egidio A. Diodati

*Assumption College*

## OVERVIEW

This case provides an introduction to the diversity-related incidents occurring recently at the U.S. Air Force Academy in Colorado Springs, Colorado. Because of the military culture of this organization, change efforts, as well as gender and religious issues, present unique challenges to effective management.

## BACKGROUND OF THE ORGANIZATION

The United States Air Force, originally known as the Army Air Corps, was part of the Department of the Army until after World War II. Because the educational requirements particular to Air Force officers could not be met by the other service academies, the Air Corp became a separate organization. The first U.S. Air Force Academy class entered in July of 1955 at a temporary location, Lowry Air Force Base, Denver, Colorado, and moved to the current location in 1958. Women, called the "eighties ladies," first entered the academy in July of 1976, as part of the class of 1980. (United States Air Force Academy Public Affairs Office, June 2005, p. 3).

Today the core curriculum at the Academy includes courses in science, engineering, social sciences, and humanities. The most popular majors include management, astronautical engineering, international affairs, political science, history, behavioral science, civil engineering, electrical engineering, and engineering mechanics (United States Air Force Academy, Public Affairs Office, June, 2005 p. 1).

Women currently represent 17.9 percent of the total 4,381 cadets. This is a fairly consistent number with the population of women at the academy ranging from 18.5 percent for the class of 2006 to 17.0 percent for the class of 2009. Female representation at the Academy parallels that of the Air Force in general. Carl Builder of the RAND organization reports that, "due to the large number of support personnel needed to run the . . . Air Force, this service has gone farther than any other service in integrating women into its ranks. Nearly 20 percent of all Air Force personnel are women and 99.7 percent of its jobs are open to women" (Zeigler & Gunderson, 2005, p. 10). Acceptance rates for women are roughly two percent lower than for males. The attrition rate for women seems to be fairly consistent with that of men, varying from less than one percent (0.1%) to 4.3 percent.

## MILITARY CULTURE

Military culture has been described as "the prevailing values, philosophies, customs, traditions, and structures that collectively, over time, have created shared individual expectations within the institution about appropriate attitudes, personal beliefs, and behaviors" (Zeigler & Gunderson, 2005, p. 8). While studies indicate that a strong traditional organizational culture can produce dysfunctional blind spots in thinking and limits on innovation, these values can also become "a stimulus for wonderful selfless action" (Zeigler & Gunderson, 2005, p. 9).

The relative importance of personnel concerns is perhaps best expressed by Carl Builder, a RAND analyst and expert on military culture. He suggests that the Air Force worships at the altar of technology . . . and would gladly sacrifice personnel to have the budget strength to stay on the cutting edge of technology.

The unique facets generally attributed to the military culture are as follows:

- **Discipline**—the quality that keeps soldiers from panicking in the face of danger. This value is culturally enforced with "punishment and repetitive drill, and enhanced with unit cohesion and strong leadership."
- **Professional ethos**—"a set of normative self-understandings which . . . . define the profession's corporate identify, code of conduct, . . . . and social worth."
- **Ceremony and etiquette**—salutes, parades, uniforms, and medals. These help form a common identity among members.
- **Cohesion and esprit de corps**—the shared sense of identity among military personnel at the unit or branch level.

(Zeigler & Gunderson, 2005, p. 8)

Differing theoretical frameworks provide differing approaches to understanding Air Force Academy culture. Ziegler and Gunderson's framework views the postmodern military as characterized by five organizational changes:

- Increasing impenetrability of civilian and military spheres structurally and culturally
- Diminution within the military services, based on branch of service, rank, and combat versus noncombat support roles, etc.

- A shift in purpose from fighting wars against a clearly identifiable opponent to missions that are not 'military' in the traditional sense
- Military forces being used in internationally authorized missions
- Military forces themselves becoming international in nature

In their research Ziegler and Gunderson (2005, p. 3, 4) report on a unique facet of military culture:

> Of the four possible "feminisms" (liberal feminism, cultural feminism, radical feminism, and postmodern feminism), military organizations generally are less threatened by and prefer the *liberal feminism* view, which essentially construes equality as sameness. *Cultural feminism,* on the other hand, has the perspective of equality as a recognition of difference. Radical feminism seeks to destroy the hierarchy of gender and has a view of equality as antisubordination. Postmodern feminism approach is the general rejection of paradigmatic approaches (2005, p. 4).

As a comment on propensity for change, research shows that most bureaucracies, including the military, are not only resistant to change, but also are designed not to change. This dread of innovation by military bureaucracies is due to the nature of the job that the armed forces perform. To them, change equals increased risk of death and destruction. These organizations will innovate only when they have failed, when pressured from the outside, and when they seek to expand (Zeigler & Gunderson, 2005, p. 7).

Geerte Hofstede's work on international cultural differences produces a framework that applies a number of dimensions to profile cultural differences within the Air Force Academy culture.

**Power Distance** is the extent to which less powerful members of organizations accept and expect that power is distributed equally or unequally. Inequality or equality is endorsed by the followers as much as by the leaders. Power and inequality are fundamental to the organization and all are aware of and act in accordance with these power distance relationships.

**Individualism/Collectivism** is the degree to which people are influenced or not influenced by their group memberships. On the individualistic side, organizational ties between individuals are loose: everyone is expected to look after him/herself and his/her immediate family. On the collectivistic side, people are integrated into strong, cohesive organizational groups that continue protecting them in exchange for unquestioning loyalty.

**Masculinity/femininity** refers to the degree the dominant culture values assertiveness compared with cultures that value caring for others and the quality of life.

**Uncertainty avoidance** deals with an organization's tolerance for uncertainty and ambiguity. It indicates to what extent a culture programs its members to feel uncomfortable or comfortable in unstructured situations.

**Long-term vs. short-term** contrasts a perception that values persistence in achieving long-term goals with one that focuses on living for the present.

(http://feweb.uvt.nl/center/hofstede/page3.htm)

Although Hofstede's five dimensions were developed for analyses of national cultures, applying them to militaristic cultures indicate that militaristic cultures tend to:

- accept greater power distances between leaders and followers,
- reinforce collectivistic behaviors,
- value the masculine traits of assertiveness and competitiveness more than the feminine traits of nurturing and collaboration,
- avoid uncertainty, generally showing more discomfort in unstructured situations, and
- espouse the long-term values of respect for tradition, fulfillment of social obligations, and protecting one's image.

## THE FIRST OF THE MAJOR ACADEMY PROBLEMS: SEXUAL ASSAULTS

In early 1993, the first set of rape allegations by women cadets and graduates surfaced. In response to these allegations, and in an attempt to prevent further problems, the Academy embarked on a number of new policies and initiatives. First, they set up a Center for Character Development to promote ethical conduct, established a twenty-four hour rape hotline, and issued a policy to "ensure [that] a climate exists that is free of discrimination, harassment, intimidation, and assault of any kind."

## THE SECOND OF THE MAJOR PROBLEMS: MORE SEXUAL ASSAULTS

Ten years later, on January 2, 2003, the secretary of the Air Force, chief of staff of the Air Force, several U.S. senators and representatives, and major media outlets received an anonymous email asserting, that "there was a significant sexual assault problem at the U.S. Air Force Academy and that it had been ignored by the Academy's leadership." One of the recipients, Sen. Wayne Allard, told the *Washington Post,* "It seems like when a woman reports a rape case that the wheels get set in motion that she gets forced out of the Academy. And not always is there a similar thing happening to a man" (Cooperman, 2005).

The 2003 investigation by the Air Force revealed that nearly all of the women who came forward in 2003 to say they were assaulted by fellow cadets in the previous decade alleged that they were punished, ignored, and/or ostracized by the commander when they spoke out.

> This subculture manifested itself through an unhealthy disregard for regulations and the law, including prohibitions regarding alcohol consumption, sexual harassment, and assault, resulting in cadet order and discipline significantly below the level expected at a premier military institution funded at taxpayer expense (Air Force Print News, September 15, 2005).

Twelve percent of the women who graduated from the Air Force Academy in 2003 reported that they were victims of rape or attempted rape while at the Academy. Sexual predation was directed mainly toward freshmen and sophomore women who were under 21 and who were blackmailed after accepting alcohol from upper class cadets. Women who complained were generally pushed out of the Academy, ostensibly for alcohol abuse and fraternization—which led to the situation in which the rapes occurred. However, the occurrence of rape at the Academy was not necessarily disproportionate to that found at other colleges and universities (Air Force Print News, 2005).

Beginning in the spring semester of 2003, new leadership at the Academy began making "sweeping changes" to the culture and environment to correct these problems. The commandant of cadets was quoted as saying, "If there is the perception of a problem in the wing, we've tried to take that head on. I will not tolerate retribution against a victim" (USAF Office of Special Investigations, 2004). These reported changes included new sexual assault reporting procedures instituted as part of an "Agenda for Change" program. Victims of sexual assault could have confidential counseling and medical care without triggering the disciplinary process, and military commanders would receive notice of a request for help, *but* not know the identity of the victim (Report of the Panel to Review Sexual Misconduct Allegations at the US. Air Force Academy, 2003).

In a March 26, 2005, memo to the secretary of the Air Force, Peter B. Teets recommended that the commanders at the Academy at the time of the alleged incidents, who were found responsible by the Air Force Inspector General's investigation and a parallel congressional investigation, not be prosecuted. He justified his recommendation with the words, "they had acted in good faith and were not intentionally or willfully derelict in their duties" in dealing with the sexual assault issue.

> Moreover, any mistakes or misjudgments that some of them may have made are mitigated by the complexity of the issues they faced, the necessity of policy tradeoffs and compromises, and the difficulty of measuring program effectiveness. Their record of missed warning signs is disturbing, but these officers acted in good faith to discharge their responsibilities ... by taking bold steps to deter sexual assaults and implement effective reporting procedures (Wikipedia: Air Force Academy Sexual Assault Scandal p. 2).

The memo went to Congress over the Easter weekend when Congress was in recess. Several members did register belated dismay over the document. The Miles Foundation, a group representing victims' rights, expressed concern over the inadequacy of the government's response.

## THE THIRD OF THE MAJOR ACADEMY PROBLEMS—RELIGIOUS INTOLERANCE

On April 28, 2003, the executive director of Americans United for the Separation of Church and State sent a fourteen-page report to Secretary of Defense Donald Rumsfeld that severely criticized the U.S. Air Force Academy for "instances of religious discrimination and the promotion of evangelical Christianity" at the school. The first paragraph of the report addresses the overall severity of the problem, as they saw it.

> We have investigated these complaints and come to the conclusion that the policies and practices constitute egregious, systematic, and legally actionable violations of the Establishment Clause of the First Amendment to the United States Constitution" (April 28, 2005, p. 1).

The report claims to be based upon reports from current and former cadets—with some confirmation from Academy faculty and administration, members of the chaplain's office—that upper-class cadets frequently pressure cadets to attend chapel and to take religious instruction (April 28, 2005, p. 1).

The fourteen-page report was broken down into sections that addressed Coerced Religious Practices, Pervasiveness of the Problem, Official Discrimination against Non-Christians and Nonreligious Cadets, Inadequate Remedial Measures, and Effect on Religious Discrimination at the U.S. Air Force Academy. In each area the report went into very specific detail to amplify the nature and scope of the problem.

Under Coerced Religious Practices, a number of critical incidents were detailed. In the first of these, a Protestant chaplain reportedly exhorted cadets attending chapel one Sunday to return to their housing and proselytize cadets who had not attended the service with the penalty for failure being to "burn in the fires of hell" (p. 9). Outside observers confirmed reports that chaplains regularly encouraged cadets to convert other cadets to evangelical Christianity (p. 2). Another complaint was that there were numerous instances in which prayer was part of mandatory official events at the Academy. A mandatory meeting of all cadets during basic cadet training was opened with a prayer, as were regular meals in the cadet dining room, awards ceremonies, and mandatory military-event training dinners.

Other forms of coercion in the report included a number of faculty members who introduced themselves to their classes as born-again Christians and who encouraged their students to become born again during the semester. In one instance, an instructor reportedly ordered students to pray before they were permitted to begin the final examination for the course. In another example, the Academy newspaper published 2003 Christmas greetings with three hundred names listed from various academic departments. These individuals declared their joint "belief that Jesus Christ is the only real hope for the world—there is salvation in no one else" (p. 4). The names included six tenured academic department heads, nine permanent professors, the then-dean of the faculty, the current dean of the faculty, the vice-dean of the faculty, the Academy's director of athletics, the Academy's head football coach, and other members of the faculty and staff.

In another example, the office of cadet chaplains sponsored a Christian-themed program related to *The Passion of the Christ* by placing a sign on each plate in the cadet dining hall indicating that "This is an officially sponsored U.S. Air Force Academy event." There were numerous reports of non-Christian cadets being subjected to harassment by upper class cadets, who often used religious epithets.

Under Pervasiveness of the Problem, it was noted that "Violations . . . are not merely aberrant acts by a few rogue individuals, but instead are reflections of systematic and pervasive religious bias and intolerance at the highest levels of the command structure" (p. 7). In the report, these general allegations were followed by specific examples including

- a number of incidents in which the Commandant of Cadets officially endorsed evangelical Christianity—his own faith—on one occasion, he wrote that cadets "are first accountable to God" (p. 7);
- the Commandant of Cadets instructing cadets that whenever he used the phrase "Airpower," they should respond with "Rock, Sir!"—invoking the parable from Matthew 7:24-29; Luke 6:46-49 (p. 6);

- that faculty and staff also contributed though such widespread practices as faculty proselytizing in the classroom and directives from Academy chaplains to proselytize other cadets (p. 7); and
- the conduct of the Head Football Coach, which included the placing of a large banner in the locker room that read "I am a Christian first and last. I am a member of team Jesus Christ!" (p. 8). Other than one minor counseling session, the coach has never been disciplined.

Under Official Discrimination Against Non-Christian and Nonreligious Cadets, the report detailed a number of problem areas. First, it mentioned the situation where Christian cadets were given "non-chargeable" passes to attend religious services or religious study sessions. These passes were not counted against the cadet's leave time. However, cadets who celebrate the Sabbath on other days of the week are not able to obtain such passes. There were reports of Saturday Sabbath worshipers who were denied passes due to mandatory attendance at football games, parades, etc. To make the situation a bit more binding, the Academy makes it a practice never to schedule events on Sundays due to potential conflict with Christian worship services (p. 9).

Moreover, the report states that Academy officials have discriminated against nonreligious students by denying them privileges that are routinely available to religious cadets. One example specifically mentioned was the Academy Commandant authorizing cadets to hang crosses and other religious symbols in their dorm rooms, while Academy regulations specifically prohibit such a display (p. 9). When one atheist cadet complained to the Academy's MEO office (similar to the EEO office in other organizations), the officer in charge first denied his complaint and then attempted to convince him to become a Catholic (p. 10).

## THE AIR FORCE RESPONSE

The response from the Air Force was seemingly of substance. First, the acting secretary of the Air Force directed the establishment of a cross-functional team to examine the issue of the religious climate at the Air Force Academy. Included in the composition of the team was Rabbi Arnold Resnicoff (only recently appointed as special assistant to the secretary of the Air Force for Values and Vision to Air Force Leadership) and Ms. Shirley A. Martinez, deputy assistant secretary of the Air Force for Equal Opportunity.

In the Executive Summary section of the final report, there is the statement that "The HQ USAF team found a religious climate that does not involve overt religious discrimination, but a failure to fully accommodate all members' needs and a lack of awareness over where the line is drawn between permissible and impermissible expressions of belief." In an attempt to describe just how limited the problem was, the Air Force report attempted to minimize the fifty-five complaints, which formed the basis of the earlier report by the Americans United for Separation of Church and State, with the statement that they were "in reality a collection of observations and events reported by about thirteen people, and purported to have taken place over a four-year period" (U.S. Air Force News Service Press Release, May 4, 2005).

The official Air Force investigation produced nine findings, which it documented with examples based on interviews and surveys from various constituencies at the Academy.

### Finding #1.

"... there was a perception of religious intolerance among some at the Academy." This was identified through surveys of cadets, faculty, and administrators.

### Finding #2.

Although there are standing DOD, Air Force, and Academy policies regarding religious accommodation, religious discrimination, and members' rights of expression, the report claims there, "is no guidance indicating the specific appropriate parameters for either the free exercise or the establishment of religion." It goes on to say, "....there are no relevant materials on culture and religion in the curriculum for new Air Force commanders".

### Finding #3.

Although the Academy had initiated a new program to enhance the climate of respect for individuals or different belief systems, the program is "not adequate, by itself, to address the issue of religious respect for the Academy community."

### Finding #4.

Cadets, faculty, and staff expressed concern about inappropriate bias toward a predominant religion and a perception of intolerance of other views. These concerns were focused in the following six examples:

- Senior faculty and staff regularly made public expressions of faith that others believed to be "inappropriately influential or coercive." As a result, some (cadets, faculty, and staff) expressed concern about the impact of religious affiliation on their career advancement. These included mandatory prayers at official functions and in sports locker rooms. A number of faculty members and coaches considered it their duty to profess their faith and to discuss it in their classrooms "in furtherance of developing cadet's spirituality" (p.36).

- A number of cadets used printed flyers and the cafeteria public announcement system to advertise "religious events."

- Some cadets have experienced religious slurs and disparaging remarks from other cadets.

- Some faculty and staff paid for their names to be included on a holiday announcement with an overtly Christian message in the campus newspaper.

- The commandant of cadets, at a voluntary Christian retreat, led cadets in a "challenge and response cheer" regarding Jesus. He later led a group of mixed-faith cadets in the same cheer. Some found it to be offensive.

- The head football coach at the Academy placed a banner on the wall of the team locker room with an overtly Christian message. Some cadets, faculty, and staff found this to be inappropriate.

**Finding #5.**

Internal control mechanisms to address cadet and staff complaints and assess trends were functioning, but not thoroughly integrated into Academy life. Cadets seemed unclear on when or how to use them.

**Finding #6.**

The Academy "does not give appropriate consideration to the diverse religious practices of cadets of minority faiths." This heightens the perception that "individuals not of the Christian faith are not being treated fairly."

**Finding #7.**

The process of granting religious accommodation requests to cadets is not standardized across the Academy.

**Finding #8.**

Kosher meals are not always available to Jewish cadets as part of their religious observance.

**Finding #9.**

The Academy's chaplain's office sponsors programs for religious education for eighteen groups that meet on Monday evenings. Many of these are conducted by outsiders who are given security badges to get on base. Some cadets, faculty, and staff expressed concern that this unlimited access to cadets "could be perceived as an institutional bias towards religious groups" (Headquarters, U.S Air Force, 2005).

## RECOMMENDATIONS

The official Air Force report recommended the following as remedies to the religious intolerance allegations and findings:

1. A policy should be developed regarding religious expression. It should provide specific guidelines to those who must exercise judgment in the area of religious expression.
2. The organization should "reemphasize policy. . . . regarding appropriate endorsement and advertising of. . . . . groups of which Air Force members may be part."
3. The organization should "reemphasize policy . . . . regarding oversight of unofficial groups that operate on Air Force bases and have access to Air Force personnel."
4. The organization will "reemphasize the requirement. . . . to address issues of religious accommodation. . . .when planning, scheduling, and preparing for operations."
5. The organization will develop a policy "that integrates cultural awareness and respect. . . . to . . . .operating Air Force units at home or deployed."
6. The organization will "expand its character development program that promotes increased awareness of and respect for diverse cultures and beliefs"[2] throughout the Academy's curriculum.
7. The organization must ensure a single point of contact "for determining what statutorily established complaint mechanism is appropriate for"[3] complaints of this nature.

8. The organization will continue its use of "internal controls to assess climate and implement corrective action."
9. The organization will "create opportunities for cadets to discuss and learn about issues of religion and spirituality."

## CONCLUSION

The case presents, via a chronology of recent events at the U.S. Air Force Academy, a series of three problems that have been reported in the media. The factual presentation is a function of research exploring a number of sources, including media reports, press statements, reports from private organizations, and official U.S. government reports. In addition, the case contains an appropriate amount of topical cultural organizational development research that is pertinent to this and many organizations being analyzed.

## DISCUSSION QUESTIONS

1. Describe the culture of the Air Force Academy as presented in this case in terms of its similarity and differences to other academic institutions.

2. List the management and organizational forces that contribute to resistance to change at the Air Force Academy.

3. Are the three major problems in this case—the 1993 sexual assaults, the 2003 sexual assaults, and the 2005 religious intolerance—related in any way? If so, how?

4. Evaluate the changes that the Academy made after the 1993 sexual assault scandal. Explain the reasons for your evaluation.

5. Evaluate the changes that the Academy made after the 2003 sexual assault scandal. Explain the reasons for your evaluation.

6. Evaluate the effectiveness of the changes made after the 2005 religious intolerance complaints. Explain the reasons for your evaluation.

7. Given the unique military culture of this organization, what recommendations would you suggest at this point in time?

---

*Writing Assignment*

Assume that you are a diversity consultant hired by the Air Force to make recommendations for preventing future sexual harassment and religious intolerance problems. Keeping in mind the military culture, what recommendations would you suggest at this time? Provide a justification for your suggestions.

## BIBLIOGRAPHY

Air Force Print News. (September 15, 2005). Officials release academy sexual-assault I.G. reports. (www.af.mil/news/story-print.asp?ID=123009362

Americans for the Separation of Church and State. (April, 2005). *Report of Americans for Separation of Church and State on Religious Coercion and Endorsement of Religion in the United States Air Force Academy.*

Baldwin, C. C. (April 29, 2005). *A Rich Heritage of Religious Freedom and Respect.* Washington: Air Force Print News.

Cooperman, A. (May 4, 2005). *Air Force Announces Task Force.* Washington Post: p. A03.

DOD Press Release. (April 28, 2005). *Watchdog Group Asks Rumsfeld, Air Force Officials, to Correct Problems.* Washington.

Dominquez, M. (June 22, 2005). *U. S. Air Force Report on the Religious Climate at the U.S. Air Force Academy.* (www.defenselink.mil/transcripts/2005/tr20050622-3104.html)

Feldman, N. (2005). *Divided by God: America's Church-State Problem-And What We Should Do About It.* New York, NY: Farrar, Straus, & Giroux.

Gentile, M. (April 29, 2005). *Air Force Focuses on Religious Respect.* Washington: Air Force Print News.

Headquarters, United States Air Force. (June, 2005). *The Report of the Headquarters Review Group Concerning the Religious Climate at the U.S. Air Force Academy.* Washington.

Hofstede, G . (n.d). A summary about my ideas about national culture differences. http://feweb.uvt.nl/center/hofstede/page3.htm

Lopez, C. T. (June 8, 2005). *Air Force Appoints Task Force to Address Religious Climate At the United States Air Force Academy.* Washington: Air Force Print News.

Lopez, C. T. (June 22, 2005). *Report: Academy Grapples with Religion in the Public Forum.* Washington: Air Force Print News.

Lopez, C. T. (June 27, 2005). *Air Force Advisor Chosen for Values, Vision.* Washington: Air Force Print News.

Lumpkin, J. J. (June 23, 2005). *Intolerance at the Air Force Academy.* Boston: Boston Globe Newspaper.

Mount, M. (May 5, 2005). *Air Force Probes Religious Bias Charges at Academy.* Washington: CNN Washington Bureau.

Report of the Panel to Review Sexual Misconduct Allegations at the US. Air Force Academy. (Sept 23, 2003). (Fowler Report) http://www.defenselink.mil/news/sep2003/d20030922usafareport.pdf

United States Air Force Academy, Public Affairs Office. (June, 2005). *U.S. Air Force Fact Sheet, United States Air Force Academy,* p. 3.

United States Air Force Office of Special Investigations. (September, 2004). *Report on Sexual Assault Allegations.* Washington.

U.S. Air Force News Service Press Release. (April 4, 2005). *Air Force Appoints Task Force to Address Religious Climate at the United States Air Force Academy.* Washington.

Wikipedia Article. (June, 2005). *Air Force Academy Sexual Assault Scandal* http://en.wikipedia.org/wiki/united_states_air_force_academy

Zeigler, S. & Gunderson, G. (2005). MOVING BEYOND G.I. JANE, *Women and the U.S. Military.* Lanham, Md.: University Press of America, Inc.

---

**Diversity on the Web**

Read the article "Naval Academy Combats Sexual Harassment" found on the following Web site.

What are the similarities and differences between what happened at the Air Force Academy in this case and the Naval Academy in this article in terms of sexual harassment issues?

http://www.military.com/NewsContent/0,13319,139837,00html?ESRC=eb.nl

# Fairfax Metropolitan Hospital: The Candidate

## M. June Allard

*Assumption College*
*Worcester State College Professor Emerita*

Fairfax Metropolitan Hospital is a moderately sized teaching hospital committed to quality care from a qualified staff. The hospital currently suffers from a lack of diversity among its staff, however—a glaring fault in nearly every unit at the hospital and one pointed out by several accrediting agencies. The hospital now seeks to develop a more diversified staff, which they define as one representing the racial/ethnic diversity of their community. In addition to diversifying, there is an urgent need to modernize the nursing department, as its outdated procedures and inefficient practices concern accreditors. Compounding the hospital's concerns is the recent retirement of the director of nursing—just as another nursing accreditation visit looms on the horizon.

## THE INTERVIEW

HR director Jorge Hansen listens as the search committee discusses a candidate they have just interviewed for the director of nursing position. The candidate is Dr. Saryn Soysa, a heavyset, pleasant young woman. Although she is very much overweight, she looks even younger than her 32 years. Originally from Sri Lanka, she has been educated in U.S. universities and is now a U.S. citizen.

Dr. Soysa's credentials are truly outstanding. She took advanced exams, graduated early from college *summa cum laude,* and completed advanced graduate work by studying full time on national and international fellowships. With a doctorate from a prestigious U.S. graduate school, this articulate young woman has already won several research grants as well as a number of awards and honors. Her work experience is appropriate for the director of nursing position, and her references laud not only her skills, but also her personality and sense of responsibility. Her credentials are superb and by far the best of all the candidates under consideration.

As the HR manager listens, themes emerge from the committee's discussion of Dr. Soysa. Typical of the comments he hears are the following:

"I am concerned about her health, given that she is so overweight."

"Did you notice *how much* she ate at lunch?!"

"It's important that we present a good public appearance . . ."

"This job involves a lot of public relations; the director has a lot of public exposure."

"Too bad our benefits don't include fitness clubs or Weight Watchers!"

"I just don't know about her . . ."

"She is qualified, but . . ."

"And she is so much younger than the other directors! Do you think she is too young to fit with them?

"Experienced nurses might not accept her . . ."

"I just don't know if she would fit well with our organization."

Someone suggests that maybe they should select one of the male candidates, since there are few male nurses in the unit and the hospital has never had a male in the nursing director's position. Someone else tentatively suggests that maybe the search should be reopened.

As the committee continues its discussion, the HR director is aware that no one is arguing for any other candidate in particular. There seems to be implicit acceptance that Saryn Soysa is by far the best qualified; easily head and shoulders above all the other candidates.

Their conversation, however, reflects reservations tinged with some prejudices. Jorge knows that the search team is conscious of its charge to diversify the nursing unit and he thinks that their comments are not masking ethnic or cultural prejudice, but rather they reflect underlying disapproval of Saryn's *weight and youth*.

Jorge has another consideration also. He is aware that his supervisor, the hospital CEO, is on shaky ground with the board of directors, and he suspects that she may think it is too risky to hire someone so young for such an important post. The board might well question her judgment in approving such a hire.

In summary, while there is universal agreement that Dr. Soysa is exceptionally qualified and the hospital really needs her expertise to modernize the nursing department, the search committee is clearly uncomfortable with her weight. They also seem to be uncomfortable with her youth although they avoid making many direct references to it. The CEO could likely be leery of her weight as well as her youth.

## THE HR MANAGER'S ETHICAL DILEMMA

Jorge ponders the situation; the final decision is his. Should he yield to the committee's reservations by hiring a less qualified candidate? Would the CEO be happy with this decision? Should he consider reopening the search even though it is extremely unlikely to yield someone so well qualified again? Would either of these alternatives be the best *ethical* decision for the hospital? Would either be the best *business* decision?

On the other hand, should Jorge ignore committee reservations and hire Saryn Soysa? If he does, how should he explain his decision to the committee and to his boss, the CEO? Would this be the best *ethical* decision for the hospital? The best *business* decision?

# DISCUSSION QUESTIONS

1. Generate a list of possible actions the HR manager might take.

2. Which action(s) would you suggest as the most appropriate for the HR manager? Why?

3. Are there legal issues here? Explain. (Refer to *Appearance and Weight Inclusion Issues in the Workplace* in this text.)

4. If Jorge hires Saryn, what message is he sending to the hospital staff? If he doesn't hire her, what message is he sending?

5. If Jorge hires Saryn, what problems is she likely to face? What problems will Jorge likely face?

6. What resources does Saryn have for dealing with the problems? What resources does Jorge have for dealing with the problems?

---

## Diversity on the Web

### Social Costs

There are considerable social costs including stigma, prejudice, and discrimination for those who are obese.

1. Research these costs noting the interrelationships of obesity, gender, age, race, and social class.

2. What impact are they having on Saryn right now?

3. If she is hired, how might they affect her in the future?

    http://www.obesityresearch.org     [2001, v.9, p.788]

    http://www.nytimes.com     [click: a) December 2, 2006 b) Business c) Darlin, Damon]

4. This case primarily involves the factors of weight and youth. Go to the following Web site and take the IAT test for weight ('Fat-Thin'). Also, take the IAT test for Age (Young-Old) and compare the two results.

5. There are those who feel that the bias against weight is stronger than the bias against race. Take the IAT test for race and the one for skin tone and compare these results against those from your tests for weight and age.

    https://implicit.harvard.edu/implicit

# Evaluating Diversity and Inclusion in the Real World: Conducting a Diversity Audit

Carol P. Harvey

*Assumption College*

**S**ince organizational change with the goal of an inclusive workplace is the theme for this text, the diversity audit is designed to be a capstone assignment that measures where an organization is in terms of its change efforts. Diversity audits are evaluations based on qualitative and quantitative information about the status of diversity within the organization. Today, many organizations conduct audits for various reasons, such as determining the effectiveness of diversity recruiting and retention efforts, measuring the value of diversity training, and surveying workers about the success of diversity initiatives, such as supplier programs and diversity councils. These audits reveal whether a gap exists between what is being done and what the organization should do in terms of diversity, and are used as a basis for action planning.

Although this assignment is not as involved as a real corporate internal diversity audit, the **content** is designed to provide students with an opportunity to visit a real organization and to gather enough information to evaluate its progress in terms of its diversity initiatives. In addition to applying material from the course, this project requires students to **process** the experience of working on a project team where they can learn to deal with the diversity of that group and develop ways to manage that diversity productively. While the team should make recommendations for improving diversity at this organization in the paper and presentation, because of possible legal ramifications, it is **not** their role to act as actual consultants.

Dividing up the work equitably and preparing the criteria and questions for the interview are part of the assignment. Do not expect your instructor to do this for the group. It is important that the group follow these steps in order.

# INSTRUCTIONS

After your instructor forms groups of 4 to 5 students, it is important to follow these steps, in order:

1. **Find an Organization that is Willing to Work with Your Group.**
   The group should meet early in the semester to brainstorm possible organizations that might be willing to participate in this project. As always, it may be easier to gain access if a group member already has an established relationship with an organization such as an internship placement, a job there, or a family member who is employed there. Notice how these connections illustrate an example of privilege. Groups should always have another alternative organization in mind just in case the first choice does not work out. Some companies may refuse because they are afraid of what students may find, are currently involved in a lawsuit, etc. Very early in the semester make contact with someone in the organization. Explain the assignment for what it is: an opportunity for students to learn firsthand how a real organization deals with diversity issues on a daily basis.

   The group needs to be realistic about this field assignment. Sometimes small companies of less than 300 employees pose difficulties because of their limited financial and human resources. In contrast, at large *FORTUNE* 500 companies, it may be difficult to find the right contacts. Some organizations may refuse to cooperate because they are afraid of what the team may learn. Even organizations that are willing to cooperate may find it difficult to schedule meeting times that work for students. So, it is imperative that the team line up both a first choice and at least one backup choice for this project and begin the process early in the semester in case the group encounters difficulties.

2. **Conduct Secondary Research.**
   Secondary research resources are materials gathered for another reason. *Internal* examples include annual reports (a good source of mission and value statements), press releases, employee handbooks, and any other materials that the organization can provide. Explain to your contact person that the group would like to be as knowledgeable as possible about the organization to maximize the time on the visit. So any material that can be sent and read by the group *before* the visit will help the group to prepare. Remember that researching an organization's Web site is a good way to begin and can offer useful information, but it is only the public face that the organization chooses to present.

   Students should also conduct thorough *external* secondary research on their organization for additional material. Utilizing various library databases, students may discover very useful information. For example, small local companies are often the subjects of newspaper articles that can be found in newspaper databases. Larger companies may have been involved in discrimination lawsuits that are detailed in legal databases, and students are not apt to be told about these on visits.

3. **Preparing to Visit the Organization.**
   Make an appointment to interview *at least* three company representatives, managers and/or employees. If you can interview people from different functions and areas and levels (human resources, training, managers, and hourly employees), it will provide different perspectives and richer data. Although all team members

do not need to go on the interview, at least two or three should participate to min-imize bias. Because many organizations are reluctant to let students tape-record interviews, it is more realistic to be prepared to take notes. Of course, multiple visits would probably provide richer data, and some organizations will give students the time for this, but many will not.

When making an appointment, it can be helpful to arrange for a tour of the organization. Student groups may discover interesting observations that contrast with the information that they will be given. For example, one student group visiting a medium-sized manufacturing plant observed that the entire manufacturing workforce was composed of Asian women. They later learned that one of the top managers believed that Asian women had small hands that made assembling electrical components easier. So he instructed his supervisors to hire only Asian women in the assembly area. Job applications from all others were immediately discarded.

Before visiting the organization, the whole group should meet to work on three items:

1. Establishing criteria (i.e., standards) for a diverse organization,
2. Preparing a list of thoughtful questions about diversity that the group will explore on the visit(s), and
3. Reviewing the semester's readings for ideas about how theory may apply to this organization. If the team has gathered, read, and thoroughly discussed the secondary data, it will help the group to accomplish these tasks more effectively and efficiently.

Examples of possible criteria that can be considered and then evaluated include, but are not limited to, topics discussed throughout the semester such as the following:

- Support for diversity from top management

- Managers held accountable for hiring, coaching and promoting diverse employees

- Diversity included in the organization's mission and/or value statements and in the organization's planning process

- Representation of diverse people (race, gender, age, ethnicity, physical and mental challenges, etc.) in all levels of the organization and the board and in advertising and publications

- Human capital programs that aid in the recruitment, support, and retention of a diverse workforce, such as special recruiting efforts, flexible work arrangements for parents and/or older workers, employee resource groups, mentoring programs, partner benefits, flexible holiday policies, etc.

- Effective diversity training that is ongoing, required for all levels of employees, and routinely updated and assessed for effectiveness

- Supplier diversity programs

- Corporate social responsibility programs that contribute resources people, financial resources, etc., to a range of causes that benefit diversity groups of people

- Evidence that the organization is inclusive, i.e., diversity is connected to the main mission of the organization

Remember that the group's criteria for what would make an inclusive diverse workplace must be tailored to the mission, size, resources, location, etc., of the organization selected. For example, a nonprofit hospital located in a very diverse community will be very different from a FORTUNE 500 company with a headquarters in New York City and branches located in many countries. Consult Table 1 in Bourne's article on "The Inclusion Breakthrough…" under "The New Baseline" for additional ideas in developing your criteria for a diverse organization.

4. **Visiting the Organization/Conducting Primary Research.**
   Make an appointment that is convenient for your contact. Dress professionally; be on time, polite, and respectful of your contact's time constraints. If the group is thoroughly prepared and is knowledgeable about the organization, it will show. Occasionally, student teams are asked that the name of the company be kept confidential. If this issue comes up, it is important that you be honest. The teacher will have to know the true identity of the organization to assess the team's work. However, a fictitious name can be used for the paper and class presentation.

   Try to gather additional information through observation. Be sure to pay attention to "subtle" cues of inclusion or lack of inclusion. (i.e., is there evidence that they really do what they say they do?). One helpful way to do this is to analyze the organization's culture in terms of Schein's levels of culture (see Box).

---

### LEVELS OF ORGANIZATIONAL CULTURE

| | |
|---|---|
| **Surface Level Artifacts** (visible) | Includes organizational structures, processes, dress, rituals, physical layout, etc. |
| **Values** (espoused & operational) | Espoused values are what the organization says it values in terms of strategies, philosophies, etc., not necessarily what they do, which are operational values |
| **Basic Underlying Assumptions** | Real source of values and behavior; Philosophies that are sometimes unconscious and difficult to change |

Adapted from Schein, E. (1997). *Organizational Culture and Leadership*. San Francisco: Jossey-Bass, p. 16–27.

---

According to Schein, in order to understand organizational culture, one must look at an organization in terms of these three levels. For example, as an outsider, you may see things (artifacts), but not really understand what these things mean, until you know more about the espoused values and the underlying assumptions. This suggests caution in interpreting what you may observe on the site visit. For example, a team visited the corporate headquarters of a large corporation lauded in the business press for its innovative diversity programs and met with the manager in charge of the national program. Her office was small, had no visible secretarial support, was set off by movable partitions and was located in a hallway. The students interpreted her physical layout as meaning that diversity really was an "espoused" (what they said), not an "operational" (what they do) corporate value. In truth, her real office was being renovated!

Sometimes teams discover interesting things on their visits about the racial, ethnic, gender, and age makeup of the various levels and divisions of the workforce. This is very helpful because some organizations may be reluctant to provide concrete numbers on the demographics of their workers. For example, is there signage in Braille, Spanish, or another local popular language? Do all the Asian workers sit together at lunch? Is this organization going beyond what is required by the Americans with Disabilities Act in terms of accessibility? However, as in the previous example, students need to dig deeper into the organizational culture in order to accurately assess the true meanings of what they see.

In another instance, a team was interviewing the manager of a store that is part of a huge national retail chain. He proudly pointed out that his organization makes it a goal to provide jobs to physically challenged workers and even featured physically challenged customers in their advertising campaigns. There was a notice encouraging physically challenged workers to apply for jobs posted in the entrance, etc. However, at this store, the team found that these workers were assigned to work *only* in the stockroom, unseen by the customers. This provides an example of an initiative (revealed through the artifact) that may be supported at corporate level (espoused), but lacks accountability to make it operational at the local level. The manager's basic assumption was that his corporation was not taking this program seriously.

Sometimes student groups can obtain interesting artifacts on the site visit(s) that will be helpful in writing their papers or can be visual aids in class presentations. Teams have returned with both useful and sometimes comical examples of how an organization promotes diversity and inclusion, such as written materials (copies of company newsletters, employee handbooks, and value statements) and artifacts (diversity coffee mugs for every member of the class, pictures of an all-white, middle-aged, male board of directors, and even a beaded diversity key chain). It is part of the learning experience for the group to determine the value of these artifacts to determine if diversity is really valued, i.e., operational, or merely an espoused value at their organization.

5. **Post-Visit Activity.**
   Once the visit is completed, the real work begins. This is the most important part of the process and may require several team meetings. Groups that do well on this assignment take ample time at this stage. The entire group should meet and debrief. In terms of diversity, what did they really see? What does it mean in terms of the organizational culture? What did they learn? How did the visit support or refute what they had learned through their secondary research? What seems contradictory? What evidence is there of true inclusion? How can the theory learned during the semester, help to explain what they know about the organization?

   After thoroughly discussing the data, the group should evaluate their organization *against their established criteria for a diverse organization*. At this point, the group may find that they omitted some factors and may want to add additional criteria.

6. **Written Report (NOTE: Your Instructor May Assign Different Length and Additional Content Requirements).**
   Each team also will prepare a 12- to 14-page paper that explains their findings in detail. The paper should be free from spelling and grammatical errors, cite all

sources and interviews in a bibliography, and contain any additional helpful material in an exhibit section (copies of organizational value statements, relevant press releases, company newsletters, etc.).

The report should detail the strengths and weaknesses of the organization's diversity initiatives and be organized as follows:

- A one-paragraph executive summary

- One page describing the company background (history, size, industry, organizational structure, etc.)

- One to two pages explaining the group's criteria for a diverse organization

- One to two pages describing the visit(s)

- The remainder of the paper should focus on evaluating the organization's efforts in terms of the diversity concepts covered in this course, particularly in Section III of this text. (i.e., Where is this organization in terms of Thomas and Ely's paradigms? In which of the four phases detailed in "The Inclusion Breakthrough ..." article is this organization in and why? What evidence is there of a business case for diversity in this organization?)

- A conclusion with the team's recommendations for change and a team grade (A, A−, B+, B, B−, etc.) for this organization's diversity and inclusion efforts.

- Bibliography, exhibits, etc.

7. **Presentation.**
The variety of student projects and the lessons about diversity management should be shared with the rest of the class. It is particularly interesting to see the different approaches and contrasts of the organizations. Each team of students should make a class presentation that details the results of their diversity audit.

At a minimum, the presentation should include a short company background, a list of the group's criteria for a diverse organization, anything particularly interesting learned from the visit(s), and an explanation of the group's evaluation of their organization, linked to the textual theory, in terms of how it attempts to manage diversity and inclusion.

It is expected that the group will use visual material (PowerPoint slides, handouts, material supplied by the organization, etc.), rehearse their presentations so that individual speakers do not repeat each other's material, not exceed the time limits set by the instructor, and be prepared to answer questions from the class.

At the conclusion of the talk, the group, *without revealing the grade that they assigned to the organization,* should ask for a show of hands from the class members as to what letter grade from A to F should be assigned to this organization. Then, they can reveal what grade the group gave the company for their diversity efforts and the rationale behind the decision.

## BIBLIOGRAPHY

Schein, E. (1997). *Organizational culture and leadership.* (San Francisco: Jossey-Bass), 16–27

## *Writing Assignment*

**Assessing Group Diversity, Process, and Conflict Resolution**

During the completion of this group project, you have had the opportunity to interact with students who may be different from you in some less visible ways. In addition to visible social identity group differences, such as race, and gender, often, differences in terms of personality, time management, leadership styles, values, etc., can cause conflict in terms of the quality, satisfaction, and completion of group projects, both in classes and in the workplace. Since you are finishing a course on "diversity" management, this is a good time to assess the issues of productivity, individual difference, and conflict resolution in terms of this work group.

Using the project journal that you have kept during the semester, write a 4–5 page paper that analyzes the group performance in terms of the group *process,* i.e., how effectively this group worked together. In your paper, be sure to answer the following questions, but do **NOT** use any actual names of group members:

- What were the primary differences in terms of working style that helped or hindered this group from accomplishing their objectives for this project?
- How did the group effectively or ineffectively deal with these differences?
- Did someone assume a leadership role? Was the leadership style effective or ineffective? Why?
- If there were conflicts or conflict avoidance in this group, apply Parker's article, "The Emotional Connection of Distinguishing Differences and Conflict" to evaluate the resolution or lack of resolution of the conflicts.
- In retrospect what could the group have done differently to produce a more effective project? What could the group have done differently to do it more efficiently?
- From this assignment what have you learned about diversity that can be applied to productively managing the differences that are "invisible" in the workplace?

### Diversity on the Web

**Evaluating Organizational Commitment to Diversity by Auditing Web Sites**

In the twenty-first century, Web sites are an important channel of communication between organizations and their external stakeholders. If an organization is serious about its commitment to diversity, one would expect that this would be reflected in the design, content and graphics, of the Web site. Potential employees, customers, suppliers, etc., often turn first to a Web site before initiating interaction with an organization. If diversity is really integral to the mission and values of an organization, information on diversity should be easily accessible, informative, and well integrated into the Web site.

Your instructor will select an industry such as health care, hospitality, manufacturing government, education, sports, etc., or specific Web sites that members of the class will use for this assignment. Then prepare a report on the following

1. Evaluate how *accessible* diversity related material is on this Web site. Is there a direct link from the home page? What type of results does entering the term "diversity" in a search box yield? Or, do you have to explore on your own? Sometimes searching under "careers" or "press releases" will produce some diversity related results. On some Web sites, students will have to explore deeply into Web pages to find material related to diversity. What does this say about the organization's commitment to diversity?

2. Evaluate the *usefulness* of the diversity information to potential employees, customers and suppliers. Is the diversity material related to the organization's business case for diversity, core values, mission, etc., the way that the organization does business? How current is the diversity-related material? For a good example explore Hewlett Packard's Web site at

   http://www.hp.com/hpinfo/abouthp/diversity/

3. Evaluate the *appropriateness* of the *photographs and graphic material* that relates to diversity. Some Web sites will feature photographs of diverse employees and customers, yet not link this material to the verbal content. Some reuse the same pictures on different pages, etc. On the Hewlett Packard Web site, notice the photos they use and the diversity value chain graphic available at

   http://www.hp.com/hpinfo/abouthp/diversity/value.html

4. Using the Web site that you were assigned for this project, assume that you are a) a potential employee, b) a potential customer and c) a potential supplier or subcontractor. What perceptions might you have about this organization's commitment to diversity based solely on the Web site? Looking at this Web site, do you think that it encourages or discourages diverse employees to apply for jobs in this organization? Why or why not?

5. What internal management issues can affect the prominence that diversity gets or doesn't get on an organization's Web site?

6. If students report their findings to the class, they can briefly demonstrate the best and worst features of the Web sites and the following question may then be used for class discussion:

   Assume that you are a (female, over 55, racial minority, person with a physical challenge, gay or lesbian, etc.) job applicant and you have read ads for job openings for which you are fully qualified in all of the companies presented in class. What perceptions might you have of each company before you even walk in the door? Would you still apply? Why or why not?

# Resources for Teaching and Learning About Diversity

## PRE AND POST COURSE ASSESSMENT TOOLS

In this section, there are pre and post course assessment options that will help the student and the instructor to assess what has been learned during this course. Completing these forms will help to measure what the class has learned during the semester. In addition, these assessments assist the instructor in measuring how well course goals were accomplished as well as serving as tools for deciding what changes need to be made in preparing future classes.

## FILM RESOURCES

"Seeing and Valuing Diversity Issues Through Film", provides a comprehensive guide to the use of popular films to illustrate diversity concepts. The article provides specific suggestions and discussion questions for the use of film scenes that correspond to the previous three sections of this text.

# Pre-Course Diversity Assessment

### M. June Allard

*Assumption College*
*Worcester State College, Professor Emerita*

This exercise examines how you view your understanding of diversity concepts. It is not an evaluation of you or your knowledge—your ratings are not measured against any standard or criterion. This is an informative exercise only.

_____          _____
Mother's Maiden Name                                     Date

# DIVERSITY CONCEPTS

Please think about what you know about diversity and indicate the extent of your current knowledge and skill by circling one of the numbers to the right of each concept.

## Diversity Concepts

| | No Skill/ Knowledge | | | | Expert Skill/ Knowledge |
|---|---|---|---|---|---|

### Section A. Factual Knowledge

- Laws and legal and ethical issues — 1  2  3  4  5

### Section B. Conceptual Knowledge

- Awareness of individual and organizational multiple social identities — 1  2  3  4  5
- The concepts of culture and the range of cultural behaviors and expectations — 1  2  3  4  5
- The formation and impact of stereotypes — 1  2  3  4  5
- Psychological theories of prejudice and discrimination — 1  2  3  4  5
- One's own cultural values, biases, and behaviors and how they may influence one's behavior and interactions in organizations — 1  2  3  4  5
- The changing workplace, including issues and challenges related to managing a diverse workforce — 1  2  3  4  5

### Section C. Procedural and Conditional Knowledge: Skills and Behaviors Used in Appropriate Conditions

- Identifying potential gains from a diverse workforce — 1  2  3  4  5
- Flexibility in management style and competency and skills to fit diverse audiences — 1  2  3  4  5
- Critical analysis (diversity audit) of a Web site or company — 1  2  3  4  5
- International and intercultural communication skills and understanding — 1  2  3  4  5
- Ethical behavior — 1  2  3  4  5
- Demonstrate understanding of the business case for diversity — 1  2  3  4  5

# DIVERSITY LEARNING SUMMARY SHEET

1. **Sections A, B, C.** Enter all of your knowledge ratings in the first column (Pre-course Ratings).

2. **Section B.** Sum your ratings on the six Conceptual Knowledge scales and divide the sum by six to obtain an average. Enter this average in the first column under AVERAGE RATING.

3. **Section C.** Sum your ratings on the six Procedural and Conditional Knowledge scales and divide this sum by six to obtain an average. Enter this average in the first column under AVERAGE RATING.

| Diversity Learning Summary Sheet | Pre-course Ratings | Post-course Ratings | Learning |
|---|---|---|---|
| **Section A. Factual Knowledge** | | | |
| ■ Laws | | | |
| **Section B. Conceptual Knowledge** | | | |
| ■ Social identities | | | |
| ■ Culture | | | |
| ■ Stereotypes | | | |
| ■ Prejudice and discrimination | | | |
| ■ Self | | | |
| ■ Workplace issues | | | |
| ❖ AVERAGE RATING | | | |
| **Section C. Procedural and Conditional Knowledge** | | | |
| ■ Diverse workforce | | | |
| ■ Flexibility | | | |
| ■ Critical analysis | | | |
| ■ Communication | | | |
| ■ Ethics | | | |
| ■ Business case | | | |
| ❖ AVERAGE RATING | | | |

## DISCUSSION QUESTIONS

1. Examining your ratings, how would you describe your diversity knowledge and skills at the beginning of the course? Are they generally high or low? Are there major differences or similarities or patterns among concepts? For which concept is your knowledge or skill the greatest? The least?

2. Examine your AVERAGES. Is your knowledge different for different types of concepts? Does it differ for factual vs. conceptual vs. procedural concepts?

# Pre Course-Checking Perceptions

## Carol P. Harvey
### *Assumption College*

RATE EACH OF THE STATEMENTS BELOW USING THE FOLLOWING SCALE:

| Strongly Agree | Agree | Somewhat Agree | Somewhat Disagree | Strongly Disagree |
|:---:|:---:|:---:|:---:|:---:|
| 1 | 2 | 3 | 4 | 5 |

_____ 1. The best way to deal with my coworkers is to treat them as I would like to be treated.

_____ 2. Because of Affirmative Action and Equal Opportunity laws, minorities and women, etc., actually have an advantage in getting jobs in the American workplace.

_____ 3. One's sexual orientation is a matter of choice.

_____ 4. The most qualified applicant usually gets the job.

_____ 5. Most employees are motivated to work harder and stay at a job by the same things, especially the salary.

_____ 6. Women who are equally qualified earn the same wages as men in the same professions.

_____ 7. It is only a matter of time before minorities and women are as equally represented as white men in the senior management of large corporations.

_____ 8. Integrating diverse workers into today's organizations is relatively easy to do.

_____ 9. I am not prejudiced against any group.

_____ 10. Because of the Americans with Disabilities Act, workers with physical and mental challenges are now employed in the workplace in proportion to their numbers in the population.

TOTAL your score: _____

# Seeing and Valuing Diversity Issues Through Film

### Joseph E. Champoux
*The University of New Mexico*

**F**ilm is a potentially rich resource for seeing and valuing the diversity issues discussed in a college class and in this text. This article details film scenes or entire films that instructors can show during class time or students can view outside of class. These scenes and films review and emphasize various aspects of diversity addressed in this course.

This article has three sections that align with the three previous sections of this book. Each entry describes a film's story line, film scene context, selected scene, and discussion questions to guide viewing the film scene or film. The entries also refer to tables in this article that give complete location information on a DVD or VHS videotape.

## SECTION I. A FRAMEWORK FOR UNDERSTANDING INDIVIDUAL PERSPECTIVES OF DIVERSITY

Individual perspectives on diversity consider such issues as diversity, perception, stereotyping, and diversity conflict. The film scenes discussed in this section give visual anchors for the topics and issues.

Table 1 shows the publication and position information for the film scenes discussed in this section. Use the scene context information and the entries in Table 1 to easily find the film scene on DVD or VHS videotape. Table 2 gives publication information for full length films described in this and other sections.

### Young Frankenstein—

A humorous film scene from *Young Frankenstein* introduces some basic diversity issues. The Monster (Peter Boyle) visits Harold the Blind Man's (Gene Hackman) home. Harold cannot see the Monster, which possibly affects his reactions.

Gene Wilder plays young Dr. Frederick Frankenstein (properly pronounced "FRONK-en-steen"), who works in his grandfather's laboratory. Marty Feldman plays

| TABLE 1   Film Scene Information | |
|---|---|
| *Bend It Like Beckham*<br>Color, 2002, 1 hour, 52 minutes, PG-13<br>Distributor: Twentieth Century Fox<br>Home Entertainment<br>DVD: Chapter 8, No More Football<br>VHS: Start: 0:24:16 — Stop: 0:28:33 — 5 minutes | *The Devil Wears Prada*<br>Color, 2006, 1 hour, 49 minutes, PG-13<br>Distributor: Twentieth Century Fox<br>Home Entertainment<br>DVD: Chapter 2, Appointment with Emily to Chapter 4, Hired (Stop: 00:10:14)<br>VHS: Not available |
| *Crash* (I)<br>Color, 2004, 2 hours, 2 minutes, R<br>Distributor: Lions Gate Home Entertainment<br>DVD: Chapter 2, Blind Fear (00:07:47 — 00:09:43)<br>VHS: Not available | *Door to Door*<br>Color, 2002, 1 hour, 31 minutes, NR<br>Distributor: Warner Home Video<br>DVD: Chapter 17, Salesman of the Year,<br>VHS: Start: 1:01:12 — Stop: 1:04:52 — 4 minutes |
| *Legally Blonde*<br>Color, 2001, 1 hour, 36 minutes, PG-13<br>Distributor: Metro-Goldwyn-Mayer Home Entertainment<br>DVD: Chapter 26, Poor Judgment<br>VHS: Start: 1:20:33 — Stop: 1:23:22 — 3 minutes | *Transamerica*<br>Color, 2005, 1 hour, 44 minutes, R<br>Distributor: Genius Products Inc.<br>DVD: Chapter 11, I Thought Your Parents Were Dead<br>VHS: Not available |
| *Mr. Baseball*<br>Color, 1992, 1 hour, 48 minutes, PG-13<br>Distributor: MCA Universal Home Video<br>DVD: Chapter 10, My Way (Stop: 01:07:04)<br>VHS: Start: 1:06:17 — Stop: 1:13:20 — 7 minutes | *12 Angry Men*<br>Black and White, 1957, 1 hour, 33 minutes, Not rated<br>Distributor: MGM/UA Home Video<br>DVD: Chapter 14, 20/20 Vision<br>VHS: Start: 1:22:11 — Stop: 1:30:08 — 9 minutes |
| *The World's Fastest Indian*<br>Color, 2005, 2 hours, 7 minutes, PG-13<br>Distributor: Magnolia Home Entertainment<br>DVD: Chapter 17 (01:25:12) to Chapter 18 (01:31:13)<br>VHS: Not available | *Young Frankenstein*<br>Black and White, 1974, 1 hour, 42 minutes PG-13<br>Distributor: Twentieth Century Fox Home Entertainment<br>DVD: Chapter 18, The Blind Hermit<br>VHS: Start: 1:07:30 — Stop: 1:12:11 — 6 minutes |

| TABLE 2 Full Length Film Information | |
| --- | --- |
| *Backdraft*<br>Color, 1991, 2 hours, 15 minutes, R<br>Distributor: Universal Home Video, Inc. | *My Big Fat Greek Wedding*<br>Color, 2002, 1 hour, 35 minutes, PG<br>Distributor: Big Wedding, LLC |
| *Crash* (II)<br>Color, 2004, 2 hours, 2 minutes, R<br>Distributor: Lions Gate Home<br>Entertainment | *Radio*<br>Color, 2003, 1 hour, 49 minutes, PG<br>Distributor: Columbia Tristar Home<br>Entertainment |
| *The Emperor's Club*<br>Color, 2002, 1 hour, 49 minutes, PG-13<br>Distributor: Universal Studios | *Remember the Titans*<br>Color, 2000, 1 hour, 54 minutes, PG<br>Distributor: Walt Disney Home Video |
| *Million Dollar Baby*<br>Color, 2004, 2 hours, 12 minutes, PG-13<br>Distributor: Warner Home Video Inc. | |

Igor (properly pronounced "eye-gore"), Dr. Frankenstein's assistant. All 1930s Frankenstein films are the targets of this hilarious spoof.

This scene begins as the camera zooms to Blind Hermit's house and pans to a lighted candle. This scene follows Little Girl's (Anne Beesley) interaction with Monster on a seesaw. He sits on it and throws her into her bedroom. The scene ends with Monster's finger on fire as he crashes through the door. Blind Hermit asks him to wait because he was intending to make espresso. A black screen closes the scene.

Think of the following questions while viewing this scene:

- Do people's differences affect the interactions of Blind Hermit and Monster? Give some examples from the scene.
- Are there any functional or dysfunctional results of acceptance or rejection of differences in the scene?
- Do you perceive any stereotyping? Explain.

## PERCEPTUAL PROCESSES

Diversity among an organization's members also brings different perceptual processes into social interactions. Some issues worthy of extensive discussion about such diversity effects include selective perception, stereotyping, and perceptual effects on communication. A scene from *The Devil Wears Prada* shows Miranda Priestly's (Meryl Streep) first meeting with applicant Andy Sachs (Anne Hathaway). It is filled with perceptual process moments, such as how Miranda's prior view of proper attire colors her initial acceptance of Andy. *My Big Fat Greek Wedding,* when viewed in its entirety, shows many perceptual process issues that can occur when different cultures collide.

### The Devil Wears Prada—

Cynical, ruthless Miranda Priestly is the world's worst boss. She rules *Runway* magazine, as its demanding editor in chief. Naïve, aspiring journalist Andy Sachs applies for a position as an assistant to Priestly. She does not know Priestly, nor has she ever heard of the magazine. Andy perceives this position as one of many on the way to a journalistic career. Her grueling first days and weeks on Priestly's staff shape Andy in significant ways that forever change her world view. Streep's extraordinary performance leaves a chilling impression of this ruthless manager.

The recommended scenes start with Andy Sachs leaving an elevator. She has arrived at the *Runway* offices for an interview with Miranda Priestly. Andy first meets Priestly's assistant, Emily Charlton (Emily Blunt). The scenes end as Andy starts to leave the building and Emily calls to her in apparent disbelief. The film continues with Andy telling her friends that she got the job.

Reflect on the following questions while viewing these scenes:

- What is Emily's perception of Andy? What does she emphasize in forming her perceptual image?
- What is Miranda Priestley's perception of Andy? What does she emphasize in forming her perceptual image?
- What is Andy's self-perception? Positive? Negative? Why?

### My Big Fat Greek Wedding—

Meet Toula Portokalos (Nia Vardalos), Greek, age 30, attractive, and single. Meet her father Gus Portokalos (Michael Constantine), a Greek man operating Dancing Zorba's, the family restaurant in Chicago. One of his goals is to have Toula marry a Greek man, but Toula has other ideas, such as taking some college classes so she can work in Aunt Voula's (Andrea Martin) travel agency. Along comes Ian Miller (John Corbett), handsome, not Greek, and vegetarian. Eventually, the two families meet with some predictable, but delightful, comic results.

Members of the two families likely have different bases of their perceptions of each other. Think of and review the following questions while watching *My Big Fat Greek Wedding:*

- What is the basis of Gus' perception of Ian at the end of the first family meeting? Does his perception change over time? Why or why not?
- What is the basis of Maria Portokalos' (Lainie Kazan) perception of Ian and his family?
- What is the basis of Aunt Voula's perception of Ian?
- What is the basis of Harriett (Fiona Reid) and Rodney (Bruce Gray) Miller's perception of Toula's large Greek family? Do they change their perception of the family over time? Why or why not?

## DIFFERENCES AND CONFLICT

Workforce diversity creates many chances for conflict to emerge, often triggered by the sharp differences among people and their perspectives. Diversity discussions can include extensive observations on the bases of conflict, conflict episodes, and conflict reduction. The original *12 Angry Men* has a jury deliberation sequence toward the end of the film that shows a positive result of conflict—bringing more information into the discussion. It also shows the various jurors' conflicting reactions and the effects of those reactions on social interactions within the group.

### 12 Angry Men—

Dramatically shows the struggle of 12 jurors trying to reach a verdict in a murder trial. The defendant is a young Hispanic man. Mr. Davis, Juror #8 (Henry Fonda), believes the defendant is innocent from the beginning of deliberations and presses for a not-guilty verdict. The characters played by each actor add to the dynamics of the conflict shown: an impatient baseball fan, Juror #7 (Jack Warden), who has tickets to a game that night; a logical, structured stockbroker, Juror #4 (E. G. Marshall); and Fonda's chief opponent Juror #3 (Lee J. Cobb).

These scenes show the events that precede the jury's final decision. They follow the angry comments by bigoted Juror #10 (Ed Begley). Juror #8 has summarized their situation with nine voting innocent and three voting guilty. These scenes begin with a shot of Juror #4 while Juror #8 says off camera, "Maybe you can tell us." Juror #4 says, "I'll try." The scenes end with Juror #3's angry response to the now 11 innocent and one guilty vote. The film cuts to Juror #8 moving around the jury table to face Juror #3 while saying, "You're alone."

Think about the following questions while viewing this film sequence:

- Various events can start a conflict episode. What was the basis of conflict among the jurors in these scenes?
- How did the jurors reduce their conflict?
- Do you expect this jury to continue in escalating conflict? Why or why not?

## SECTION II. A FRAMEWORK FOR UNDERSTANDING SOCIAL IDENTITY PERSPECTIVES ON DIVERSITY

People have unique personalities that define them as individuals. They can have membership in multiple groups, further adding to their personality complexity. Those groups are defined by the person's sex, age, ethnicity, cultural heritage, sexual orientation, social class, religion, and physical/mental challenges. This section describes film scenes that visually anchor group identity aspects of diversity and intercultural communication. Table 1 has the information needed to find these scenes on a DVD or VHS videotape. Use the table information, the scene description, and the scene context information for each film to locate the recommended scenes.

## INTERCULTURAL COMMUNICATION

People from different cultures present issues about intercultural communication and cultural differences as the basis of diversity in organizations. Miscommunication can easily happen when people from different cultures interact with each other. Some scenes from *Mr. Baseball* show Jack Elliot's (Tom Selleck) visit to Hiroko Uchiama's (Aya Takanashi) traditional Japanese family. Jack makes several cultural errors, leading to humorous negative results.

## Mr. Baseball—

The New York Yankees trade aging baseball player Jack Elliot to the Chunichi Dragons, a Japanese team.[1] This lighthearted comedy traces Jack's bungling entry into Japanese culture. It exposes his cultural misconceptions, which almost cost him everything—including his new girlfriend, Hiroko Uchiyama. After Jack slowly begins to understand Japanese culture and Japanese baseball, his teammates finally accept him. This film shows many examples of Japanese culture, especially its love for baseball.

Unknown to Hiroko's father, she and Jack develop an intimate relationship. Unknown to Jack, Hiroko's father is "The Chief" (Ken Takakura), the Chunichi Dragons' manager. These scenes take place after "The Chief" has removed Jack from a baseball game. It shows Jack dining with Hiroko, her grandmother (Mineko Yorozuya), grandfather (Jun Hamamura), and father. The film continues with a dispute between Jack and Hiroko. Jack also learns from "The Chief" what he must do to succeed on the team.

Keep the following questions in mind while viewing these scenes from *Mr. Baseball:*

- Does Jack Elliot behave as if he had cross-cultural training before arriving in Japan?
- Is he culturally sensitive or insensitive? Why or why not?
- What do you propose that Jack Elliot do for the rest of his time in Japan?

## Bend It Like Beckham—

Jesminder "Jess" Kaur Bhamra (Parminder Nagra), the youngest daughter of orthodox Sikh parents, lives in a middle-class London suburb. She has a secret passion for football (soccer) that outrages her mother (Shaheen Khan), who discovers Jess playing with some young men. A cultural tradition says Jess should marry into an approved family. Instead, Jess pursues football, especially after befriending Juliette ("Jules") Paxton (Keira Knightley). Jess and Jules become teammates on the Harriers, a local team. Her hero is football superstar David Beckham (hence the film's title). Jess's non-traditional behavior blooms into outstanding football talent.

These scenes begin with Jess running onto a grassy area in her football uniform. They follow Jess's successful tryout for the Harriers. They end after Jules turns to leave saying, "Jess, come on. Are you playing?" Tony (Ameet Chana) follows her as Jess looks on. The film continues with a shot of the family home and a commercial aircraft flying overhead.

Use the following questions as guides while watching the *Bend It Like Beckham* scenes:

- What is Jess's mother's view of the proper roles for young Sikh Indian women?
- Does Jess accept those roles? Why or why not?
- What is Jess's father's (Anupam Kher) perception of proper gender roles for Jess?

## Crash (1)—

Several lives intersect over a 36-hour period in Los Angeles, California. A carjacking, sexist police encounters, illegal searches, multiple social class interactions, and racial

---

[1]From Our Feature Presentation: Organizational Behavior 1st edition by CHAMPOUX. 2005. Reprinted with permission of South-Western, a division of Thomson Learning: www.thomsonrights.com. Fax 800 730-2215.

tensions all appear in this highly charged film. Many people interact over the 36 hours, highlighting a Los Angeles reality. Superb acting, writing, direction, and cinematography create an almost unparalleled, gripping experience.

This scene occurs early in the film. It follows the gun-buying interaction involving the gun store owner (Jack McGee), Dorri (Bahar Soomekh), and her father Farhad (Shaun Toub). Anthony (Chris "Ludacris" Bridges) quickly emerges from a restaurant, saying to Peter Waters (Larenz Tate), "Did you see any white people waitin' an hour and 32 minutes for a plate of spaghetti?" This scene ends as Anthony and Peter comment on feeling no fear. The film continues with them drawing guns and stealing the Cabots' (Sandra Bullock and Brendan Fraser) vehicle.

Consider the following questions while watching this scene:

- Carefully note Anthony's description to Peter of their restaurant experience. Do stereotypes appear to affect his reactions to the restaurant event and his perception of the approaching Cabots? If *yes,* which stereotypes did he use?
- Did Jean Cabot react because she was cold or because of the two approaching black men? Note some examples from the scene to support your position.

### The World's Fastest Indian—

Burt Munro (Anthony Hopkins) spent a lifetime restoring his beloved 1920 Indian motorcycle. Now he is ready to make a timing run at Bonneville Salt Flats, Utah. Burt makes the long boat trip from Invercargill, New Zealand to Utah. Against almost impossible odds (especially the officials) and limited budget, Burt sets a speed record that remains a legend.

These scenes begin with a crew pushing the red "Flying Cabaccus" from the inspection and check-in area. Burt and his new acquaintances push his 1920 Indian (#35) into the inspection area. The scenes follow Burt's first meeting with Jim Enz (Christopher Lawford) on the salt flats. These scenes end after an official says he is too old to run his Indian. Burt responds by noting that he feels 18 years old and says to Mike McFarland (Gavin Grozer), another official, "And I give you a run for your money, young fella." The film cuts to Burt checking his motorcycle that is now hitched to his car. Rolly Freed (William Lucking) and Marty Dickerson (Walton Goggins) offer to help.

Think about these questions while watching the scenes from *The World's Fastest Indian:*

- Carefully watch the officials' behavior early in the scenes. Does Burt's age and the age of his motorcycle appear to affect the officials' reactions? Note some specific examples.
- Do the officials dismiss the importance of Burt's desire to make his timing run because of his presumed age? Explain.
- Assume you have not seen this film. What do you expect the officials to decide about Burt making a timing run? Explain your reasoning.

### Transamerica—

Sabrina "Bree" Claire Osbourne (Felicity Huffman) always knew he (she) was not a man, despite having a son from an earlier affair. He (she) undergoes psychological counseling and takes hormonal medications to prepare for sex change surgery. The sudden arrival of her 17-year-old son Toby (Kevin Zegers) severely disrupts his (her) well-laid plans. A road trip from New York to Los Angeles has many revealing moments for both of them. Add an undesirable though memorable visit with Bree's parents in Phoenix, Arizona, where she discovers herself, her son, and her new sexuality.

These scenes follow Sammy Many Goats (Forie Smith) picking them up after the hitchhiker (Grant Monohon) stole Bree's car. Bree and Toby walk toward her parent's home. Sammy drives away. The scenes end as Bree's mother (Fionnula Flanagan) tells Bree's sister Sidney (Carrie Preston) to stop picking on her. The film cuts to a restaurant with the entire family arriving.

Consider the following questions while viewing these scenes:

- Assess the acceptance or rejection of Bree's sexual orientation by each family member: her mother Elizabeth, her father Murray (Burt Young), and her sister Sidney. Give examples from the scenes to support your answers.

### Door to Door—

Bill Porter (William H. Macy) has cerebral palsy, a disease that impairs his physical functioning, but not his mental functioning. Determined to land a sales job, he offers to take the Watkins Company's most undesirable territory. He touched the hearts of many during his daily round of activities—bus drivers, shoe shiners, and the hotel bellman who ties his necktie each day. Bill never gives up. This touching film has many images of a tough, determined spirit. Based on a true story, this film dramatizes Bill Porter's role in selling Watkins products. To see the real Bill Porter and Watkins products, visit www.billporter.com.

This scene begins after Shelly Brady's (Kyra Sedgwick) graduation from Portland State University. It starts with a dark screen, followed by the titling, "November 1989" and "I Love being a Salesman." The scene shows a Watkins Company gathering for Chuck's (Bill Dow) retirement and an award. Bill Porter reports to Chuck. View this scene in two steps.

1. Start the scene as suggested but stop after Peter Schaeffer (David Lewis) pats Chuck on the chest and walks away in disbelief (DVD: Stop: 01:00:11; VHS: Stop: 1:02:11). Consider the first question in the list below.
2. Continue with the scene to its end while thinking about the next two questions in the list below.

The film continues with Bill and Shelly making their deliveries. Shelly lifts a box from her vehicle and hands it to her daughter Michelle (Samantha Cantner).

While viewing this scene from *Door to Door,* assume you have not seen this film and answer the questions below:

- After first meeting Bill, does Peter Schaeffer, his incoming manager, assume Bill can attain high sales performance? Explain.
- At what level would you predict Bill's sales performance, knowing that he has cerebral palsy?
- Do you expect his fellow sales people to support his sales efforts? Why or why not?

## Legally Blonde[2]—

Elle Woods' (Reese Witherspoon) boyfriend, Warner Huntington III (Matthew Davis), wants to go to Harvard Law School instead of keeping their relationship alive. Elle pursues him vigorously by applying to and being accepted to Harvard Law School. This is a charming comedy, dedicated to blonde women everywhere in the world.

These scenes follow the successful use of Elle's hunch about key witness Enrique Salvatore (Greg Serano) in Brooke Windam's (Ali Larter) trial. She enters the law offices area and learns that Professor Callahan (Victor Garber) wants to see her in his office. These scenes end in the elevator as Elle holds her forehead. The film cuts to Elle leaving the elevator in the lobby where she meets Emmett (Luke Wilson) and tells him she is quitting the internship.

Consider the following questions while viewing the *Legally Blonde* scene:

- Does Professor Callahan sexually harass Elle? If *yes,* what is the evidence in these scenes?
- If these scenes show sexual harassment, what type of harassment is it? *Quid pro quo* harassment or hostile environment harassment?
- Did Elle behave appropriately or inappropriately in Professor Callahan's office? Give examples.

# SECTION III. A FRAMEWORK FOR UNDERSTANDING ORGANIZATIONAL DIVERSITY AND INCLUSION

Watch the full-length films described in this section to visually anchor diversity knowledge. The text for each film includes a film description and question-based guides for what the film shows. Each film gives an engaging cinematic experience and has rich visual anchors of diversity issues. Table 2 shows publication information for each film discussed in this section.

## Crash (2): Diversity/Perception/Ethics—

*Crash* shows a 36-hour period in Los Angeles. Multiple social class interactions and racial tensions all appear in this highly charged film.

Think of and review the following questions while watching *Crash:*

- Which diversity dimensions does this film vividly show? Consider all possibilities such as age, gender, social class, race, and the like.
- Does stereotyping appear anywhere in the film? Give examples.
- Is stereotyping a basis for any conflict incidents shown in the film? Note some examples.
- Are there any moments of acceptance of differences in the film? Please explain.

## Million Dollar Baby: Accepting Differences/Valuing Diversity—

Maggie Fitzgerald (Hilary Swank) walks into Frankie Dunn's (Clint Eastwood) gym intending to become a boxer. Frankie does not easily accept the idea of training a

[2]From Our Feature Presentation: Human Resource Management 1st edition by CHAMPOUX. 2007. Reprinted with permission of South-Western, a division of Thomson Learning: www.thomsonrights.com. Fax 800 730-2215.

female fighter. Combined with a long-time estrangement from his daughter, Frankie adjusts slowly to Maggie's aspirations. Scrap (Morgan Freeman), an ex-boxer, works in the gym and knows that Frankie's gruff exterior hides a caring person.

Reflect on the following questions while watching *Million Dollar Baby:*

- Early in the film, Frankie says to Maggie, "I don't train girls." He completely rejects her as a possible boxing trainee. At what point does Frankie begin to accept Maggie? Note examples of acceptance.
- Does Frankie change his training methods because Maggie is female or, does he use the same methods he uses with male boxers?
- Maggie suffers serious spinal injuries during her welterweight title match in Las Vegas, Nevada. Does this result suggest that women should not be allowed to fight? Why or why not?
- Throughout this film, contrast Scrap's behavior with Frankie's behavior toward Maggie. Does Scrap accept female boxers more than Frankie? Why or why not?

### Remember the Titans: Diversity and Performance—

Coach Herman Boone (Denzel Washington) becomes the first black football coach at newly integrated T. C. Williams High School in Alexandria, Virginia, in 1971. This change moves former coach Bill Yoast (Bill Patton) to the role of assistant coach. Conflict between the coaches and players appears early in the season. Based on a true story, this engaging film shows the struggle between black and white coaches and black and white players to build an effective, winning team.

Here are some questions to think about while watching *Remember the Titans:*

- Does the film's portrayal of black-white relationships in 1971 Virginia appear believable to you? Why or why not?
- Have you experienced any similar incidents in your life or in the area where you live? Please note some specific examples.
- Predict some results for intra-team relationships after they leave for camp. Do you expect acceptance of their differences or continued conflict over their differences? Explain.
- Does Coach Boone recognize and use his team's diversity to its advantage? Please note some specific examples from different sections in the film.

### The Emperor's Club: Ethics and Social Responsibility in Organizations—

William Hundert (Kevin Kline), a teacher at Saint Benedict's Academy for Boys, believes in teaching his students about living a principled life. He also wants them to learn his beloved classical literature. New student, young Sedgewick Bell (Emile Hirsch), challenges Hundert's principled ways. Bell's behavior during the seventy-third annual Mr. Julius Caesar Contest causes Hundert to suspect that Bell leads a less than principled life, a suspicion reinforced years later during a repeat of the competition.

The film offers several examples of ethical and unethical behavior. Carefully observe the behavior of the characters noted below while viewing *The Emperor's Club*.

- Does young Sedgewick Bell behave ethically or unethically? Note specific examples.

- Does older Sedgewick Bell (Joel Gretsch) behave ethically or unethically? Note specific examples.
- Does Headmaster Woodbridge (Edward Herrmann) behave ethically or unethically? Note specific examples.
- Does William Hundert behave ethically or unethically? Note specific examples.

### Radio: Mental Ability and Team Work—

Cuba Gooding, Jr., plays James Robert "Radio" Kennedy, a mentally disabled resident of Anderson, South Carolina, in 1976. Based on a true story, Radio becomes a friend of Coach Harold Jones (Ed Harris) and helps inspire the football team and town to a higher behavioral standard. Excellent acting and script sensitively show the difficult, delicate, and sometimes ridiculed behavior of a mentally disabled person. The real James Robert "Radio" Kennedy appears at the end of the film and during the closing credits (DVD Chapter, 28, 26 Years Later; VHS: 1:45:38).

Use the following questions as reflective guides while viewing *Radio:*

- Pause the film at the end of a football practice (DVD Chapter 3, James Robert Kennedy, at 00:07:07; VHS videotape at 0:08:11). Radio has just taken the football that went over the fence. The film continues with Mary Helen (Sara Drew), Coach Jones's daughter, arriving home late. Assess the likely reaction of Coach Jones to Radio and the likely reaction of his team members. Acceptance, rejection, or ridicule? Answers to these questions appear later in the film.
- Coach Jones gives Radio a role during the team's activities while competing and while practicing. Do team members accept or reject Radio? Do townspeople accept or reject Radio? Note examples for each question.
- Johnny Clay (Riley Smith) is the player who tries to retrieve the football from Radio early in the film. He also tricks Radio into going into the girls' locker room later in the film (DVD Chapter 21, The girls' locker room incident; VHS Start 1:12:01 – Stop 1:18:06). Does he eventually accept Radio? Why or why not?
- Despite his mental disability, does Radio positively contribute to team functioning? Note some specific examples.

## SUMMARY

This article described film scenes and entire films that focused on various diversity issues and topics. Each film scene or film offered visual representations of theories, concepts, and discussions that appear in other sections of this book.

# Post-Course Diversity Assessment

M. June Allard

*Assumption College*
*Worcester State College, Professor Emerita*

**T**his exercise examines how you view your understanding of diversity concepts. It is not an evaluation of you or your knowledge—your ratings are not measured against any standard or criterion. This is an informative exercise only.

_____          _____
Mother's Maiden Name                                Date

# DIVERSITY CONCEPTS

Please think about what you know about diversity and indicate the extent of your current knowledge and skill by circling one of the numbers to the right of each concept.

| Diversity Concepts | | | | | |
|---|---|---|---|---|---|
| | *No Skill/ Knowledge* | | | *Expert Skill/ Knowledge* | |

*Section A. Factual Knowledge*

| | | | | | |
|---|---|---|---|---|---|
| ∎ Laws and legal and ethical issues | 1 | 2 | 3 | 4 | 5 |

*Section B. Conceptual Knowledge*

| | | | | | |
|---|---|---|---|---|---|
| ∎ Awareness of individual and organizational multiple social identities | 1 | 2 | 3 | 4 | 5 |
| ∎ The concepts of culture and the range of cultural behaviors and expectations | 1 | 2 | 3 | 4 | 5 |
| ∎ The formation and impact of stereotypes | 1 | 2 | 3 | 4 | 5 |
| ∎ Psychological theories of prejudice and discrimination | 1 | 2 | 3 | 4 | 5 |
| ∎ One's own cultural values, biases, and behaviors and how they may influence one's behavior and interactions in organizations | 1 | 2 | 3 | 4 | 5 |
| ∎ The changing workplace, including issues and challenges related to managing a diverse workforce | 1 | 2 | 3 | 4 | 5 |

*Section C. Procedural and Conditional Knowledge: Skills and Behaviors Used in Appropriate Conditions*

| | | | | | |
|---|---|---|---|---|---|
| ∎ Identifying potential gains from a diverse workforce | 1 | 2 | 3 | 4 | 5 |
| ∎ Flexibility in management style and competency and skills to fit diverse audiences | 1 | 2 | 3 | 4 | 5 |
| ∎ Critical analysis (diversity audit) of a Web site or company | 1 | 2 | 3 | 4 | 5 |
| ∎ International and intercultural communication skills and understanding | 1 | 2 | 3 | 4 | 5 |
| ∎ Ethical behavior | 1 | 2 | 3 | 4 | 5 |
| ∎ Making the business case for diversity | 1 | 2 | 3 | 4 | 5 |

# DIVERSITY LEARNING SUMMARY SHEET

1. **Sections A, B, C.** Enter all of your knowledge ratings in the second column (Post-course Ratings).

2. **Section B.** Sum your ratings on the six Conceptual Knowledge scales and divide the sum by six to obtain an average. Enter this average in the second column under AVERAGE RATING.

3. **Section C.** Sum your ratings on the six Procedural and Conditional Knowledge scales and divide this sum by six to obtain an average. Enter this average in the second column under AVERAGE RATING.

| Diversity Learning Summary Sheet | | | |
|---|---|---|---|
| | *Pre-course Ratings* | *Post-course Ratings* | *Learning* |

**Section A. Factual Knowledge**

- Laws

**Section B. Conceptual Knowledge**

- Social identities

- Culture

- Stereotypes

- Prejudice and discrimination

- Self

- Workplace issues

❖ AVERAGE RATING

**Section C. Procedural and Conditional Knowledge**

- Diverse workforce

- Flexibility

- Critical analysis

- Communication

- Ethics

- Business case

❖ AVERAGE RATING

## DISCUSSION QUESTIONS

1. Examining your ratings and graphs, describe your diversity knowledge and skills at the end of the course, i e., are they generally high or low? Are there major differences or similarities or patterns among concepts?

2. For which concept is your knowledge or skill the greatest? The least?

3. Examining your AVERAGES, is your knowledge different for different types of concepts, i. e., for factual vs. conceptual vs. procedural concepts?

## ADDITIONAL INSTRUCTIONS FOR STUDENTS WHO MADE PRE-COURSE RATINGS
## LEARNING

Compute your learning for each concept by subtracting your pre-course ratings from your post-course ratings and enter the differences in the learning column of the diversity learning summary sheet.

## DISCUSSION QUESTIONS

1. Eamining your Diversity Learning Summary Sheet and graphs, describe your *learning* about diversity.

2. For which concepts is learning the greatest for you? The least for you? Explain.

# Post Course-Checking Perceptions

## Carol P. Harvey
### *Assumption College*

RATE EACH OF THE STATEMENTS BELOW USING THE FOLLOWING SCALE:

| Strongly Agree<br>**1** | Agree<br>**2** | Somewhat Agree<br>**3** | Disagree<br>**4** | Strongly Disagree<br>**5** |
|---|---|---|---|---|

_____ 1. The best way to deal with my coworkers is to treat them as I would like to be treated.

_____ 2. Because of Affirmative Action and Equal Opportunity laws, minorities and women, etc., actually have an advantage in getting jobs in the American workplace.

_____ 3. One's sexual orientation is a matter of choice.

_____ 4. The most qualified applicant usually gets the job.

_____ 5. Most employees are motivated to work harder and stay at a job by the same things, especially the salary.

_____ 6. Women who are equally qualified earn the same wages as men in the same professions.

_____ 7. It is only a matter of time before minorities and women are as equally represented as white men in the senior management of large corporations.

_____ 8. Integrating diverse workers into today's organizations is relatively easy to do.

_____ 9. I am not prejudiced against any group.

_____ 10. Because of the Americans with Disabilities Act, workers with physical and mental challenges are now employed in the workplace in proportion to their numbers in the population.

TOTAL your score: _____

# CONTRIBUTORS

**Jeanne M. Aurelio,** D.B.A., is a professor of Management at Bridgewater State College. She has consulted with numerous corporations and federal agencies on topics including organizational performance, diversity, managerial effectiveness, and performance counseling. Her areas of specialization include organizational culture and leadership.

**Carlo Baldino** is a retired high school English teacher. Carlo has published numerous newspaper articles on race and racism. He was the winner of two New England Press Association Awards for "coverage of a racial or ethnic issue" and "educational reporting."

**Joseph E. Champoux,** PhD, is a Regents Professor of Management at the Robert O. Anderson School of Management of the University of New Mexico. His research activities focus on film as a teaching resource and enhancements for online courses. He has published articles in several scholarly journals, eleven book chapters, and thirty print or electronic books.

**Gina Colavecchio** is employed in the Marketing Department at FirstComp Insurance in Rhode Island. She has a BS from Rhode Island College and an MBA from Assumption College. Her recent projects include the development of a marketing manual, the construction of an online company store, and the development of incentive programs.

**Egidio A. Diodati** is an associate professor of Management at Assumption College. Professor Diodati provides consulting services to corporations in the areas of network communications, market research, marketing, and management.

**Colleen Fahey,** PhD, is an associate professor of Economics at Assumption College. Her research interests include local government finance and structure as well the economic modeling of competition in internet retailing. She has published in journals such as *Social Science Quarterly* and the *Journal of Economics and Business*.

**Steve Farough,** PhD, is an Associate Professor of Sociology at Assumption College, where he teaches social theory and courses on race and gender. His current research is on white masculinities.

**Michael M. Harris,** PhD, is professor of Management, and fellow of the International Business Institute at the University of Missouri–St. Louis. His interests include workplace diversity, human resource management, and international management. He recently edited a book on international human resource management (Erlbaum).

**Diane Holtzman** teaches Business Studies at The Richard Stockton College of New Jersey and Public Relations at Rowan University. Currently she is completing her doctorate in Organizational Leadership at Nova Southeastern University.

**John Howard,** PhD, is professor of American Studies at King's College, University of London. He is the author of *Men Like That: A Southern Queer History* (University of Chicago Press, 1999) and the editor of three other volumes.

**Gerald Hunt,** PhD, is the chair of the Human Resources Management and Organizational Behavior Department in the School of Business at Ryerson University in Toronto, Canada. He teaches in the areas of Organizational Behavior and Industrial Relations. His research focuses on the response of labor unions to a more diverse labor market.

**Evonne Kruger,** PhD, is an associate professor of Business Studies at The Richard Stockton College of New Jersey. A graduate of Temple University, her areas of expertise are strategic management, managerial decision making, and community engagement.

**Richa Kumari** is a management consultant, trainer, and author specializing in leadership, human resource management, and diversity issues. She is coauthor of *Practicing Leadership: Principles and Applications 3rd ed.* (John Wiley & Sons, 2005) and several other publications, including a monthly newspaper column on inclusive leadership.

**Christopher Laib** is the assistant director of the University of Massachusetts Dartmouth Student Activities, Involvement & Leadership Office. He has presented numerous training sessions to student leaders and staff members dealing with diversity, ethics, and organization/team development.

**Deborah Larsen** is a senior vice president for Bank of America in their Central Massachusetts Commercial Banking Group and has more than 20 years of banking experience. She has taught numerous classes for the American Institute of Banking.

**Jeanne M. McNett,** PhD, is a professor at Assumption College in the Business Studies Department. She served on the team that established the first public university for women in Saudi Arabia; has worked with companies such as Mitsubishi, Nippon Express, and Sony; and has published in the area of international management and teaching.

**Joyce McNickles** is an assistant professor of Human Development and Human Services at Anna Maria College. She teaches courses in Social Inequality, Social Work, Sociology, and Multicultural Education. She is currently pursing an EdD in Social Justice.

**Marc S. Mentzer,** PhD, is an associate professor of Industrial Relations and Organizational Behavior at the University of Saskatchewan. His research has appeared in such journals as *Canadian Journal of Administrative Sciences, Canadian Review of Sociology & Anthropology, Organization Studies,* and *Ethnic Groups.*

**M. E. (Pete) Murphy** is an assistant professor of Management at Assumption College. He is a professional engineer and manager with a long career in the international energy industry. He has professional interests in improving applied management skills.

**Carole G. Parker,** PhD, is a retired associate professor of Management from Seton Hill University. She has served on the staff of the Gestalt Institute of Cleveland.

**Asha Rao,** PhD, is an assistant professor of Management at Rutgers University. Her research focuses on issues of cross-cultural conflict and its resolution in joint venture negotiations, multinational management, and domestic diversity.

**Pam Sherer,** PhD, is an associate professor of Management at Providence College. Her research interests include diversity, faculty development practices, collaborative learning, and pedagogy.

**Arthur Shriberg,** EdD, is a professor of Management and Entrepreneurship at Xavier University, and a noted author, newspaper columnist, speaker, and humorist. As a leadership and diversity consultant he has worked in more than 150 corporate, governmental, healthcare, not-for-profit, and educational settings. His most recent book is *Practicing Leadership: Principles and Applications 3rd ed* (John Wiley & Sons, 2005).

**Charles Dwaine Srock** is an instructor of Business Studies at the Richard Stockton College of New Jersey, specializing in OB, management skills, and organizational development. He is completing his doctorate in Management at Capella University.

# INDEX